DAMAGED

OXFORD EARLY MUSIC SERIES

THE GUITAR AND ITS MUSIC

THE GUITAR AND ITS MUSIC

FROM THE RENAISSANCE TO THE CLASSICAL ERA

JAMES TYLER
AND PAUL SPARKS

OXFORD
UNIVERSITY PRESS

This book has been printed digitally and produced in a standard specification
in order to ensure its continuing availability

OXFORD
UNIVERSITY PRESS

Great Clarendon Street, Oxford OX2 6DP

Oxford University Press is a department of the University of Oxford.
It furthers the University's objective of excellence in research, scholarship,
and education by publishing worldwide in

Oxford New York

Auckland Cape Town Dar es Salaam Hong Kong Karachi
Kuala Lumpur Madrid Melbourne Mexico City Nairobi
New Delhi Shanghai Taipei Toronto
With offices in
Argentina Austria Brazil Chile Czech Republic France Greece
Guatemala Hungary Italy Japan South Korea Poland Portugal
Singapore Switzerland Thailand Turkey Ukraine Vietnam

Oxford is a registered trade mark of Oxford University Press
in the UK and in certain other countries

Published in the United States
by Oxford University Press Inc., New York

Parts I and II © James Tyler, 2002
Part III © Paul Sparks, 2002

ISBN 978-0-19-816713-6

Printed and bound by CPI Antony Rowe, Eastbourne

For Joyce and Tobey,

and

in memory of

Pauline Geller and Robert Spencer

PREFACE

More than twenty years ago I wrote a modest introduction to the history, repertory, and playing techniques of the four- and five-course guitar: *The Early Guitar: A History and Handbook*. Since its publication (Oxford, 1980), many performer-scholars of Renaissance and Baroque music have expanded their repertories and research to include early guitar music and topics. Awareness of the guitar's history and repertory has grown appreciably in the Classical guitar world as well, although, as some of the most recent writings on the subject indicate, many guitarists continue to harbour basic misconceptions concerning the nature of the early guitar. Some still think that the vihuela was 'the early guitar', and find it difficult to accept that for musicians and theorists in the sixteenth century the guitar was actually a small, treble-range, four-course instrument. Some find it equally troubling that the later and larger five-course guitar, for much of its most attractive, complex, and virtuoso solo repertory, often requires tunings and stringing arrangements that are radically different from that of the modern instrument.

Having significantly expanded my research on the early guitar and its music over the past twenty years, I decided that it was time to publish a new book on the subject. This, in part, to address in a more systematic (and, I hope, more convincing) fashion than I did in *The Early Guitar* the fundamental issues described above, and to recant or reaffirm certain views that I had previously endorsed; but mainly to share new research and proffer some new ideas on the development of the early guitar and its vast repertory, to amend and expand the annotated lists of primary sources previously published in *The Early Guitar*, and to furnish additional source lists and information, which performers and researchers may find useful.

Since my work has focused primarily on the guitar and its music from *c.*1550–*c.*1750 (Parts I and II of the present book), I am deeply indebted to Paul Sparks, my collaborator on other recent writings on the guitar and a prior book for Oxford University Press (*The Early Mandolin*, 1989), for contributing Part III. Some readers may notice that there is a greater emphasis on organology in his portion of the book than in mine. There are good reasons for this. While essential to a study of the guitar in the second half of the eighteenth century (a period of transition in which numerous instruments survive in their original state), it is not as relevant to a study of the principal guitar type of the sixteenth century, the four-course instrument—no examples of which survive! As for the five-course Baroque guitar, while there are a number of extant instruments, there are also many opinions as to which features of any particular example are original—so many opinions that a separate book on the subject is probably warranted. In any case, the richest sources of information on the two main guitar types of the mid-sixteenth to mid-eighteenth century seem to be the publications and manuscripts containing their music and the writings of contemporary theorists. Accordingly, what these sources tell us about the nature of the instruments and their roles in the music-making of their times is at the heart of Parts I and II.

James Tyler

Pasadena, California
September 2001

Information about the guitar during the second half of the eighteenth century has been conspicuously absent from the standard histories. The period has usually been dismissed in a few curt paragraphs as a time when the old five-course Baroque instrument had fallen into widespread disuse throughout Europe, when the low E string had not yet been added (except by a handful of experimental makers), and when very little guitar music was being written or published. In short, the guitar between 1750 and 1800 has generally been presented to modern readers as a musical Sleeping Beauty, lying dormant and unloved as it awaited the onset of the nineteenth century, when Fernando Sor and Mauro Giuliani would finally arrive to breathe new life into it.

As Part III of this study will demonstrate, those widely held perceptions simply do not correspond to the facts. Far from falling into disuse, the five-course guitar remained very popular until the early years of the nineteenth century, above all in France. Guitars with a sixth course tuned to E were being manufactured in Spain prior to 1760, and they became the standard form in that country long before the eighteenth century ended, remaining so well into the nineteenth century. Furthermore, an enormous amount of guitar music was published between 1750 and 1800, mainly accompaniments to vocal music, but also a considerable quantity of instrumental pieces. Admittedly, the guitar was seldom heard in the formal environs of the concert hall at this time; neither were many solo virtuoso showpieces being composed for it (as they had been for guitars in the Renaissance and Baroque). Far from being a Sleeping Beauty, however, the instrument was a vital and indispensable part of music-making in France, Italy, the Iberian Peninsula, and South America throughout the second half of the eighteenth century.

In Part II and Appendix III of this book James Tyler has recommended new sources of guitar repertory from his period to players of the modern instrument. I hope that my contribution will persuade players of both the modern guitar and the five-course Baroque guitar that many pieces from the latter decades of the eighteenth century deserve rehabilitation and can become a legitimate and meaningful part of their instrument's repertory. Whether they play an old or modern type of instrument, I am confident that musicians will want to explore this little-known repertory, especially some of the fine duets, trios, and songs, which, if played with sensitivity and an awareness of the appropriate style, will help to illuminate yet another side of the multifaceted personality of the guitar.

Paul Sparks

Leven, Beverley, East Yorkshire
September 2001

ACKNOWLEDGEMENTS

Many friends, colleagues, and mentors have helped and encouraged me over the years. I am grateful to the late Robert Spencer for his extraordinary kindness in allowing me access to his rich private library; the late Howard Mayer Brown and the late John M. Thomson for encouraging me to write about the instruments I play; Professors Brown, John Ward, and John Walter Hill for their innovative, thought-provoking research; and Nina Treadwell and Rogério Budasz for bringing much relevant information in their own areas of research to my attention.

I thank Dr Daniela Fattori, Associate Director of the Biblioteca Civico in Verona; Dr Rudolf Hopfner, Director of the Musical Instrument Collection at the Kunsthistorisches Museum in Vienna; Dr André P. Larson, Director of America's Shrine to Music Museum at the University of South Dakota in Vermillion; Ingrid Leis of the Gesellschaft der Musikfreunde in Vienna; Jenny Nex, Assistant Curator of the Royal College of Music's Museum of Musical Instruments in London; Frank and Leanne Koonce of Phoenix for helping me to secure and permitting me to reproduce illustrations; Bonnie J. Blackburn for copy-editing; Bruce Phillips for his support of the project; and Sophie Goldsworthy, Jacqueline Smith, Michael Wood, and Julia Bryan Chukinas of Oxford University Press for seeing the book through to publication.

Most of all, I thank my greatest source of inspiration, my wife Joyce.

J.T.

I am indebted to many people who, during my research for this book, have offered me their help, advice, and encouragement. In particular, I should like to thank Alex Timmerman for drawing my attention to several guitars of the late eighteenth century, and for providing me with photographs; Laurence Libin and Stewart Pollens for supplying me with a photograph of the Alonso guitar; and James and Joyce Tyler for drawing my attention to various source materials, and for helping to keep me enthused throughout this book's lengthy gestation period.

I should also like to thank Kathy Adamson, librarian at the Royal Academy of Music, London, for allowing me access to items from the collection of the late Robert Spencer; Ephraim Segerman, Mimmo Peruffo, and Barry Pratt for sharing with me their expertise on string-making; David Roberts for his critique of the first outline of my work; Jorge Felix for his help with locating research materials in Portugal; Jeremy Montagu for advice about eighteenth-century strings and guitars; John Mackenzie for many useful discussions; Luis Gásser and Brian Jeffery for information about Fernando Sor; and everybody at Oxford University Press who helped with the publication of this book.

Lastly, I should like to thank my wife, Tobey Burnett, for everything.

P.S.

CONTENTS

LIST OF ILLUSTRATIONS

LIST OF TABLES

Sources of Guitar Music *c*.1600–*c*.1750

LIST OF MUSICAL EXAMPLES

LIST OF ABBREVIATIONS

Bibliographical

AcM	*Acta musicologica*
AMw	*Archiv für Musikwissenschaft*
AnMc	*Analecta musicologica*
CNRS	Centre National de la Recherche Scientifique
EM	*Early Music*
FoMRHI	*Fellowship of Makers and Restorers of Historic Instruments*
Grove 6	*The New Grove Dictionary of Music and Musicians*, 6th edn. (1980)
GSJ	*Galpin Society Journal*
IAML	International Association of Music Librarians
IMS	International Musicological Society
JAMS	*Journal of the American Musicological Society*
JLSA	*Journal of the Lute Society of America*
LSJ	*Lute Society Journal*
ML	*Music & Letters*
MQ	*Musical Quarterly*
MT	*Musical Times*
NG II	*The New Grove Dictionary of Music and Musicians*, 2nd edn. (2001)
NRMI	*Nuova rivista musicale italiana*
PRMA	*Proceedings of the Royal Musical Association*
RBM	*Revue belge de musicologie*
RdMc	*Revista de musicología*
RISM B/VI	Répertoire international des sources musicales: *Écrits imprimés concernant la musique*, ed. François Lesure (Munich: Henle Verlag, 1971)
RISM B/VII	Répertoire international des sources musicales = Boetticher 1978
S.P. E.S.	Studio per Edizioni Scelte

Library Sigla

A—Austria

A-Ila	Innsbruck, Landesregierungsarchiv
A-Klse	Klagenfurt, Schlossbibliothek Ebental
A-KR	Kremsmünster, Benediktiner-Stift Kremsmünster, Musikarchiv
A-Wn	Vienna, Österreichische Nationalbibliothek

B—Belgium

B-Bc	Brussels, Conservatoire Royal de Musique
B-Br	Brussels, Bibliothèque Royale Albert 1er

CH—Switzerland

CH-Bu	Basel, Bibliothek des Frey-Grynäischen Instituts
CH-N	Neuchâtel (Neuenburg), Bibliothèque publique et universitaire de Neuchâtel
CH-Zz	Zürich, Zentralbibliothek

CZ—Czech Republic

CZ-Bm	Brno, Moravské Zemské Múzeum, Oddělení Dějin Hudby
CZ-Pdobrovského	Prague, Národní Muzeum, Dobrovského (Nostická) Knihovna
CZ-Pnm	Prague, Národní Muzeum, Ceské Hudby
CZ-Pnm	Prague, Národní Muzeum, Hudební Archiv
CZ-Pnm	Prague, Národní Muzeum, Hudební Oddělení
CZ-Pu	Prague, Státní Knihovna, Universitní Knihovna

D—Germany

D-B	Berlin, Staatsbibliothek zu Berlin – Preußischer Kulturbesitz, Musikabteilung
D-DEsa	Dessau, Stadtarchiv
D-DO	Donaueschingen, Fürstlich Fürstenbergische Hofbibliothek
D-DÜk	Düsseldorf, Goethe-Museum, Anton und Katharina Kippenberg-Stiftung
D-HR	Harburg (Schwaben), Fürstlich Öttingen-Wallerstein'sche Bibliothek, Schloss Harburg
D-KIl	Kiel, Schleswig-Holsteinische Landesbibliothek
D-LÜh	Lübeck, Bibliothek der Hansestadt Lübeck, Musikabteilung
D-Mbs	Munich, Bayerische Staatsbibliothek
D-Mmb	Munich, Städtische Musikbibliothek
D-MZfederhofer	Mainz, private library of Hellmut Federhofer

D–Rp	Regensburg, Bischöfliche Zentralbibliothek
D–W	Wolfenbüttel, Herzog August Bibliothek, Musikabteilung

DK—Denmark

DK–Kk	Copenhagen, Det kongelige Bibliotek
DK–Sa	Sorø, Sorø Akademi, Biblioteket

E—Spain

E–Bbc	Barcelona, Biblioteca de Cataluña
E–GRu	Granada, Universidad, Biblioteca General
E–Mn	Madrid, Biblioteca Nacional

F—France

F–Dc	Dijon, Bibliothèque du Conservatoire
F–G	Grenoble, Bibliothèque municipale
F–Pa	Paris, Bibliothèque de l'Arsenal
F–Pc	Paris, Bibliothèque Nationale (Fonds Conservatoire)
F–Pm	Paris, Bibliothèque Mazarine
F–Pn	Paris, Bibliothèque nationale de France
F–Po	Paris, Bibliothèque-Musée de l'Opéra
F–Psen	Paris, Bibliothèque du Sénat
F–Psg	Paris, Bibliothèque Sainte-Geneviève
F–TLm	Toulouse, Bibliothèque municipale

GB—Great Britain

GB–Cfm	Cambridge, Fitzwilliam Museum
GB–Ckc	Cambridge, Kings College, Rowe Music Library
GB–Cmc	Cambridge, Magdalene College (Pepys Library)
GB–En	Edinburgh, National Library of Scotland
GB–Ge	Glasgow, Euing Music Library
GB–Gm	Glasgow, Mitchell Library
GB–Hadolmetsch	Haslemere, Carl Dolmetsch Library
GB–Hu	Hull, Hull University, Brynmor Jones Library
GB–Lam	London, Royal Academy of Music
GB–Lbl	London, British Library
GB–Llp	London, Lambeth Palace Library
GB–Lspencer	London, private library of Robert Spencer (now in the library of the Royal Academy of Music; see GB–Lam)
GB–Ob	Oxford, Bodleian Library

HR—Croatia

HR–Zs   Zagreb, Glazbeni archiv nadbiskupskog bogoslovnog sjemeništa

I—Italy

I-BA	Bari, private library
I-BIad	Bitonto, Biblioteca Vescovile Mons. Aurelio Marena
I-Bc	Bologna, Civico Museo Bibliografico Musicale
I-COc	Como, Biblioteca Comunale
I-Fc	Florence, Conservatorio di Musica 'Luigi Cherubini'
I-Fn	Florence, Biblioteca Nazionale Centrale
I-Fr	Florence, Biblioteca Riccardiana
I-Gl	Genoa, Biblioteca dell'Istituto (Liceo) Musicale 'Niccolò Paganini'
I-IE	Jesi, Biblioteca Comunale
I-Mc	Milan, Conservatorio di Musica 'Giuseppe Verdi'
I-Mt	Milan, Biblioteca Trivulziana e Archivio Storico Civico
I-MOe	Modena, Biblioteca Estense
I-MOs	Modena, Archivio di Stato
I-Nc	Naples, Conservatorio di Musica S. Pietro a Majella
I-Nn	Naples, Biblioteca Nazionale 'Vittorio Emanuele III'
I-NOVi	Novara, Istituto Civico Musicale Brera
I-OS	Ostiglia, Fondazione Greggiati
I-PAc	Parma, Conservatorio di Musica 'Arrigo Boito'
I-PEas	Perugia, Archivio di Stato
I-PEc	Perugia, Biblioteca Comunale Augusta
I-PESc	Pesaro, Conservatorio di Musica 'Gioacchino Rossini'
I-PIa	Pisa, Archivio di Stato
I-PLcom	Palermo, Biblioteca Comunale
I-Raa	Rome, Biblioteca del Pontificio Ateneo Antoniano
I-Rn	Rome, Biblioteca Nazionale 'Vittorio Emanuele II'
I-Rsc	Rome, Conservatorio di Musica S. Cecilia
I-Rvat	Rome, Biblioteca Apostolica Vaticana
I-TI	Termini-Imerese, Biblioteca Comunale Linciniana
I-Tn	Turin, Biblioteca Nazionale Universitaria
I-Tr	Turin, Biblioteca Reale
I-Vnm	Venice, Biblioteca Nazionale Marciana
I-VEc	Verona, Biblioteca Civica

MEX—Mexico

MEX-Mn	Mexico City, Biblioteca Nacional
MEX-Msaldívar	Mexico City, private library of the Saldívar family

NL—The Netherlands

NL-DHgm	The Hague, Gemeentemuseum
NL-DHk	The Hague, Koninklijke Bibliotheek

P—Portugal

P-Cug	Coimbra, Biblioteca Geral da Universidade
P-Lcg	Lisbon, Fundação Calouste Gulbenkian
P-Ln	Lisbon, Instituto da Biblioteca Nacional e do Livro

PL—Poland

PL-Kj	Kraków, Biblioteka Jagiellońska
PL-Wn	Warsaw, Biblioteka Narodowa

RA—Argentina

RA-BArm	Buenos Aires, Ricardo Rojas Museum

RUS—Russia

RUS-Mrg	Moscow, Rossijskaja Gosudarstvennaja biblioteka
RUS-SPa	St Petersburg, Rossijskaja akademiia nauk biblioteka
RUS-SPsc	St Petersburg, Rossijskaja nacional'naja biblioteka

S—Sweden

S-N	Norrköping, Stadsbiblioteket
S-SK	Skara, Stifts- och Landsbiblioteket
S-Skma	Stockholm, Kungliga Musikaliska Akademiens Bibliotek
S-Sr	Stockholm, Riksarkivet

US—United States of America

US-BRp	New York, Brooklyn Public Library, Art and Music Division
US-CA	Cambridge, Harvard University Music Libraries
US-CAe	Cambridge, Harvard University, Eda Kuhn Loeb Music Library
US-Cn	Chicago, Newberry Library
US-Cum	Chicago, University of Chicago, Music Collection
US-LAtyler	Los Angeles, private library of James Tyler
US-LAuc	Los Angeles, University of California, W. A. Clark Library
US-NYp	New York, Library and Museum of the Performing Arts, Music Division, New York Public Library at Lincoln Center

US-PHalbrecht	Philadelphia, Otto E. Albrecht private collection
US-PHu	Philadelphia, University of Pennsylvania Libraries
US-R	Rochester, Eastman School of Music, Sibley Music Library
US-Wc	Washington, DC, Library of Congress, Music Division

PART I

THE GUITAR IN THE SIXTEENTH CENTURY

Introduction

What was the nature of the instrument that sixteenth-century Spaniards, Italians, Frenchmen, and Englishmen knew as the *guitarra*, *chitarra*, *guiterre*, and gittern, respectively? Was the Spanish *vihuela de mano* considered a guitar? What did Italian musicians in the late sixteenth century mean by the terms *chitarra spagnola*, *chitarriglia*, *chitarrino*, *chitarra italiana*, and *chitarra napolitana*?

According to documentary evidence, including contemporaneous sources of music for the instrument, the typical sixteenth-century guitar was a small, figure-8-shaped, four-course,[1] treble-range instrument, tuned a fourth or more higher and about one-third the size of a modern Classical guitar. Later in the century the Italians would also refer to it as chitarrino, chitarra italiana, and chitarra napolitana. The somewhat larger five-course guitar, which the Italians called the chitarra spagnola, first appeared in the third quarter of the sixteenth century. The still larger, six-course, lower-range, figure-8-shaped Spanish vihuela de mano,[2] and its Italian counterpart, the *viola da mano*, were not considered guitars. Indeed, as will be seen, all available evidence from the sixteenth century indicates that the guitar had its own separate and distinct character, function, tunings, and repertory, and that sixteenth-century players, theorists, and composers regarded the vihuela not as a guitar but as a figure-8-shaped Spanish equivalent of the lute.

---

[1] A course usually comprises two or more strings; however, the first course was often a single string.

[2] For information about the Spanish vihuela de mano, see Corona-Alcade (1990), and about the Italian viola da mano, Tyler (1980*a*), ch. 1.

I

Spain: *La Guitarra de quatro órdenes*

In his set of variations on the *Conde Claros* ground[1] for vihuela (*Delphin de musica . . .* 1538), the excellent Spanish composer Luis de Narváez (*fl.* 1530–50) provides conclusive evidence that the guitar and vihuela were regarded as two distinct instruments in sixteenth-century Spain. He specifically heads one section of his fifteenth variation 'contrahaciendo la guitarra' (in imitation of the guitar), and for this section employs only the four inner courses of the vihuela, which comprise the interval pattern (though not the pitches) of the four-course guitar.

More evidence from mid-sixteenth-century Spain is provided by Juan Bermudo (*c.*1510–*c.*1565), who published a book of music theory, *El libro primo de la declaracion de instrumentos*, in Osuna in 1549 and an expanded edition, *El libro llamado declaracion de instrumentos musicales*, in 1555.[2] Bermudo is the source of the earliest tuning information we have for the guitar. He also explains the procedures for intabulating pre-existing vocal and instrumental music for the guitar, vihuela, and *bandurria*.[3] He describes the guitar as smaller than the vihuela ('mas corto', ch. 65), and as generally having only four courses,[4] with an interval pattern resembling the second to fifth courses of a vihuela. The specific tunings for guitar given in Ex. 1.1 are found in *Libro quarto* (ch. 65). Roman numerals designate the courses.

As illustrated, in both the 'temple a los nuevos' (new tuning) and 'temple a los viejos' (old tuning),[5] the first three courses are in unison and the fourth has a bourdon (*bordón*)—a thicker, gut 'bass' string, tuned an octave below its thinner companion in the same course. Notice that the difference between the new and old tunings involves only the fourth course and whether it is tuned a fourth or a fifth lower than the third. In

---

[1] A ground is a harmonic pattern or sequence of harmonies.

[2] All citations refer to the later edition of the book.

[3] The bandurria in the 16th c. was a very small treble-range instrument related to the guitar. It had three courses, probably of gut, tuned either in fifths or a fourth and a fifth. For further details, see Bermudo (*Libro quarto*), chs. 48 and 49. See also Tyler (1980*a*), 107.

[4] Bermudo (*Libro segundo*), ch. 32: 'La guitarra commun tiene quarto ordenes de cuerdas . . .'. He adds that in Spain he has seen a guitar with five courses, and explains that the additional course is placed before the *first* course, and that the interval between these two courses is a fourth.

[5] In *Libro segundo*, ch. 32, Bermudo mentions that the old tuning is more suitable for the old romances and strummed music of the time: 'Este temple mas es para romances viejos, y Musica golpeada: que para Musica de el tiempo.'

EX 1.1. Juan Bermudo's guitar tunings (1555)

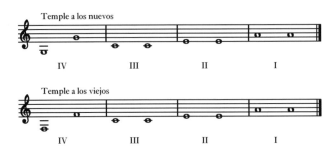

the 'temple a los nuevos' the lowest actual pitch is just *g* below middle *c*, the same as on a violin. Other sixteenth-century sources corroborate both of these high-pitched tunings for the guitar.[6]

Bermudo also gives specific, nominal tunings for the vihuela (see Ex. 1.2).[7] Notice that they are identical to the standard tunings for the lute, or, as Bermudo calls it, the 'vihuela de Flandes'.[8] Notice, too, that while the second (*a´*) tuning indicates the same high pitch for the vihuela's first course as for the first course of the guitar, the vihuela's remaining five courses descend nearly to the bottom of the bass clef. Hence, in his explanation of the procedure for intabulating pre-existing music for the guitar or the vihuela, when Bermudo remarks that one may imagine ('ymaginar') the instrument to be at any pitch level one chooses,[9] what he means is that one may mentally transpose the pitch to whatever level is necessary to fit the music comfortably onto the instrument's fingerboard. As his tuning charts make clear, however, he regarded the guitar and vihuela tunings given above (and below) as the 'standard' ones.

Later in the chapter Bermudo alludes again to the smallness of the guitar in comparison to the vihuela: 'A player can better display his skill [at setting two- or three-part music in tablature] with the knowledge and use of the guitar than with that of the vihuela, because it is a smaller instrument.'[10] He mentions that the octave stringing of the guitar's fourth course is traditionally called *requinta*, that the instrument has ten frets, and that one usually plays two- or sometimes three-part music on it. He then reconfirms the guitar's tuning 'a los nuevos' as: *g g´– c´c´– e´e´– a´ (a´)*.

In discussing the relative tunings of the vihuela, the 'discante',[11] and the guitar in *Libro quarto* (ch. 69), Bermudo states that the guitar is to be tuned 'at an octave above the vihuela so that the *quinta* [the thin upper string of the fourth course] is tuned to the

---

[6] See below, Chs. 2–4.   [7] Bermudo (*Libro quarto*), chs. 55 and 56.

[8] Bermudo (*Libro quarto*), ch. 65: 'el laud o vihuela de Flandes' (the lute or Flemish [i.e. foreign] vihuela).

[9] Bermudo (*Libro quarto*), ch. 65.

[10] 'De mayor abilidad se puede monstrar un tañedor con la intelligencia, y uso de la guitarra: que con el de la vihuela, por ser instrumento mas corto' (ch. 65). The entire *Libro quarto* is translated in Espinosa (1995–6), 1–139.

[11] The 'discante' is a small, six-course vihuela, tuned a fourth higher than the normal vihuela. Bermudo says that

Ex. 1.2. Bermudo's vihuela tunings (1555)

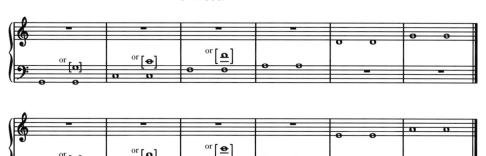

second fret of the fourth course of the vihuela'.[12] Since a typical vihuela is tuned *GG* – *cc* – *ff* – *aa* – *d′d′* – *g′g′*, Bermudo's instructions again point to a guitar with its octave fourth string at *g′*, and reaffirm the high-pitched tuning that he gave in chapter 65.[13] In chapter 85, after sharing with us his hypothetical tuning for a proposed five-course guitar, he reiterates that the guitar in common use in his day is the four-course guitar tuned to *a′*.

With this important information from Bermudo's endlessly fascinating treatise in mind,[14] we turn to the earliest dated source of music for the guitar, Alonso Mudarra's tablature book *Tres libros de musica en cifras para vihuela . . . y algunas fantasias pora guitarra . . .* (Seville, 1546). Mudarra (*c.*1510–80) was raised in the households of the nobility, where he undoubtedly performed his earliest compositions. Like many vihuelists, he was regarded as a courtier; but later in life he also became a cleric. Indeed, in the same year that his *Tres libros de musica* was published he was appointed canon at Seville Cathedral.[15] Like Bermudo, who includes him among Spain's greatest players,[16] Mudarra describes the guitar as having ten frets, and a bourdon on the fourth course (fo. 21).[17] However, unlike Bermudo, he does not specify nominal tunings for either the guitar or the vihuela.

one can tune the 'discante' a fourth higher than a vihuela, the sixth course of the smaller instrument being the same pitch as the fifth course of a vihuela. This means that the 'discante' is tuned even higher than the guitar.

[12] 'la guitarra en octava de la vihuela, que viniesse la quinta de la guitarra con el segondo traste de la quarta de la vihuela'.

[13] Despite the numerous 16th-c. references to the guitar as a small high-pitched instrument, many modern writers still maintain that the four-course guitar had a tuning identical with the top four strings of a modern classical guitar.

[14] In *Libro quarto*, ch. 66, Bermudo also includes some intriguing material from the writings of two authors from ancient times, Boethius and Nicomachus, concerning the tuning of a so-called 'guitar of Mercury', and gives his own theoretical tuning for it.   [15] 'Mudarra, Alonso' in *Grove 6*.   [16] Bermudo, *Libro segundo*, ch. 35.

[17] Although Mudarra and Bermudo mention the use of a bourdon on the fourth course, in some contemporary Italian sources only a thin pair of upper octave strings is indicated for the fourth course (see below, Ch. 4).

In addition to vihuela solos, songs to the vihuela, and a solo for harp or organ, *Tres libros de musica* includes six solos for the four-course 'guitarra'.[18] The first is a fantasia in imitative style using the 'temple viejo'; this is followed by three more fantasias in 'temple nuevo'. All four compositions are quite substantial and of the same high quality as Mudarra's music for vihuela. The fantasias are followed by a *Pavana*, which uses the harmonic material of the Italian Pavana del Duca (as does the vihuela solo on fo. 18). The final guitar solo is a set of two variations[19] on an Italian harmonic pattern, the Romanesca, which bears the title of the popular Spanish song text 'O guardame las vacas'.

Another vihuelist, Miguel de Fuenllana, was born in *c.*1525 and died as early as 1585 or as late as 1605.[20] Despite having lost his sight in babyhood, he became one of the most celebrated vihuelists of his day.[21] His tablature book, *Libro de musica para vihuela, intitulado Orphenica lyra . . .* (Seville, 1554), is dedicated to Prince Philip, who two years later would become Philip II, ruler of Spain and the Spanish Kingdoms (including Milan, Naples, and about half of the New World). The book includes Fuenllana's compositions for the typical six-course vihuela, as well as nine items for a five-course instrument ('vihuela de cinco ordenes'),[22] and nine for the four-course 'guitarra'.

The first guitar piece appears to be an intabulation of a section of a Credo entitled *Crucifixus, a tres* (that is, in three-part writing). A setting of a *villancico* by Juan Vásquez entitled *Covarde cavallero* follows. Although its vocal melody part is embedded in the tablature, it can be read without difficulty because the relevant tablature numbers are printed in red ink. This clever format enabled the piece to be performed either as a guitar solo, or with the vocal line both played and sung, probably by the guitarist. The text of the song is set beneath the appropriate notes of tablature. Fuenllana used the same format for the next piece, *Passeavase el Rey moro*, a famous *romance* that tells of the Spanish conquest of the Moorish city of Granada in 1491–2.[23]

Following the vocal intabulations are six fantasias in two- and three-part counterpoint for guitar, three of them marked with the letter 'D', for *dificile*, and the others

---

[18] The entire volume is published in facsimile in Tyler (1980*d*).

[19] The variation was an instrumental form used widely in the 16th c., not just in Spain, but also in Italy and England.

[20] Jacobs (1978), pp. xix–xxv.

[21] Bermudo, *Libro segundo*, ch. 35.

[22] Fuenllana gives no indication of nominal pitches for the tuning of this vihuela, but the tablature for the instrument shows that it has the interval pattern of a guitar rather than the top five courses of a standard vihuela. The five-course instrument was probably as large as other vihuelas and, possibly, was the forerunner of the 17th-c. Spanish guitar.

[23] There is a quasi-facsimile of this piece, including the red numbers, in Wolf (1919), 161. The facsimile edition of the entire Fuenllana volume (Geneva: Minkoff Reprints, 1981) does not include the red numbers, which renders it useless for the many vihuela and guitar pieces in the book that use this format.

marked 'F', for *facile*. In truth, none of these complicated fantasias, which frequently demand wide left-hand stretches, can be regarded as easy, not even on the small four-course guitar. Like his fantasias for vihuela, Fuenllana's guitar pieces are composed in a strict, contrapuntal style that is virtually devoid of ornamental passagework.

Regrettably, little Spanish music survives for the four-course guitar after the mid-sixteenth century, but there is important evidence that the instrument continued to be widely used in Spain for the remainder of the sixteenth and well into the seventeenth century: a little booklet by Juan Carlos Amat (*c.*1572–1642), first published in 1596, entitled *Guitara española de cinco ordenes . . . y a la fin se haze mencion tambien de la guitarra de quarto ordenes*. While there is no extant copy of the first edition, the original letters of approval, dated 15 June 1596 in Barcelona, are reprinted in the earliest surviving edition (Lérida, 1626). As its title indicates, Amat's booklet mainly concerns the five-course Spanish guitar; however, the author ends with a brief chapter on the four-course instrument,[24] in which he explains how his system of chord symbols can be used for both types of guitar.[25]

Evidently, only two genuine 'guitars' survive from the sixteenth century,[26] both Iberian and both five-course instruments. One, by the Portuguese maker Belchior Dias of Lisbon,[27] is a small, beautifully crafted instrument dated 1581, with a string length of 55.4 cm (see Pl. 1.1). Interestingly, the theoretical five-course guitar discussed by Bermudo in *El libro llamada declaracion de instrumentos musicales*[28] was also quite small, to judge by his proposed tuning for it: $f - g - c' - f' - g'$. It is not known who made the other guitar, but details of its construction and decoration suggest that Dias was the maker of this superb undated instrument as well.[29] It is much larger than the 1581 guitar, with an approximate string length of 70 cm (see Pl. 1.2). Experts believe it was built in about 1590. There are no contemporary sources to tell us what the Spanish or Portuguese called this instrument in the late sixteenth century, unless one was Fuenllana's 'vihuela de cinco ordenes'; but in Italy it was known as the chitarra spagnola.

---

[24] In his chapter heading Amat calls the four-course guitar 'Guitarra de siete cuerdas', by which he means a guitar with seven strings (arranged in four courses, the first being a single string).

[25] Chord-symbol systems and Amat are discussed in Ch. 9.

[26] For further details, see Evans (1977), 27.

[27] London, Royal College of Music.

[28] Bermudo, *Libro quarto*, ch. 85.

[29] U. S., private collection, formerly in the collection of Robert Spencer. See Tyler (1980*a*), 37 (pl. 6).

PL. 1.1. Small five–course guitar by Belchior Dias
(Lisbon, 1581). London, Royal College of Music,
Museum of Musical Instruments

PL. 1.2. Five-course guitar, attributed to Belchior Dias, *c.*1590.
Collection of Frank and Leanne Koonce

2

France: The Creation of the Repertory

Whereas in Spain the music for guitar was limited to a few items found in the vihuela books, French publishers produced substantial collections exclusively for the *guiterre* (or *guiterne*).[1] And not only was there far more of it, but the French repertory was considerably more varied, comprising fantasias, intabulations of vocal music, songs to the guitar, and dance music, all composed in a style that involved a much greater degree of ornamental passagework than is found in the Spanish sources. French composers further augmented the guitar's repertory by providing solos that could also be used as parts in ensemble versions of the pieces.

It all began on 8 November 1548, when the Parisian music printer Nicholas Du Chemin was granted a privilege by Henri II to print all kinds of music, including tablatures for lutes and guitars ('Lutz, guiternes'). Apparently, Du Chemin never used the royal privilege to print music for plucked instruments, but others did. On 12 November 1550 the printer and renowned type designer Robert Granjon obtained a similar royal privilege, and by 23 December he had contracted with the long-established printer Michel Fezandat[2] of Paris to publish music jointly. One of the earliest products of their partnership was a beautifully printed series of four tablature books for guitar (designed by Granjon himself). First editions of the initial two books in the series, Guillaume Morlaye's *Le premier livre de chansons, gaillardes, pavannes . . . en tabulature de guiterne* and *Le second livre de chansons, gaillardes, paduanes . . . en tabulature de guiterne*, probably printed between 1550 and 1551, are lost.[3] However, later editions, from 1552 and 1553 respectively, have survived. As its full title indicates, the third book in the series, *Le troysieme livre contenant plusiers duos, et trios . . . en tabulature de guiterne, par Simon Gorlier, excellent joueur* (Paris, 1551), is by the excellent player Simon Gorlier, while the fourth book, *Quatriesme livre . . .* (Paris, 1552), is by Morlaye. Copies of both survive. It is not known why the partnership of Granjon and Fezandat was dissolved on 27 February 1551, but Fezandat's imprint appears alone on the final book in the series, as well as on the aforementioned second editions of *Le premier livre* and *Le second livre*.

---

[1] All the 16th-c. French printed sources are reproduced in facsimile in Tyler (1979*b*) and Tyler (1980*c*).
[2] Among other things, Fezandat is noted for being Rabelais's publisher.
[3] Brown (1965), 124, 138, and 148.

The Lyonnaise musician Simon Gorlier (*fl.* 1550–84) was also a printer and bookseller. His collection in the Granjon and Fezandat series (*Le troysieme livre*) consists entirely of tablature settings of well-known chansons by Pierre Certon, Pierre Sandrin, Jacotin (surname unknown), Claudin de Sermisy, and Clément Janequin, as well as a duo from a mass by Josquin. In general, Gorlier's guitar intabulations tend to preserve the essential features of the original material. His addition of some light embellishment in the form of running passagework echoes the style of the majority of contemporary French lute intabulations. Like similar lute publications, Gorlier's guitar anthology probably was intended as a means by which amateur players could become familiar with some of the 'classics' of the chanson repertory that were performed at court. This is not to say that *all* the music in the collection was intended for the amateur market, however. Gorlier ends his anthology with a lengthy and exacting 249-bar intabulation of Clément Janequin's famous four-part chanson *La Bataille*.[4] A showpiece for any instrument, it is all the more impressive on the simple four-course guitar.

Gorlier refers to the guitar's diminutive size and lack of complexity several times in the preface to his anthology, and he justifies having spent so much time and effort preparing music for it (rather than the larger and more complex six-course lute) by alluding to the guitar's Classical associations:

The Ancients were satisfied with such instruments as the Guitar, which they called *Tetrachordes* because it had four strings. Not that I claim to prefer it to other instruments, but at least, if merely in honor and memory of Antiquity, I wanted to show that it had its own limits for reproducing music in two or three voices or parts, as well as does a larger instrument.[5]

In an 'advertissement' to the reader (fo. 19ᵛ), he describes the effort it took to intabulate *La Bataille* for the guitar, and speaks again of the instrument's size: 'because some people might think that such a small instrument, I mean "small" in both senses, hardly deserves such trouble as I have spent . . .'.[6]

Gorlier's attitude towards the guitar was not shared by Guillaume Morlaye (*c.*1510– after 1558), the composer-intabulator of the other three guitar books in the series—at least not in print. First cited in official Parisian records of 1541 as a merchant, Morlaye appears to have been a shareholder in a merchant ship that plied the lucrative African slave trade. He is cited again in the 1550s, but as a lute player and teacher with close ties to the Parisian art world and to the artist François Clouet in particular.[7] Morlaye

---

[4] For a description of *La Bataille*, see Wolzien (1983).

[5] 'les antiques se sont contentez de telz ou semblables instruments qu'est la Guiterne, qu'ilz appelloient Tetrachordes, pource qu'ilz ne contenoient que quatre chordes. Non que ie la pretende preferer aux autres instrumens, mais pour le moins i'ay bien voulu donner a cognoistre, ne fust ce qu'a l'honneur & memoire de l'antiquité qu'elle a aussi bien ses limites propres & convenables, pour recevoir l'harmonie de deux ou trois voix, ou parties qu'un plus grand instrument . . .' (fo. 1ᵛ); translation in Heartz (1960), 466.

[6] 'pour autant qu'il semble à plusiers que si petit instrument, i'entens de l'une & l'autre petitesse, ne merite tel labeur que ie y ay employé . . .'. Translation in Heartz (1960), 466.

[7] Clouet was a highly esteemed French portrait painter at the court of François I.

described himself as a pupil of the renowned Italian lutenist Alberto da Ripa (*c.* 1500–51), who was employed at the French court during the reigns of both François I and Henri II. He prepared an edition of his teacher's lute music, which was published by Fezandat after the lutenist's death in 1551. On 13 February 1552 Morlaye was granted a privilege to print music for the lute and other instruments, and entered into a publishing partnership with Fezandat on 19 April 1552.

The first of his guitar collections, *Le premier livre de chansons, gaillardes, pavannes . . . en tabulature de guiterne* (see Pl. 2.1), begins with two substantial fantasias of good quality and moderate difficulty. These are followed by eight intabulations, with embellishment, of chansons by Boyvin (given name unknown), Julien Belin, Sermisy, Janequin, and Sandrin. A pavan–galliard pair follows, which is based on well-known Italian grounds, the Passamezzo antico and the Romanesca respectively. The next pavan–galliard pair is also built on the Passamezzo antico ground. Next is a separate galliard based on a chanson by Pierre Certon entitled *Puis que nouvelle affection*. It is followed by three more galliards, presumably by Morlaye himself. Another galliard, entitled *Les cinque pas*, is a ground that was known in Italy as 'Rocha el fuso'. It is followed by three further galliards, two unidentified and the third based on Certon's chanson *O combien est heureuse*. The next piece is a *Buffons* based on the Italian Passamezzo moderno, and the next a *Conte clare*, which is the famous Spanish ground *Conde Claros*.[8] The collection ends with four French *branles* and two *allemandes*.

Morlaye's *Le second livre de chansons, gaillardes, paduanes . . . en tabulature de guiterne* opens with two lengthy fantasias of considerable merit, followed by eight more chanson intabulations. Next come two settings of a popular dance piece, *Branle. Tin que tin tin*, also known as *Tintelore* in France and 'Essex Measures' in England. The pavan in the subsequent two pavan–galliard pairs is the Passamezzo antico, and the next single galliard a Romanesca. They are followed by six more galliards, the first built on another Italian ground, La gamba, and the other five still unidentified. Then come six French branles, the second of which is found also in an Italian guitar source of 1549, where it is labelled 'fantasia'.[9] The fourth branle contains the same musical material as the third, but bears the rubric 'a corde avallée', which simply means that for this piece the fourth course should be tuned a tone lower than normal (i.e. Bermudo's old tuning). The branles are followed by a *Hornpipe d'Angleterre*, which turns out to be the popular English ground 'Wakefield on a greene'.[10] Morlaye concludes his international selection of pieces with an Italian *Villanesque*, two *Contre-clare*s, and an *Allemande* (*Lorraine*).

[8] See Ward (1992), ex. 43 and ex. 117.
[9] Barberiis (1549). This source is discussed in Ch. 4.
[10] See Ward (1992), ex. 44 and App. F, no. 322.

LE
PREMIER LIVRE DE
CHANSONS, GAILLARDES, PAVANNES,
Branfles, Almandes, Fantaifies, reduictz en tabulature de Guiterne
par Maiftre Guillaume Morlaye ioueur de Lut.

A PARIS.
De l'Imprimerie de Robert GranIon & Michel Fezandat, au Mont
S. Hylaire, à l'Enfeigne des Grandz Ions.
1 5 5 2.
Auec priuilege du Roy.

PL. 2.1. A typical four-course guitar illustrated on the title page
of Guillaume Morlaye, *Le premier livre . . .* (Paris, 1552)

The fourth and final book in the series, Morlaye's *Quatriesme livre*, is also the most interesting.[11] It opens with two extraordinary fantasias, which the composer ascribes to his teacher Alberto da Ripa.[12] Both are extended works that attest to Alberto's exceptional contrapuntal skills, and seem to have been conceived for guitar rather than arranged for it.[13] Neither piece has been found in any other source. The second of the two is marked 'a corde avallée' and, hence, requires the richer sonority produced by the aforementioned re-tuning down of the fourth course.

The collection continues with intabulations of three chansons (two by Sandrin), followed by three Italian *villanesche* (three-voice pieces from Naples, composed in a distinctive, popular style). The first of the Italian pieces, *Non é pieu fedé*, is anonymous,

---

[11] Although a listing of the contents of all four books in the series can be found in Brown (1965), 124, 127, 138–9, and 148, many of the pieces are identified and described here for the first time.

[12] Styled Albert de Rippe.

[13] Both also contain a number of printing errors that need correcting before the pieces can be played from the facsimile edition.

PL. 2.2. First page of *La Seraphine* from Guillaume Morlaye,
Quatriesme livre . . . (Paris, 1552), fo. 15ᵛ

but the second and third, *Chi dira mai* and *Oy mé dolente*, are by Giovanni Domenico
da Nola, one of the period's best-known and most influential composers of Neapolitan
song. The inclusion of these *villanesche* in Morlaye's collection is just one indication of
the widespread popularity the genre enjoyed in the mid-sixteenth century.

    The next two items are both marked 'a corde avallée'. The first, *La Seraphine*, is one
of the gems of the four-course guitar repertory (see Pl. 2.2). It is in six sections: the
first three are built on a beautiful, almost mesmerizing (but unidentified) Italianate
harmonic pattern, while the final three consist of variations on the Italian Romanesca.
The second item is a fine setting of the Spanish *Conde Claros*. These are followed by
three noteworthy pavans. Still another pavan, entitled *Chant d'orlande,* comes next;
this one is in seven-bar phrases and has little melodic interest, which suggests that it
might be a harmonic formula over which certain poetic forms were recited—a long-
standing Italian practice. As the title of the piece implies, the poetry accompanied by
Chant d'orlande could well have been stanzas from the Ferrarese court poet Lodovico
Ariosto's famed epic poem *Orlando furioso*. The final pieces for guitar include four

galliards, the third a setting of the Italian La gamba ground,[14] and two French branles, the second a setting of the well-known Italian popular tune 'Scaramella', which originated in the fifteenth century.

Significantly, the rest of the book is devoted to music for the cittern (*cistre*), a small, four-course, wire-strung, plectrum-played instrument, which became popular in the fifteenth century and remained so until the nineteenth. The French cittern, like the guitar, was a treble-range instrument, but the former had triple stringing for its third and fourth courses and a tuning of $a'a'a - g'g'g - d'd' - e'e'$, which is first encountered in the early fifteenth century.[15] Morlaye's book is the earliest surviving printed source of cittern tablature. Unlike his guitar music, the pieces for cittern are of no musical import, and are mentioned here only because Morlaye's inclusion of them is evidence of a perceived connection between the guitar and cittern that existed in the minds of sixteenth-century musicians (and, as will be seen, seventeenth-century musicians as well).

Undoubtedly, the Morlaye and Gorlier series inspired the publication of another series: five guitar books by the Parisian lutenist, composer, and music printer Adrian Le Roy (*c.*1520–98). Le Roy was associated with such renowned Parisian court composers as Pierre Certon, Jacques Arcadelt, Claude Le Jeune, Guillaume de Costeley, and Claude Goudimel, and also with the literary circle of the Comtesse de Retz, which included the esteemed humanist-poets Pierre Ronsard, Antoine de Baïf, and Mellin de Saint-Gelais, whose texts he set to music and whose laudatory dedications to him can be found in several of his works. On 14 August 1551 Le Roy and his cousin Robert Ballard (*c.*1525–88) obtained a privilege from Henri II to print and sell all sorts of music, and throughout his career, Le Roy would be recognized for the quality and range of the music he published, much of it in collaboration with the aforementioned composers and poets. It is found as part music, tablatures for solo lute, cittern, and guitar, and collections of songs for lute and voice and guitar and voice.

One of Le Roy and Ballard's first productions was also the first in a series of tablature books for the guitar, *Premier livre de tablature de guiterre . . .* (Paris, 1551),[16] a collection of fantasias, chanson intabulations, pavans, galliards, allemands, and branles, which also contains an extremely valuable additional feature. For many of the pieces a second version marked 'plus diminuée' (more embellished) is provided, thereby preserving an important record of ornamentation practice in sixteenth-century France. Furthermore, as many of the pieces were printed elsewhere in ensemble or part-song

---

[14] Considering the number of Italian artists and musicians that were employed by the French crown, e.g. the 'school' of Fontainebleau, Leonardo da Vinci, and Alberto da Ripa, it is not surprising to find so many Italianate items in the French guitar books.

[15] Tyler (1974) and Tyler (2000*a*).

[16] Le Roy also may have published a tutor in 1551, *Briefe et facile instruction pour apprendre la tabulature à bien accorder, conduir et disposer la main sur la guiterne*. No copy survives, but it may have been translated into English. See Brown (1965) under [1551]₄ and below, Ch. 3.

versions, they can be performed either as guitar solos or as ensemble pieces with guitar. For example, the set of 'Branles de Bourgongne' from the *Premier livre* is also found in Claude Gervaise's book of ensemble dance music in four and five parts, *Troisieme livre de danceries* (Paris, 1557).[17] Combining the guitar solo versions from the set with the bass lines and some inner parts from Gervaise's ensemble versions results in consort pieces rather like those described by Bermudo,[18] in which the guitar part becomes the embellished treble line of the ensemble version. This style is somewhat analogous to the lute-dominated mixed consort from later in the sixteenth century.

Le Roy's *Second livre de guiterre, contenant plusieurs chansons en forme de voix de ville . . .*[19] is also interesting. The term 'voix de ville' on the title page refers to a vocal genre in which courtly poetry is set to an intentionally simple, almost popular melody or chord pattern. Often a standard dance rhythm is used, which explains why the names of dances frequently appear beside the song titles. Seventeen of the twenty-three items for voice and guitar were composed by Le Roy, while the other six are Le Roy's settings for voice and guitar of four-part chansons by Sandrin, Certon, and Mithou.[20] At least three of the texts, 'O combien est heureuse', 'Helas mon dieu', and 'Puisque nouvelle affection', are odes by Saint-Gelais;[21] while 'Pour m'eslonger' and 'Mes pas semez' are laments, the former, also by Saint-Gelais,[22] using the Romanesca ground.

Le Roy formatted the guitar songs in the following manner: the unadorned vocal line is presented in staff notation with one verse of text beneath the appropriate notes and all the remaining verses printed below the piece; the guitar accompaniment, which incorporates an embellished version of the vocal line, appears in tablature on the facing page (see Pl. 2.3). This format implies that the pieces can be performed either vocally or as guitar solos. Vocal performance, with the singer executing the more or less plain version of the piece—Pierre Certon's *J'ay le rebours*, for example—and the guitarist playing the embellished accompaniment, results in a musical experience that is both sensuous and moving. Because English and French music for lute and voice from the late 1580s onwards tends to present the voice part as an independent line, some modern writers doubt that the earlier guitar accompaniments would have doubled the voice.[23] However, as Véronique Lafargue K has convincingly shown,[24] this style of accompaniment was not at all uncommon in the sixteenth century.

---

[17] Most of the Parisian four-part dance collections mentioned in this chapter have been published in modern edition by London Pro Musica Editions.

[18] Bermudo, *Libro quarto*, ch. 69.

[19] The first edition was published in 1551 or 1552; however, only a later edition from 1556 survives.

[20] Le Roy later published the majority of these pieces in four-part form in his *Premier livre de chansons en vau de villle* (Paris, 1573).   [21] Heartz (1972), 155–6.   [22] Brooks (1999), 428–30.

[23] Heartz (1972) and Le Cocq (1995).   [24] Lafargue K (1998).

CHANSON.

'A Y le rebours de ce que ie fouhaite, I'ay conuerty en ioye contrefaite Tout le plai-

fir q̃ perdre craignoye tãt:I'ay du mal tãt tãt, Que le cœur me fend De voir l'amour defaite.   I'ay du

Ma douleur n'eſt moins grande que ſecrette,
Mon bien perdu ſans eſpoir ie regrette,
Qui me ſouloit l'eſprit rendre content:
I'ay du mal tant tant.

Plus ie congnois l'amour ſeure & perfaite,
Plus me deplaiſt de la voir imperfaite,
Si i'en ai ris, i'en pleure bien autant:
I'ay du mal tant tant.

Vn cœur leger plus qu'une girouette,
Qui ne tient plus promeſſe qu'il ait faite,
A ruiner ma fermeté pretend:
I'ay du mal tant tant.

Pour ſon plaiſir changement il accepte,
De mon ennuy moins faire la recepte:
Car vraye amour,ou vie ou mort attend:
I'ay du mal tant tant.

Pour ſuiure amour & eſtre de ſa ſecte,
I'ay tous ces mots,ſans qne nul en excepte,
Et tous ces biens paſſez vois regrettant:
I'ay du mal tant tant.

Fy des beaux chants & des vers du poete,
I'aime trop mieux Hieremie le prophete,
A uec luy vois mourir en languiſſant:
I'ay du mal tant tant.

PAVANNE

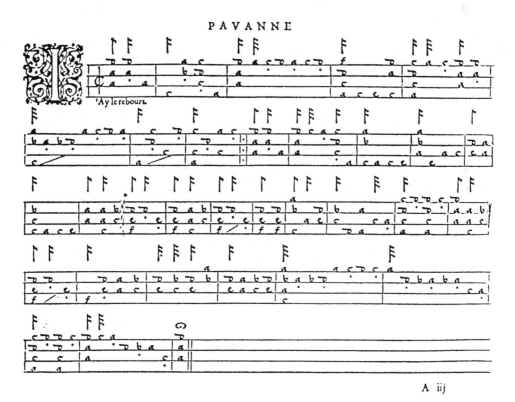

'Ay le rebours.

A iij

PL. 2.3. *J'ay le rebours* by Pierre Certon from Adrian Le Roy,
Second livre . . . (Paris, 1556), fos. 2ᵛ–3

Le Roy's *Tiers livre de tabulature de guiterre, contenant plusiers préludes, chansons, basse-dances, tourdions, pavanes, gaillardes, almandes, bransles . . .* (Paris, 1552) is similar in content and style to his *Premier livre*, except that in the third book, instead of opening with two fantasias, he gives two brief free-form preludes and also includes a somewhat old-fashioned dance sequence (more characteristic of the beginning of the century than the middle). The latter comprises a 'Basse-dance', a 'Demi basse-dance', and a triple-metre 'Tourdion'. The basse dance is Clément Janequin's delightful chanson *Il estoit une fillette*, regularized into basse-dance metre, and carries the title of the chanson. The same chanson was arranged previously as a four-part pavan entitled *La Gaiette*, and is found in the dance collection *Musique de joye* printed by Jacques Moderne in Lyons (no date, but definitely from the 1540s). It appears also as a 'Ronde' in Tylman Susato's four-part dance collection published in Antwerp in 1551. Another of Le Roy's chanson-dance arrangements for guitar, entitled *Bransle gay. Je ne seray jamais bergere*, is also found in Moderne's collection,[25] and several others appear in similar Parisian prints of the time. As previously suggested for the items with four-part concordances in Le Roy's first book, combining the embellished guitar parts from his third book with the bass and inner lines from the ensemble versions can result in some truly delightful-sounding Renaissance consort music.

   The fourth book in the series, *Quart livre de tablature de guiterre . . . composées par M. Gregoire Brayssing de augusta . . .* (Paris, 1553), is exceptional in many respects. It is the work of Gregor Brayssing (*fl.* 1547–60) of Augsburg, a German lutenist who was probably in the service of the Elector Johann Friedrich of Saxony. Upon Friedrich's defeat by Emperor Charles V in 1547 at Mühlberg, Brayssing left Germany. He is not heard of again until 1553, the year his book was published in Paris by Le Roy and Ballard. Little else is known about him, but he was apparently active in the same Parisian music circles as Le Roy, and was a friend of Etienne du Tertre, the composer of many chansons and an ensemble dance collection of 1557. Brayssing later became friends with Loys Bourgeois, a composer and theorist known for his psalm settings, his role in the development of the Calvinist Psalter, and his didactic manual *Le droict chemin de musique* (Geneva, 1550). Brayssing himself intabulated five psalms for solo guitar, including one by Josquin; the others have not been identified.

   His 1553 collection opens with six contrapuntal fantasias. Several are lengthy and all are gems of the four-course guitar repertory. These are followed by the aforementioned psalm settings (each with its Latin title followed by an approximate translation into French), which are finely wrought and lightly embellished with passagework. Next come Brayssing's intabulations of six chansons by Jean Maillard, Sandrin, Boyvin, Arcadelt, Sandrin, and Mathieu Sohier, respectively; and Sebastian Festa's late Italian frottola *O passi sparsy* (a setting of Petrarch's sonnet) which was known and loved throughout Europe.

[25] No. 28.

Brayssing's book concludes with two rather long pieces that are singled out for mention on its title page. The first is a perennial favourite, Janequin's 207-bar descriptive chanson *L'Alouette/Or sus vous dormés trop*, with its imitation of a singing lark; the second is a programme piece in the 'battle' genre, 189 bars long, composed by Brayssing himself, and entitled *La guerre*. The latter piece carries the rubric: 'Veldt schlacht Wieder loblicher Churfurst herzogk Johans Friderich Von Sachsen vor Mulberg gefangen ist Worden', which refers to the above-mentioned battle of 1547 involving his probable former patron Johann Friedrich of Saxony.

The fifth and final book in the series, Le Roy's *Cinquiesme livre de guiterre, contenant plusieurs chansons a trois & quatre parties . . .* (Paris, 1554), is a voice and guitar collection similar in format to the *Second livre* and very *au courant*. Of its twenty-three items, fourteen are three-part pieces by the renowned Franco-Flemish composer Jacques Arcadelt (*c.*1505–68). Two of them, *Que te sert amy* and *J'ay tant bon credit*, appear here in print for the first time; three others were published by Le Roy in the previous year in three-voice versions; and all the remaining items were published by him in the same year in three-part versions. Apart from the chansons by Arcadelt, there are two by Pierre Certon not found elsewhere; two by Le Roy himself; and one each by De Bussy (given name unknown) and Laurent Bonard. Five of the texts can be ascribed to Saint-Gelais. While most of the items are presented with the original top part (superius) in staff notation for the singer, at least three, *Quand viendra la clarté*, *Je ne sçay que c'est*, and *Amour me sçauriez*, all by Arcadelt and with texts by Saint-Gelais, have the original tenor part notated in staff notation. As is typical for chanson intabulations in this format, the guitar tablatures contain the complete chanson, including a lightly embellished version of the tenor melody line.

The copies of Le Roy's five printed books found in the Bibliothèque Mazarine in Paris are all bound together with an appendix of eight folios of manuscript tablature for guitar (F-Pm Rés. 44. 108).[26] Apparently, most of the music contained on the manuscript folios was copied directly from the printed books in *c.*1560. Another, later, French manuscript for lute and cittern (F-Pn Rés. 1109)[27] also includes five guitar tablatures that were copied from Le Roy's printed books. The collection for four-course guitar published in Antwerp in 1570 by Pierre Phalèse and Jean Bellère under the Latin title *Selectissima elegantissimaque, Gallica, Italica et Latina in guiterna ludenda carmina . . .*[28] includes ninety-two items pirated from Le Roy's books I–V, as well as the tablature parts for his voice and guitar pieces, but not the vocal parts in staff notation. The remaining sixteen items in the Phalèse and Bellère publication also seem to be by Le Roy, but are not from any of his surviving books.[29]

---

[26] See RISM B/VII, 278.   [27] See Goy et al. (1991), 89–91.

[28] For a description and list of contents, see Brown (1965), 248–50. An apparent second edition dated 1573 is described on p. 268.

[29] They are possibly from Le Roy's lost 1551 tutor.

The Phalèse and Bellère print begins with instructions in Latin for tuning and playing the guitar. Some scholars have surmised that they were from Le Roy's lost tutor; however, Dobson, Segerman, and Tyler[30] have shown that they are actually a very bad adaptation for guitar of Sebastian Vredeman's cittern instructions from a 1568 publication that was also printed by Phalèse. Ironically, these garbled, misleading instructions serve as another indication of how closely associated the guitar and cittern were in the minds of sixteenth-century musicians.

The two published series by Morlaye, Gorlier, Le Roy, and Brayssing comprise an extensive and varied selection of music for an instrument that had become, by this time, a true fixture in the musical life of France. Just how popular the guitar had become is revealed in a short anonymous treatise entitled *Discours non plus melancoliques*... (Poitiers, 1556).[31] Its author observes that formerly the lute was used more than the guitar; however, during the last twelve or fifteen years everyone has taken to the guitar, and today there are more guitarists in France than in Spain.[32] He also mentions that the lute and guitar have their strings arranged in double courses, except for the first, which is single, and thus corroborates Bermudo's statement that the guitar has seven strings in four courses. After explaining how to divide up the vibrating string length of a lute from nut to bridge in order to find the proper places for the tied frets, he says that you end up with a string length of two or three feet ('pié'), but when you calculate the fretting for a guitar, you are working with a string length of only a foot and a half.[33]

A manuscript from about 1585 (F-Pn MS fr. 9152), intended by its author Jacques Cellier as a didactic discourse on a wide range of subjects, includes some fascinating information about the guitar. On fo. 190 there is a precise drawing of a four-course guitar with seven pegs and strings and seven frets.[34] Below the drawing is a tuning chart in staff notation together with tuning instructions. On the chart Cellier designates the course numbers in reverse of the order used today: that is, his first course is our fourth and his fourth our first (see Ex. 2.1). This manner of designating courses

Ex. 2.1. Jacques Cellier's tuning chart (*c.*1585)

[30] Dobson et al. (1974). A reprint of Phalèse's Latin instructions are in Heartz (1963).

[31] The treatise is reprinted in Vaccaro (1981), 459–64. Dobbins (1992), 59 and 269 suggests that the author is the literary figure Bonaventure des Périers (d. *c.*1544).

[32] 'duquel [the lute] en mes premiers ans nous usions plus que de la Guiterne: mais despuis douze ou quinze ans en ça, tout nostre monde s'est mis a Guiterner . . . trouverés aujourdui plus de Guiterneurs en France, qu'en Espagne'. Text in Vaccaro (1981), 459.

[33] 'Tu as fait la ligne EF de deus ou trois pié long, mais tu as une Guiterne . . . qui n'a pas un pié & demy de corde . . .'. Text in Vaccaro (1981), 464.

[34] Reproduced in Turnbull (1974), pl. 19.

Ex. 2.2. Interpretation of Cellier's tuning

was not uncommon in sixteenth-century sources. His tuning instructions are: 'The thick string [of the lowest-pitched course] of the guitar is tuned with the following [course] at [the interval of] a fourth [higher]. And the following [course] with the third [course] at [the interval of] a third and the third [course] with the fourth [or highest course] at [the interval of] a fourth'.[35] This, as we have seen, is the standard interval pattern of a typical four-course guitar.

The three changes of clef indicated on Cellier's tuning chart can be interpreted as representing the three intervals mentioned in his instructions. The first interval is a fourth from *g* below middle *c´*. The second, despite the different octave given by the new clef, is the third from *c* to *e*. The next is puzzling because the clef indicates the expected interval of a fourth, but Cellier gives the pitches as *a* and *d´*, which make no sense in this interval pattern. Either his intention here was merely to show the interval pattern without defining a specific pitch, or he has made a mistake in the designation of the pitch. If the former, and Cellier included the staff notation merely as a graphic representation that was not meant to be taken literally, and if Cellier's starting pitch *g* seems a reasonable one, then the end result is a tuning that is identical with Bermudo's *temple a los nuevos*.[36] (See Ex. 2. 2.)

Of course, a third interpretation might be that the *a* (the nominal pitch of the first course of a typical four-course guitar)[37] is meant to be followed by a fifth course at *d´*. After all, Bermudo had theorized about a small five-course guitar in 1555. Nevertheless, this interpretation no longer seems probable, especially since another copy of Cellier's manuscript (GB–Lbl Add. MS 3042) has only the drawing of the guitar and the written instructions (fo. 145ᵛ), and no chart suggesting a fifth course. There is no convincing evidence that the five-course guitar was known in sixteenth-century France. On the other hand, as this chapter has shown, the quality and extent of the published repertory for the four-course instrument certainly attest to *its* widespread use and immense popularity in France.

---

[35] 'La grosse corde de la guiterne saccorde avec la suivante a la quarte. Et la suivante avec la troizieme a la tierce & la tierce avec la quarte a la quarte.'

[36] See Ch. 1. This interpretation supersedes the one in Tyler (1980*a*), 36.

[37] Heartz (1963) interprets the chart as being for a five-course guitar, as have other writers, including Tyler (1980*a*).

3

England: '. . . yused of gentilmen, and of the best sort . . .'

Not long after it was introduced in France, the guitar also became known in England. It is first cited in Thomas Whythorne's autobiography. Whythorne reports that when he went to London in 1545, he 'learned to play on the Gittern, and Sithern which ii instruments were then strange in England, and therefore the more desired and esteemed'. The gittern, he writes, 'was an instrument . . . yused of gentilmen, and of the best sort in thoz days'.[1] One such gentleman was England's Secretary of State, Sir William Petre, who owned and took lessons on a 'gyttron' in 1550. An engraved portrait of Robert Dudley, Earl of Leicester, dated 1568, in which a small guitar is included among the objects symbolic of his interests and pursuits, suggests that he too was a gentleman occupied with the guitar.[2]

While it should never be assumed that the name by which an instrument is known in one period signifies the same instrument in another period,[3] one can be reasonably certain that from the mid-sixteenth to the early seventeenth century in England 'gittern' meant guitar. In Richard Perceval's *Dictionarie in Spanish and English* (London, 1599) the phrase 'Tañér guitárra' is translated as 'to play on the Gitterne'. It also seems likely that the various spellings of the English term were derived from the various spellings of the contemporary French term 'guiterne'. In Randle Cotgrave's *Dictionarie of the French and English Tongues* (London, 1611), 'Guiterne' or 'Guiterre' is translated as 'a Gitterne'.[4] In this respect, it is significant that the copies of Le Roy's series of books for *la guiterne* that are preserved in the British Library were purchased 'new' by an Englishman.[5]

Sixteenth-century English music sources also lend support to the view that the gittern was a typical four-course guitar. The earliest is a fragment found at the beginning of Raphe Bowles's lute manuscript, dated 1558 (GB–Lbl Stowe 389). Written in French tablature for an unnamed four-course instrument with the expected intervals

---

[1] Quoted in Heartz (1963), 16. See Osborn (1962), 11, 21–3.

[2] Heartz (1963), 16, 19–20 and pl. IIa.

[3] For example, about a century later in England the name 'gittern' seems to indicate a wire-strung instrument much like a cittern. See Ward (1979–81), 9–15.

[4] Heartz (1963), 3–4.

[5] Ward (1979–81), 16.

of a four-course guitar (nominal pitches not given), it is the opening of a Passamezzo antico set in the style of the Le Roy and Morlaye guitar publications. A manuscript for keyboard belonging to Thomas Mulliner (GB–Lbl Add. MS 30513) also contains nine pieces for cittern ('Cytherne' or 'Sitherne') and a fragment and two pieces for 'gitterne' (added at the very end in about 1560). The last require an instrument with four courses tuned to guitar intervals and echo the style of contemporary French guitar pieces (that is, four-note chords alternating with running single-line passages). The music comprises anonymous, untitled settings of the Italian harmonic grounds Chi passa and Passamezzo antico; the fragment appears to be the opening bars of a setting of the Romanesca.[6] A larger selection of twenty-one anonymous pieces is included in the Osborn Manuscript of *c.*1560, now in the Beinecke Library at Yale University in New Haven, Connecticut (US–NH Osborn Music MS 13). In French tablature, these pieces are for an unnamed four-course instrument tuned to guitar intervals; nominal pitches are not given. Several titles are in English including 'The hedgynge hay', 'Pardye', and 'Whane raging love'; many others are settings of Italian harmonic grounds. Among the pieces labelled 'Matizine', 'gallyard', 'quando claro', 'saltarello', 'pavana', et al. are ones that appear to be the musical support for texts by the Earl of Surrey and Thomas Wyatt.[7]

Some of the pieces in the Osborn Manuscript are similar in style to the French guitar repertory, but a number are comprised of full four-note chords throughout. The presence of the latter pieces has led John Ward to posit that the music in this manuscript was intended for two different instruments: a four-course guitar for the typical French-style settings and, for the chordal pieces, an 'old-fashioned wire-strung English gittern that was played with a plectrum'.[8] He argues that these chordal pieces are 'clearly wedded to the use of a plectrum'.[9] The problem with this theory is that there is no evidence that a wire-strung English gittern was in use during the time of the manuscript. The evidence that Ward presents is from an entire century later.[10] As for the necessity of using a plectrum to play the chordal pieces, Bermudo (1555) refers to 'Musica golpeada' (struck or strummed music) for the four-course guitar with no mention of a plectrum. According to Bermudo, strumming the guitar was a long-standing tradition in Spain.[11] Moreover, it is known that when Prince Philip of Spain

---

[6] For bibliographic details and further information on the pieces in the Bowles and Mulliner manuscripts, see Ward (1979–81), 110–12.

[7] For a description and thematic index of these pieces, see ibid. 112–29.

[8] Ward (1992); i: Text; ii: Music. See i. 36.

[9] Ibid. i. 36.

[10] Ibid. i. 28. See also Ward (1979–81), 6–15. Ward cites as evidence a manuscript by Sir Peter Leycester dated 1656 (Cheshire Record Office, DLT/B33). In the mid-17th century the instrument known as a 'Gittyrne' apparently was 'a Treble Psittyrne'. However, I do not accept this as evidence that the English gittern of a century earlier was also a treble cittern.

[11] Bermudo, *Libro segundo*, ch. 32. See also above, Ch. 1 n. 5. A later source, Cerreto (1601), also mentions strumming on the four-course guitar. (See below, Ch. 4.)

was at the English court for a brief time during his marriage to Mary Tudor (1554–8), some of his own court musicians were with him.[12] All evidence from the mid-sixteenth century found to date seems to suggest that the four-course repertory in the Osborn manuscript is for one instrument—a guitar—played in both the French lute style and the Spanish chordal strumming style.[13]

As for the size of the guitar, there are only a few clues in English sources. The aforementioned 1568 portrait of the Earl of Leicester shows what looks to be a very small guitar, assuming the scale of the instruments is comparable to that of the other surrounding objects. From around the same time, the remarkable inlaid designs on the top of the so-called 'Eglantine table' depict, among other things, a lute, cittern, and four-course guitar.[14] These inlays are clearly meant to be realistic representations; since the relative dimensions of the lute and cittern (instruments about which we have a great deal of information) are accurate, the representation of the guitar in relation to them should be reliable. Not surprisingly, the guitar is shown as being quite small—considerably smaller than the lute and somewhat smaller than the cittern. Its comparative string length has been estimated at 38 cm,[15] which is consistent with the information found in the French and Spanish sources.

Other important information concerning the guitar in sixteenth-century England is contained in publications associated with the enterprising English printer James Rowbotham. It is known that in 1568–9 Rowbotham published *A briefe and plaine instruction for to learne the Tablature, to Conduct & dispose the hand unto the Gitterne*, now lost. From the wording of the title, it appears as if Rowbotham's publication was an English translation of Adrian Le Roy's 1551 guitar tutor *Briefve et facile instruction pour apprendre la tablature à bien accorder, conduire et disposer la main sur la guiterne*,[16] also lost—except for the pieces pirated (or rescued, depending upon how one views the matter) by Pierre Phalèse (1570). A publication of Rowbotham's that does survive, *A Briefe and easye instru[c]tion to learne the tablature to conducte and dispose thy hande unto the Lute* (1568), is definitely known to be a translation of another of Le Roy's lost tutors.[17]

In *c*.1977 eight pages of Rowbotham's lost gittern book were recovered.[18] Four of them, now in the Van Pelt Library of the University of Pennsylvania in Philadelphia (no shelf number), are headed 'An instruction to the Gitterne' and contain incomplete

---

[12] See 'Habsburg' (3) in *Grove 6*.

[13] Full chordal strumming with the fingers was a central stylistic feature of five-course guitar music and technique as well.

[14] Illustrated in Collins (1976), 275–9. Segerman (1976), 485 gives estimates of the string lengths of the 'Eglantine' instruments.

[15] Segerman (1976), 485.

[16] Ward (1979–81), 16–17 and Brown (1965), 130 and 238.

[17] Phalèse (1570) is discussed above, Ch. 2. See also Brown (1965), 248–50. For a description of Rowbotham's lute print, see Brown (1965), 229–30.

[18] Ward (1979–81), 107–8.

pieces in French tablature for a four-course instrument tuned to guitar intervals. The captions on two of the pages are in French, 'Plus diminués' and 'Plus fredonnes', which indicate here, as they do in some of Le Roy's lute publications, that these are the more embellished and the much more embellished versions (in terms of the rapidity of the passagework and the smaller note values) of well-known pieces. The plain versions of the pieces are not among the fragments preserved here. Neither are there titles on the fragments, although one is an exact concordance of the complete 'Plus diminués' version of the *Almande. Les bouffons* from Phalèse's 1570 print, and is followed by the 'A' section of the 'Plus fredonnes' version of the same piece.

Not long after the existence of the Philadelphia fragments became known, another two pages were recovered in Shrewsbury by Peter Duckers, who, several months later, found two more.[19] Astonishingly, the four new pages turned out to be from the same section of the book as the previously recovered Philadelphia fragments. It is now possible to assemble a hypothetical sequence of the pages as follows: a Philadelphia page containing a short untitled prelude (to demonstrate the major mode) and a tuning chart; followed by a Duckers page containing an almost identical piece of music (to demonstrate a flattened mode, 'b mol') entitled 'Petitte fantasie dessus l'accord', the opening measures of which have been torn away. These are followed by another Duckers page (with the folio number 14) on which the 'Petitte fantasie' continues; another Philadelphia page on which it still seems to continue; and another Duckers page (with the folio number 15) on which it ends. The 'Petitte fantasie' is a fine 76-bar piece. It would not be difficult to reconstruct its missing opening bars.

On the same Duckers page is *Les buffons*, which turns out to be the plain version of the piece mentioned previously in the description of the Philadelphia fragments. It is an exact concordance of the plain version of the *Almande. Les bouffons* from Phalèse's 1570 print. The next Philadelphia page contains the aforementioned 'Plus diminués version of *Les buffons*, and the Philadelphia page which follows, the aforementioned 'A' section of the 'Plus fredonnes' version of the piece. The 'B' section of this version would have been on the next page, which, unfortunately, is still missing, and the final Duckers page contains the last eight measures of it. The 'Plus fredonnes' versions of this and other Le Roy pieces are not included in the Phalèse print, perhaps because he judged them to be too difficult for his clientele.

An estimate of the size and contents of the Rowbotham print can be made by comparing what remains of it to a similar extant publication by Le Roy entitled *Breve et facile instruction pour apprendre la tablature, à bien accorder, conduire, et disposer la main sur le Cistre* (Paris, 1565).[20] This tutor opens with an engraved illustration of a distinctively decorated cittern. Since Phalèse (1570) includes an illustration of a guitar that is

---

[19] I am immensely grateful to Peter Duckers for contacting me about the pages and enclosing photocopies with his letters of 19 Oct. 1986 and 1 Jan. 1987. These pages later became part of the collection of the late Robert Spencer.

[20] Brown (1965), 218–19.

PL. 3.1. Four-course guitar illustrated in Marin Mersenne,
Harmonie universelle (Paris, 1636), copied from Pierre Phalèse (1570)

engraved in a style identical to Le Roy's cittern (see Pl. 3.1), it is reasonable to assume that he obtained it from Le Roy's lost 1551 guitar tutor, and that the same guitar illustration might have appeared in the Rowbotham gittern print as well.

The cittern book continues with sixteen instructions for stringing the instrument, reading tablature, fingering, and understanding the rhythmic signs and their correlation to staff notation values (for example, ♪ = ♩, ♪ = ♩, etc.). Tuning instructions and a tuning chart follow. It is entirely possible that the Rowbotham gittern print contained the same type of instructions, although, as previously mentioned, a short prelude in the major mode precedes the tuning chart on the first of the recovered pages of the Rowbotham gittern print. In both books music follows the instruments' respective tuning charts. In total the cittern book comprises twenty-four folios (48 pages).

The tuning chart from the Rowbotham gittern print contains what seems at first to be some quite baffling information (see Ex. 3.1). Had they been meant to be taken literally, the pitches shown on the chart would suggest an instrument much larger than the size indicated by most other sixteenth-century sources. Not that an instrument with a string length long enough for the highest pitch *d′* (that is, a whole tone below modern guitar *e′*) is completely out of the question.[21] However, negotiating the rapid 'fredonnes', not to mention the demanding left-hand stretches so prevalent in this style of music, on a large instrument would have presented Rowbotham's clientele with a rather unrealistic challenge. Indeed, it is highly unlikely that the pitches were intended to be taken as the actual pitches of the guitar, especially since the concept of an absolute pitch standard had yet to be explored in the sixteenth century. Clearly, the

---

[21] A woodcut by Tobias Stimmer from the 1570s of a woman playing a large four-course seven-string guitar is reproduced in Turnbull (1974), pl. 18. Michael Praetorius (*Syntagma musicum II . . .*, 1619), 28 gives, in staff notation, this same *d′* tuning, as well as one a fourth higher.

Ex. 3.1. James Rowbotham's tuning chart (1601)

tuning chart was intended only as a graphic illustration of guitar intervals,[22] and Rowbotham's guitar was the same small high-pitched instrument described in the many contemporary sources and treatises that have been surveyed thus far.

Which leads to the question: in the absence of an absolute pitch standard, how was the actual pitch to which a guitar (or any sixteenth-century instrument) could be tuned determined? Apparently that depended on several factors of a quite pragmatic nature: the instrument's size, the strength of its construction, and the quality of the gut strings that the player had on hand. In other words, as Ward has explained so excellently, actual pitch was relative, not absolute.[23]

Rowbotham's gittern book seems to have been the only printed source of guitar music from sixteenth-century England. However, the fact that it was published at all indicates, at the very least, a perceived demand for guitar music in England during this period—otherwise, would Rowbotham or any other commercial publisher have taken the financial risk? As this print and the manuscripts discussed in this chapter show, interest in the four-course guitar began in England around the middle of the century, influenced, quite possibly, by the 1554 marriage of Mary Tudor to Prince Philip of Spain, and, most definitely, by the transmission of French guitar music to England via the guitar-playing English aristocracy.

---

[22] See the discussion of the Cellier tuning chart above, Ch. 2. Another, albeit later, example of a staff notation tuning chart representing only a graphic illustration of guitar intervals is found in Marin Mersenne, *Harmonicorum libri XII* (Paris, 1648), 27. Here the tuning of the five-course guitar is shown, with pitches that are a fifth lower than expected. Later, however, in his written explanation, Mersenne gives the expected nominal pitches for the instrument.
[23] Ward (1982).

4

Italy: *La Chitarra da sette corde*

Guitar music is first encountered in Italy on the final pages of Melchiore de Barberiis's fifth lute publication, *Opera intitolata contina* (Venice, 1549). Barberiis (*fl. c.* 1545–50) was a priest at Padua Cathedral, the town's principal music centre, and, according to the book's title page, was a most excellent lute player ('sonator di Lauto eccellentissimo'). Regrettably, apart from the sparse information found in his own publications, we know almost nothing about Barberiis's life; however, we do know a great deal about the cosmopolitan town in which he lived and worked.

Padua was part of the Republic of Venice and renowned for its university, which was founded in 1222. From the outset Padua University attracted students from all over Europe and England, especially law students, whose liberal arts education included music.[1] By the sixteenth century Padua had become a mecca for lutenists, whose services were much in demand by a large student population eager for lute lessons. Like his colleague Antonio Rotta, Barberiis was probably one of Padua's many lute teachers and, with five publications to his credit,[2] part of the town's vibrant cultural scene, which, of course, also included members of the Paduan nobility and other wealthy patrons of musical, literary, and scientific endeavours.

It is entirely possible that Barberiis was introduced to the four-course guitar and its French repertory by one of his French, Flemish, or English students. There are four short guitar pieces at the end of his 1549 lute book. Although each is marked 'Fantasia', the pieces are actually simple dances in regular four-bar phrases. The first is found, note for note, in Guillaume Morlaye's *Le second livre . . .* (second edition, Paris, 1553; first edition, now lost, *c.* 1550–1), where it is entitled 'bransle'.[3] The third consists of lightly embellished statements of the Italian Bergamasca and Passamezzo antico grounds. The second and fourth fantasias have not yet been identified. Stylistically, all four are similar to the dance music found in the Morlaye and Le Roy prints, and in this regard the manner in which Barberiis presents the tablature for 'la Chitara da sette corde' (a frequent designation for the typical four-course guitar) is both unu-

---

[1] 'Padua' in *Grove 6*.

[2] Barberiis was the composer of five of the ten volumes of lute music produced by the Venetian printer Girolamo Scotto. One of the other volumes is by Francesco da Milano, regarded as the greatest lutenist-composer of his time. Another of the volumes is by Antonio Rotta. For details of this series, see Brown (1965), 76–7 n. 1.

[3] It is piece no. 23 in the 1553 edition.

sual and telling. As expected, the preceding lute pieces are notated in Italian-style tablature with the top line of the staff representing the sixth course of the lute and numbers on the lines representing the frets to be held down. For the guitar pieces, however, while numbers are used as in Italian-style tablature, the top line in Barberiis's four-line guitar tablature represents the first course of the guitar,[4] as in French-style tablature. To avoid confusion, either Barberiis or the publisher Scotto carefully marked the top line of each of the four pieces 'canto'. This precaution was apparently lost on the typesetter, however, as there are an inordinate number of printing errors in these four short pieces.

A fascinating manuscript, most likely Florentine, is preserved in the Brussels Bibliothèque du Conservatoire (MS Lit. XY no. 24135). It probably was begun in around 1540 as a cantus partbook for the madrigals and motets of such composers as Arcadelt and Francesco Corteccia; but it is obvious that additions were made to it over the course of many years.[5] Included in its miscellaneous contents is a section in Italian tablature for four-course guitar that was probably added in the 1570s. The music is very simple; most of the pieces have no barlines or rhythm signs, and it is clear that they are the work of an amateur scribe, notating as best she[6] could, an aide-memoire for future reference. Nevertheless, the contents, which have not been identified or discussed previously, offer not only an anthology of some of the guitar's most popular repertory, but also some valuable ancillary information.

The manuscript contains twenty short guitar pieces in all, beginning on folio 14 with an untitled setting of the Bergamasca in triple time, followed by a setting of Ruggiero. Folio 14^v includes a piece entitled *La franchina*, which is a setting of the popular *commedia dell'arte* song *La bella Franceschina*. Folio 15 contains a setting of the *Cavalletto zoppo*, which is the accompaniment to a popular song based on the Passamezzo antico ground. Nothing is known about *Malgarita* on folio 15^v. Folio 16^{r-v} contains an *Aria da cantare*, a harmonic formula to which poetry was sung.[7] Not surprisingly, the harmonies are that of the most frequently used ground for this practice, the Romanesca. An unidentified *Pavana* appears next (fo. 17), followed by two untitled and unidentified pieces on folios 17^v and 18. The next two pieces are entitled *Lirum* and *Ciciliana* (fos. 18^v and 19); and on folio 19^v there is a *Matacinata*, the Italian version of the French *Matachines*, a semi-ritual dance that generally portrays a mock battle or sword fight. The folk-religious version of the *Matachines* survives to this day in Mexico and elsewhere.[8] The music for the Italian *Matacinata*, as for the other sixteenth-century versions, consists of two bars of I and two bars of IV, with an off beat or

---

[4] I have encountered this unusual tablature style only in one other source, Luis Milan's book of 1535, which is for the six-course vihuela.

[5] Fenlon and Haar (1988), 145–6.

[6] There is evidence that the manuscript came from a convent.

[7] This traditional Italian practice was mentioned in Ch. 2 in connection with Morlaye's *Quatriesme livre*, 1552.

[8] For more information, see 'Matachin' in *Grove 6*.

syncopated rest from bar 3 into 4. The four bars are repeated again and again until the dance ends.[9]

The next piece (on the same folio), entitled *Buratinata*, has just as simple a harmonic scheme as the *Matacinata*. Folio 20 contains fragments of music in staff notation, and the two tablatures after that are settings of the 'Rug[g]iero' ground (fo. 20ᵛ) and *Liram* (fo. 21). The latter does not contain the same musical material as the aforementioned *Lirum*. This section of the manuscript ends with a piece whose title is extremely difficult to decipher: 'Capritio novo [next word unreadable] Ricardo [?] Pallav.no' (fo. 21ᵛ).

Most of the remaining folios have been ruled for music, but are blank until almost the end of the manuscript, where four additional pieces for a four-course instrument appear in a different and much neater hand. Like the other tablatures, these have no bar lines or rhythm signs. The first item is entitled *La Violina* (fo. 64) and consists of a single-line melody. The piece uses the interval pattern of the four-course guitar; if it did not, given the similarities in appearance of Italian violin tablature and Italian four-course guitar tablature, it could be mistaken for a violin piece. The remaining items are chordal in style, beginning with a *Vilan Spagnolo* (fo. 64) consisting of one statement of the four-bar ground. Generally called 'Villan di Spagna' (the Spanish peasant), it is found in countless versions spanning two centuries. On the same folio is yet another statement of the 'Rug[g]iero' ground; and finally, on folio 64ᵛ, a piece entitled *Spagnoleto*, the ubiquitous three-section ground and melodic pattern, which became exceedingly popular in the seventeenth century (when it was arranged many hundreds of times for lute and guitar).[10] Despite its title, the Italian Spagnoletta does not seem to have originated in Spain.

A document dating from around the time of the latest pieces in the Brussels manuscript contains one of the earliest specific references to the five-course instrument, known in Italy as the Spanish guitar (chitarra spagnola). In a letter of 31 January 1579 the eminent patron of the arts Cardinal Del Monte[11] professed to sing to the 'chitarra Spagnola'.[12] Although it cannot be said with absolute certainty that he was referring to the five-course instrument, many later documents confirm this use of the term.[13]

Italian references to the use of guitars in a theatrical context began appearing during the last decade or so of the sixteenth century. The most spectacular politico-cultural event of the time, the 1589 wedding in Florence of the Grand Duke Ferdinand

[9] There are two chords in this piece, which, if they are not scribal errors, seem to indicate the need for a guitar with a fifth course.

[10] It was revived in the 20th c. by Ottorino Respighi, who set it for orchestra in the third of his suites of *Ancient Airs and Dances*, where it is called 'Siciliana'.

[11] Francesco Del Monte (1549–1626). Caravaggio was one of his protégés.

[12] Quoted in Christiansen (1990), 28.

[13] No qualifying adjective is found in the title of a guitar book printed in the 1580s—Girolamo Giuliani's *Intavolatura de chitarra* (*c.*1585), listed in Brown (1965), 359; since it is now lost, the nature of the guitar for which it was written cannot be determined.

Ex. 4.1. Scipione Cerretto's tuning chart (1568–9)

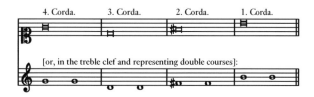

de' Medici and the French princess Christine of Lorraine, included six sumptuously staged *intermedi* (that is, entertainments that combined breathtaking visual effects, costumes, music, dance, and poetry), performed between the acts of Girolamo Bargagli's comedy *La pellegrina*.[14] These musical productions not only commemorated an alliance that was of great political import, they were also a showcase for the latest development in Italian vocal and accompaniment style, which modern scholars have termed 'monody'.

The final *intermedio*, subtitled 'Il dono di Giove ai mortali di Ritmo e Armonia' (Jove's gift to mortals of Rhythm and Harmony), ended with a lavish production number involving a large cast of singers and dancers. Composed by Emilio de' Cavalieri (*c.* 1550–1602), the artistic director of the entire event, the 'Ballo', entitled 'O che nuovo miracolo' (O what fresh wonders), comprised a series of sections in which a mixed chorus alternated with a trio of women singers, one of whom was the acclaimed virtuosa Vittoria Archilei (1550–*c.* 1620). Each of the three women accompanied themselves on instruments, 'Margherita' on a tambourine, Vittoria on a 'chitarrina . . . alla Spagnola', and Lucia Caccini on a 'chitarrina . . . alla Napolettana'.

A Neapolitan printed source from 1601 helps to clarify the nature of the last instrument, providing details of its tuning and stringing arrangement, as well as offering fascinating insight into the procedure for intabulating polyphonic music on the tiny four-course instrument. The source, *Della prattica musica vocale et strumentali*,[15] is by the composer, theorist, and lutenist Scipione Cerreto (*c.* 1555–1633),[16] who provides a tuning chart and instructions for a 'chitarra à sette Corde', which he also refers to by the provocative nickname 'bordelletto alla Taliana' (little Italian brothel-house guitar) (see Ex. 4.1). Note that the tuning is re-entrant, that is, the pitch of the fourth course is higher than the third, and that the lowest pitch indicated is *d'* above middle *c'*. Cerreto's guitar is a true treble-range instrument. Its normal pitches are even higher (by one tone) than the ones indicated by Bermudo (1555) and the sixteenth-century

---

[14] For a discussion of the Florentine *intermedi* see D. P. Walker (1963), which includes an edition of all of the music. For full documentary detail, see also Saslow (1996). And for related information and new musical examples, see Treadwell (2001), chs. 4 and 5.

[15] Cerreto (1601), *Libro quarto*, ch. 8.   [16] 'Cerreto, Scipione' in *Grove 6*.

Ex. 4.2. Cerretto's example of an intabulation for guitar (1601)

French sources. Even though there is no bourdon on the fourth course (as called for by both Bermudo and Mudarra, 1546), the interval arrangement is similar to that of the *temple a los viejos* and *a corde avallée* tuning, except the fourth course is up a fourth instead of down a fifth.

In his commentary Cerreto states that 'the guitar of seven strings is imperfect because there are no low notes on it as on a lute'; however, he says 'whenever you want to intabulate [part music] the low notes can be transposed up an octave or fifteenth higher'.[17] To illustrate, he provides a short musical example in four-part counterpoint, and beneath it an intabulation of the piece using standard Italian tablature. Cerreto's example is given in Ex. 4.2, along with an editorial transcription of the tablature into staff notation showing the arrangement of the voice lines for the four-course guitar.

Cerreto then provides another chart, which correlates in staff notation each note on the guitar fingerboard up to the tenth fret, and confirms the re-entrant tuning indicated on his previous tuning chart. In addition he comments on the practice of strumming the four-course guitar (as opposed to the lute-style technique he used for his intabulations): 'And when the instrument will be sounded chordally with all the fingers of the right hand, it will make a beautiful effect, but this method of playing needs much practice to learn.'[18]

The distinction between Spanish and Neapolitan guitars was one that would persist into the next century, when the small four-course guitar was often labelled 'Napoletana', and the five-course 'Spagnola'. Of course, the diminutive form 'chitarrina' for the Spanish guitar used in Cavalieri's ballo 'O che nuovo miracolo' suggests that it too was a small instrument, similar perhaps to the Iberian five-course guitar by Belchior Dias, dated 1581, discussed in Chapter 1. Records indicate that both guitars used in the Florentine *intermedi* had to be sent up from Rome, presumably because guitars were not yet common in the north of Italy, whereas they were already well established in the south.

It is perhaps worth mentioning that the harmonic pattern of Cavalieri's 'O che nuovo miracolo', known as the Aria di Firenze (or Ballo di Fiorenza, or Ballo del Gran Duca, among other similar names), made a truly indelible impression on Grand Duke Ferdinand's wedding guests. Not only was it an immediate 'hit', but it also became an international 'pop standard'. Since two guitars seem to have played featured roles in the ballo's first performance, it is not altogether surprising that virtually every volume of guitar music for the next seventy years included at least one setting of it.[19]

After working in Florence for many years, Cavalieri returned to his native Rome, where his sacred opera (the earliest for which all the music survives) *Rappresentatione di Anima, et di Corpo* (Drama of the Soul and the Body) was performed in February

---

[17] 'la Chitarra à sette Corde Strumento imperfetto, per causa che in esso non vi sono tutti le voci grave, come habbiamo nel Strumento del Liuto: Ma tuttavia volendosi intavolare potrassi transportare le Notule gravi per Ottava, ò Quintadecima alta . . .' (p. 320).

[18] 'E quando tale Strumento si sonarà arpiggiando con tutte le dita della mano destra, farà anco bello effetto, ma questo modo di sonare si può imparare con lunga prattica' (p. 321).

[19] There are also innumerable non-guitar settings by such composers as G. Frescobaldi, A. Banchieri, and G. B. Buonamente. For an exhaustive study of the Aria di Firenze, see Kirkendale (1972). Respighi's modern setting for orchestra is in the second suite of his aforementioned *Ancient Airs and Dances*, where it is called 'Laura soave'.

1600. The publisher's preface to the original score gives detailed information on how Cavalieri wanted his work to be performed: 'It will be good if [the character] Pleasure, with his two companions, have instruments in their hands, playing while they sing, and also playing their Ritornelli. One can have a chitarrone, another a chitarrina alla spagnuola, and the third a small tambourine with bells in the Spanish style.'[20] Cavalieri remains consistent in his use of the diminutive form for the Spanish guitar, and, as will be seen in Chapter 6, small five-course guitars were indeed used in Italy well into the seventeenth century .

It is ironic that the only written-out guitar music to survive from sixteenth-century Italy consists of the few short pieces at the conclusion of Barberiis's lute book and the simplistic offerings in the Brussels manuscript. Ironic, because, as will be seen in the next two chapters, it was in Italy that a notation system for the guitar associated with monody was created, and from Italy that solo guitar music of the highest order and, arguably, the greatest influence would soon emerge.

---

[20] 'Il Piacere con li due compagni, sarà bene, che habbiano stromenti in mano suonando mentre loro cantano, & si suonino i loro Ritornelli. Uno puotrà havere un Chitarone, l'altro una Chitarina Spagnuola, e l'altro un Cimbaletto con sonagline alla Spaguola, che facci poco romore . . .'. For a translation of the entire preface, see MacClintock (1979), 183–6.

5

Italy: The Role of the Guitar in the Rise of Monody

Music historians have recounted at length the rise of the new style of Italian solo song, known today as monody, and its new approach to accompaniment called basso continuo. Especially well chronicled are those activities that occurred in the north Italian cities of Florence, Ferrara, and Mantua. Much has been written about the 'Florentine Camerata', a circle of noblemen and intellectuals who met regularly to discuss and formulate theories on the nature of ancient culture and music, and how the latter might have been performed. An influential figure at these gatherings was the singer-composer Giulio Caccini (c.1545–1618), whose patrons were the Medici and whose 1602 publication *Le nuove musiche*, a book of solo songs with basso continuo accompaniment and a preface on the performance of 'the new music', is considered by many to be central to the rise of monody. As the new century dawned, Caccini, the singer-composer Jacopo Peri (1561–1633), Emilio de' Cavalieri, and others put monody to brilliant use in their creation of another Italian innovation, opera, thereby ensuring that Italian style would influence music production throughout Europe for another century.[1]

What very few scholars have investigated, however, is the degree to which these revolutionary developments in the north of Italy rested on the performing practices of the south, particularly Naples and Rome. Recent ground-breaking research by Howard Mayer Brown and, especially, John Walter Hill has demonstrated the singular importance of south Italian singing and accompanying practices, including the flexible sprezzatura (an artistic, seemingly nonchalant use of rubato and other dramatic devices to express the emotional content of song texts); the incorporation of recitational style and improvised, florid ornamentation; and the style of accompaniment, wherein simple harmonies derived from the bass line were played on a chordal instrument, often by the singer.[2] Hill has noted also that many of the performers and composers employed at the northern courts, who played leading roles in the development of monody, were either Roman, Neapolitan, or trained by south Italians. These

---

[1] For two typical accounts of these developments, see 'Monody' in *Grove 6* and Palisca (1989).
[2] Brown (1981) and Hill (1997), ch. 3.

included, among others, the soprano (and guitarist) Vittoria Archilei; Cavalieri and Caccini; Melchior Palantrotti, the bass singer in Peri's opera *Euridice* (1600); the soprano (and guitarist) Ippolita Recupita; and a singer regarded by Monteverdi as the finest of the time, Adriana Basile, who often accompanied herself on the guitar.[3]

Apparently, it was common practice in sixteenth-century Rome and Naples to sing poetry to the accompaniment of standard recitational formulas.[4] Sometimes these formulas were composed for a specific occasion, using a simple harmony and a neutral, almost chant-like melodic line; but more often than not a stock harmonic ground, such as the Romanesca, Tenor di Napoli, Ruggiero, or Passamezzo antico, played on a lute, cittern, or, above all, a guitar, was used to support the text.[5] This style of singing a text to a chord pattern (not necessarily with a high degree of melodic profile) may be likened somewhat to a mid-twentieth-century coffeehouse poet or folk-club vocalist, intoning or singing to a standard blues chord progression. Of course, in the Renaissance the practice was not confined to popular culture; indeed, the most celebrated court singers cultivated it to the level of high art.

In the 1520s vocal genres native to Naples and Rome and composed in a popular style began to be known and appreciated throughout Italy as well as in other parts of Europe. Called *napolitana*, *canzona alla napolitana*, *villanesca*, *villanella*, and *villotta*, they usually appeared as part music for three or four voices; however, a small number have survived as solo songs with instrumental accompaniment. The few examples encountered previously in the French four-course guitar sources, such as *La pastorella mia* by Jacques Arcadelt in Le Roy's fifth book (1554), showed that the prevailing style of accompaniment was virtually the same as for the lute,[6] that is, the guitar played an intabulation of the lower two or three parts and the top (melody) line was sung. Since the three parts usually were very limited in range, the four-course guitar's lack of a bass range did not present a great problem. Bass lines were easily adapted to fit the guitar, as Cerreto's example in the previous chapter demonstrates.

By the 1570s and 1580s the villanella and canzonetta publications of such renowned madrigalists as Orazio Vecchi (*c.*1563–1628) and Luca Marenzio (*c.*1553–99), combined with the continuing Neapolitan and Roman output, comprised a vast repertory; and there is much evidence to suggest that some of the later examples were performed as solo songs with instrumental accompaniment.[7] Not surprisingly, the instrumental accompaniment often involved the five-course Spanish guitar, which, as we saw in the previous chapter, was already in use in the south.

---

[3] Hill (1997), 70.   [4] Ibid. 84.

[5] For further information, see Hill (1997), 61–5, 84, and 105 and Coelho (1995*b*). Certain recitational formulas are also found in French sources for the four-course guitar. See above, Ch. 2.

[6] This type of 'lute song' is discussed in Mason (1997).

[7] Hill (1997), 84, 105, and 167 cites Vincenzo Giustiniani's *c.*1628 description of the emergence of monody in Rome in the context of recitational formulas and the accompanied solo performance of villanellas, arias, and madrigals.

An important manuscript dating from *c.*1585–1600, which contains examples of this repertory, is preserved in Bologna in the Biblioteca Universitaria (I–Bu MS 177/IV). It is a partbook for the top line ('canto' is written at the beginning of each piece)[8] of forty villanella- or canzonetta-type strophic songs. Three of the song texts, 'Non per viver da lunge Amor' (fos. 14ᵛ–15), 'Mentre l'aquila sta mirand'il sole' (fos. 15ᵛ–16), and 'Non vegio, al mondo cosa' (fos. 25ᵛ–26), were cited in 1588 by Giovanni del Tufo as songs that were frequently sung in the streets of Naples (*Ritratto . . . della nobilissima città di Napoli*). The first two texts are found in poetry manuscripts of the 1580s.[9] The third, despite its canzonetta-like setting in this source, is actually a *lauda* to the Virgin Mary, which is found in a different musical setting in Cosimo Bottegari's 'lute book'[10] (actually, 'viola da mano book'),[11] which he began in 1574. The Bologna canto part has a concordance in a four-part setting by the Neapolitan composer Scipione Dentice,[12] and there is another musical setting of the text in one of the earliest and most important sources of monody, a manuscript from *c.*1590–1600 preserved in the library of the Brussels Conservatoire (B–Bc MS 704, pp. 233–4).

The works of several of the most celebrated composers of the late sixteenth century are included in the Bologna partbook. Orazio Vecchi, a north Italian composer influenced by south Italian style, is represented by his widely known canzonetta *Mentre io campai contento* (fos. 38ᵛ–39), first published in 1580. Arguably the most famous example of early monody, Giulio Caccini's *Amarilli mia bella*, is also found here (fos. 37ᵛ–38), but in what may have been a three- or four-voice version and from a much earlier date than his famous 1602 setting for solo voice and basso continuo.[13] The Bologna canto part is virtually identical with the vocal line of the solo version. Two other composers, Paolo Quagliati and Luca Marenzio, who were working in Rome in the 1580s, are also represented: Quagliati by his canzonetta *La prima volta ch'io viddi tanta beltà* (fo. 30ᵛ), published in 1588, and Marenzio by his villanella *Dicemi la mia stella* (fos. 7ᵛ–8).

Significantly, the Bologna manuscript is also the earliest known document containing examples of a quasi-continuo notational system, devised specifically for the guitar, known as *alfabeto*. In this system the intended harmonies are symbolized by letters of the alphabet, which usually appear above the appropriate notes of the melody line. As shown in Ex. 5.1, each of the letters (as well as a few additional signs) represents a specific finger pattern on the guitar fingerboard, and thus a specific block harmony

---

[8] The other two or three partbooks do not survive.

[9] Cardamone (1981), 116.

[10] MacClintock (1965), no. 36.

[11] Tyler (1980*a*), 24.

[12] See RISM 1599[6]. This publication is an anthology of sacred music by several Neapolitan and Roman composers. It should not be assumed that Dentice's piece was composed in the very year the book was published. The composers represented in the anthology were mainly active in the 1580s.

[13] For a full discussion of the origins of *Amarilli mia bella* and a brief description of I-Bu MS 177/IV, see Carter (1988).

Ex. 5.1. Example of *alfabeto* notation. The resolution of the *alfabeto* chords into staff notation employs a tuning and stringing without bourdons. This arrangement was often associated with Rome and Naples

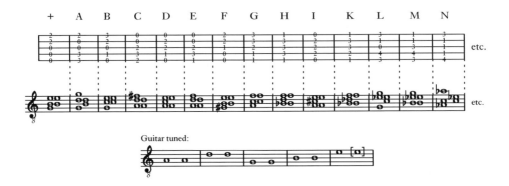

Guitar tuned:

(chord).[14] When the chords are played on a guitar without bourdons, any inversions are virtually inaudible. Even on a Baroque guitar strung *with* bourdons, the effect is still one of nearly inversion-free block harmonies.

  Alfabeto notation is found above sixteen of the Bologna manuscript's forty canto parts, including Marenzio's aforementioned *Dicemi la mia stella*. This piece was first published in the composer's 1584 collection of three-part *villanelle*,[15] in which the top part is identical with the Bologna canto part, except without the *alfabeto*. Example 5.2 is a transcription of Marenzio's villanella using the Bologna canto part and its *alfabeto* notation, together with the second and third parts from Marenzio's original printed version. As the transcription and the *alfabeto* chart show, unlike the earlier style of accompaniment in which the lutenist or guitarist played a near-literal intabulation of the lower parts, *alfabeto* notation merely provides the guitarist with an indication of the correct harmonies to play, that is, block chords that follow faithfully the harmonies implied in the part-writing. Hence, while it cannot be said with absolute certainty that Marenzio's *Dicemi la mia stella* was performed from the Bologna partbook as a solo song, what *is* certain is that someone's intention in around 1590 was to play a continuo-type accompaniment to it on guitar. Of course, the idea that guitar *alfabeto* pre-dates other systems of continuo notation belies the received impression from modern reference works that *alfabeto* made its first appearance in a 1606 print.[16] Nevertheless, there is no reason to doubt the dating of the Bologna manuscript or to suspect that its *alfabeto*, which is in the same hand as the rest of the music and text, was added later. As

[14] A more detailed explanation of the *alfabeto* system can be found below, Ch. 6.

[15] Luca Marenzio, *Il primo libro delle villanelle* (Venice, 1584).

[16] For example Carter (1988), 255. The reference is to Girolamo Montesardo, *Nuova inventione d'intavolatura . . .* (Florence, 1606), which is discussed in Ch. 6.

Ex. 5.2. Luca Marenzio's *Dicemi la mia stella* with canto line and *alfabeto* chords from I-Bu MS 177/iv

this and other sixteenth-century manuscripts (discussed below) bear out, the *alfabeto* system was already in use years prior to its first appearance in print, particularly in the Kingdom of Naples.

That Naples was a province of Spain during the sixteenth century and ruled by viceroys on behalf of the Spanish crown fuels the notion that the Spanish guitar was introduced in Rome by way of Naples. Likewise, the Bologna manuscript, with its apparent southern provenance, and other manuscripts with definite Neapolitan origins lend strong support to the notion that the *alfabeto* system was invented on Spanish-ruled Italian soil. Admittedly, there was a similar system in use in Spain known as 'Catalan cifras' (numbers), which was invented by Juan Carlos Amat and first appeared in print in 1596;[17] however, there is no evidence that this system was known or used in Italy, not even in Naples.[18]

The *alfabeto* system probably arose in direct response to the innovative changes in musical style that were taking place during the last quarter of the sixteenth century, and the guitar probably appealed to some of the early monodists because it was able to meet many of the demands of the new style. For example, monodic style required a chordal instrument whose technique allowed it to accompany the singer in as clear and transparent a manner as possible, so that the words of the song could be heard and understood without difficulty. Moreover, as the new style evolved and monodists began to experiment with unusual or unexpected harmonic shifts in the accompaniment, the chordal instrument also had to be very flexible in terms of the 'keys' in which it could play. Of course, any chord-playing instrument of the period could fulfil these requirements—although keyboard instruments (especially the harpsichord) do require tempered tuning systems,[19] which means that if the harmony moves away from the key in which it began, the remote chords will sound out of tune. Gut-strung plucked instruments, such as the lute and theorbo, which have movable, tied-on, gut frets and normally use equal temperament,[20] can play most chords quite well in tune without their frets having to be readjusted. However, on those instruments, some keys tend to be much more difficult physically for the left hand to deal with than others, and the more challenging chord shapes, with fewer convenient open strings available, can lose resonance.

The guitar, on the other hand, could meet many of the demands of monodic style with little difficulty. Because it has only five courses, a great many chords are a lot easier to negotiate on the guitar than on the lute or theorbo. Like those instruments, it has movable gut frets that are tuned in equal temperament; however, since it is comparatively easy to shift most chord shapes up and down the guitar's long fingerboard,[21] playing in tune in remote keys is almost as straightforward as the more common ones. By its very nature, the guitar encourages the player to think about harmony in the 'new' way rather than in terms of traditional counterpoint. Being able to play block

[17] Amat (1596) is lost; the 1626 edition is discussed at length in Ch. 9.
[18] Similarly, there is no evidence that the Italian *alfabeto* system was known or used in Spain before the late 17th c.
[19] See 'Temperaments' (1–3) in *Grove 6*.   [20] See 'Temperaments' (4) in *Grove 6*.
[21] See the discussion of shifted chords in Ch. 6.

chords on it with ease made the guitar an ideal tool for the early monodists, and the invention of *alfabeto* enabled them to notate, and hence transmit widely, a style of guitar accompaniment that may well have been a traditional unwritten Neapolitan practice.

Another Neapolitan *alfabeto* manuscript that pre-dates the notation's first appearance in print is entitled 'Libro de cartas y Romances Espanoles' (I-Rvat Chigi cod. L. VI. 200).[22] It is dated 1599 and dedicated to the Duchess of Traetta. Traetta was a fiefdom of Naples, located about 70 kilometres north-west of that city. Modern writers have identified the woman who was its duchess in 1599 as either Isabella Gonzaga[23] or Lucretia Orsini;[24] however, the famous dancing master Fabritio Caroso dedicated a dance to 'Cornelia Caraffa Caetana, Duchessa di Traetto' in his 1581 publication *Il ballarino*, and the same dance to 'Camilla Caetana Caetana, Duchessa di Traetto' in his 1600 reworking of the book.[25] As Caroso's livelihood probably depended to some extent on his keeping track of who was who at the various courts, it seems reasonable to assume that his identification of Camilla (Cornelia's daughter) as the duchess in question is reliable. Unfortunately, little biographical information has been found about either of them.

The celebrated Neapolitan singer Adriana Basile (*c.*1590–*c.*1640) may have been the child prodigy who lived in the household of the Duke and Duchess of Traetta from at least 1599. If so, she also may have sung from her patroness's manuscript of Spanish songs, while accompanying herself on the harp or guitar.[26] Ten years later, Adriana was the subject of the following excerpt from a letter to Vincenzo Gonzaga, the Duke of Mantua, from Gioseppe Fachoni, a representative of the Gonzaga court:

My brother recently told me that he was on the trail of a Neapolitan who has all these qualities: she plays the harp excellently and has a good voice and can sight-read any kind of madrigal with such assurance that no singer is more talented than she. And what is even better, she plays the guitar very well and sings in Spanish and has such a repertory that between the Italian and the Spanish she knows more than 300 works by heart. She is young, about nineteen years old. She would have been taken on by important cardinals who wanted her, but because she is too striking and beautiful they reneged.[27]

---

[22] For full details, see Acutis (1971), 6 and Hill (1997), 70–4.

[23] Hill (1997), 42. Isabella Gonzaga was the wife of Luigi Carafa della Marra (*c.*1570–1630), who became Duke of Traetta *c.*1614.

[24] Larson (1985), 101. The duke at this time was Luigi Caetano d'Aragona (*c.*1554–*c.*1613), as Larson indicates. He was a friend of Gesualdo, travelled with him to Ferrara in 1594, and was known to be a music lover.

[25] See Fabritio Caroso, *Il ballarino* . . . (Venice 1581). In the 'Tavola', the ballo 'Conto dell'Orco' is dedicated to 'Cornelia Caraffa Caetana, Duchessa di Traetto'. In the second, expanded edition, entitled *Nobiltà di dame* . . . (Venice, 1600), the same ballo is dedicated to 'Camilla Caetano Caetano, Duchessa di Traetto', who, according to the *Dizionario biografico degl'italiani* (in the entry for Filippo Caetani) was the daughter of Luigi Caetano and Cornelia Carafa, the Duke and Duchess of Traetta.   [26] Hill (1997), 70.

[27] Translated in Parisi (1989), 134. The letter is quoted in full on pp. 181–2. The relevant portion reads: 'Mio fr'ello mi ha detto che un pezzo fa sta su la pratica d'una Napolitana quale ha tutte q'ste qualità: sona di Arpa in eccelenza, e vi canta al libro ogni sorte di madrigali con tal sicurezza che non vi' è cantante nissuno che la sup[era]re è quello che è

After Vincenzo's prolonged negotiations for her services, Adriana moved with her family to the ducal court in Mantua, and soon became one of Italy's most admired and acclaimed singers of monody.[28]

The Traetta manuscript contains no staff notation, only the texts of Spanish songs, most of them with *alfabeto* notation above the appropriate words. Many of the texts[29] are typical late sixteenth-century *romances*, such as 'Rio de Sevilla', a three-part setting of which is found in a *cancionero* manuscript in Turin (I-Tn MS I-14) dating from the 1580s or 1590s.[30] A number of the texts were still in use in the early years of the seventeenth century and frequently appear in manuscripts with guitar *alfabeto*. While many have still not been identified, one of the Traetta texts, 'Entre todos los remedios', is found in an anonymous two-part setting[31] in a contemporaneous manuscript now in Kraków (PL-Kj MS 40163).[32]

The Kraków manuscript is a highly interesting *cancionero* containing thirty, mainly three-part, settings of Spanish and some Italian texts.[33] Many are the only known settings of those texts.[34] Fifteen of the pieces have *alfabeto*, including some that are music concordances of pieces in the 1599 Traetta manuscript. The aforementioned treble and bass setting of 'Entre todos los remedios' (in soprano and bass clefs) appears without *alfabeto* in the Kraków manuscript; however, the Traetta *alfabeto* given above the text concordance fits the Kraków version almost perfectly, confirming that we are dealing with the same late sixteenth-century piece in both manuscripts. Ten pieces are without text; seventeen have Spanish texts, and three Italian. For one of the songs the middle part is marked 'tenor', and for two of them the lowest part is marked 'basso'.

For most if not all the Kraków pieces the tune seems to be in the tenor part and the top part is a discant. In this regard, the placement of the *alfabeto* is significant: *alfabeto* is usually found above the melody line, perhaps because the singer often accompanied her/himself. For all fifteen of the relevant pieces in this manuscript the *alfabeto* is written above the tenor part and duplicated above the bass part,[35] but it never appears above the top part. This double helping of *alfabeto* chords suggests either the involve-

---

il meglio sona di chittaria beniss.mo e canta a la spagnola, et il tal coppia che tra le Italiani e Spagnole sa più di trecento opere a la mente; è giovane di dicenove anni in circa; sarebbe stata presa da cardinali principali che la volevano, ma per essere troppo vistosa, e bella sono restate.'

[28] See 'Basile, Adriana' in *Grove 6*.

[29] For a discussion of a selection of the texts in the Traetta manuscript and others, see Baron (1977).

[30] For a discussion of the Turin manuscript, see Etzion (1988), 68–9.

[31] For all the three-part pieces in this manuscript the lowest line is on the the recto side of the opening and the other two parts on the the previous verso of the opening. For *Entre todos los remedios* the two parts are both on the verso of the opening and only the remaining verses are on the recto side. This suggests that the piece is complete in two parts.

[32] Formerly in the Berlin State Library.

[33] Inventoried in Kirsch and Meierott (1992), 208–13, a bibliography of tablatures. It was first mentioned in Wolf (1919), 215, and again in Boetticher (1978), who listed it as lost in the Second World War.

[34] Although I have found settings of four of the texts from the Kraków manuscript in other *cancioneros*, I have not yet found any music concordances.

[35] There are many discrepancies between the two sets of *alfabeto*, but none serious.

ment of two guitarists, or, more likely (since the parts are not in score but in choirbook format), that a single guitarist has been given the choice of reading from either the tenor line for self-accompaniment, or, like later basso continuo players, the bass line. It is conceivable that these pieces were performed without the discant, as guitar-accompanied solo songs.

Although the Kraków manuscript contains mainly Spanish texts with a few Italian ones mixed in, it is likely to be another late sixteenth-century Neapolitan or south Italian (rather than Spanish) source[36]—late sixteenth-century because of its contents and the archaic style of its staff notation, and Neapolitan or south Italian, again because of its contents but also the presence of Italian *alfabeto* rather than Spanish *cifras*. It will be recalled that the 1599 Traetta manuscript, which is unquestionably a Neapolitan source, is made up entirely of Spanish texts, has concordances in the Kraków manuscript, and, of course, has *alfabeto*.

The Kraków, Traetta, and Bologna manuscripts all provide evidence of the connection between the Kingdom of Naples (or southern Italy) and the earliest use of *alfabeto*. These precious manuscripts contain the beginnings of a notation system created especially for the guitar to accompany the solo voice, a system developed in response to the new way of thinking about harmony that would also result in the development of another system of accompaniment for chordal instruments—basso continuo.

---

[36] See Kirsch and Meierott (1992), 213.

PART II

THE SPANISH GUITAR
(*c*.1600–*c*.1750)

Introduction

The special relationship between the five-course chitarra spagnola and the new monodic style intensified during the first quarter of the seventeenth century, giving rise to a plethora of manuscripts and printed collections for solo voice with guitar *alfabeto* (and occasionally a bass line for another instrument). At the same time, an equally extensive repertory of dances, short introductions, and interludes for solo guitar, featuring an improved *alfabeto* system, was introduced. Beginning in the 1630s, the Spanish guitar's ever-growing popularity inspired new generations of professional guitarists to create a mixed tablature format that combined lute-type and *alfabeto* notation, and a solo repertory, much of which is of the highest order.

One hundred and eighty printed and manuscript collections of solo music for the five-course guitar survive from seventeenth-century Italy alone. This number does not include the innumerable reprints of the published items, neither does it take into account Italian music found in French, English, and Spanish tablature sources. In addition, there are over 250 extant Italian sources of vocal music with guitar *alfabeto* accompaniment. While the combined output from France, England, the Low Countries, Scandinavia, Germany, and the Austrian Empire (including Bohemia), Spain, Portugal, and the New World amounts to barely more than half the total number of Italian sources, in terms of quality its contribution to the repertory is monumental.

To put the size of the repertory in perspective, the total number of manuscripts and printed books for guitar from the seventeenth century alone, preserved in libraries throughout Europe and in the United States and Mexico, is substantially greater than the number for either lute or keyboard. Regrettably, many of these sources have yet to be examined, few have been inventoried, and comparatively little has been done in the way of bibliographical concordance gathering. It is very much hoped that this study and the annotated checklists (Tables 6.1–10.1) provided in the following five chapters will prove useful to the scholars who are working to remedy this neglect.

As many modern players of the Baroque guitar are aware, there never was a standard tuning or stringing arrangement for the instrument, and only rarely does a composer provide the precise tuning and stringing arrangement required for the performance of his music. But even if he does, it cannot be assumed that the same tuning and stringing is appropriate for *all* early guitar music. In order to decide which will best serve the stylistic demands of the specific music to be played, familiarity with all the tuning and stringing options used in the Baroque is essential. These fundamental details are discussed at length in the chapters that follow.

Finally, the interpretation of *alfabeto* sources can pose a problem for researchers, performers, and editors alike. The innumerable sources of *alfabeto* chord solos from the first quarter of the seventeenth century, and the equally large number of vocal sources consisting of text with *alfabeto* but no staff notation are not always easy to interpret. Indeed, many examples can be dealt with only by referring to other settings of the same pieces found in staff notation. This procedure, too, is discussed in the chapters that follow.

6

Italy: The Creation of the Repertory

The Manuscript Sources of Vocal Music in Staff Notation with Guitar Alfabeto

The last quarter of the sixteenth century saw the invention of *alfabeto* notation that was used in conjunction with vocal music—both the light, three-voice forms (*villanelle* and *canzonette*) and the late sixteenth-century monodies with Italian and Spanish texts. By the end of the sixteenth century *alfabeto* was well established, and by the early seventeenth could be found in one of the chief sources of classic monody, I-Fc MS C. F. 83, 'Codex Barbera'.

Of Florentine provenance and dating from about 1600–20, the 'Barbera manuscript' consists mainly of solo songs with a vocal line and a bass line, the latter displaying the sparse numbers and accidentals of the recently developed system of figured bass for continuo accompaniment. Sixteen of the manuscript's 106 pieces also incorporate *alfabeto* letters above the vocal line. These include Giulio Caccini's *Al fonte al prato al bosco*, *Non ha il ciel' cotanti lumi*, and *Ohime begl'occhi*, as well as Peri's *Bellissima regina* and Raffaello Rontani's *Ho si fort'il cor legato*. With the exception of *Ohime begl'occhi*, which is a through-composed solo madrigal, these are all *canzonette*, which, together with other types of strophic song, form the greater part of the repertory of *alfabeto*-accompanied monody. A similar manuscript from the same period, also found in Florence (I-Fn Magl. XIX 25), likewise contains several examples of early monody with basso continuo and guitar *alfabeto*. One is Domenico Brunetti's *Circe crudele*, which is also found (without *alfabeto*) in his printed collection *L'Euterpe* (1606); concordances have not yet been found for the other pieces. The checklist in Table 6.1 (see p. 85) includes these manuscripts and other similar sources.

The Printed Sources of Alfabeto *Solos*

The year 1606 also marks the first appearance in print of music for solo guitar, Girolamo Montesardo's *Nuova inventione d'intavolatura per sonare li balletti sopra la chitarra spagniola senza numeri, e note; per mezzo della quale da se stesso ogn'uno senza maestro potrà imparare* (New invention of tablature for playing dances on the Spanish guitar; without numbers [i.e. the numbers used in Italian-style lute tablature] or notes [staff notation]; by means of which you can learn [to play] by yourself without a teacher). Published in Florence, this simple instruction book is important because it is the first to provide a rhythmic stroke system along with the *alfabeto*. It also marks the first appearance of a chart explaining the *alfabeto* system, in which the corresponding Italian-style lute tablature is presented beneath each of twenty-three letters and four other symbols. These letters and symbols represent precise left-hand chord formations and fingerboard positions (see Pl. 6.1).

Since the *alfabeto* system had been in use for at least twenty years prior to Montesardo's publication, it is unlikely that his new invention was the *alfabeto* chord notation itself; rather, it was probably his notation for rhythmic strumming. It consists of a horizontal line, above and below which the *alfabeto* letters (both upper and lower case) are printed (see Ex. 6.1 on p. 54). A letter below the line means a strummed down stroke of the right hand, and a letter above the line an upstroke. An upper-case letter is meant to equal about twice the time value of a lower-case one. No metrical signs or bar lines are provided. Montesardo's strumming notation is basic—so basic that, unless a modern player is already familiar with the dances and grounds from this period, some rhythmic uncertainty is inevitable, particularly in the pieces in triple metre.

Of course, most early guitarists were familiar with such traditional dances and popular harmonic grounds as the Villano di Spagna, Ruggiero, Bergamasca, Ciaccona, Pavaniglia, Mattacino, Ballo [or Tenore] di Napoli, Spagnoletta, Paganina, La monica, Canario, and Ballo del Gran Duca. And, since the publication's newer items also included dances, Montesardo's specific rhythmic strumming patterns would have been helpful in interpreting them, and the remaining items—examples of the traditional I–IV–V–I Passacaglia chord pattern—as well. The latter often were used as introductions and interludes between the verses of other pieces; indeed, Montesardo sometimes calls them 'ritornelli'. Many examples are found in the *alfabeto* song manuscripts; however, the strumming style associated with the ritornellos and dances may not always be appropriate for the accompaniment of the *alfabeto* songs themselves. Amongst the hundreds of sources of monody with *alfabeto*, only one contains rhythmic stroke signs.[1] Of course, strumming is clearly appropriate for the accompa-

---

[1] Sanseverino, *Il primo libro d'intavolatura per la chitarra spagnuola* (1622). See below, pp. 58–9.

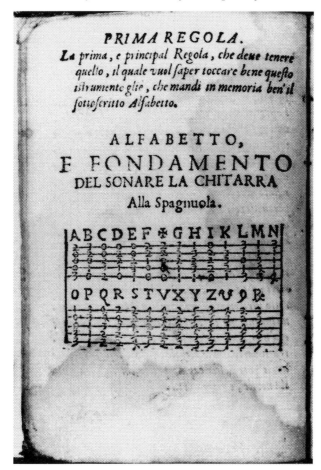

PL. 6.1. *Alfabeto* chart from Girolamo Montesardo,
Nuova inventione . . . (Florence, 1606), fo. 3v.
Vienna, Gesellschaft der Musikfreunde

niment of some vocal music, particularly those pieces classified as popular dance song, such as *La dolce partite de vida de mi vida*, the last item in Montesardo's book. For this piece he does include his rhythmic strumming notation, but omits the text.

Although Montesardo's chord solos are rudimentary, they probably represent the earliest appearance of an actual repertory for the five-course guitar. Since these pieces do not carry the melody, but are in essence the 'chord charts' for common material, the dances can be performed either as solos or as rhythmic backing for ensemble versions. Significantly, Montesardo gives many of the introductions and interludes in several different *alfabeto* 'keys'. This suggests that not only was the early guitarist

Ex. 6.1. *Ballo di Napoli* by Girolamo Montesardo (1606)

	a		b		a	
Aa AA		Bb BB		CABC	Aa AA	*

	a	a		c		c	
Aa AA			Cc CC		[I]HOI	Cc CC	*

	d		a		b		a
Dd DD		Aa AA		Bb BB		CABC	Aa AA[.]

expected to be ready to play an 'intro' and ritornellos for virtually any piece that s/he might be asked to accompany, but to play them in any 'key' requested.

Montesardo's book also offers some tuning and stringing information (fo. 5ᵛ), the former vague, but the latter quite specific. For tuning, the player is instructed to begin by adjusting the fifth course to a convenient ('conveniente') pitch, and then to tune the remaining courses by interval; no nominal pitches are given. However, when describing the use of a bourdon ('cordone') and its neighbouring upper octave ('canto'), Montesardo makes clear his preference for octave stringing on both the fourth and fifth courses. This stringing of the five-course guitar with bourdons was common practice in the early seventeenth century; but other options would soon emerge in Italy and elsewhere.

Girolamo Montesardo's real name was Girolamo Melcarne,[2] and Montesardo was the name of the town in the territory of Naples where he was born. An early citation identifies him as organist at the Roman church of Santa Maria in Trastevere in the year 1603,[3] a post later held by Girolamo Frescobaldi. It is unclear whether he was actually working in Florence when his guitar instruction book was published there in 1606. His name is not found on the roster of musicians employed at the Medici court; however, his book is dedicated to Francesco Buontalenti, presumably a relative of Bernardo Buontalenti, the renowned scenery and costume designer for the 1589 Florentine *intermedi*. A year after its publication Montesardo was engaged as a singer at San Petronio in Bologna, and the following year began a brief tenure as *maestro di cappella* at the cathedral in Fano. As a composer of sacred music he published two volumes in 1608 and 1612, and some of his motets are included in the anthologies of other composers. He also published secular vocal music, including an anthology best described as a musical tribute to Florence (1608). Its contents include a monody by Peri, which the composer later published himself, and one by Caccini that is unique to this source.[4] By 1611 Montesardo had returned to Naples, where in 1612 he published

---

[2] Carter (1987), 28. [3] A church record of that year is cited in Hammond (1983), 333.
[4] Kirkendale (1993), 174 and 240. For a discussion of Montesardo (1608), see Carter (1985).

another secular work, *I lieti giorni di Napoli*, a collection comprising music for two and three voices with guitar *alfabeto*. He did not include his rhythmic strumming notation for any of the items in this volume.

Montesardo's was the first of many chord solo books published throughout the seventeenth century and later. Foriano Pico's *Nuova scelta di sonate per la chitarra spagnola* was long thought by several scholars to be the second, with a publication date judged to be 1608. However, it recently has been proved that this book originated much later in the century—most likely 1698, although it does appear to be a reprint of much earlier material.[5] Pico's *alfabeto* chord chart, for example, seems to be related to Flaminio Corradi's chord chart of 1616 (see below, Table 6.5). Further, on pages 2–10, the information Pico offers on the *trillo* and *repicco* (two elements of right-hand technique used for the rhythmic embellishment of *alfabeto* chords)[6] are from Tomasso Marchetti's *Il primo libro d'intavolatura* . . . published in Rome by Catalani in 1635 (see note 9). Pico's style of notating moveable chords, which is similar to that found in a series of manuscripts by Francesco Palumbi that could date from as early as *c.*1600 (discussed below), also points to his or his publisher's having drawn the introductory text and music from much earlier sources.

Pico includes versions of a number of the traditional dances found in Montesardo's book and the early manuscripts, and also some new items, such as a *Marchetta* (a Sicilian ground), a *Perugina*, and a *Tarantella*. The Ballo di Mantova appears as a chord solo or, perhaps, a chordal accompaniment, since Pico's version lacks the piece's well-known catchy tune. Also found in innumerable later sources of guitar music,[7] it probably originated in a late sixteenth-century theatrical work performed at the Mantuan court. The earliest version of the complete piece (including the melody, bass, and implied harmonies) is Giuseppino Cenci's canzonetta *Fuggi fuggi da questo cielo*, which is found in a manuscript dating from *c.*1600.[8]

---

[5] See Gary Boye: 'The Case of the Purloined Letter Tablature: The Seventeenth-Century Guitar Books of Foriano Pico and Pietro Millioni', *Journal of Seventeenth-Century Music*, Volume 11, no. 1, 2006. Boye convincingly re-dates the Pico book to 1698 and gives detailed information on the printed material and its relationship to that of Pietro Millioni. Boye seems unaware, however, that Pico used the complete text (though not the music) of Tomasso Marchetti's *Il primo libro* of 1635, and that another edition of the book (although without Marchetti's name) was printed in 1648 by the same publisher (Catalani).

[6] For a discussion of these and other details of *alfabeto* performance practice, see App. I, Weidlich (1978), and Jensen (1980).

[7] In addition to the countless solo guitar and keyboard versions of it, the Ballo di Mantova was also arranged for all sorts of instruments, including xylophone in G. B. Ariosti, *Modo facile di sonare il sistro* . . . (Bologna, 1686 and later editions), and for ensembles. Biagio Marini published a trio sonata on the theme in 1655. For an edition of Gasparo Zanetti's 1645 ensemble version and further concordances, see Tyler (1984*a*).

The tune of the Ballo is so distinctive that it became known throughout Europe, eventually entering the realm of folk music, wherein each country claimed it as its own. Smetana, for example, used it as the principal theme of *Má Vlast*, assuming it was a Slavic folksong, and a version of it forms the basis of the Israeli national anthem.

[8] For an edition of the song, which is found, without *alfabeto*, in the 'Barbera manuscript' (I-Fc MS C. F. 83, fo. 158, *c.*1600), see Hill (1997), ii, no. 156. Several different texts were sung to it, the two most widely known being 'Fuggi, fuggi da lieti amanti' and 'Fuggi, fuggi dolente core'.

In the most important section of his book (33–48), a new system is introduced, one not found in Montesardo for shifted chords, that is, basic *alfabeto* chord shapes played in higher positions on the fingerboard. In this system, numbers beside the letters tell the player the fret at which the chord shape is to be played; hence, H5 means that the basic H chord (B flat major at the first fret) is to be played up at the fifth fret, which produces a D major harmony. (For a full explanation of this system, see App. I.)

This new system has at least three advantages. First, because some of the shifted chords are the same as those represented by some of the later letters of the alphabet (for example, H2 is the same chord as letter R, and H3 as letter Z), it is unnecessary to memorize the complete *alfabeto*. Secondly, the shift system facilitates the notating of chords of the same harmony in different positions and inversions. (The guitar's modern chord-name system would benefit from this sophisticated feature!) Thirdly, whereas the simpler *alfabeto* system allowed composers to notate only the basic harmonies, the shift system made it possible for them to include a melody line as the highest note of each shifted chord. Pico illustrates this feature in *La moda, La mia donna importuna, La bella Margarita, Va pur, superba va, La cotognella*, and other pieces that were just becoming popular around the time his book was published.

Improvements also were made to Montesardo's rhythm notation system. By adding short vertical lines above and below Montesardo's horizontal line to represent the up and down strokes ('botte') of the right hand, and by placing the *alfabeto* letters at the appropriate points above the horizontal line, he designed what was intended to be a much less cluttered, easier to read system. Unfortunately, Pico's printer, in addition to making numerous other errors, put many of the stroke signs in backwards; and since Pico, like Montesardo, provides no metre signs or bar lines, his book is actually no easier to read than Montesardo's. In some of the earlier material used by Pico, these stroke signs are in their correct positions.[9]

The tuning information is just as ambiguous as Montesardo's. The player is instructed to tune the fifth course to a comfortable pitch, and the other courses by frets, using the tuning of the fifth course as a starting point. Unlike Montesardo, Pico says nothing about the use of bourdons and octaves, so the player must decide on the appropriate stringing arrangement for his music: with a bourdon on the fourth course, or without—with a bourdon on the fifth course, or without?

On the other hand, the descriptions of how to play the *trillo* and *repicco* are clear. The presentation of a series of *alfabeto* chords to be used expressly for accompanying

---

[9] Portions of the text of Pietro Millioni's *Corona del primo, secondo, e terzo libro . . .* (Rome, 1631 and its 1635, 1636, and 1638 editions) are used by Pico. He also used the entire text of Tomasso Marchetti's *Il primo libro . . .* (Rome: Catalani, 1635), which is not listed in RISM, but in the Library of the Royal Academy of Music, London (ex Spencer). Thus, it is probable that Marchetti also plagiarized Millioni! The item listed in RISM as anonymous 1618[21] is dated incorrectly. It is actually an edition of Marchetti's *Il primo libro* without the author's name. There is a facsimile of Marchetti's 1660 edition (Geneva: Minkoff Reprints, 1981).

the *Letanie de' Santi* (Litany of the Saints) offers some interesting and unique performance practice ideas. His final section, an anthology of pieces with its own title page (*Villanelle nuove . . .*), consists of guitar *alfabeto* for six song texts, 'Ahi che morir mi sento', 'Al fiero gioco', 'Ben ch'ogn'hor con lieto core', 'Non più morte cor mio', 'Occhietti amati che m'accidete', and 'Pensai col partire'. Several of the texts are found in sources dating from between 1604 and 1627. All in all, Pico offers us so much in the way of new and valuable material that it is particularly frustrating not to have any information about him other than that he was likely to have been a Neapolitan.

Another Italian centre under Spanish rule during this period, Milan, like Naples, was actively involved in the publication of guitar *alfabeto* books. Published in Milan in 1620,[10] Giovanni Ambrosio Colonna's first book, *Intavolatura di chitarra alla spagnuola . . .*, was the first in an excellent series of four guitar publications.[11] Colonna (*fl.* 1616–37) dedicated it to Giulio Cesare Borromeo (1593–1638), Count of Arona, an important military leader to whom Giovanni Paolo Foscarini also dedicated a piece in his guitar book of *c.*1630. Since Colonna came from a family of printers, it is not surprising that the layout and presentation of his music is clear and mostly error-free. His first book provides brief instructions on reading the tablature, which is similar to Pico's, as well as an explanatory *alfabeto* chart that includes the shifted chords also encountered in Pico.

The music begins with I–IV–V–I Passacaglias in all the letters ('keys', major and minor), presented both in simple form and embellished ('passeggiati'). For the latter, passing and shifted chords are added. These pieces are followed by settings of all the expected dances of the time (for example, the 'Chiaccona', 'Zarabanda', and 'Vilan di Spagna'), most of them presented in more than one key. Colonna then offers a succession of dances and grounds dedicated to various local dignitaries, ending with the *Aria alla piemontesa* as sung by ('cantata dal') Francesco Gabrielli 'detto Scapino'. Gabrielli (1588–1636) was a renowned actor in the *commedia dell'arte*, who created the comic character Scapino in the early seventeenth century.[12] A contemporary engraved portrait by Carlo Biffi (1633) depicts him holding his *commedia* mask in one hand and a guitar in the other. On its frame are a few more guitars and a great number of unusual and exotic instruments, all of which Gabrielli reputedly played or invented.[13] There are several pieces associated with Scapino in other guitar sources, and a posthumous edition of one of his poetic monologues has *alfabeto* above the text.[14]

---

[10]   Its dedication is dated 12 Dec. 1619.

[11]   The last book in the series was published in 1637.

[12]   See Kenneth and Laura Richards, *The Commedia dell'Arte* (Oxford, 1990), 109–26.

[13]   It is found in the Biblioteca Ambrosiana, Milan, and is reproduced in *Enciclopedia dello spettacolo* (Milan, 1958), v. 804–5.

[14]   *Infirmità, testamento, e morte di Francesco Gabrielli detto Scappino . . .* (Verona, Padua, and Parma, 1638). A modern edition (without *alfabeto*) is found in Vito Pandolfi, *La commedia dell'arte: storia e testi* (Florence, 1957–61), ii. 111–17.

At the end of the book is a most interesting section entitled 'Regola per incordare le Chitarre per sonare di concerto' (Rule for tuning guitars for playing in consort). Here Colonna describes three guitars, the smallest and largest tuned a fifth apart, and the middle one tuned a tone higher than the largest. He gives no nominal pitches; however, if the middle guitar has a top string at *e′*, then the larger one would be at *d′* and the smaller at *a′*. Colonna says that if the larger guitar plays an *alfabeto* letter I, the next an A, and the smallest a C, they will agree on the harmony; and they do. Played with Colonna's tunings for each of the guitars, these letters produce a G major chord. The implication here is that the *alfabeto* system is immensely practical, since guitars of different sizes can play the same piece together if each guitarist reads the letters designated for his or her size instrument.

Benedetto Sanseverino's *Intavolatura facile . . .* was also published in 1620 in Milan, and it too contains many of the same dances and passacaglias found in the majority of *alfabeto* guitar books. However, this book is of historical importance because it introduced three notable new features to the *alfabeto* tablature that make reading and interpreting it much easier: (1) metre signs; (2) bar lines; and (3) along with the *alfabeto* letters and stroke signs, actual note-heads, stems, and flags, as found in mensural notation. Sanseverino provides a comprehensive description of these new features, including an explanation of proportional relationships. His tuning and stringing information is also of great interest, and for several reasons. Like Montesardo, he declares his preference for bourdons and octaves on the fourth and fifth courses and indicates that the first course is a single string. However, Sanseverino also includes a chart in staff notation that reveals the nominal pitches he had in mind. Since these pitches indicate a tuning with the top string at *d′*, we know that Sanseverino's guitar was tuned a whole tone lower than the top five strings of a modern guitar. This tuning is also indicated in several later sources, discussed below.

A number of noteworthy *alfabeto* solos are also included in the 1620 edition, among them *Saltarello de Santino*,[15] which appears in no other source, and *Aria sopra Vezzosetta*, which is dedicated to Carlo Cantù, a singer at the Duomo in Milan.[16] For a subsequent edition, published in Milan two years later under the title *Il primo libro d'intavolatura per la chitarra spagnuola*, Sanseverino added six vocal pieces containing text and *alfabeto* but no staff notation. The first of these is a dance song version of the Aria del Gran Duca entitled *Dimmi Amore*.[17] Two more dance songs follow, *Poi che vol'amor* and *Balletto. Qui dov'è 'l fiore d'ogni beltà*, both apparently unique to this source. The next piece is the well-known Spanish song (*ayre*) *Quando yo me en amore*,

---

[15] Presumably Santino Garsi (d. 1603), the famed lutenist at the Farnese court in Parma.

[16] Probably the father of the famous *commedia dell'arte* actor of the same name (1604–76), who created the comic character Buffetto and was employed at the court of Parma. Sanseverino appears to have had Parmese connections as well. For a portrait of the actor, see the frontispiece to Tyler (1980a).

[17] See Kirkendale (1972), 59–50.

found elsewhere in a three-voice version with *alfabeto* (PL-Kj 40163, *c.*1590–1620),[18] and in four versions containing only text and *alfabeto* (I-Fn MS 2973 and I-MOe MSS 2, 3, and 115). The *alfabeto* for the three-voice version is virtually identical with Sanseverino's. This suggests that he, like the author of the manuscript, used the harmonies in the three-part version to create the guitar *alfabeto*, which in his version accompanies a single voice.

The text of the next piece, *Caldi sospiri*, is found in several other versions, including two settings consisting only of text and *alfabeto* (in I-Fn MS Magl. XIX 143 and GB-Lbl Add. MS 36877); a voice, basso continuo, and *alfabeto* setting by Raffaelo Rontani (in I-Fn MS Magl. XIX 24); and an anonymous setting for voice and basso continuo (in I-Mc MS S. B. 196/6) with an apparent connection to the Mantuan court. Sanseverino's *alfabeto* chords fit this last version of *Caldi sospiri* perfectly. His final vocal item, *Capelli d'oro d'Amor*, has a concordance in a manuscript containing song texts and *alfabeto* (GB-Lbl Add. MS 36877). Sanseverino's vocal settings are unique in the *alfabeto* song repertory for having rhythmic strumming signs above the words, and his book is the 'exception which proves the rule' that rhythmic strumming signs are never found in the *alfabeto* vocal sources!

Virtually all the *alfabeto* solo books contain the same core repertory of dances and passacaglias in plain or embellished versions and in a variety of keys. However, each book also adds something new and intriguing to the repertory, and many offer details of technique, tuning, interpretation, and their authors' circumstances that make even the humblest of these publications of value to present-day performers and scholars. In this respect Giovanni Battista Abatessa's books are typical. For example, in his 1627 book Abatessa (d. after 1652), who is likely to have been born in the town of Bitonto (near Bari), then part of the Kingdom of Naples,[19] reveals some important information on guitar technique. He says that when strumming the guitar, the right hand should be up near the neck of the instrument. He also gives instructions on playing the *trillo* and *repicco*, and on tuning. In his 1635 book he includes a solo entitled *Sinfonia del Grandi*, presumably referring to Alessandro Grandi (*c.*1580–1630), one of the best monody composers of the age, as well as five songs in staff notation, variously for one, two, and three voices, each with a sparsely figured bass line and guitar *alfabeto*. His 1652 book contains instructions on how to tune an 'arpetta'[20] to the guitar.

---

[18] This Neapolitan manuscript was discussed in Ch. 5.

[19] For more about Abatessa and a thematic index of his tablatures, see Lospalutti (1989).

[20] This term could mean a small harp, or, possibly, the small appendage found on some guitars—an extension of the guitar's body containing a small number of diatonically tuned strings to be played in the manner of a harp. Abatessa refers to only eight strings. There is a drawing of a guitar with this appendage in an 18th-c. vocal MS (P-Ln Col. Pomb. MS 82, fo. 75), where it is labelled a 'Tyorba Christalina'. I am indebted to Rogério Budasz for bringing this reference to my attention. An extant Spanish instrument from the late 18th c. by Rafael Baza (Granada) has this appendage on the upper right bought on the treble side. It is in London, Victoria and Albert Museum, No. 12/12. The 'arpetta' is also referred to in Antonio di Micheli (1680 and 1698). See Table 6.2.

Another Neapolitan guitarist, Fabritio Costanzo (*fl.* 1627), published a collection
that is mainly for guitar quartet, that is, it comprises thirty quartets, four duos, and
sixteen solos. The quartets are printed in table-book format for each opening, with
two of the *alfabeto* parts on one page and the other two on the opposite page. Laid flat
on a table, the book can be read by each pair of guitarists while facing each other.
Costanzo calls for guitars at four different pitch levels—the three indicated by
Colonna for his medium-size, smaller, and larger guitars, and another tuned to a
higher pitch than Colonna's medium-size instrument. For each piece Costanzo provides an *alfabeto* part in the proper 'key' for each of the guitar tunings; hence, four
guitarists adept at rhythmic strumming should be able to create from the music in this
collection a quite dramatic and exciting suite in the popular style.

In his book of *alfabeto* chord solos, *Intavolatura di chitarra spagnuola libro
secondo* . . . (Macerata, 1629),[21] Giovanni Paolo Foscarini (*fl.* 1620–49) adds two guitar
duos, one trio, and some original solo compositions (including a selection of pieces
designated 'Francese') to the core repertory. At the conclusion of the book, which he
dedicated to one Giulio Francesco Brancaleone in Macerata on 30 October 1629, he
also provides some information about himself: 'Dell'Accademico Caliginosi detto il
Furioso, Musico e Sonatore, di Liuto, e Tiorba; della Venerabile Compagnia del
Santissimo Sacramento d'Ancona'. This inscription tells us that the composer's 'academic' name was 'Il Furioso', that he was a member of a literary association in Ancona
known as the 'Caliginosi', and that he was a musician (composer) and a lute and
theorbo player connected to the religious confraternity of the Holy Sacrament in the
same city. It was not until a much later publication that Foscarini identified himself by
name.[22]

Francesco Corbetta (*c.*1615–81) of Pavia apparently was a resident of Bologna when
his first book of guitar music, *De gli scherzi armonici* . . ., was published there in 1639.
He signed his dedication to Odoardo Pepoli on 4 September 1639 in Bologna and
inscribed many of the pieces to local dignitaries. Although it consists mainly of
alfabeto solos, which, like those of Sanseverino, are printed with metre signs, bar lines,
and mensural notes, Corbetta's book also includes eight pieces in mixed tablature (discussed later in the chapter). Like Costanzo, he describes the procedure for tuning four
guitars of different sizes and pitch levels together, but does not reveal what the nominal pitches are; however, if it is assumed that one of his four guitars corresponds to
Costanzo's medium-size model with its first course tuned to *e´*, then his other three
guitars would have been tuned a fourth lower, a semitone lower, and a second higher in
relation to the first guitar.

[21] Apparently, no copies of Foscarini's *Intavolatura di chitarra spagnuola libro primo* . . . have survived.
[22] In some of the older bibliographies, e.g. Wolf (1919), he is listed as 'Caliginoso'. For a discussion and assessment
of Foscarini's works, see Danner (1974).

The Florentine guitarist Antonio Carbonchi (*fl.* 1640–3) published his extraordinary second book, *Le dodici chitarre. . .*, in Florence in 1643.[23] It contains a total of seventy-two pieces, forty of which are for solo guitar, and the remaining thirty-two for twelve different-size guitars! Amazingly, Carbonchi furnishes parts for each of the latter pieces in twelve different *alfabeto* keys. He also provides tuning instructions for the twelve guitars, each a semitone apart, going through a complete chromatic scale. Though one doubts the viability of such an ensemble (then or now), it should be noted that two, three, or, indeed, up to twelve guitarists reading from the appropriate *alfabeto* parts for their size instruments can play in harmony from Carbonchi's remarkably precise notation.[24]

Another collection that is of interest for a variety of reasons is Carlo Calvi's publication *Intavolatura di chitarra e chitarriglia . . .* (Bologna, 1646). As Calvi indicates on its title page, he is not the composer but the compiler of the music of two excellent teachers ('duo eccellenti professori'), one of whom appears to be Francesco Corbetta. Calvi's book includes Corbetta's 1639 *alfabeto* chart and the aforementioned instructions for tuning four guitars of different sizes and pitch levels together. The music he divides neatly into two parts; the first part, entirely in *alfabeto*, is for chitarriglia, and the second, comprising twenty pieces in Italian-style lute tablature, is for chitarra. The music for chitarriglia includes what appear to be simplified versions of some of the *alfabeto* items found in Corbetta's 1639 book.

Calvi's use of the term 'chitarriglia' implies that he is differentiating between a smaller guitar and the presumably larger 'chitarra'. A manuscript dated 1649 (F-Psg MS 2344, fo. 84ᵛ), one of the rare sources to provide a specific tuning for any size guitar, includes a tuning, in both tablature and staff notation, for a small guitar (with no bourdons on either the fourth or fifth course)[25] (see Ex. 6.2); while another, later manuscript source (A-Wn MS S. M. 9659, fo. 3)[26] provides, in tablature and staff notation, two specific high-pitch tunings for a small guitar *with* bourdons (see Ex. 6.3).

At the conclusion of the *alfabeto* section of his book, just before the section of lute-style tablature begins, Calvi writes: 'Le seguente Suonate possono servire anche per la Chitarriglia, ma sono veramente per la Chitarra' (The following pieces can serve also for the *chitarriglia*, but are really for the *chitarra*). This statement reinforces Calvi's distinction between the two sizes of guitar, while, at the same time, informing the player that the music in this section can be played on either of the sizes. Indeed, because Calvi used lute-style tablature, which is not pitch-sensitive and simply shows

---

[23] Carbonchi's first book, *Sonate di chitarra spagnola* (Florence, 1640), contains no *alfabeto* and is discussed below under the heading 'The Printed Sources of Solos in Italian Mixed Tablature'.

[24] Carbonchi's multi-guitar tuning instructions can also be found, translated into English, in a manuscript that was used in Restoration England, GB-Ob Mus. Sch. C 94, 'The De Gallot MS', *c.* 1660–84, fo. 138, discussed on p. 116.

[25] This is a French source and the term 'guitarre' is used.

[26] This is a manuscript from *c.* 1700 in French tablature.

Ex. 6.2. Tuning chart from F-Psg MS 2344. The tablature chart begins with the third course open; the unisons are implied for the remaining courses. The nominal tuning is determined by the pitches given for the treble and bass viols

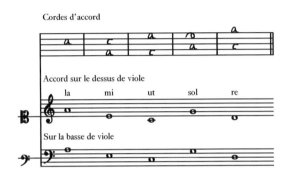

the player where on the fingerboard to put her/his fingers, the music can be played on any guitar, regardless of its size or pitch level.

A number of manuscripts, as well as other printed sources, also use the term 'chitarriglia',[27] but precisely what is meant by it is still unclear. In most of the songbooks in which it is used,[28] a tuning at *e'* for the instrument's highest course is indicated, assuming the *alfabeto* was meant to be played in the same key as the vocal and bass parts. Since this is the typical tuning for a medium-size guitar, the implication is that many songbook composers may have used the terms 'chitarriglia' and 'chitarra spagnola' interchangeably.

The publications of *alfabeto* solos, which often included song texts with *alfabeto* notation, flourished mainly during the first half of the seventeenth century; however, first editions were still being published as late as 1680. The last of these, *La nuova chitarra . . .*, was published in Palermo by the Sicilian guitarist and priest Antonio di Micheli in the year of his death, 1680. Not only is it an extensive anthology of *alfabeto* solos and Sicilian song texts with *alfabeto*, it also offers a significant amount of valuable instructional material concerning tuning, shifted chords, transposition, cadences, scales, reading from the bass line, and continuo practice.[29] There were numerous reprints and later editions of many of the *alfabeto* publications, including at least thirteen of the ubiquitous Millioni and Monte book, the last of which appeared in 1737!

---

[27] Manuscripts such as I-Bc SM AA/360. fo. 93; I-VEc MS 1560 [S. Pesori]; and US-LAtyler, 'Libro di Varie canzonette da cantare sù la Chitariglia' (an *alfabeto* songbook written by Alberto Fiorini, *c*.1620).

[28] Such as B. Borlasca, *Canzonette a tre voci . . .* 1611; C. Milanuzzi, *Secondo scherzo . . .* 1622 ['Chitarra alla Spagnola' on the title page and 'Chitariglia' in the preface]; E. Guazzi, *Spiritosi affetti . . .* 1622; B. Marini, *Scherzi, e canzonette . . .* 1622; B. Marini, *Madrigaletti . . .* 1635; F. Gabrielli, *Infermità, testamento, e morte . . .* 1638.

[29] For a study of Micheli's book, see Failla (1979).

Ex. 6.3. Tuning chart from A–Wn MS S. M. 9659

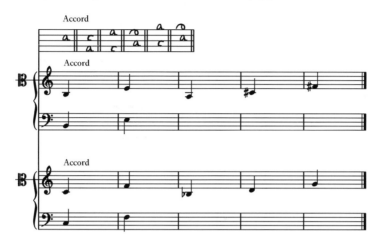

An annotated checklist of all known printed sources of *alfabeto* solos, with the exception of several books by Giovanni Paolo Foscarini and Stefano Pesori, can be found in Table 6.2 (p. 86). The Foscarini and Pesori publications are not included because, although they contain some *alfabeto* solos, they are primarily sources of solos in Italian mixed tablature.[30]

The Printed Sources of Solos in Italian Mixed Tablature

The creation of the ingenious system known today as mixed tablature enabled composers to notate in one tablature system every technique and musical nuance that could be expressed in either Italian lute tablature or *alfabeto* notation independently, including fully melodic single-line passages, rhythmic strumming, high-position chords, slurs and trills, and so on.

Giovanni Paolo Foscarini seems to have been the first to introduce this 'nuova inventione', as he called it, in his publication of *c.*1630, *Il primo, secondo, e terzo libro della chitarra spagnola*. Although some important bibliographic details are omitted from its title page (such as its date and place of publication), much of this book is handsomely engraved, including the title page, a portrait of Foscarini (see Pl. 6.2), and all the music; only the composer's instructional material is typeset. It is entirely possible that Foscarini engraved the music plates himself. The idiosyncratic appearance of the tablature suggests personal involvement, and the book undoubtedly would have cost

---

[30] For a full explanation of mixed tablature, see App. I.

PL. 6.2. Portrait of Giovanni Paolo Foscarini from
I quatro libri della chitarra spagnola, n.p., *c*.1632

him far less to publish if a professional engraver had been required only for the elaborate title page and portrait. It is also likely that Foscarini owned the plates, since the
same ones were used repeatedly to produce the individual presentation copies that
appeared between *c*.1630 and 1649. Most of the title pages for these 'editions' feature
ornate escutcheons or shields, which served as empty frames that could be filled in by
hand each time the composer found a prospective patron.

    Beginning with his *c*.1630 publication, *Il primo, secondo, e terzo libro della chitarra
spagnola*, Foscarini's entire output is *this* publication with alterations made to its title
page, changes of dedicatee for certain pieces, and the addition of Books 4 and 5 (in
several astounding instances *without* altering the original title)! Although its title page
indicates that it contains his first three books, while Book 1 (which is entirely in
alfabeto) might actually contain the same material as his lost first book, Book 2
has none of the music found in his completely typeset *Libro secondo . . .* of 1629 (men-

tioned in the previous section). Moreover, the typeset instructional material found in his 1629 publication has been greatly revised and expanded in the new work.

A copy of the original *c.*1630 edition is found in Berlin (D-B). Its contents match the information given on the title page, and the hand-drawn coat of arms on the lower escutcheon, which is quartered and features ships and two Moors' heads, is believed to be Foscarini's. The same coat of arms also appears in the lower escutcheon of later editions. The coat of arms in the upper escutcheon has not been identified, and there is no formal dedication. The engraved title page resembles other Roman ones of the period, and some of the individual pieces are dedicated to such important Roman personages as 'Don Paolo Orsini, Duca di Bracciano' and 'Abbate D. Virginio Orsini', as well as the aforementioned 'Giulio Cesare Borromeo', count of Arona (near Milan). By this time Foscarini apparently had left Macerata for Rome, a city that offered many more career opportunities to the freelance musician.[31]

An expanded edition of the original collection, which includes Book 4, appeared *c.*1632. Despite the addition of Book 4, this version, a copy of which is preserved in London (GB-Lbl), has the same title page as the original *c.*1630 print of Books 1–3; however, the coat of arms of the Roman patron of the arts Paolo Borghese has been added to the top escutcheon. The aforementioned arms in the lower escutcheon, believed to be Foscarini's, remain. Book 4 contains pieces dedicated to Prince Flavio Orsini, the Roman poet and opera librettist Fabio dalla Corgna, and Giuseppe Cesari, 'Cavagliere d'Arpino', a highly important Roman painter and colleague of Caravaggio.

Another copy containing Books 1–4 (Library of the Royal Academy of Music, London, ex Spencer) has an altered version of the original title page that reads *I quatro libri della chitarra spagnola* . . . . The lower escutcheon has been changed to a crowned shield held by two standing angels, and there is no coat of arms within the frames of either the upper escutcheon or lower shield. Unlike the copy in the British Library, this one has an engraved 'Tavola' (list of contents).

As previously mentioned, Book 1 (pp. 1–14) consists entirely of *alfabeto* solos, notated simply and without bar lines. It is comprised of core repertory, such as the Tenor di Napoli, La monica, Folia, Paganina, and Spagnoletta. Book 2 (pp. 15–37) begins with two pieces in Italian-style lute tablature labelled 'Toccata' and 'Corrente', and composed in lute style. All the remaining items in Book 2 represent the earliest pieces found in the new mixed tablature. These range from free-form *capricci*, to elaborate versions of the Passacaglia and Folia, to a variety of dance forms notated with single-line passages, strummed *alfabeto* chords, slurs, parallel tenths, and other examples of Baroque guitar idiom, sometimes all in the same piece. Book 3 (pp. 38–78) begins with five pieces composed in lute style and notated in Italian-style lute tablature, including a Pavaniglia and a Corrente; these are characterized by elaborate

---

[31] Hill (1997) and Hammond (1994) provide detailed accounts of the Roman music scene in Foscarini's day.

melodic variations. All the remaining items in Book 3 are in mixed tablature, including a number of free-form pieces, harmonic grounds, and dance forms. Many of the latter are uncharacteristically complex, with striking harmonic colours and daring suspensions.

The latest of the books, Book 4 (pp. 79–102), is entirely in mixed tablature and consists mainly of solos that are even more elaborate than those in Book 3. Several entitled 'Corrente francese' might actually be French. The one on page 42, for example, is Foscarini's arrangement of a courant for lute by Ennemond(?) Gautier (found in GB-Cfm MS Mus. 689, fo. 37 and RUS-SPa MS O. 124, fos. 58ᵛ–59ʳ). There is also a short sinfonia for two guitars and a toccata in a scordatura tuning. The *tavola* is on pages 103–4. All the pieces are relatively short, and selecting and performing several of them in a suite, as was the custom in the seventeenth century, makes for an enjoyable and worthwhile musical experience.

Another copy of the *c.*1632 edition (CZ-Pnm) has the *c.*1630 title page and a formal, printed dedication to a Bohemian nobleman at the Habsburg court in Prague dated 25 April 1638 in Rome. The coat of arms of Venislao di Michna has been drawn in by hand in the upper escutcheon, and Foscarini's own is in the lower. There is another edition in Bologna (I-BcV33), which contains Books 1–3 but has the title page from an edition of Books 1–4, *I quatro libri*! The upper escutcheon on this title page has been altered to a square shape, which has been filled in with an unidentified coat of arms, and the lower shield has been altered and is filled in with Foscarini's. This copy also has a typeset *tavola*, which includes only the contents of Books 1–3. There is no dedication or publication date, but this copy is probably from *c.*1638 as well.

The expansion of Foscarini's original *c.*1630 publication continued: *Li cinque libri della chitarra alla spagnola . . .* , as its title indicates, incorporates a fifth book. This edition has a newly designed title page, which bears a striking resemblance to the title page of Michelangelo Galilei's lute book (Munich, 1620). Its formal dedication to Charles [III] of Lorraine, Duke of Guise, is dated 25 September 1640 in Rome, and Charles's coat of arms is printed rather than drawn in by hand. The new engraved plates for Book 5 are in the same hand as the plates for Books 1–4.

Book 5 (pp. 103–35) contains more high-quality toccatas and dance settings in mixed tablature, as well as a few in simple lute tablature. One of the latter (the 'Ciacona' on p. 107) is actually an arrangement of a lute piece, *Chiacona Mariona alla vera spagnola*, from Alessandro Piccinini's posthumous lute book of 1639. Book 5 also contains two *sinfonie* for guitar and basso continuo; a chart containing the *alfabeto* letters that guitars tuned to different pitches must play in order to produce the same harmony; three pages of tables designed to help players make their own intabulations from staff notation; and four more to help them learn to play from a figured bass ('per sonare sopra la parte'). This last series of tables is much more detailed than any of the charts found in the *alfabeto* books, and is probably the first serious attempt at continuo instruction for the guitar.

There is a copy in Madrid (E-Mn) of an edition containing Books 1–5, which, inexplicably, has the same title page as the edition in the Royal Academy of Music (ex Spencer) containing only Books 1–4. Another title page for an edition containing Books 1–5 also appeared at this time, *Inventione di toccate sopra la chitarra spagnuola*. This one is found on a copy in Termini-Imrese (I-TI), which has two different dedications, one dated 4 November 1640 in Rome and the other 20 October 1649 in Venice.

Foscarini was probably in Paris in 1647, the year his Italian translation of Johannes Kepler's great scientific work *Harmonices mundi* (1619) was published there under the title *Dell'armonia del mondo*. In his preface Foscarini reveals that at one time he had worked in Brussels, the capital of the Spanish Netherlands, at the court of Albert and Isabella.[32] Since Albert died in 1621, this must have occurred very early in Foscarini's career. He also says that he was in the service of Francesco Perretti (1597–1655), a nephew of the rich and powerful Cardinal Montalto, one of the great Roman music patrons of the time.[33] If, in fact, he was in Paris in 1647, Foscarini could well have been among the Italian singers and musicians who took part in Luigi Rossi's opera *Orfeo*, which was performed there on 2 March 1647. We know from the cast list and detailed synopsis of each act that the continuo instruments used in the production included four harpsichords ('cimbali'), four theorbos ('tiorbe'), two lutes ('liuti'), and two guitars ('chitarre').[34] Might one of the guitarists have been Giovanni Paolo Foscarini?

The eight pieces in mixed tablature included in Francesco Corbetta's first book, *De gli scherzi armonici . . .* (Bologna, 1639), reveal that the young guitarist was already a skilled practitioner of the newer style. Although not as sophisticated as the music contained in his subsequent two books, these pieces are fine additions to the repertory, nicely printed (typeset) and easy to transcribe.

He dedicated his second book, *Varii capricii per la ghittara spagnuola*, to Carlo Gonzaga II, ninth Duke of Mantua and Monferrato (1629–65), on 30 October 1643 in Milan. Since Carlo was only 14 years old in 1643, his duchy was still under his mother's rule. Corbetta probably dedicated his book to Carlo in the hope of receiving a court appointment, perhaps as guitar teacher to the young duke. The book has an engraved portrait of the composer, beneath which is the information that he was a member of the Accademia degli Erranti in Brescia (founded in 1620), that his academic name was 'Il Capricioso',[35] and that he was 28 years of age. The music is engraved, and composed entirely of mixed tablature. It begins with a toccata and a series of sixteen 'passachali' in several different keys. Corbetta's passacaglias, like

---

[32] Albert Ernst, Archduke of Austria (1559–1621), was married to Isabella, the Infanta of Spain (1566–1633), daughter of Philip II. They ruled the Spanish Netherlands together from their court in Brussels.

[33] Hill (1997) is a comprehensive study of Montalto's music patronage.

[34] Found in I-Rvat Barb. Lat. 4059, fo. 131ᵛ and US-I Ml. 95.067, fo. 89ᵛ.   [35] Paolini (1980), n. 5.

Foscarini's, are not the simple I–IV–V–I introductions first encountered in the *alfabeto* books but modern vehicles for harmonic variation that display an imaginative use of dissonance, unexpected harmonies, and scale passages.[36]

The passacaglias are followed by eight suites in different keys, each consisting of an 'almanda', a corrente, and a 'sarabanda', in that order. The sarabands are in the French style (typically, with repeated sections and the characteristic ♩ ♩. ♩ rhythm), and quite unlike the simple, lusty Spanish Zarabanda. One of the suites is in a special scordatura tuning and, consequently, is notated in lute-style tablature without *alfabeto*. There follows a 'Follia' with three variations, the last of which features slurred parallel sixths. Corbetta then provides two charts, the first designed to help the guitarist read from a figured bass and the second to make 4–3 and 7–6 cadences. He ends the book with two *sinfonie* for guitar and another, unspecified instrument to play the figured bass; the second of the two is an especially rewarding performance piece.

Corbetta may have been in the Spanish Netherlands when his fourth book,[37] *Varii scherzi di sonate per la chitarra spagnola*, was published; the dedication to the Habsburg Archduke Leopold Wilhelm of Austria was signed in Brussels, 1 January 1648. Since there is no record of his having been employed at the Brussels court at this time, Corbetta may have dedicated the book to Leopold Wilhelm in the hope of securing an important court appointment.

Like his second book, *Varii scherzi di sonate . . .* also begins with an *alfabeto* chart, followed by ten 'passachaglie' in various keys. A superb 'Chiacona' follows, with an exciting and imaginative array of variation techniques, such as tessitura changes, intricate rhythmic play, and slurred passagework. Corbetta next presents five suites, each of which begins with a short 'Prelud', followed by an 'Almanda', and a varying number of sarabands or correntes. The fifth suite is in a scordatura tuning and therefore notated in lute-style tablature without *alfabeto*. Its 'Prelud' is followed by a Gigue and a 'Passachalo'. Next come five individual 'Correnti Francese', three 'Sarabande Francese', and a set of 'Follias', all in mixed tablature. The book ends with continuo instruction charts.

The influence of French style is very apparent in Corbetta's fourth book. The *alfabeto* chart at the beginning of the book explains the letters using both Italian and French tablature.[38] His correntes and sarabands are all '[à la] Francese'. He uses the French terms 'prelud[e]' and 'gigue' instead of toccata and *giga*. Of course, the book is also full of Italian-style music; but this, unquestionably, is the last of his publications about which that can be said. Accordingly, his 1671 and 1674 publications are

---

[36] Corbetta may have found inspiration for his 1643 collection from Angelo Michele Bartolotti's forward-looking first book of guitar solos published in 1640. For a discussion of Bartolotti's music, see pp. 69–72.

[37] A possible third book by Corbetta from around 1650, *Guitarra espanola y sus diferencias de sones*, believed lost, may recently have been recovered; it is discussed along with other printed books from 17th-c. Spain in Ch. 9.

[38] For a discussion of the importance of French style on Corbetta's music, see Paolini (1983).

discussed in the chapters dealing with the Spanish guitar in England and France respectively.

Following Foscarini's *c.*1630 and Corbetta's 1639 publications came another note-worthy addition to the guitar's solo repertory in mixed tablature, the Bolognese guitarist Angelo Michele Bartolotti's *Libro primo di chitarra spagnola . . .* (Florence, 1640). Bartolotti (*c.*1615–81) dedicated his book to the Florentine Duke Jacopo Salviati on 9 August 1640.[39] The wording of the dedication makes it clear that he truly was in Salviati's service, and the fact that the copy preserved in London (GB-Lbl) once belonged to a certain Giulio Medici[40] invites speculation that he was the guitar teacher of other members of the Florentine aristocracy as well.

In his very first book Bartolotti displays a level of artistic skill and creativity not previously encountered. It includes an ingenious set of passacaglias in which each piece ends in a key that is the starting point for the next piece. The set moves through even the remotest keys, and, if played in its entirety (forty-eight pages), is comparable to Bach's *Wohltemperirte Clavier*, but for guitar. Another innovation is Bartolotti's use of scale passages wherein the individual notes are divided up amongst all the courses, giving the harp- or bell-like effect of notes cascading or ringing one into the other. Thirty-four years later Gaspar Sanz called this effect 'campanelas'. Although Bartolotti provides no details of tuning or stringing, this particular technique requires a guitar that is strung without a bourdon on the fifth course (that is, with both strings tuned an octave higher than the fifth string of a modern guitar), and probably with none on the fourth course either. If a guitar strung with bourdons is used, these courses should at least be arranged so that the upper octave string is in the outer position, and thus easily accessible to the right hand. The desired effect cannot be achieved if the lower string of the course sounds first or at the same time as the upper. The set of passacaglias is followed by variations on the Ciaccona, and six suites in various keys, each consisting of an *allemanda*, two *corrente*, and an Italian-style *sarabanda*. Bartolotti ends the book with variations on the Folia.

He is next cited as a theorbist at the court of Queen Christina in Stockholm and Uppsala, where he was a member of a special ensemble of Italian singers and musicians that included Pietro Reggio (1632–85) and Vincenzo Albrici (1631–96).[41] Records show that Bartolotti was employed in Sweden between 30 November 1652 and 12 July 1654.[42] Christina abdicated on 6 June 1654 and journeyed to Rome, where

[39] Salviati was a Florentine nobleman who is known to have been a patron of music. See Kirkendale (1993), 390.

[40] Coelho (1995*a*), 78 tentatively identifies Giulio Medici as a member of the Medici family, who also owned a Florentine lute manuscript (I-Fn MS Magl. XIX 105) dated 1635, which contains a single guitar piece (fo. 13ᵛ).

[41] Two manuscripts dated 1654 include instrumental music by Albrici and have indications for guitar continuo: S-Uu Instr. mus. ms. i. hs. caps. 1. 10 and 11. 25. See Mason (1989), 81.

[42] Payroll lists from the Swedish court are quoted in E. Kjellberg, 'Kungliga musiker I Sverige under stormaktstiden' (diss., Uppsala University, 1979), 298–310. For an idea of the sort of music Bartolotti was performing during this period, see the MS collection now in Oxford (GB-Och MS 377) consisting of cantatas by the Roman composers Luigi Rossi, Giacomo Carissimi, and Antonio Cesti. According to the inscription on its front cover, the MS

she planned to convert to Catholicism and become a patroness of the arts. Evidently, Bartolotti followed her, first to Innsbruck, where he was employed at the Habsburg court of Archduke Ferdinand Karl, 1655–6.[43] During this period he may have travelled to Rome, where his second book, *Secondo libro di chitarra . . .*, was published, though without a date or publisher's name. It is dedicated to Queen Christina, and her coat of arms appears on its title page. Christina may have financed the publication, or perhaps Bartolotti dedicated the book to her in the hope of securing her future patronage.

His second book displays both his maturity as a composer and his consummate mastery of Baroque guitar idiom in works that achieve an artistic level not equalled until much later in the century. It opens with an *alfabeto* chart in both Italian and French tablature and the most comprehensive explanation encountered to date of Baroque guitar technique. The execution of arpeggiated, simultaneous, and separated chords; trills, mordents, and appoggiaturas; *tenuto*; and other stylistic elements found in his tablature are all carefully explained both in words and tablature charts. The music that follows is organized by key, but not in suites. Bartolotti provides a prelude for almost every key, and each is followed more or less randomly by up to twenty-two pieces consisting of various dance forms. It is up to the performer to create suites by choosing first a prelude and then several other items in the same key. Including the preludes, there are about 140 high-quality pieces from which to choose.

The Prelude in D minor (pp. 69–70) is particularly impressive (see Pl. 6.3). It begins with an arpeggiated flourish, followed by scalar sequences in free rhythm and virtuoso, cascading scale passages that end dramatically on the dominant. A fugal section in two-part contrapuntal writing follows, which builds to a gigue-like section in triple metre. This, in turn, develops to the point where any semblance of a steady metre dissolves in a highly dramatic torrent of notes, which come to a peaceful resolution on D major. Here and throughout the collection, the composer combines French dance forms with Italian expressiveness, virtuosity, and melodic emphasis to stunning effect.[44]

Bartolotti probably became well acquainted with French dance music during his years of service at the Stockholm court; in addition to the Italian band Christina also employed a corresponding French one.[45] France under Louis XIII and his wife Marie de' Medici had become a powerful political force internationally; and since political

belonged to Bartolotti: 'Musica del Sig.r Angelo Michele / Uno di Musici della Capella / di Reyna di Svecia / Upsalia Marti 21 / 1653.

[43] Chauvel (1984), [4]. Bartolotti would have known at least one of the cantata composers in his MS personally: Antonio Cesti was the choirmaster at the Innsbruck court during the very time Bartolotti was there. See Kirkendale (1993), 415.

[44] Although both of Bartolotti's superb publications are available in facsimile (Chauvel, 1984), the composer deserves a modern edition of his complete works.

[45] Christina's French ensemble included the violinist Pierre Verdier (1627–1706).

PL. 6.3. *Prelude* by Angelo Michele Bartolotti, from *Libro secondo* . . . (Rome *c.*1655/6), 69–70

dominance, economic prosperity, and patronage of the arts went hand in hand in those days, French style had begun to exert a significant influence on European music and culture. Not surprisingly, we next encounter Angelo Michele Bartolotti in Paris, where he would hold a lifetime position as theorbo player at the court of Louis XIV[46] and, as will be seen in the next chapter, would continue to compose for the theorbo and guitar.

Antonio Carbonchi's second book (Florence, 1643), comprising music for one to twelve guitars in *alfabeto* notation, was discussed in the previous section; his first, also published in Florence, had appeared three years earlier. Entitled *Sonate di chitarra spagnola con intavolatura franzese*, it is dedicated to the Medici prince Mattias of Tuscany (1613–67), Governor of Siena, who was noted for his patronage of music.[47] Carbonchi's first book, like his second, is unusual. All the music, whether composed in the *pizzicata* (lute) style or the *battuta* (strummed) style, is notated in French-style lute tablature. Carbonchi's use of 'intavolatura franzese' should not be too surprising, however, considering the close cultural and political ties between France and Tuscany. Indeed, Marie de' Medici (1573–1642) was still the Dowager Queen of France at this time.

The simple pieces in Carbonchi's collection are his versions of the Passacaglia (in many keys), the Ciaccona, the Spagnoletta, and other popular Italian dances and dance songs, such as the *Aria di Scappino*, *Clorida*, and the *Correntina alla Genovese*; a selection of Spanish items, including *Escaraman* and *Mariona*; French pieces, such as *L'Avignona*; and two popular songs with quasi-French titles, *Dupon Monami* and *Quamvolevò Madame*. Other pieces have family or given names in their titles, including the *Corrente Orsina* and *Sarabanda Anna*. A piece with the latter title is also found in Corbetta's 1648 book.

Ferdinando Valdambrini contributed two outstanding books of music to the Baroque guitar repertory. The first, entitled *Libro primo d'intavolatura di chitarra a cinque ordini*, was published in Rome in 1646 and dedicated to a clergyman, Don Paolo Savelli, Abbot of Chiaravalle. In the preface Valdambrini explains the signs that appear in his music and states that the same ones were used by the great Roman theorbist Girolamo Kapsperger (*c*.1580–1651).[48] He also describes how arpeggios and other technical devices are performed and gives the stringing arrangement to be used for his

[46] See Chauvel (1984), Introduction.

[47] Although nothing is known of Carbonchi, it is likely that he was a guitar teacher to Florentine society. The manuscript I–Fn Magl. XIX 143 seems to be an autograph (owned by 'Antonio Bracci, fiorentino' and inscribed, on fo. 1ᵛ, '. . . da me Ant.o Carboni . . .'). Another manuscript (D–B Mus. ms. 40085) also contains pieces by Carbonchi, and instructional material in three others (I–MOe Campori 612, I–PEc MS 586, and GB–Ob Mus. Sch. C 94) is taken from Carbonchi's two printed works.

[48] Kapsperger apparently published two books of guitar solos, now lost: *Intavolatura di chitarra* and *Intavolatura di chitarra spagnola pizzicata*. No dates are given for these works. The second, to judge by its title, appears to have been either in lute style or, possibly, mixed tablature. See O. Wessely, 'Der Indice der Firma Franzini in Rom', in *Beiträge zur Musikdokumentation: Fr. Grasberger zum 60. Geburtstag* (Tutzing, 1975), 141. On the importance of Kapsperger see Coelho (1983).

Ex. 6.4. Tuning chart from Francesco Valdambrini, *Libro primo* (1646)

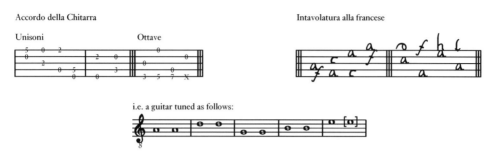

music. By means of a tablature chart that shows which notes are unisons and which octaves, he explains that (for his music) the guitar should be strung without bourdons, that is, it should have a totally re-entrant tuning with the pitches of both the fourth and fifth courses an octave higher than the fourth and fifth strings of a modern guitar. He does not give a nominal tuning, but his continuo charts show that he meant the first course to be tuned to *e′* (see Ex. 6.4). This is the same tuning and stringing arrangement preferred by the later Spanish guitarist Gaspar Sanz,[49] who described it as the normal tuning and stringing arrangement used by the Roman guitarists with whom he had studied.

Like many guitar books of the time, Valdambrini's *Libro primo* . . . begins with charts designed to help the guitarist learn to read from a continuo bass line as well as to play cadence figures. The first music consists of five toccatas in different keys. Despite having bar lines, they are rhythmically free and exploit many of the techniques that are unique to the Baroque guitar, such as cascading scales, slurred parallel sixths, and extended, slurred scale passages. The toccatas are followed by a series of thirteen *corrente*, the final eight of which have a section of variations labelled 'partita'. Then come twelve melodious *balletti*, six *gagliarde*, and an *alemana* with its *partita*. The next item is a *Battaglia*, which, like many other pieces in the 'battle' genre, is a virtuoso showpiece. Covering six pages, it employs all known elements of Italian Baroque guitar technique, and quotes many popular tunes, such as 'Girometta', 'Clorida', 'Tulurù', and 'Fra Jacopino', to name a few. The book's final three pieces, a *Capona*, a *Sarabanda*, and even a *Ciaccona*, seem rather tame after the *Battaglia*.

Valdambrini's second book, entitled *Libro secondo d'intavolatura* . . ., was also published in Rome. The only surviving copy has the year 1647 inked in by hand on its title page. It has the same type of instructional material as his first book, but is more detailed. Valdambrini's advice on how to play a *trillo*, *mordente*, *tremolo*, and *finta* is especially useful. As expected, the music begins with a series of twelve passacaglias,

---

[49] Sanz and his music are discussed in Ch. 10.

each in a different key. All are substantial, high-quality compositions, as are the remaining pieces—twelve *capone* and three *ciacconi*. A conscientious guitar teacher, Valdambrini concludes the book with another chart for reading a figured bass line and one that explains how to convert *alfabeto* chords into French tablature.

In the same year that Valdambrini's first book appeared (1646), the first in a series of seven guitar books by Giovanni Battista Granata (*c.*1625–*c.*1685) of Turin was published in Bologna. Entitled *Capricci armonici sopra la chitarriglia spagnola*, it contains dance movements, such as a 'Corrente Francese', 'Sarabanda', 'Alemanda Francesa', and 'Balletto Francese', as well as a few free-form pieces labelled 'Capriccio musicale', 'Sinfonia', and 'Toccata'. Regrettably, the music is insubstantial and disappointing, and Giacomo Monti's typesetting is rife with printing errors.

Granata was a barber-surgeon by profession, that is, he was licensed to deal not only with hair, but also with minor medical procedures, such as bloodletting for therapeutic purposes.[50] He was also an amazingly prolific composer. His second book, *Nuove suonate di chitarriglia spagnuola piccicate, e battute*, appeared in *c.*1650 (without a publisher's name or date). Sadly, the music (twenty-one engraved plates) is just as dismal as the music in his first. His third book, *Nuova scielta di capricci armonici*, published in Bologna in 1651, employs a greater degree of idiomatic guitar technique and includes a pleasant sonata for guitar and basso continuo. His fourth, *Soavi concenti di sonate musicale*, published in Bologna in 1659, is the most interesting of the seven collections. It contains much fine and original solo music, including five suites of random dance movements for five different scordatura tunings and some rare pieces for a theorboed guitar.[51] There is also an excellent extended sonata for violin, guitar, and continuo, and instructions for guitarists on how to play continuo and cadence figures.

His fifth book, *Novi capricci armonici musicali . . .*, published in Bologna in 1674, is of interest because it opens with twelve individual dance pieces in various keys for guitar, violin, and 'viola' (da gamba). In these the violin part more or less doubles, or reinforces, the guitar's melodic line, and the viola da gamba plays the bass line (a sketchy version of which is also incorporated in the guitar part). This type of trio arrangement, in which a plucked instrument plays what is essentially a solo with its treble and bass reinforced by other instruments, had become common by this date in French and German lute circles, and would later be taken up by Vivaldi.[52] The remaining thirty-two pieces are solos—random dance forms that are not organized into suites but

---

[50] Granata's profession is discussed in Dell'Ara (1979), 11–12.

[51] This instrument was a five-course guitar with an extra, extended neck and peghead for seven unfingered bass or diapason strings tuned diatonically down to *A* at the bottom of the bass clef. Other sources for a similar instrument are: GB-Ob Mus. Sch. C94 (De Gallot guitar MS *c.*1660–84), which contains twelve pieces for 'la guittare Theorbée' with seven basses; I-Nc MS 1321 ('Canzoni e madrigali . . .', *c.*1650), which contains nineteen pieces for a 'catarra' with eight basses; GB-Lam, ex Spencer (a MS entitled 'Sonate per il Chitarrone Francese del Sig.ᵣ Ludovico Fontanelli 1733') for a theorboed guitar with five basses. For additional information, see also Pinnell (1979).

[52] See Vivaldi's lute trios RV 82 and RV 85.

grouped mainly by tonality. The music is good, though unexciting. The same can be said of his final two books, published in Bologna in 1680 and 1684 respectively.[53]

A publication well worth investigating is the Bolognese guitarist Domenico Pellegrini's *Armoniosi concerti sopra la chitarra spagnuola* . . . (Bologna, 1650). Pellegrini was also a composer of cantatas,[54] both sacred and secular. That he regarded himself primarily as a professional guitarist is made clear in the preface to his 1650 publication: '. . . per mia particolar professione, io suono la Chitarra'. His book opens with some useful explanatory material on arpeggiation, dynamics, slurring, and ornamention. The music that follows comprises free-form pieces (three toccatas and a *ricercata*), dance forms (four *allemande*, two *balli*, four *brandi*, eleven *corrente*, and six *sarabande*), three grounds with variations (a 'Chiaccona', a Passacaglia, and a Romanesca), and an 'Aria'. The Passacaglia is substantial (208 variations) and modulates through all the keys before returning to the one in which it began. Well worth studying and performing, it is a tour-de-force reminiscent of Bartolotti's passacaglias (1640), described above.

Another piece worthy of note is the *Battaglia Francese*, about which Pellegrini comments in his preface: '. . . I have transcribed many things from French lute tablature, despite the fact that I have never been in France, nor [have I] ever heard the trumpet played on the battlefield. In case you may wonder how I could nevertheless produce a battle piece, I should tell you that I found it necessary to take an example from a virtuous gentleman who had composed a similar piece.'[55] This elaborate work calls to mind Valdambrini's *Battaglia* published four years earlier. Perhaps he is the 'virtuous gentleman' whose *battaglia* was the inspiration for the present piece. That one of Pellegrini's other pieces, the *Alemanda quarta* (49), is dedicated to the same clergyman to whom Valdambrini dedicated his 1646 book ('Abbate D. Paolo Savelli') seems to support this idea.

Less worthy is a book by the Ferrarese guitarist Francesco Coriandoli (d. 1670), *Diverse sonate* . . . (Bologna, 1670). Not only is the music in this collection mediocre, but one must slog through a multitude of printing errors in order to discover how truly undistinguished it is.[56] On only a slightly higher plane are the two books by Francesco Asioli of Reggio (Emilia), *Primi scherzi di chitarra* . . . and *Concerti armonici per la chitarra spagnuola* . . ., both published in Bologna in 1674 and 1676 respectively. Somewhat more promising is Giovanni Bottazzari's *Sonate nuove per la chittarra*

[53] The treble and bass parts for both of Granata's final books were printed in separate partbooks, now lost.

[54] Pellegrini's earliest surviving publication is *Pietosi affetti il terzo libro* . . . (Venice, 1646). Nothing is known of his first two, now lost. See Vecchi (1977).

[55] 'hò tradotto molti mottivi d'intavalatura di Liuto alla Francese: non essendo io stato mai in Francia, ne havendo udito come si suonano le trombe nelle Battaglie. E perche resti sodisfatto chi potrebbe interrogarmi sopra di questo, m'è stato d'huopo il pigliarne esempio da qualche virtuoso, che habbia composto di simil materia' (fo. 5).

[56] The printer was Giacomo Monti, who also published Granata's error-filled 1646 book. To be fair, Monti was also the publisher of Pellegrini's 1650 book, which, though not error-free, is much more reliable. Clearly, proof-reading was the responsibility of the composer.

spagnola . . ., published in Venice in 1663. Bottazzari's dances, though organized mainly by tonality, are not necessarily intended as set suites. Sophisticated technical devices are employed, such as cascading scales and extended slurred passages, and several groups of pieces are in five different scordatura tunings.

The publications of Italian mixed tablature end with Ludovico Roncalli's outstanding contribution to the repertory, *Capricci armonici sopra la chitarra spagnola* . . ., printed in Bergamo in 1692. Roncalli is a composer about whom nothing is known, except the snippets of information found in his book. According to the title page he was a count, apparently from Bergamo, which was then part of the Republic of Venice. He dedicated his book to Cardinal 'Panfilio' in July 1692, in Bergamo. Benedetto Pamphili (1653–1730) is remembered today as the patron of Arcangelo Corelli, Alessandro Scarlatti, and the young George Frideric Handel in Rome. At the time of Roncalli's publication (and as its title page indicates), he was the papal legate to Bologna (1690–3); nothing in Roncalli's dedication indicates, however, that Pamphili was, or had ever been, his patron.

The music in this meticulously engraved publication is a series of nine formal suites, each in a different key, and each beginning with a *Preludio*, followed by an *Alemanda*. Various dance forms, including the *Corrente*, *Gigua*, *Sarabanda*, *Minuet*, and *Gavotta*, follow, but in no set order. Two of the suites end with a set of variations on the Passacaglia. It is fitting that Italy's seminal contribution to the solo repertory for Spanish guitar ends with Roncalli. His music is so finely crafted and has such enormous melodic appeal that it compares favourably with some of the best contemporaneous Italian music for other instruments—even the violin sonatas of Corelli.

The music sources discussed in this section, together with all known printed sources of guitar repertory in mixed tablature, are included on the annotated checklist in Table 6.3.

The Manuscript Sources of Alfabeto *Solos and Songs, and Solos in Mixed and Lute-Style Tablature*

Dealing with manuscript sources is considerably more difficult than printed ones for two main reasons. First, it is rare to find a manuscript that indicates the year in which it was written (and, indeed, most were written over a number of years); secondly, most manuscripts do not identify the author, and neither is the name of the original owner always present to aid in the search for its provenance. In some fortunate instances various distinguishing marks are present, such as a coat of arms, an original shelf number, or a striking and distinctive handwriting, and these serve as clues. Usually, however, the only way to determine the date and provenance of a manuscript is to compare it with other sources of the same repertory that *are* dated and provide additional clues.

On the other hand, manuscripts frequently offer invaluable information that is not found in the printed sources, such as specific details of tuning and stringing. As we have seen, the typical tuning information found in printed sources instructs the player to start with the fifth course and tune it to a pitch that suits the instrument; then to place a finger on the fifth fret and tune the fourth course to that pitch; and so on, until all the courses are tuned. A tablature chart is usually provided to illustrate the written instructions. Taken at face value, this information could easily lead a modern player to the conclusion that the Baroque guitar had bourdons on the fourth and fifth courses— which, indeed, is the stringing preferred by several of the guitarists we have encountered, including Montesardo (1606). However, several manuscript sources that present precisely the same tuning chart come to an entirely different conclusion. For example, in an *alfabeto* manuscript (F-Pn Rés. Vmc. MS 59) from *c.*1620–30 it is explained in this manner (fo. 2):

Note that on the fifth course its two strings are always tuned in unison, stopping the third course at the second fret and tuning it to the fifth course open as you see here. The fourth course is tuned a fourth higher by stopping the seventh fret [of the fourth course] with the [open] fifth course producing a unison [*sic*: clearly an octave is meant here] or, by stopping the fifth course at the fifth fret, with the fourth course [open], making a unison. The third course is tuned a fourth higher by stopping [it] at the second fret [and tuning it] with the open fifth course. The second course is tuned a third higher by stopping [it] at the third fret [and tuning it] with the fourth course in unison. The first course is tuned a fourth above the second course [by stopping it] at the third fret, [making that note] an octave above the third course [open].[57]

This description shows how deceptive the tuning charts and explanations found in most *printed* guitar books can be. The manuscript author's explanation of the same basic tuning chart reveals that his or her guitar has a re-entrant tuning with no bourdons at all—which, in fact, is the stringing arrangement preferred by some of the period's most excellent guitarists, including, as previously noted, Ferdinando Valdambrini (1646).

As the majority of printed sources that offer deceptive tuning charts and instructions tend to be *alfabeto* books, some modern writers have concluded that all music containing *alfabeto*, including music in mixed tablature, should be performed on a

---

[57] The key to understanding these instructions is realizing that the anonymous author of the MS numbers the courses in reverse order; i.e. the first course ('prime') is the fifth course and the fifth course ('quinta') is the first course. This reverse ordering is not unusual (cf. I-BcAA/360, fo. 109). Please note that, to avoid confusion, I have adjusted the order in my translation:

' Nota che le prime due corde sempre s'accordano in voce pari tastandole al sec.° o terzo tasto o a voto come si vede qui.

' Le seconde s'accordano una quarta voce sop. tastate al settimo tasto, con le prime a voce pari o vero al quinto quelle prime con le secondo con voce uguale[.]

' Le terse s'accordano una quarta sotto, tastate al secondo tasto colle prime a voto[.]

' Le quarte s'accordano una terza sopra taste al terzo tasto con le seconde a voce pari[.]

' La quinta s'accorda una quarta sopra le quarta al terso tasto un ottava le terse'[.]

guitar with bourdons. Yet, the manuscript calling for a guitar with no bourdons and a re-entrant tuning contains only music with *alfabeto*, and Valdambrini's music is in mixed tablature. In fact, most sources of mixed tablature, even those in which specific tuning instructions like Valdambrini's are not provided, tend to require a re-entrant tuning of at least the fifth course, without which the many unique effects typical of the style are difficult to achieve.

Another manuscript (I-Bc AA/360) from *c.*1640–80 contains a tuning chart in staff notation[58] for an *e´*-tuned guitar with a totally re-entrant stringing arrangement and a third course comprised of one *g* string at the normal pitch and the other an octave higher! This may seem strange in and of itself; however, it starts to make sense when applied to some of Roncalli's music (1692). Although he gives no tuning instructions, Roncalli's tablature often seems to call for an upper octave note on the *g* course! This use of an octave on the third course is corroborated in yet another manuscript (I-MOe MS Campori 612), in which the same tuning chart in tablature is explained using staff notation.[59]

Although most guitar manuscripts are anonymous, the authors of a number of them can be identified. There is a manuscript in Verona (I-VEc MS 1434) entitled *Libro dell' ill.^mo conte Paulo Canossi – Veronese*. The coat of arms of the Veronese Count Paulo Canossi appears in full colour, and at the bottom of the title page is the name of the manuscript's author, 'Fran.^co Palumbi Maestro di chitarra'. Another manuscript, now in Paris (F-Pn MS Español 390), is dedicated to Filippo Roncherolle and has the name of the author inscribed on the title page: 'Franc.º Palumbi'. Both manuscripts contain many of the same Italian, Spanish, and Sicilian song texts with *alfabeto*. Both also contain *alfabeto* solos written in a cursive, highly distinctive, almost flamboyant hand (see Pl. 6.4).

Indeed, Palumbi's handwriting is so idiosyncratic there can be little doubt that he is also the author of four other manuscripts that until now have been considered anonymous.[60] These are I-Fn Landau-Finaly 175 and I-Fr MSS 2793, 2804, and 2849, all four of which contain much of the same material as the two signed Palumbi manuscripts. A small portion of another manuscript, I-Fc 2556, is written in the same hand,[61] while yet another, I-Fr 2951, though not in Palumbi's hand, has so much material in common with his manuscripts, it is likely to have been copied from one of them.

Nothing concrete is known about the life of this 'Maestro di chitarra', but from the combination of Spanish, Sicilian, and Italian song texts with *alfabeto* in his manuscripts, it can be surmised that Francesco Palumbi came from southern Italy. Perhaps, like so many of the Italian guitarists and singers of the time, he was a Neapolitan who

---

[58] Although the tuning is expressed in the bass clef, the reference to the fifth course being tuned to 'a la mi re' of a 'spinetto' and the context of the description show that the guitar in question is not a bass guitar but one at normal pitch.

[59] See Jensen (1980), 20, 35–6, and pl. IV.

[60] e.g. RISM B/VII, 118–21.   [61] Kirkendale (1972), 81.

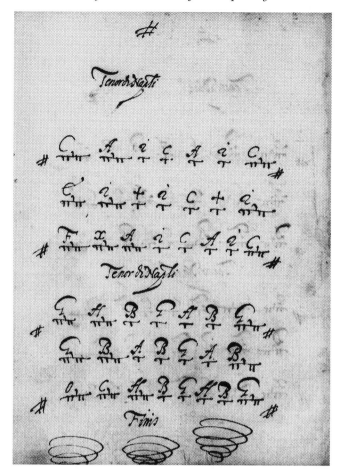

PL. 6.4. Two settings of the *Tenor di Napoli* on the
alfabeto letters C and G by Francesco Palumbi
(Verona, Biblioteca Civica, MS 1434–82.3, fo. 17ᵛ)

travelled to the northern courts to increase his employment opportunities. This supposition is supported not only by the four Florentine manuscripts cited above, but also
by the aforementioned Verona manuscript (I-VEc MS 1434), which is dedicated to
one of his aristocratic Veronese students.

As for their dates, all the *alfabeto* solos contained in the Palumbi manuscripts,
including settings of such traditional dances and harmonic formulas as the 'Pasa-
caglio', 'Roggiero', 'Villan di spagna', Sarabanda, Folia, Romanesca, Ballo del Gran
Duca, Spagnoletta, Calata, Tordiglione, and Tenor di Napoli, are also found in manuscript sources from the late sixteenth century, as well as in the earliest printed *alfabeto*

books, Montesardo (1606) and Pico (1698). Palumbi's song texts with *alfabeto* that have concordances in the Duchess of Traetta manuscript, dated 1599 (I–Rvat Chigi L.VI. 200),[62] including *Salen mis suspiros*, *Vuestros ojos dama*, *Ay que contento*, and *A la moça bonita ciquitta*, are also helpful in the dating of his manuscripts, as are the eight that have concordances in the Neapolitan *cancionero* manuscript from *c.*1590–1620, now in Kraków (PL–Kj 40163),[63] including *Moçuela del valle*, *O si volassen*, *Bulliçioso*, *Frescos ayres del prado*, and *Llegamos a Puerto*. These concordances point to an earlier date than the ones most recently cited.[64] Indeed, the earliest of the Palumbi manuscripts could be from *c.*1600–10 and the others no later than *c.*1620.

Unquestionably, the manuscript sources of *alfabeto* solos and songs, and of the song texts with *alfabeto*, are fascinating documents with much to tell us about early Baroque performance practice. It is hoped that scholars will one day embark on as detailed and systematic a study of them as they have of other repertories, and that the annotated checklist provided in Table 6.4 will prove useful.

The Printed Songbooks with Alfabeto

There is also a vast repertory of printed songbooks containing arias, *canzonette*, madrigals, laments, and other vocal forms, that include guitar *alfabeto* as an accompaniment option. The music is generally found in score form for solo voice (occasionally two or three voices) with a figured bass line and *alfabeto* above the vocal line. This repertory includes publications by some of the most revered composers of the time, such as Sigismondo d'India, Stefano Landi, and Alessandro Grandi. There are also books by Andrea Falconieri, Girolamo Kapsperger, Carlo Milanuzzi, Giovanni Battista Vitali, and many others. Composers contributing individual items to the repertory include Claudio Monteverdi (five arias with *alfabeto* in Milanuzzi, 1624 and RISM 1634[7], all unique to the prints in which they are found); Girolamo Frescobaldi (RISM 1621[15]); Domenico Mazzocchi (RISM 1621[16]); and Francesco Cavalli (RISM 1634[7]).

Despite the evidence for its widespread use found in the many guitar books that provide instruction tables for playing both *alfabeto* chords and continuo from a figured bass line,[65] modern writers and editors rarely mention the guitar as an option for accompanying solo song. Certainly, its tunings often prevent it from sounding the true bass note; however, an idiomatic continuo accompaniment for guitar can be stunningly effective when combined with a lute or theorbo playing the true bass line.

[62] Discussed in Ch. 4. [63] Discussed in Ch. 4.

[64] For example, Hill (1997), 70 suggests a dating of *c.*1630 for F–Pn 360, and RISM B/VII, 119 a dating of *c.*1660–70 for I–Fr 2804.

[65] Most of the songbooks printed in Venice by Vincenti provide a chart that correlates the notes of a bass line with the appropriate *alfabeto* letter (chord) to play over it. Nicola Matteis's book (1680 and 1682) is probably the most useful and detailed of the continuo treatises of the period. It is available in a facsimile edition (Monte Carlo: Éditions Chanterelle, 1980). Strizich (1981) is a useful guide for readers of Italian, and N. North, *Continuo Playing on the Lute, Archlute and*

It is impossible to include a detailed and systematic study of this huge repertory in the present book, but the annotated checklist in Table 6.5 should provide scholars with a useful starting point for such a study. In addition to the sources of published songbooks with a vocal line, a figured bass line, and *alfabeto*, the list also includes the published sources of song texts with *alfabeto* only. This supplements the list of printed sources of *alfabeto* solos, where song texts with *alfabeto* also appear (see Table 6.2). The complete contents of most of the books can be found in Lesure and Sartori (1977), and there is additional information in RISM B/I; other references are given for those entries not included in either of these sources.

The Four-Course Guitar in Seventeenth-Century Italy

Although the five-course guitar took precedence in seventeenth-century Italy, the four-course guitar was not completely ignored, and mention of it must be included in this chapter. By now commonly known as the chitarrino, chitarra alla napolitana, or chitarra italiana, the four-course guitar remained of sufficient interest to warrant the printing of its own *alfabeto* chart in Pietro Millioni's *Corona del primo, secondo, e terzo libro* . . . (Rome, 1631).[66] After dealing first with the 'chitarra spagnola', Millioni goes on to explain how to finger the same *alfabeto* chords on a 'chitarrino', or 'chitarra Italiana' (p. 8), for which he provides a four-line tablature chart. The chord shapes for the four-course guitar are the same as for the five-course instrument, except, of course, without the fifth course. (See Pl. 6.5 for an example of a mid-seventeenth-century chitarrino.)

An anonymous source published in Rome in 1645 is entitled: *Conserto vago di balletti, volte, corrente, et gagliarde, con la loro canzone alla franzese. Nuovamente posti in luce per sonare con liuto, tiorba, et chitarrino à quarto corde alla napolitana insieme, ò soli ad arbitrio, e diletto de' virtuosi, et vobile professori, ò studiosi di questi instrumenti, composti da buono, ma incerto auttore. Libro primo.*[67] The title is quoted here in full because of the useful information it offers: 'Delightful consort of ballettos, voltas, correntes and galliards with their canzonas ('canzone alla franzese'). Newly printed for playing on the lute, theorbo, and four-course Neapolitan-style guitar: [The pieces] can be played separately as solos ad libitum and are for the enjoyment of virtuous and noble teachers or students of these instruments; [the music is] composed by a good, but anonymous author'.

Theorbo (Bloomington: Indiana University Press, 1987), is an indispensable source for all players of plucked instruments.

[66] Subsequent editions are dated 1635, 1636, and 1638.   [67] Discussed in Cavallini (1978a).

PL. 6.5. Chitarrino by Giovanni Smit (Milan, 1646).
Vienna, Kunsthistorisches Museum, SAM 49

After a brief explanation of the various markings found in the tablature (for right-hand fingering, *tenuto*, arpeggiation, slurring, the *trillo*, and so on), the music is presented in three separate parts, all in Italian-style lute tablature, including the guitar part. Its title notwithstanding, the music is actually one suite of pieces comprising a *balletto*, a *volta*, a *corrente*, a *gagliarda*, and a *canzona* (labelled 'Ricercata' in the theorbo and guitar parts). Each seems to be based on the same musical material—the popular ground More Palatino, which was known in France as *En revenant de S. Nicolas,* and in some Italian sources, such as Frescobaldi's *Il primo libro di capricci* . . . (Rome, 1624, no. 7), as *Or* [or *Poi*] *che noi rimena.*

As for the individual parts, the lute's seems to be entirely self-sufficient, containing enough melody and bass to be convincing as a solo. The theorbo part mainly doubles the bass of the lute part, but it too could pass as a solo. The guitar part, however, is so elaborate, so full of decorative filigree, that it makes sense only when played over a basic version of the ground, such as the lute part.

No tuning information is provided for the guitar, but the tablature clearly establishes its relationship to the other instruments, whose nominal tunings, of course, are known. The guitar tablature indicates that its tuning configuration is that of the Spanish *temple a los viejos* or French *a corde avallée,*[68] and that if the lute's first course is *g′*, the relative pitch of the guitar's first course is *a′*. However, since the lute and theorbo tablatures indicate that they should both be tuned to the same pitch level, and since the Italian theorbo was normally tuned in *A,* in this particular instance it is likely that the lute also would have been tuned to *A.*[69] If so, then the guitar's first course would have been a tone higher at *b′*, and its tuning identical to Cerreto's of 1601.[70]

Seventeenth-century manuscript sources for the four-course guitar are as scarce as the printed ones. One, formerly in the collection of the late Robert Spencer and now in the library of London's Royal Academy of Music, dates from about 1620 and contains Italian lute-style tablature for four-course guitar in the first half (fos. 1–12) and Italian tablature for violin in the second (fos. 16ᵛ–22ᵛ). At the end of the manuscript (on fo. 32ᵛ)[71] there is a tablature tuning chart for the 'chitarra semplice' with the instruction to first tune the fourth course as you please ('Prima accordarete la 4. a come piacer a voi'). It then shows in tablature a fret check for the remaining intervals. Normally, this would result in the typical interval configuration of the four-course guitar. However, on folio one there is a chart giving the names of the courses ('corde') as 'canto' for the first, 'sottana' for the second, 'mezzana' for the third, and 'cantine' for the fourth. The diminutive form 'cantine' strongly suggests that the fourth course is meant to be at the

---

[68] 'Temple a los viejos' is discussed in Ch 1. and 'a corde avallée' in Ch. 2.

[69] Although the Italian lute typically was tuned in *G,* there are some sources that also indicate an *A* tuning, including I-Bc MS AA/360, an Italian lute MS from the same time as *Conserto vago* . . . . See Coelho (1995a), 222.

[70] Discussed in Ch. 4.

[71] The pages at the end of each half contain blank staves.

higher octave, which would produce a re-entrant tuning similar to Cerreto's, but in the Spanish *temple a los nuevos* interval configuration![72]

Among the twenty-five guitar pieces included in this manuscript are *La zoppa*, *La gerometta*, *Rose e viole*, *Norcina*, *Dama d'amor*, *Bruscello*, and *Giardin d'amore*. All are in lute-style tablature that appears to have been written by a novice. The four-course guitar section ends with two songs, 'e diventato questo cor meschino' and 'da poi che tu mi ho tradire', the texts of which are written under the tablature.[73]

---

[72] Discussed in Ch. 1.

[73] The violin section contains similar material. Two further MSS containing pieces for four-course guitar (amongst pieces for the five-course guitar and other instruments) are I-IE Mus. Ms. Plan, 6² (early 17th c.; see Fabris (1982), 107–8) and I-Bc MS AA/360, fo. 159ᵛ (*c.* 1640–80; see Coelho (1995*a*), 62–3). Another manuscript, I-PEc MS 586 by Antonio Carbonchi (*c.* 1635–40), contains tuning information (fo. 6) for a 'chitarrino a sette corde', which seems to indicate a tuning in *g*´ (see RISM B/II, 280–1).

TABLE 6.1. *Italian manuscript sources of vocal music in staff notation with* alfabeto

Location	Source	Remarks
I–Bu	MS 177/IV	Neapolitan? *c.*1580–1600. Canto partbook for 16th-century *napolitane, villanelle*, and *canzonette*
I–Fc	MS C. F. 83	Codex Barbera; Florentine, *c.*1600–20
I–Fn	MS Magl. XIX 24	Florentine, *c.*1620. Music mainly by R. Rontani
I–Fn	MS Magl. XIX 25	Florentine, *c.*1615
PL–Kj	Mus. ms. 40163	Neapolitan *cancionero, c.*1590–1620. Three-voice Spanish songs
US–Wc	MS M. 2. 1. I 8. case	*c.*1650. Anonymous cantatas and duets; one piece, *Alcina abbandonata*, has *alfabeto*

TABLE 6.2. *Italian printed sources of* alfabeto *solos*

Dates in square brackets indicate books that are now lost.

1606	Montesardo, Girolamo, *Nuova inventione d'intavolatura per sonare li balleti sopra la chitarra spagnuola* . . . (Florence)
1620	Colonna, Giovanni Ambrosio, *Intavolatura di chitarra alla spagnuola* . . . (Milan)
1620	Colonna, Giovanni Ambrosio, *Il secondo libro d'intavolatura di chitarra alla spagnuola* . . . (Milan)
1620	Sanseverino, Benedetto, *Intavolatura facile delli passacalli, ciaccone* . . . (Milan)
1622	Milanuzzi, Carlo, *Secondo scherzo delle ariose vaghezze* . . . (Venice) An *alfabeto* songbook; the concluding section contains 26 guitar solos. Later edn.: 1625 (Venice).
1622	Sanseverino, Benedetto, *Il primo libro d'intavolatura* . . . (Milan) An expanded edition of 1620 (Milan). Also contains texts with *alfabeto* and songs in staff notation with *alfabeto*.
1623	Colonna, Giovanni Ambrosio, *Il terzo libro d'intavolatura* . . . (Milan)
1623	Milanuzzi, Carlo, *Terzo scherzo* . . . (Venice) An *alfabeto* songbook; the concluding section contains 38 guitar solos.
[1624]	Millioni, Pietro, *Il primo, secondo, et terzo libro d'intavolatura* . . . (Rome) Cited in Marin Mersenne, *Harmonie universelle* . . . (Paris, 1636), fo. 96ᵛ. A later edn. from 1627 survives entitled *Quarta impressione del primo* . . . (Rome).
*c.*1625	Monte, Lodovico, *Vago fior di virtù* . . . (Venice)
1627	Abatessa, Giovanni Battista, *Corona di vaghi fiori* . . . (Venice)
1627	Aldigatti, Marc'Antonio (da Cesana), *Gratie et affetti amorosi* . . . (Venice) An *alfabeto* songbook containing 48 brief guitar solos. (Facs. edn.: Bologna: Università degli Studi di Bologna, 1979).
1627	Colonna, Giovanni Ambrosio, *Intavolatura di chitarra spagnuola del primo, secondo, terzo et quarto libro* . . . (Milan)
1627	Costanzo, Fabritio, *Fior novello. Libro primo di concerti di diverse sonate* . . . (Bologna)
1627	Millioni, Pietro, *Seconda impressione del quarto libro d'intavolatura* . . . (Rome) The date of the first edn. is not known. Later edn.: 1635 (Rome).
1627	Millioni, Pietro, *Prima impressione del quinto libro* . . . (Rome)
*c.*1627	Millioni, P. and Monte, L., *Vero e facil modo d'imparare a sonare* . . . (Venice) 16 of the 38 solos pirated from Millioni, 1627. Later edns.: 1637 (Rome and Macerata); 1644 (Venice); 1647 (Rome and Macerata; facs. edn.: Bologna: Forni Editore, 1977); 1652 (Venice); 1659 (Venice); 1666 (Venice); 1673 (Venice); 1673 (Venice and Macerata); 1678 (Venice); 1678 (Venice), entitled *Novissime canzonette* . . . reprints most of the solos; 1684 (Venice); 1737 (Venice).
1629	Foscarini, Giovanni Paolo, *Intavolatura di chitarra spagnuola libro secondo* . . . (Macerata)
1631	Millioni, Pietro, *Corona del primo, secondo, e terzo libro d'intavolatura* . . . (Rome) For further information, see Gary Boye: 'The Case of the Purloined Letter Tablature: The Seventeenth-Century Guitar Books of Foriano Pico and Pietro Millioni', in *Journal of Seventeenth-Century Music*, Volume 11, no. 1, 2006, n. 33. Also gives *alfabeto* instructions for four-course guitar.

1635   Abatessa, Giovanni Battista, *Cespuglio di varii fiori* . . . (Orvieto)
Later edn.: 1637 (Florence) Also contains songs in staff notation with *alfabeto*.

1635   Marchetti, Tomasso, *Il primo libro d'intavolatura* . . . (Rome)
Later edns.: 1648 (Rome) no author's name on title page; 1660 (Rome; facs. edn.: Geneva: Minkoff Reprint, 1981). Also contains texts with *alfabeto*. (For more details, see Ch. 6 n. 9.)

1637   Colonna, Giovanni Ambrosio, *Intavolatura . . . del primo, secondo, terzo, & quarto libro* . . . (Milan)
Facs. edn.: Bologna: Forni Editore, 1971. These are not reprints of Colonna 1620 and 1623.

1637   Sfondrino, Giovanni Battista, *Trattenimento virtuoso disposto in leggiadrissime sonate per la chitarra* . . . (Milan)

1639   Corbetta, Francesco, *De gli scherzi armonici* . . . (Bologna)
Also contains eight pieces in mixed tablature.

1639   Trombetti, Agostino, *Intavolatura di sonate* . . . (Bologna)

1639   Trombetti, Agostino, *Libro secondo d'intavolatura* . . . (Bologna)

1643   Carbonchi, Antonio, *Le dodici chitarre . . . libro secondo* . . . (Florence)
Facs. ed.: Florence: S.P.E.S., 1981.

[1645]   Abatessa, Giovanni Battista, *Intessatura di varii fiori* . . . (Naples)
Later edn.: 1652 (Rome and Lucca).

1646   Calvi, Carlo (compiler), *Intavolatura di chitarra e chitarriglia* . . . (Bologna)
Facs. edn.: Florence: S.P.E.S., 1980. The first half contains *alfabeto* solos for 'chitarriglia' and the second half Italian-style lute tablature for 'chitarra'.

c.1650   Abatessa, Giovanni Battista, *Ghirlanda di varii fiori* . . . (Milan)

1653   Banfi, Giulio, *Il maestro della chitarra* . . . (Milan)
The first half is in *alfabeto* and the second mixed tablature.

1677   Ricci, Giovanni Pietro, *Scuola d'intavolatura* . . . (Rome)
Also contains texts with *alfabeto*, songs in staff notation with *alfabeto*, and music for 'mandola' in staff notation.

1678   Anonymous, *Novissime canzonette musicali de diversi auttori* . . . (Venice)
A collection of texts with *alfabeto* followed by *alfabeto* solos, some pirated from Millioni and Monte, *Vero e facil modo . . . c.*1627.

1680   Micheli, Antonio di, *La nuova chitarra* . . . (Palermo)
Later edn.: 1698 (Palermo). Also contains Sicilian texts with *alfabeto*.

1698   Pico, Foriano, *Nuova scelta di sonate per la chitarra spagnola* . . . (Naples)
See n. 5 for further bibliographical information. Also contains texts with *alfabeto* and songs in staff notation with *alfabeto*. (Facs. edn.: Geneva: Minkoff Reprint, 1981).

TABLE 6.3. *Italian printed sources of solos in mixed tablature*

---

*c.*1630   Foscarini, Giovanni Paolo, *Il primo, secondo, e terzo libro della chitarra spagnola* . . . [Rome]

Book 1 is entirely in *alfabeto*, and Books 2 and 3 in mixed tablature. A later copy of Books 1–3 from *c.*1638 (I-BcV33) carries the title page of *I quatro libri della chitarra spagnola . . . c.*1632.

*c.*1632   Foscarini, Giovanni Paolo, *I quatro libri della chitarra spagnola* . . . [Rome]

The music is the same as the first three books of the *c.*1630 edn., but with the addition of a fourth book of mixed tablature. The GB-Lbl copy carries the original *c.*1630 title page, *Il primo, secondo, e terzo libro* . . . A later edn. of *c.*1634 (GB-Lam, ex Spencer) carries the title page of *I quatro libri* . . . in an altered state. A later copy (CZ-Pnm) has a dedication date of 1638, but carries the original *c.*1630 title page of *Il primo, secondo, e terzo libro* . . .

1639   Corbetta, Francesco, *De gli scherzi armonici trovati, e facilitati in alcune curiosissime suonate sopra la chitarra spagnuola* . . . (Bologna)

Though it contains primarily *alfabeto* solos, there are also eight solos in mixed tablature.

1640   Bartolotti, Angelo Michele, *Libro p.º di chitarra spagnola* (Florence)

Facs. edn.: Geneva: Minkoff Reprint, 1984.

1640   Carbonchi, Antonio, *Sonate di chitarra spagnola con intavolatura franzese* (Florence)

Facs. edn.: Florence: S.P.E.S., 1981. Mixed tablature converted into French-style lute tablature with rhythmic stroke signs.

1640   Foscarini, Giovanni Paolo, *Li cinque libri della chitarra alla spagnola* . . . (Rome)

The music is the same as in *I quatro libri . . . c.*1632, but with the addition of a fifth book of mixed tablature. Facs. edn.: Florence: S.P.E.S., 1979. A *c.*1640 copy (E-Mn) carries the title page of *I quatro libri* . . .

1640   Foscarini, Giovanni Paolo, *Inventione di toccate sopra la chitarra spagnuola* (Rome)

Same as *Li cinque libri* . . . but with a different title page. The I-PLcom copy has two dedications, one dated 4 Nov. 1640 in Rome, and the other 20 Oct. 1649 in Venice.

1643   Corbetta, Francesco, *Varii capriccii per la ghittara spagnuola* . . . (Milan)

Facs. edn.: Florence: S.P.E S., 1980.

1646   Calvi, Carlo (compiler), *Intavolatura di chitarra e chitarriglia* . . . (Bologna)

Facs. edn.: Florence: S.P.E.S., 1980. The first portion is entirely in *alfabeto* for 'chitarriglia' and the second in Italian-style lute tablature for 'chitarra'.

1646   Granata, Giovanni Battista, *Caprici armonici sopra la chittarriglia spagnuola* . . . (Bologna)

Facs. edn.: Florence: S.P.E.S., 1978.

1646   Valdambrini, Ferdinando, *Libro primo d'intavolatura chi chitarra a cinque ordini* . . . (Rome)

*c.*1647   Valdambrini, Ferdinando, *Libro secondo d'intavolatura di chitarra a cinque ordini* . . . (Rome)

1648   Corbetta, Francesco, *Varii scherzi di sonate per la chitara spagnola* . . . (Brussels)

Facs. edn.: Florence: S.P.E.S., 1983.

1648   Pesori, Stefano, *Galeria musicale . . . compartita in diversi scherzi di chittariglia* (Verona)

Facs. edn.: Verona: A.M.I.S., 1989.

*c.*1648   Pesori, Stefano, *Lo scrigno armonico opera seconda* . . . (Mantua?)

Most of the music is on single engraved plates, and there are discrepancies between the only two known copies (GB-Lbl and I-Bc). Facs. edn.: Florence: S.P.E.S., 1986.

*c.*1650   Corbetta, Francesco, (?) *Guitarra española* . . . [Missing title page]

Probably published in Madrid. This could be Corbetta's lost book. Sixty-two of its eighty-four pages are reprinted from his 1648 book; the remaining pages contain new works. Sold at Sotheby's, London, on 20 Nov. 1991. Present whereabouts unknown. See Ch. 6, n. 37.

c.1650   Granata, Giovanni Battista, *Nuove suonate di chitarriglia spagnuola piccicate, e battute . . .* (Bologna)
        Facs. edn.: Bologna: Forni Editore, 1991.

1650   Pellegrini, Domenico, *Armoniosi concerti sopra la chitarra spagnuola . . .* (Bologna)
        Facs. edn.: Florence: S.P.E.S., 1978.

c.1650   Pesori, Stefano, *Toccate di chitarriglia, parte terza . . .* (Verona)
        I-VEc MS 1560 appears to be a manuscript copy of most of the material from his previous printed books. The MS is dated 1650.

c.1650   Pesori, Stefano, *I concerti armonici di chitarriglia . . .* (Verona)
        Contains much material from Pesori's previous publications.

1651   Granata, Giovanni Battista, *Nuova scielta di capricci armonici . . . opera terza . . .* (Bologna)

1653   Banfi, Giulio, *Il maestro della chitarra . . .* (Milan)
        Half is in *alfabeto* and the rest in mixed tablature.

c.1655–6   Bartolotti, Angelo Michele, *Secondo libro di chitarra . . .* (Rome)
        Facs. edn.: Geneva, Minkoff Reprint, 1984.

1659   Granata, Giovanni Battista, *Soavi concenti di sonate musicali per la chitarra spagnuola . . . opera quarta . . .* (Bologna)
        Facs. edn.: Monte Carlo: Éditions Chanterelle, 1979.

1663   Bottazzari, Giovanni, *Sonate nuove per la chitarra spagnola . . .* (Venice)
        Facs. edn.: Florence: S.P.E.S., 1984.

1670   Coriandoli, Francesco, *Diverse sonate ricercate sopra la chitarra spagnuola . . .* (Bologna)
        Facs. edn.: Florence: S.P.E.S., 1981.

1674   Asioli, Francesco, *Primi scherzi di chitarra . . .* (Bologna)
        Facs. edn.: Florence: S.P.E.S., 1984.

1674   Granata, Giovanni Battista, *Novi capricci armonici musicali in vari toni per la chitarra spagnola, violino, e viola concertati, et altre sonate per la chitarra sola. Opera quinta . . .* (Bologna)
        Facs. edn.: Bologna: Forni Editore, 1971.

c.1675   Pesori, Stefano, *Ricreationi armoniche overo toccate di chitarriglia . . .* (Verona?)
        Contains much material from Pesori's earlier books. Found in this publication is a printed list of his students dated 1675.

1676   Asioli, Francesco, *Concerti armonici per la chitarra spagnuola . . .* (Bologna)

1680   Granata, Giovanni Battista, *Nuovi sovavi [sic] concenti di sonate musicali in varii toni per la chitarra spagnola, et altre sonate concertate a due violini, e basso. Opera sesta . . .* (Bologna)
        The separate partbooks for the violins and basso are lost.

c.1680   Matteis, Nicola, *Le false consonanse della musica per poter apprendere a toccar da se medesimo la chitarra sopra la parte . . .* (London)
        An extensive treatise on learning to play continuo on guitar, it also contains five solos in mixed tablature converted into French tablature. The same music plates were used in a re-edited English version of 1682, *The False Consonances of Musick . . .* (London). Facs. edn.: Monte Carlo: Éditions Chanterelle, 1980.

1684   Granata, Giovanni Battista, *Armonici toni di vari suonate musicali concertante, a due violini, e basso, con la chitarra spagnola, opera settima . . .* (Bologna)
        The separate partbooks for the violins and basso are lost.

1692   Roncalli, Lodovico, *Capricci armonici sopra la chitarra spagnola . . .* (Bergamo)
        Facs. edn.: Monte Carlo: Éditions Chanterelle, 1980.

TABLE 6.4. *Italian manuscript sources of* **alfabeto** *solos and songs, and solos in mixed and lute-style tablature*

Location	Source	Date	Remarks
A–Wn	MS 10248	*c.*1665–90	MS belonging to Orazio Clementi. French-style lute tablature with *alfabeto*. RISM B/VII, 359
D–B	Mus. Ms. 40085	*c.*1645	Anon. (A. Carbonchi?). *Alfabeto* solos and texts with *alfabeto*. RISM B/VII, 23
D–Rp	MS AN 63	*c.*1650	MS belonging to Domenico Romani. *Alfabeto* solos. RISM B/VII, 299
F–P	private library	*c.*1620	Anon. 16 folios of *alfabeto* solos
F–Pn	MS Español 390	*c.*1610–20	'Libro di villanelle Spagnuol et Italiane et Sonate spagnuole'. MS by Francesco Palumbi, dedicated to Filippo Roncherolle. *Alfabeto* solos; Spanish, Italian, and Sicilian texts with *alfabeto*. Esses (1992), 169
F–Pn	Rés. Vmc. MS 5	*c.*1680	Anon. Guitar solos in Italian-style lute tablature. RISM B/VII, 267–8
F–Pn	Rés. Vmc. MS 6	'1703'	Mandola music by Matteo Caccini and fragments of *alfabeto* guitar solos. RISM B/VII, 268
F–Pn	Rés. Vmc. MS 59	*c.*1620–30	Anon. *Alfabeto* solos and texts with *alfabeto*; tuning and technical information
F–Pn	Rés. Vmf. MS 50	*c.*1590–1610	Anon. Tuscan MS. 13 *alfabeto* solos, 1 text with *alfabeto* in a lute MS. Coelho (1995), 128–9
GB–HAdol-metsch	MS II. C. 23	*c.*1640	Anon. Medici provenance. Lute MS with guitar solos in *alfabeto* and in mixed tablature. RISM B/VII, 133
GB–Lam	(ex Spencer)	'1698'	MS belonging to Domenico Veterani. *Alfabeto* solos, 4 pieces in mixed tablature, and a few for lute and mandola
GB–Lam	(ex Spencer)	'1733'	'Sonate per il Chitarone Francese' by Ludovico Fontanelli for theorboed guitar. Spencer (1976)
GB–Lbl	Add. MS 36877	*c.*1623	'Villanelle di più sorte con l'intavolatura per Sonare, et cantare sù la chitarra alla spagnola', compiled by Giovanni Casalotti. Texts with *alfabeto*. RISM B/VII, 184–5; Hill (1997), 169–71, 394–402

Location	Source	Date	Remarks
I-BA	private library	'1683'	Anon. *Alfabeto* solos. Fabris (1995), 411
I-BIad	MS V. E. 45	c.1650	Anon. [G. B. Abatessa?]. *Alfabeto* solos. Lospalluti (1989)
I-Bc	MS AA 346	c.1630	Anon. addition to Pietro Millioni, *Prima scielta de villanelle* (Rome, 1627). RISM B/VII, 49
I-Bc	MS AA 360	c.1640–80	Anon. 7 *alfabeto* solos, 1 text with *alfabeto*, 6 solos in mixed tablature. Coelho (1995), 62–3
I-Bc	MS Q 34	'1613'	MS by Giovanni Amigoni. *Alfabeto* and bass chart in a MS miscellany. Jensen (1980), 157
I-Bc	MS V 280	c.1614–18	'Libro de sonate diversi alla chitarra spagnola . . .'. *Alfabeto* solos, texts with *alfabeto*, lute-style pieces. RISM B/VII, 48–9
I-COc	MS 3.1.11	mid-17th c.?	Anon. *Alfabeto* solos, mixed tablature. Fabris (1982), 116
I-Fc	MS B. 2521	mid- 17th c.	Anon. *Alfabeto* solos. Fabris (1982), 116
I-Fc	MS B. 2556	mid-17th c.	'Questo libro di sonate di chitara, e di Giovanni Antonii e W'. *Alfabeto* solos, texts with *alfabeto*, 1 lute-style piece. RISM B/VII, 117–18
I-Fn	MS Fondo Landau-Finaly Mus. 175	c.1610–20	Anon. [Francesco Palumbi]. *Alfabeto* solos; Italian, Sicilian, and Spanish texts with *alfabeto*. RISM B/VII, 115–16
I-Fn	MS Fondo Landau-Finaly Mus. 252	'1625'	'Questo libro di sonate di chitarra spagnuola è di Atto Celli da Pistoia'. *Alfabeto* solos, texts with *alfabeto*. RISM B/VII, 116–17
I-Fn	MS Magl. VII. 618	mid-17th c.	Anon. Texts with *alfabeto*. *MT* (June 1979), 489; Boetticher (1979), 203
I-Fn	MS Magl. VII. 894	mid-17th c.	Anon. *Alfabeto* solos. *MT* (June 1979), 489; Boetticher (1979), 203
I-Fn	MS Magl. VIII. 1222bis	c.1623	Anon. [Roman?]. *Alfabeto* solos, texts with *alfabeto*. Hill (1997), 171–2, 403–13
I-Fn	MS Magl. XIX. 105	'1635'	Anon. [Florentine]. Lute MS belonging to Giulio Medici. 1 *alfabeto* solo. Coelho (1995), 78–80
I-Fn	MS Magl. XIX. 137	early 17th c.	Anon. Basso continuo, a few guitar pieces in lute-style tablature. RISM B/VII, 111; Jensen (1980), 103

TABLE 6.4. *continued*

Location	Source	Date	Remarks
I-Fn	MS Magl. XIX. 143	*c.*1640	Florentine MS belonging to Antonio Bracci with material by A. Carbonchi. *Alfabeto* solos, texts with *alfabeto*. RISM B/VII, 112
I-Fr	MS 2774	*c.*1620	Anon. 'Intavolatura della chitarra spagnola'. *Alfabeto* solos, Italian and Spanish texts with *alfabeto*. Baron (1977), 21–2; RISM B/VII, 118; Jensen (1980), 18, 158
I-Fr	MS 2793	*c.*1610–20	Anon. [Francesco Palumbi]. *Alfabeto* solos, Italian and Spanish texts with *alfabeto*. Baron (1977), 21; RISM B/VII, 118–19
I-Fr	MS 2804	*c.*1610–20	Anon. [Francesco Palumbi]. MS belonging to Guglielmo Altoviti. *Alfabeto* solos, Italian and Spanish texts with *alfabeto*. Baron (1977), 21; RISM B/VII, 119–20
I-Fr	MS 2849	*c.*1610–20	Anon. [Francesco Palumbi]. *Alfabeto* solos, texts with *alfabeto*. RISM B/VII, 120–1
I-Fr	MS 2868	*c.*1620–40	Anon. Florentine MS belonging to Mario Belli. *Alfabeto* solos. Kirkendale (1993), 359
I-Fr	MS 2951	*c.*1620–30	Anon. (same hand as MS 2952). *Alfabeto* solos, Italian and Spanish texts with *alfabeto*. Baron (1977), 21; RISM B/VII, 121; Passaro (1992)
I-Fr	MS 2952	*c.*1620–30	Anon. (same hand as MS 2951). *Alfabeto* solos, Italian and Spanish texts with *alfabeto*. RISM B/VII, 122; Passaro (1992)
I-Fr	MS 2973	*c.*1610–20	Anon. *Alfabeto* solos, Italian and Spanish texts with *alfabeto*. Baron (1977), 21, 33, 35, 37; RISM B/VII, 122–3; Jensen (1980), 52–3
I-Fr	MS 3121	mid-17th c.	Anon. MS '. . . sonate della chitarra spagnuola . . .' belonging to Filippo Baldinotti. *Alfabeto* solos, texts with *alfabeto*. RISM B/VII, 123
I-Fr	MS 3145	'1609'	Anon. MS 'Intavolatura della chitarra spagniola . . .' belonging to Mariotto Tallocci. *Alfabeto* solos, texts with *alfabeto*. RISM B/VII, 123–4; Fabris (1995), 392
I-IE	Mus. Ms. Plan. 3	'1682'	Anon. MS belonging to Gio. Francesco Fioroni. Mixed tablature. Fabris (1982), 106–7

Location	Source	Date	Remarks
I-IE	Mus. Ms. Plan. 6/2	early 17th c.	Anon. *Alfabeto* solos, mixed tablature for both guitar and 'chitarrino'. Fabris (1982), 107–8
I-Mc	Fondo Noseda. Coll.: 48/A	mid-18th c.	Anon. The second portion (fos. 191–246) contains the *alfabeto* accompaniments for the preceding 478 pieces for a 'chitarr'a penna overo leuto con l'ottava' (18-c. Neapolitan mandolone). Fabris (1982), 108–13
I-Mt	Cod. 55	*c.*1640–50	Anon. [Stefano Pesori?]. Later section (pp. 140–98) of an earlier vocal MS. *Alfabeto* solos, mixed tablature. Fabris (1982), 114
I-MOe	MS 2	early 17th c.	Anon. Spanish texts with *alfabeto*. Acutis (1971), 7; Baron (1977), 21, 23
I-MOe	MS 3	early 17th c.	Anon. Spanish texts with *alfabeto*. Acutis (1971), 7; Baron (1977), 21, 23
I-MOe	MS 115	early 17th c.	Anon. Spanish texts with *alfabeto*. Acutis (1971), 6–7; Baron (1977), 21
I-MOe	MS Campori 612.γ.L.10.21	mid-17th c.	Anon. Florentine MS [Antonio Carbonchi?] belonging to Onorio Marinari. *Alfabeto* solos. Jensen (1980), 34–6, 158
I-MOe	MS Campori app. 719	mid-17th c.	Anon. 'Poesie musicali'. Texts with *alfabeto*. Wenland (1976), 188
I-MOe	MS Mus. E. 323	*c.*1680–1700	Anon. [Modenese?] MS with engraved portraits of James II of England and his queen, Maria of Modena. Most of the music is copied from Francesco Corbetta's 1643 book. Mixed tablature. Boetticher (1979), 201
I-MOe	MS Mus. F 1528	*c.*1665	Anon. 'Raccolta di balli per la chitarra spagnuola'. Mixed tablature, 1 piece in lute-style tablature, 1 text with *alfabeto*. Boetticher (1979), 201–2
I-MOs	MS Busta Numero IV/3	*c.*1660–80	Anon. Large, multi-sectioned MS with Italian tablature for violin and viola da gamba, 10 *alfabeto* solos, including one associated with the name Pietro Bertacchini (*c.*1641–94). RISM B/VII, 211; Coelho (1995), 102–3
I-Nc	MS 1321	*c.*1650	Anon. Vocal MS associated with the composer Fabio Costantini (*c.*1570–1644). Italian lute-style tablature for a 13-course theorboed guitar. Fabris (1982), 115–16

TABLE 6.4. *continued*

Location	Source	Date	Remarks
I-Nc	MS 7664	1607–23	Anon. MS belonging to Francesco Quartiron. 1 guitar solo in Italian-style lute tablature in a MS for lute and cittern. Fabris (1982), 114–15; Fabris (1995), 393
I-Nn	MS Mus. MS XVII. 30	1622–9 and 1635	Anon. MS belonging to Antonio Alvarez di Toledo, and later Adriana Basile-Barone. Spanish texts with *alfabeto*. Fabris (1982), 116
I-NOV	MS (no shelf no.)	*c.*1650–80	Anon. Mixed tablature. Baron (1977), 24–5; Fabris (1982), 116
I-OS	MS Musiche. B.4582	*c.*1700	Anon. Mixed tablature. Fabris (1982), 117; Fabris (1995), 403
I-PAc	MS 1506/1	*c.* 1604–12	Anon. MS [now missing?] belonging to Ginevra Bentivoglio. Italian and Spanish texts with *alfabeto*. Acutis (1971), 8, 35; Baron (1977), 21
I-PEas	MS (Fondo Sermattei della Genga)	*c.*1650	Anon. Mixed tablature. Fabris (1987), 94
I-PEc	MS 586	*c.*1640	Anon. [Antonio Carbonchi]. *Alfabeto* solos and some in mixed tablature. RISM B/VII, 280–1
I-PESc	MS Pc. 40	'1650'	Anon. *Alfabeto* solos. RISM B/VII, 282
I-PIa	MS (no shelf no.)	'1622'	'Scelta di intavolature sopra la chitarra alla spagnuola cioè da sonare, cantare, ballare, e altro', compiled by Andrea Franci di Pistoia. *Alfabeto* solos. Fabris, (1987), 80
I-Raa	MS (no shelf no.)	*c.*1650	'Ballata di Michel Angelo del Violino'. Keyboard MS with a few *alfabeto* solos. Silbiger (1980), 113
I-Rn	MS Mus. 156/1–4	early 17th c.	Ensemble music in staff notation by Stefano Landi and others; 'chitarrino' part (bass clef) for a 2-part canzona by 'Sig.r Gio:'. Fabris (1982), 118–19
I-Rsc	MS A. 247	1618–23	Anon. *Alfabeto* solos, texts with *alfabeto*. RISM B/VII, 306–7; Hill (1997), 164, 377
I-Rvat	MS Barb. Lat. 4177	mid-17th c.	Anon. Roman MS belonging to Carlo Barberini. *Alfabeto* solos, 1 text with *alfabeto*. RISM B/VII, 305–6
I-Rvat	MS Barb. Lat. 4178	mid-17th c.	Anon. Roman MS belonging to Nicolò Barberini. *Alfabeto* solos. RISM B/VII, 306

Location	Source	Date	Remarks
I-Rvat	MS Chigi cod. L. VI. 200	'1599'	Anon. Neapolitan MS belonging to the 'Duchessa di Traetta'. Spanish texts with *alfabeto*. Acutis (1971), 9; Baron (1977), 24; Hill (1997), 70–4
I-Tn	MS Foà 9	c. 1630	'Intavolatura della chitarra spag.a'. MS belonging to Desiderio Blas. *Alfabeto* solos, texts with *alfabeto*. RISM B/VII, 331–2; Esses (1992), 169–70
I-Vnm	MS Italiano classe IV. No. 1793	1657–66	Anon. lute MS, 1 *alfabeto* solo. RISM B/VII, 338; Coelho (1995), 162–3
I-Vnm	MS Italiano classe IV. No. 1910	c. 1630	Anon. MS belonging to Francesco Riccio. *Alfabeto* solos, texts with *alfabeto*. Many concordances with I-Fr MS 2849. RISM B/VII, 388–9
I-VEc	MS 1434 (82.3)	c. 1610–20	'Libro dell'ill.mo Conte Paulo Canossi – Veronese' by 'Fran[ces]co Palumbi Maestro di chitarra'. *Alfabeto* solos; Italian, Sicilian, and Spanish texts with *alfabeto*. Fabris (1982), 117
I-VEc	MS 1560	'1650'	'Toccate di chittariglia' by Stefano Pesori, dedicated to Felippo Gianfelippi. *Alfabeto* solos, song texts with *alfabeto*, mixed tablature, lute-style tablature. RISM B/VII, 339–40; Boetticher (1979), 202
US-LA tyler private library		c. 1620	'Libro di varie canzonette da cantare sù la chitariglia', compiled by Giovanni Alberto Fiorini da Carpi. Texts with *alfabeto*
US-R	MS Vault ML 96. M. 435	c. 1680–5	MS copy of Nicola Matteis, *Le false consonanse . . .* (c.1680). RISM B/VII, 303–4; Ward (1979–81), 20
US-Wc	MS M. 2. 1. T2. 17B	'1657'	Anon. MS belonging to Jacinto Petti di Radicondoli. *Alfabeto* solos, texts with *alfabeto*, mixed tablature; lute-style tablature. RISM B/VII, 346–7

TABLE 6.5. *Italian printed songbooks with* alfabeto

1610   Kapsperger, Giovanni Girolamo, *Libro primo di villanelle* . . . (Rome)
        Facs. edn.: Florence: S.P.E.S., 1979.

1611   Borlasca, Bernardino, *Canzonette a tre voci* . . . (Venice)

1612   Montesardo, Girolamo, *I lieti giorni di Napoli* . . . (Naples)
        Facs. edn.: New York: Garland Publishing, Inc., 1986.

[1613] Giaccio, Orazio, *Armoniose voci* . . . (Naples)
        Later edns.: [1618], 1620.

1613   (Various), *Orfeo. Musiche de' diversi autori* . . . (Venice)
        Cavallini (1989), 35–6.

1614   Marinoni, Girolamo, *Il libro primo de motetti a una voce* . . . (Venice)

1616   Corradi, Flaminio, *Le stravaganze d'amore* . . . (Venice)
        Later edn.: 1618.

1616   D'Aragona, Paolo, *Amorose querele* . . . (Naples)

1616   D'Aragona, Paolo, *Soavi ardori* . . . (Naples)

1616   Falconieri, Andrea, *Libro primo di villanelle* . . . (Rome)

1616   Salzilli, Crescenzio, *La sirena libro secondo* . . . (Naples)

1616   Salzilli, Crescenzio, *Amarille libro terzo* . . . (Naples)

1616   Sanseverino, Benedetto, *El segundo libro de los ayres* . . . (Milan)

1618   Caccini, Francesca, *Il primo libro delle musiche* . . . (Florence)
        Facs. edn.: New York: Garland Publishing, Inc., 1986.

1618   Giaccio, Orazio, *Laberinto amoroso* . . . (Naples)

1618   Romano, Remigio (compiler), *Prima raccolta di bellissime canzonette* . . . (Vicenza?)
        Texts with *alfabeto*. RISM 1618[17]. Later edns.: 1621 (not in RISM; GB–Lam, ex Spencer); 1622 (RISM
        1622[18]). Romano's 1619 compilation, *Aggionata ai versi* . . . (Vicenza), contains no *alfabeto*. Formerly in
        the collection of R. Spencer, it is now in the library of the Royal Academy of Music, London.

1618   Stefani, Giovanni (compiler), *Affetti amorosi* . . . (Venice)
        RISM 1618[15]. Later edns: 1621 (RISM 1621[17]), 1623 (RISM 1623[9]), 1626 (RISM 1626[13]).

1619   Falconieri, Andrea, *Musiche* . . . *libro sexto* . . . (Venice)

1619   Kapsperger, Giovanni Girolamo, *Libro secondo di villanelle* . . . (Rome)
        Facs. edn.: Florence, S.P.E.S., 1979.

1619   Kapsperger, Giovanni Girolamo, *Libro terzo di villanelle* . . . (Rome)
        Facs. edn.: Florence, S.P.E.S., 1979.

1619   Rontani, Raffaello, *Le varie musiche* . . . *libro terzo* . . . (Rome)

1620   Landi, Stefano, *Arie a una voce* . . . (Venice)

1620   Olivieri, Giuseppe, *La pastorella Armilla* . . . (Rome)

1620   Romano, Remigio (compiler), *Seconda raccolata di canzonette* . . . (Vicenza)
        Texts with *alfabeto*. RISM 1620[22]. Later edns.: [1622] (RISM [1622][19]).

1620   Rontani, Raffaello, *Varie musiche* . . . *libro quarto* . . . (Rome)
        Later edn.: 1625.

1620	Rontani, Raffaello, *Varie musiche . . . libro quinto . . .* (Rome) Later edn.: 1625.
1620	Stefani, Giovanni (compiler), *Scherzi amorosi . . .* (Venice) RISM 1620[13]. Later edn.: 1622 (RISM 1622[12]).
1620	Vitali, Filippo, *Musiche . . . libro terzo . . .* (Rome)
1621	India, Sigismondo d', *Le musiche . . . libro quarto . . .* (Venice) Facs. edn.: New York: Garland Publishing, Inc., 1986.
1621	Veneri, Gregorio, *Li varii scherzi . . .* (Rome)
1621	(Various), *Giardino musicale . . .* (Rome) RISM 1621[15].
1621	(Various), *Raccolta di varii concerti musicali . . .* (Rome) RISM 1621[16].
1622	Guazzi, Eleuterio, *Spiritosi affetti . . . libro primo . . .* (Venice)
1622	Marini, Biagio, *Scherzi, e canzonette . . .* (Parma) Facs. edn.: Florence, S.P.E.S., 1980.
1622	Milanuzzi, Carlo, *Primo scherzo delle ariose vaghezze . . .* (Venice) Later edn.: 1625.
1622	Milanuzzi, Carlo, *Secondo scherzo delle ariose vaghezze . . .* (Venice) Later edn.: 1625.
1622	Romano, Remigio (compiler), *Terza raccolta . . .* (Vicenza) Text with *alfabeto*. (RISM 1622[20]).
1622	Vitali, Filippo, *Arie a 1. 2. 3. voci . . .* (Venice)
1622	(Various), *Vezzosetti fiori . . .* (Rome) RISM 1622[11]. Facs. edn.: New York: Garland Publishing, Inc., 1986.
1623	Ghizzolo, Giovanni, *Frutti d'amore . . . libro quinto . . .* (Venice)
1623	Giamberti, Giuseppe, et al., *Poesie diverse . . .* (Rome) RISM 1623[13].
1623	India, Sigismondo d', *Le musiche . . . libro quinto . . .* (Venice) Facs. edn.: New York: Garland Publishing, Inc., 1986.
1623	Kapsperger, Giovanni Girolamo, *Libro quarto di villanelle . . .* (Rome) Facs. edn.: Florence, S.P.E.S., 1979.
1623	Manzolo, Domenico, *Canzonette . . .* (Venice)
1623	Milanuzzi, Carlo, *Terzo scherzo delle ariose vaghezze . . .* (Venice)
1623	Romano, Remigio (compiler), *Nuova raccolta . . .* (Venice) Texts with *alfabeto*. RISM 1623[11]. Later edn.: 1625 (RISM 1625[9]).
1623	Rontani, Raffaello, *Le varie musiche . . . libro primo . . .* (Rome)
1623	Stefani, Giovanni (compiler), *Concerti amorosi . . .* (Venice) RISM 1623[10].
1624	Aranies, Juan, *Libro segundo de tonos y villancicos . . .* (Rome)
1624	Berti, Giovan Pietro, *Cantade et arie . . .* (Venice) Facs. edn., New York: Garland Publishing, Inc., 1986.

TABLE 6.5. *continued*

1624   Milanuzzi, Carlo, *Quarto scherzo delle ariose vaghezze . . .* (Venice)
            Facs. edn.: New York: Garland Publishing, Inc., 1986.

1624   Romano, Remigio (compiler), *Canzonette musicali . . .* (Venice and Turin)
            Texts with *alfabeto*. RISM 1624[13].

1624   Romano, Remigio (compiler), *Seconda raccolta . . .* (Venice and Turin)
            Texts with *alfabeto*. RISM 1624[14].

1624   Romano, Remigio (compiler), *Quarta raccolta . . .* (Venice and Turin)
            Texts with *alfabeto*. RISM 1624[15].

1625   Minischalchi, Guglielmo, *Arie . . . libro primo . . .* (Venice)
            Later edn.: 1627.

1625   Romano, Remigio (compiler), *Prima (–Quarta) raccolta . . .* (Pavia)
            Texts with *alfabeto*. RISM 1625[8].

1626   Grandi, Alessandro, *Cantade et arie . . . libro terzo . . .* (Venice)
            Facs. edn.: New York: Garland Publishing, Inc., 1986.

1626   Romano, Remigio (compiler), *Residuo alla quarta parte . . .* (Venice)
            Texts with *alfabeto*. RISM 1626[16].

[1626]   Severi, Francesco, *Arie . . . libro primo . . .* (Rome)

[1626]   Stefani, Giovanni, *Ariette amorose . . .* (Venice)
            Hill (1997), 165.

1627   Aldigatti, Marc'Antonio, *Gratie et affetti amorosi . . .* (Venice)
            Facs. edn.: Bologna: A.M.I., 1979.

1627   Berti, Giovan Pietro, *Cantade et arie . . . libro secondo . . .* (Venice)

[1627]   Fasolo, Giovanni Battista, *Barchetta passaggiera . . .* (Rome)

1627   Landi, Stefano, *Il secondo libro d'arie musicali . . .* (Rome)
            Facs. edn.: Florence: S.P.E.S., 1980.

1627   Millioni, Pietro, *Prima scielta di villanelle . . .* (Rome)
            Texts with *alfabeto*.

1627   Minischalchi, Guglielmo, *Arie . . . libro secondo . . .* (Venice)

1627   Obizzi, Domenico, *Madrigali et arie . . . libro primo . . .* (Venice)

1628   Crivellati, Domenico, *Cantate diverse . . .* (Rome)

[1628]   Del Giudice, Cesare, *Madrigali concertati . . .* (Palermo)

1628   Fasolo, Giovanni Battista, *Il carro di Madama Lucia . . .* (Rome)

1628   Fedele, Giacinta, *Scielta di villanelle . . .* (Vicenza)
            Texts with *alfabeto*.

1628   Milanuzzi, Carlo, *Sesto libro delle ariose vaghezze . . .* (Venice)

1628   Sabbatini, Pietro Paolo, *Il sesto [libro]* (Bracciano)

1628   Tarditi, Orazio, *Amorosa schiera d'arie . . .* (Venice)

[1629]   Grandi, Alessandro, *Cantade et arie . . . libro quarto . . .* (Venice)

(1620s)   Missing title page; bound with Rontani 1625 (I-Rvat)

1630   Kapsperger, Giovanni Girolamo, *Libro quinto di villanelle . . .* (Rome)

1630   Milanuzzi, Carlo, *Settimo libro delle ariose vaghezze* . . . (Venice)

1630   Minischalchi, Guglielmo, *Arie . . . libro terzo* . . . (Venice)
       Facs. edn.: New York: Garland Publishing, Inc., 1986.

1632   Kapsperger, Giovanni Girolamo, *Li fiori libro sesto* . . . (Rome)

1633   Camarella, Giovanni Battista, *Madrigali et arie* . . . (Venice)

1633   Pesenti, Martino, *Arie a voce sola . . . libro secondo* . . . (Venice)

1634   Valvasensi, Lazzaro, *Secondo giardino d'amorosi fiori* . . . (Venice)

1634   [Various], *Arie de diversi* . . . (Venice)
       RISM 1634⁷.

1635   Fontei, Nicolo, *Bizzarrie poetiche* . . . (Venice)

1635   Marini, Biagio, *Madrigaletti . . . libro quinto* . . . (Venice)

1635   Milanuzzi, Carlo, *Ottavo libro delle ariose vaghezze* . . . (Venice)

1636   Fontei, Nicolo, *Bizzarrie poetiche . . . libro secondo* . . . (Venice)
       Facs. edn.: New York: Garland Publishing, Inc., 1986.

1636   Pesenti, Martino, *Arie a voce sola . . . libro terzo* . . . (Venice)
       Facs. edn.: New York: Garland Publishing, Inc., 1986.

1636   Sances, Giovanni Felice, *Il quarto libro delle cantate et arie* . . . (Venice)

1637   Landi, Stefano, *Il quinto libro d'arie* . . . (Venice)

1638   Busatti, Cherubino, *Arie a voce sola* . . . (Venice)

1638   Gabrielli, Francesco, *Infermità, testamento, e morte* . . . (Verona, Padua, and Parma)
       Text with *alfabeto*.

1640   Kapsperger, Giovanni Girolamo, *Libro settimo di villanelle* . . . (Rome)

1641   Laurenzi, Filiberto, *Concerti et arie* . . . (Venice) Facs. edn.: Florence, S.P.E.S., 2000

1641   Sabbatini, Pietro Paolo, *Varii capricii, e canzonette* . . . (Rome)

[1641] Ziani, Pietro Andrea, *Il primo libro di canzonette* . . . (Venice)

1643   Milanuzzi, Carlo, *Nono libro delle ariose vaghezze* . . . (Venice)

1644   Busatti, Cherubino, *Settimo libro d'ariette* . . . (Venice)

1646   Tarditi, Orazio, *Arie a voce sola* . . . (Venice)

1650   Sabbatini, Pietro Paolo, *Prima scelta di villanelle a una voce* . . . (Rome)
       Later edn.: 1652.

1652   Sabbatini, Pietro Paolo, *Prima scelta di villanelle a due voci* . . . (Rome)

1652   Sabbatini, Pietro Paolo, *Seconda scelta di villanelle a una voce* . . . (Rome)

1657   (Anon.), *Canzonette spirituali, et morali* . . . (Milan)
       RISM 1657¹.

[1659] (Anon.), *Nuove canzonette musicali* . . . (Venice)
       Texts with *alfabeto*. Wolf (1919), 191.

7

France: The Royal Guitarists

During the mid-sixteenth century, musicians, printers, and poets associated with the French court developed a sizeable repertory for the four-course guitar that was both charming and distinctive, and the instrument enjoyed a decades-long period of immense popularity. By the dawn of the seventeenth century, however, the guitar had fallen so out of fashion that it had to be virtually reintroduced—this time as the five-course Spanish guitar, and this time, it seems, by a Spanish guitarist, Luis de Briceño.

The Spanish presence at the French court had increased markedly with the betrothal of the 10-year-old Louis XIII (1601–43) and the 10-year-old Spanish Infanta, Anne of Austria (1601–66), daughter of Philip III. Briceño (dates unknown) evidently travelled in high courtly circles in both countries. He is first cited in connection with a book written in Spanish by 'Le Sieur de Moulère' for Louis XIII that was published in Paris in 1614.[1] The wedding of Louis and Anne took place in 1615, and it is quite possible that Briceño was part of an advance delegation sent to Paris to prepare for the bride's arrival.

In 1626 Briceño published a guitar book in Paris that was also in Spanish. His *Metodo mui facillissimo para aprender a tañer la guitarra a lo español . . .*, dedicated to a French noblewoman, 'Madama de Chales', presents music in a chordal notation similar to Italian *alfabeto*, but with the chords represented by a cipher system, evidently of Briceño's own devising.[2] According to his preface, the collection comprises 'Romances, Seguidillas, Chaconas, Çaravandas, Pasacalles, Gallardas romanescas, Satiras, Liras, Cançiones, Zampa palos, guineos, Pavanas, Otavas y quartillas . . ., la morisca, las folias de ocho maneras, el rastreado el Ay ay ay, letrillas de theatro, la dança de la Hacha, amorosas en dachas, seguidillas en Eco, el saltaren, y el cavallero Español'. Most of these are popular dance songs with Spanish texts.

In addition, Briceño provides the following instructions for tuning the guitar (fo. 5^r):

First, put the two thirds [the third course] in unison. Then put a finger on e [the fourth fret in French tablature] and adjust the open seconds [second course] to them in unison. For the first [course] finger a d [on it] and tune to the same sound at the octave with the open third course.

---

[1] Esses (1992), 50.
[2] Briceño's system differs from the earlier one devised by Juan Carlos Amat. Both are discussed in Ch. 10. See also App. I.

For the fourths [fourth course] finger the d on the second course and tune the fourth course open to the sound of them. For the fifths finger a c [second fret] on the third course and tune the open fifths to the same sound.[3]

In other words, Briceño (unlike Montesardo and Sanseverino) favoured a totally re-entrant tuning (without bourdons) for his chord solos.

At a time when the ultra-genteel French school of lutenists founded by Ennemond Gautier (*c.*1575–1651), the first in a family of illustrious seventeenth-century luten-ists, had just begun to take hold, one cannot help but wonder how the French courtiers reacted to Briceño, his popular-style music, the Spanish guitar, and (although there are no stroke signs in his book) the presumably robust, rhythmical strumming style in which he played it. Of course, as the many arrangements of French lute pieces found in guitar manuscripts demonstrate, French lute style eventually would be incorpo-rated into guitar music, and some French lutenists would take up the guitar.

One such lutenist was Estienne Moulinié[4] (1599–1676), who published five collec-tions of *airs de cour* for solo voice and lute. In the collection entitled *Airs de cour avec la tablature de luth et de guitarre . . .* (Paris, 1629), he included one French, five Spanish, and five Italian songs with guitar accompaniment. These accompaniments are in French-style lute tablature with mensural notes above the five-line staff to indicate rhythm. Although there are no actual stroke signs, the presence of full chords virtually throughout these songs suggests an attempt at notating strumming technique. For the most part Moulinié's guitar songs are as fine as his lute songs. Interestingly, some seem to require a performing style with *sprezzatura*, as the Italians described it, that is, with the rhythmic liberties and expressiveness expected of a solo singer, particularly a self-accompanied one.

One of the Italian guitar songs in Moulinié's book, *O stelle homicide* (see Pl. 7.1), is found in numerous contemporary *alfabeto* sources, and first appeared in French lute books and manuscripts as an elegant courant under the title *La belle homicide*.[5] One of the Spanish songs, *Ribericas del rio mansanares*, is found in the earlier Kraków *cancionero* manuscript (PL-Kj MS 40163, *c.*1590–1620) and the Palumbi manuscripts, discussed in the previous chapter. Another of the Spanish songs,

---

[3] 'Primeramente poner las dos Terçeras en Unison. despues poner el dedo in una E. y ajustallas con las Segundas en A. en Unison.

Por la prima. poner el dedo sobra una D. y haçer que suene aun mesmo son en Octava con las Terçeras en A.

Por las Quartas. poner el dedo sobre una D. delas Segundas y haçer que suenen en Unison con las Quartas en A.

Por las Quintas. poner el dedo sobre una C. delas Terçeras y haçer que suenen con las Quintas en A. aun mismo son'.

Briceño and his guitar book will be discussed further in Ch. 10.

[4] This is the composer's own spelling of his name. Moulinié was also a singer and is the composer cited in the previous chapter in connection with the notation used by Antonio Carbonchi in his first guitar book (Florence, 1640).

[5] For example, see the concordances to Ennemonde Gautier's version in *Œuvres du Vieux Gautier*, ed. A. Souris (Corpus des Luthistes Français, 19; Paris: CNRS, 1966).

A I R

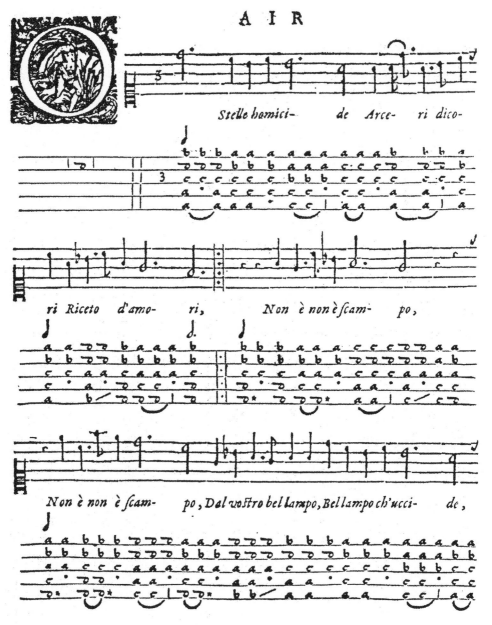

Stelle homici-   de Arce- ri dico-

ri Riceto d'amo-   ri,   Non è non è scam-   po,

Non è non è scam-   po, Dal vostro bel lampo, Bel lampo ch'ucci-   de,

PL. 7.1. Opening of *O stelle homicide* by Estienne Moulinié,
Airs de cour . . . (Paris, 1629), fo. 26ᵛ

Repicavan las campanillas, first appeared in Moulinié's own four-part version in his *Airs de cour* collection of 1626. The text of the song refers to the ringing of the church bells for King Louis XIII and Queen Anne.[6]

The renowned French mathematician, physical scientist, philosopher, and music theorist Marin Mersenne (1588–1648) provides some fascinating details about the guitar in his monumental treatise on music theory and performance practice *Harmonie universelle* . . . (Paris, 1636). Indeed, his discussion of musical instruments includes a veritable mini-treatise on the guitar (*Livre second*, fos. 95–7). It begins with a description of the four-course instrument, illustrated by a picture from Phalèse's 1570 anthology (see above, Pl. 3.1 and Chs. 2 and 3). The author's retrospective approach makes it clear that the four-course guitar was no longer in use in France in 1636. He then describes the five-course guitar in reference to a detailed engraving of the instrument (with only eight frets), a tuning chart in staff notation, and a combined chart for both Italian *alfabeto* and Spanish *cifras* (see Pl. 7.2). He notes that although the guitar normally has ten pegs for the five courses, guitarists often use only a single string for the first course. Referring to the tuning chart in staff notation, he indicates that the guitar has a totally re-entrant tuning (no bourdon on either the fourth or fifth course),[7] and, surprisingly, that the first string is at d'.[8] He goes on to discuss some of the instrument's physical features, proportions, and playing technique. He states that a flat back is just as common as a convex one, and makes a disparaging remark about the thinness of the guitar's sound. He explains the combined *alfabeto* and *cifras* chart using Italian-style lute tablature for the former and French-style for the latter. The *cifras* system he describes is based on Briceño's rather than Amat's. His discussion of right-hand technique involves the number of down or up strokes to play when reading stroke signs, and which fingers to use. Here, he is attempting to explain the Italian rhythmic ornament *repicco*. He goes on to say that dynamics are achieved by playing near the bridge, at the heel of the neck, or anywhere in between.

In the next chapter Mersenne again explains Italian *alfabeto* and Spanish *cifras*, and gives two short examples from a book by 'Pierre Million' (Pietro Millioni), now lost, which was published in Rome in 1624. The examples are from a song text with *alfabeto*, 'Una vecchia sdentata', and a galliard for solo guitar. He also cites 'Ambroise Columna' (Giovanni Ambrosio Colonna) and his 1627 book, which was printed in

---

[6] In the Netherlands numerous texts of a political nature were sung to the tune of *Repicavan las campanillas*. For details, see Baak Griffioen (1991), 303–6.

[7] Clearly, much of Mersenne's information comes from Briceño. Unlike his compatriot Amat, whose guitar is tuned to e' and has bourdons on both the fourth and fifth courses, Briceño used no bourdons at all.

[8] In addition to Mersenne, other sources that indicate a d' tuning are: in Italy, with bourdons on the fourth and fifth courses, Sanseverino (1620); I-Fc MS C.F. 83 (Barbera MS), 99; and I-Fr MS 2774 (see Jensen (1980), 18). In France, Carré (1671), 27, with a bourdon on the fourth course only; and D–B Mus. ms. 40631, fo. 4 (late 17th c.), with no indication of bourdons. And in Germany, Kremberg (1689), with bourdons on the fourth and fifth courses. See App. II.

PL. 7.2. Diagram from Marin Mersenne, *Harmonie universelle*
(Paris, 1636), Book II, fo. 95ᵛ

Milan, as well as a 'Seigneur Louys', whose book was printed in Paris in 1626. The latter, of course, is Luis de Briceño.

Mersenne then singles out a French guitarist for mention. 'Monsieur Martin', who, he says, plays the guitar perfectly, has devised a notation in French tablature in which the mensural notes above the staff show not only the rhythm of the piece, but also the direction of the right-hand strokes. He illustrates the notation with two of Martin's chord solos, an *Allemande* and a *Sarabande*, in which the top note of each chord carries the melody (see Pl. 7.3).

Martin's system works well for his pieces, as it would for any guitar music that is completely chordal. However, modifications to the tablature became necessary when

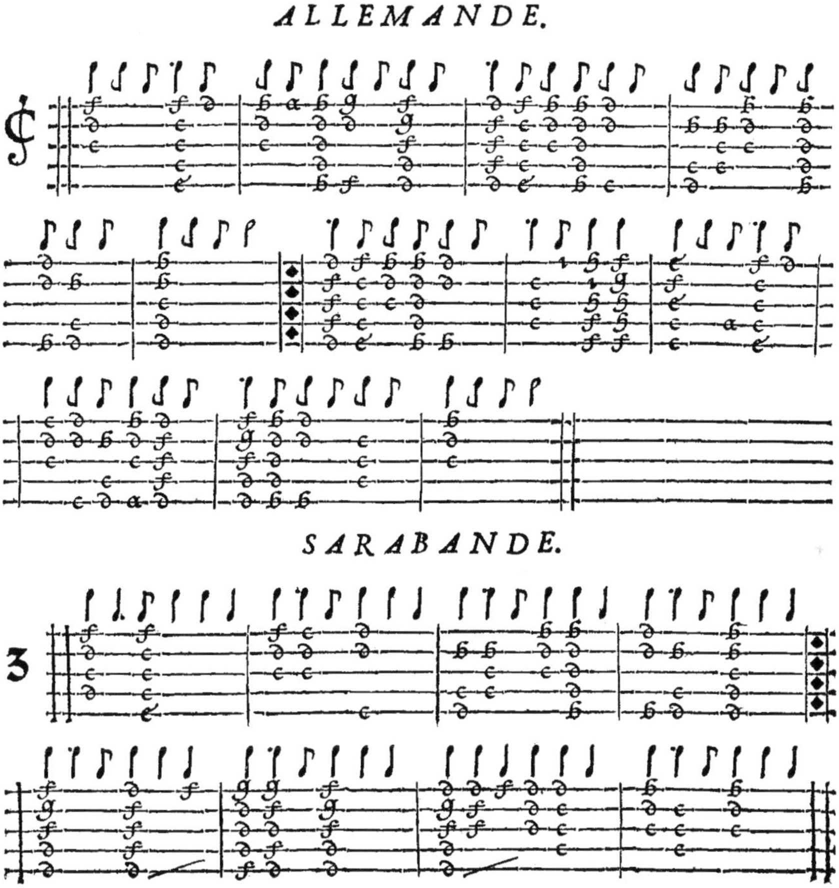

PL. 7.3. *Allemande* and *Sarabande* by 'Monsieur Martin' from Marin Mersenne, *Harmonie universelle* (Paris, 1636), Book II, fo. 97ᵛ

such stylistic elements as cascading scales, slurred parallel sixths, and single-line passages were introduced to the French repertory (as they had been to the Italian in
*c.*1630). Accordingly, by mid-century, French guitar tablatures began to appear in
which Martin's mensural notes for rhythm and stroke direction were placed *within* the
five-line staff (immediately after the relevant chords), while the mensural notes for
single-line and cascading scale passages were printed above the staff.

Mersenne includes a Latin version of the five-course guitar information from
Harmonie universelle in another of his publications, *Harmonicorum libri XII . . .* (Paris,
1648).[9] The illustration in the latter shows a different, chunkier, and less elongated
five-course instrument than the one in *Harmonie universelle*, and the tuning chart in
staff notation has a rather ambiguous clef shape, which, if interpreted as an alto *c* clef,
indicates a totally re-entrant tuning, but at the nominal pitch of *e´*. He also includes
the same detailed diagrammatic engraving of the guitar, with the tuning chart in staff
notation and the combined chart for both Italian *alfabeto* and Spanish *cifras*, and more
or less the same written commentary as in the earlier book. After explaining the
alfabeto and *cifras* chart, however, he offers as an example a complete verse from the
song *Cancion a la Reyna de França* from Briceño's 1626 book. He then gives the same
Allemanda and *Sarabanda* by Monsieur Martin that appeared in *Harmonie universelle*
(although, here, as indicated, both are spelled with a final 'a' instead of 'e'), and
remarks that the saraband is commonly accompanied by castanets ('Castaneolas').
Regrettably, he offers no further details about Monsieur Martin, who presumably was
a guitar teacher to the Parisian aristocracy.

Three important French manuscripts from the mid-seventeenth century that are
the first to display the fully developed French guitar tablature system described above
have received little attention. They belonged to 'Monsieur Dupille, commiss^re des
guerres' (Commissioner of War) and are preserved in the Bibliothèque Sainte-
Geneviève in Paris (F-Psg MSS Rés. 2344, 2349, and 2351). Each contains some quite
distinctive repertory. For the most part French, there are also a few popular pieces of
Italian and Spanish origin. The first manuscript, dated 1649, is the largest of the three
and contains mainly dance pieces—branles, sarabands, courants, and gavottes, which
bear such titles as *Branles de St. Nicolas*, *La Sylvie*, *Petite royale*, *Les Feuillantines*, *La
Chabote*, *La Tricotets*, *Marion pleure*, and *La Fronde*. Many have song texts written
beneath the tablature. While not technically demanding, these pieces represent an
important addition to the French guitar repertory from around the time of Louis
XIII, a repertory comparable to that for the French lute in this period and including
many of the same titles.

All three manuscripts contain many details that should be of interest to guitarists.
For example, the simple 'Chacona' at the beginning of MS 2344 is a strummed

---

[9] *Liber primus*, 27–30.

I–IV–V–I sequence with clearly notated *repicci*, something not seen in a printed source until twenty-two years later in Corbetta's *La Guitarre royalle*. Manuscript 2349 has a tablature tuning chart (fo. 4ᵛ) headed 'accord de guitarre par unison', which indicates that the author tuned his or her guitar without bourdons. An examination of the music reveals that in every piece the melodic line is distributed amongst all the courses, and only makes sense if both strings of both the fourth and fifth courses are tuned at the upper octave.

This tuning is also preferred by the author of MS 2344 (fo. 84ᵛ). The same chart (beginning with the tuning of the third course) is given, as is a reference in staff notation for checking the guitar's tuning with that of a treble viol ('dessus de viole') and a bass viol ('basse de viole'). The nominal pitches given for the viols indicate that the guitar which played the music in this manuscript was tuned to *a´*, a fourth higher than expected. This high tuning, implying a small instrument, has been encountered previously.[10] It should be noted, however, that in the same manuscript there are two pieces with bass vocal parts in staff notation that imply the use of a larger guitar tuned to *e´*. There are at least two possible explanations for this apparent anomaly. The first (and most obvious) is that the author had two different-size guitars in mind; the second (and most likely) is that, regardless of the nominal pitches given for the instrument's solo music, when it came to accompanying the voice, the singer and guitarist simply agreed on a pitch level that suited the ranges of both.[11]

Throughout Louis XIII's reign the guitar was seen and heard both in chamber recitals and in the court ballets that were such a vital part of the social and political ritual established by the king and his council.[12] According to contemporary court records and pictorial evidence, these productions often involved guitarists. A drawing of one of the *entrées* in the *Ballet des Fées des Forêtes de Saint-Germain* of 1625 shows eight guitarists in contemporary Spanish costume striding onstage in pairs. The caption reads: 'Entrée des Espagnolz joueurs de guitaire'.[13] Evidently, one of the guitarists was the king himself.[14]

After Louis XIII's death in 1643, the new chief minister of France, Cardinal Mazarin (Giulio Mazzarini, formerly a Roman diplomat), sent to Italy for a guitarist to teach the young future king, Louis XIV.[15] The guitar teacher's identity is unknown, but Foscarini was in Paris from at least 1647, the year his Italian translation of Kepler's *Harmonices mundi* was published there, and he appears to have had contacts in France from an even earlier date. His guitar books from the 1630s indicate a familiarity with

---

[10] See the discussion on the 'chitarriglia' in Ch. 6.

[11] For an excellent discussion of this issue see H. W. Myers, 'Pitch and Transposition', in *A Performer's Guide to 17th-Century Music* (New York: Schirmer Books, 1997), 325–40.

[12] See Isherwood (1973), ch. 2 and Benoit (1992), 334.

[13] Reproduced in Anthony (1973), pl. 2 and Baron (1975), 31.

[14] Baron (1975), 13.

[15] This is according to Jacques Bonnet (1644–1723), a historian and former member of the king's council. See *Histoire de la musique . . .* (Paris, 1715), 131.

French lute music, and his engraved portrait shows him with a classic French-style goatee and lace collar.[16]

Some scholars have contended that the guitar teacher in question was Francesco Corbetta;[17] however, there is no evidence of his presence at the French court before 1656, by which time Bernard Jourdan de la Salle[18] had held the post of guitar master to the king for six years.[19] Indeed, Corbetta's presence in Paris is documented by the guitarist himself in the Italian preface to his 1671 book *La Guitarre royalle*. He refers to another of his books, now lost, 'which was printed here in Paris in 1656 where it pleased his Majesty to allow me to be in an *entrée* of several guitars for a ballet composed by the most famous Signor Gio. Battista Lulli. . .'.[20] Lulli, of course, was the young Florentine musician and dancing master who would later become the most influential composer at the French court, Jean-Baptiste Lully (1632–87). The ballet referred to by Corbetta is *La Galanterie du temps*, which was presented under Cardinal Mazarin's auspices and featured Louis XIV as one of the dancers.[21]

The names of the other guitarists involved in the *entrée* are not known; however, François Martin (c.1620–c.1688) may well have been one of them. His manuscript collection *Airs de cour et airs à boire* (F-Pn) was composed during the period 1645–80.[22] Individual airs appear in print between 1658 and 1678. His one instrumental book, *Pièces de guitairre, à battre et à pinser . . .* (Paris, 1663), was the first collection of French guitar music to be published in Paris in the seventeenth century. And, according to the royal printing privilege at the end of the book, he was in the employ of the 'Duc d'Orleans', the king's brother.

Although a modest little book of some twenty pages, Martin's *Pièces de guitairre . . .* was engraved by Bonnart and is of a very high quality. Presented in the now standard French guitar tablature, it is divided into two suites, which, as its title page indicates, are in two different styles, the strummed style ('à battre') and the lute style ('à pinser'). The first suite consists of melodic chord solos—a *Prélude, Alemende, Courante, Sarabande, Gavotte, Gigue*, and *Passacaille*, which look simple, but, with their many passing notes, discords, and sophisticated harmonic effects, are as difficult to play as similar pieces found in the contemporary French lute repertory. Martin's tablature contains

[16] See Pl. 6.2. Compare Foscarini's portrait with that of Henry II, Duc de Montmorency, and Louis de Bourbon, Compte de Soissons, reproduced in Baron (1975), 14.

[17] For example, H. Charnassé, 'Corbett', in Benoit (1992), 180.

[18] Jourdan was born in a province of Cadiz, Spain. Apparently, nothing further is known about him, except that he remained guitar master to the king until his death in 1695. See Benoit (1992), 320.

[19] After Bernard Jourdan de la Salle died, his son Louis inherited the post; when he died in 1720, Robert de Visée was appointed 'maître de guittarre du Roy', a post that he, in turn, passed on to his son. See H. Charnassé, 'Visée, Robert de', in Benoit (1992), 728.

[20] 'che fecci stampare l'anno 1656 qui in Parigi dove si compiaque sua Maestà di admetermi in una entrata di piu Chitare d'un Balleto composo dal famosissimo S.ʳ Gio. Battista Lulli . . .'. See Corbetta (1671), 4.

[21] See Keith (1966), 79.

[22] See David Tunley's entry on François Martin in *Grove 6*. Tunley apparently was unaware of Martin's guitar book, the sole copy of which is in F-Psg. For chronological reasons the 'Monsieur Martin' cited by Mersenne (1636) is unlikely to be 'François Martin', but could be François's father.

precise markings, including an *x* on the relevant tablature line(s) to indicate which courses not to strike during a strum. He also includes *tenuto* markings, for holding down initial chords while playing passing notes, as well as ornament signs and other technical details for advanced players. Stylistically, the only comparable guitar music is found in Corbetta's second *Guitarre royalle* of 1674, to which Martin's compares most favourably. His second, lute-style suite, consisting of a *Prélude*, *Alemande*, *Courante*, *Gigue*, *Sarabande*, *Gavotte*, and *Bourrée*, exhibits an equally high degree of finesse. Although Martin provides no tuning information, the presence of cascading scale passages suggests that a re-entrant tuning is appropriate for his music.

Eight years later the nobleman Antoine Carré, 'Le Sieur de la Grange', published his own slim volume, *Livre de guitare . . .* (Paris, 1671), which he dedicated to the 'Princesse Palatine', Sophia,[23] daughter of Frederick V, Elector Palatine, and the English princess Elizabeth Stuart (also known as the 'Winter King and Queen of Bohemia'). Carré's music consists of preludes, dance movements, *passacailles*, and *chaconnes*. The latter are the traditional Spanish and Italian type—major-mode, dance-like variations on a four-bar ground. He groups his pieces by key, but does not arrange them in suites. Carré's music is first-rate. He is especially adept at using high notes along with open courses to achieve tone colour. His tablature and staff notation tuning chart (on p. 27), which begins with the tuning of the third course, indicates a totally re-entrant tuning at the nominal pitch of *d´* for the first course. However, in an appended section on continuo playing, and in what may well be the first documented mention of this stringing arrangement, he instructs the player to put a bourdon on the fourth course ('fault mettre a la guitare une octave au quattriesme'). The implication is that for playing continuo (though not his solos), Carré advocates the use of a bourdon.

Carré published a second book in Paris *c.*1675, entitled *Livre de pieces de guitarre et de musique . . .*, which he dedicated to a member of the Dutch aristocracy, Mary, Princess of Orange (mother of William III of the Netherlands, who was crowned King of England in 1689). A larger collection than his first, it contains solo music of the same high calibre, as well as a most interesting suite of consort pieces for a treble ('dessus') in French violin clef, a bass, and two guitars. The suite includes an *Ouverture*, *Air de ballet*, *Danse pour deux Arlequins*, *Sarabande*, *Menuet*, *Chacone*, and *Air de Sarabande*. The first guitar part ends with a solo, *Tombau*.

Mention was made previously of Corbetta's 1671 publication *La Guitarre royalle . . .* (Paris), which he dedicated to Charles II of England. Having travelled to London in 1661 in the wake of Charles's restoration to the throne, Corbetta returned to Paris in 1670, where he was granted a privilege to publish the book. It is a substantial collection of his music, composed in the French style and using French guitar tablature. As it pertains to the English court, it is discussed in the next chapter along with other guitar music associated with England.

---

[23] Sophia (1630–1714) was the mother of the first Hanover king of England, George I, Handel's patron.

Corbetta dedicated his second book of French guitar music, *La Guitarre royalle...*
(Paris, 1674), to Louis XIV. The music is predominantly in the strummed style,
described previously in connection with François Martin's first suite in his 1663 publication. Corbetta's pieces are not arranged in suites, but are grouped by key. Along
with the sarabands, minuets, folias, allemands, and the like are some ceremonial
pieces, such as a *Fanfare* and *Trompette Tambour de France et de Suisse: La prise de
Mastricht* (referring to a battle won by Louis's army). An interesting feature of the
book is the inclusion of a second guitar part ('contrapartie') for the first twelve solo
pieces, which means, of course, that they also can be played as duets.[24]

Corbetta comments on both *Guitarre royalle* books in the preface to the second,
which is addressed to 'amateurs de la guitarre':

In order to satisfy the inclination that I have always had for the guitar, I have travelled throughout Europe to see those who played it professionally. And as they asked me to publish some
compositions based on their style of playing, I have published several books to satisfy them.
Two years ago I had a book published[25] containing various different styles of guitar playing.
There were pieces for indifferent players in it and ones for those who pride themselves on playing well. Now that I have the opportunity of publishing new compositions, I wish to keep to the
style which most pleases his Majesty. This style is the most chromatic, the most delicate, and
the least awkward. I hope that the great monarch, who has honoured me from time to time
with his commands, will add to my happiness the honour of his approbation and his protection. If you consider them to have some merit, either for themselves alone or because of
the custom of the French of always following in the tracks of their great king, I shall be most
grateful.[26]

Here, Corbetta not only offers extraordinary insight into Louis XIV's taste in guitar
music, he also reveals how a musician-courtier paid homage to a royal patron, and just
how accommodating a composer had to be to succeed at court.

According to the preface of Rémy Médard's book, *Pieces de guitarre . . .* (Paris,
1676), he was a follower of Corbetta (fo. 3ᵛ). Médard's book is an interesting collection

---

[24] Note that the facsimile edition (Bologna: Forni Editore, 1971) does not include the second guitar parts, which
were printed in a separate partbook. Those, however, are available in another facsimile edition, Florence: S.P.E.S.,
1983.

[25] Corbetta is referring to the first of his *Guitarre royalle* books, published in 1671. Although the publishing
privilege for the second is dated 22 Dec. 1673, the book was not actually printed until 12 Jan. 1674.

[26] 'Pour satisfaire l'inclination que j'ay tousjours euë pour la Guitarre, J'ay voulu voir en plusieurs endroits de
l'Europe ceux qui en faisoient profession: Et comme ils me prioient avec instance de donner au public quelques
compositions suivant leur maniere. J'en ay fait imprimer a plusieurs fois pour les contenter. Il y a deux ans que Je fis
parestre un Livre qui contenoit differentes sortes de manieres. Il y a voit des pieces pour ceux qui jouoient
mediocrement de cet Instrument et pour ceux qui se picquent d'en bien jouer. Aujourdhuy que l'occasion se
presente de donner encore quelques Nouvelles compositions, J'ay voulou me conformer a la maniere qui plaist le
mieux a sa Maiesté, veuque parmis les autres elle est la plus cromatique, la plus delicate, et la moins embarassante.
J'espere que ce Grand Monarque qui m'a quelquesfois honoré de ses Commandemens, ajoustera a ma felicité
l'honneur de son approbation et de sa protection. Pour vous si vous en faites cas par leur propre merite, ou par la
coustume des François de marcher tousiours sur les traces de leur grand Roy Je vous en seray tous iours oblige...'
(p. 4).

of preludes, sarabands, minuets, and the like that require the same degree of technical skill as the music in Corbetta's two books of French-style music. Unlike Corbetta's, however, Médard's music is distinguished by its ingratiating melodies, and foreshadows the *galant* style of Visée and Campion. Médard provides no tuning instructions; however, the stylistic features present in his tablatures, such as the elaborate cascading scale passage that adorns one of his sarabands, which he calls 'campanelle' (little bells), strongly suggest a totally re-entrant tuning. One of Médard's preludes is indicated as having 'accors cromatiques' (chromatic chords) to be played in an improvised, arpeggiated style. This, presumably, was the sort of piece referred to by Corbetta as Louis XIV's favourite kind of guitar music. Médard also includes 'contra partie' for two of his sarabands, so they can be performed as duets.

Another musician who brought fresh ideas to the guitar repertory was Henry Grenerin, a theorbist cited as one of the king's chamber musicians as early as 1641.[27] Grenerin played in court ballets, such as the *Ballet de Psyché* in 1656 and the *Ballet de l'impatience* in 1661, and published a collection of theorbo music and instructions for continuo in 1668.[28] Years later he published his guitar book *Livre de guitarre . . .* (Paris, 1680), dedicated to the Prince de Condé, who many years earlier had led a revolt by the nobility against the Queen Mother, Anne of Austria, that forced Cardinal Mazarin briefly into exile. This was one of a series of public uprisings known as the 'frondes'. The unrest was over by 1654, and presumably Condé's relationship with the royal family had improved sufficiently by 1680 for Grenerin to dedicate a book to him.

Grenerin's music is organized into sixteen suites by key, each with an *allemande* followed by other dance forms in no set order. Eleven of the suites begin with a prelude. In addition to the guitar solos there are three 'Sinphonie' for a trio ensemble comprising two violins and a bass instrument. The bass line has continuo figures for a theorbo, and there is a separate guitar part in tablature. The book also contains three vocal pieces, two for SATB and one for SAB, with a figured bass and a guitar part in tablature. In addition Grenerin supplies detailed instructional tables for guitarists learning to play figured bass and cadences. Grenerin gives no tuning instructions; however, his solos are composed in an idiom that strongly recommends the tuning with a bourdon on the fourth course and placed in the inner position.

The placement of the bourdon string(s) is an important issue. When playing single-line melodic passages (such as cascading scales) on a guitar with a bourdon on the fourth course, for example, many apparent anomalies in the melody line can be resolved (or avoided) if the guitarist decides to pluck only the upper octave string of the course and not the lower (see Pl. 7.4). Playing only the upper of the two is made a great deal easier if the lower octave string (bourdon) is placed in the inner position.

---

[27] François Lesure, 'Trois instrumentalistes français au xviie siècle', in *RdM* 37 (1955), 186–7.
[28] *Livre de théorbe contenant plusieurs pieces. . .* (Paris, 1668).

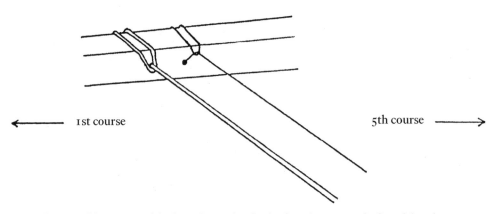

←——————   1st course   5th course   ——————→

PL. 7.4. Placement of the bourdon string in the fourth course of a Spanish guitar

This stringing arrangement is not mentioned in the seventeenth-century guitar books; however, verification of the practice can be found in an authoritative source: the surviving drawings of the illustrious instrument maker Antonio Stradivari. On a drawing of one of his guitars from around 1700, not only does he indicate the string gauges, but also the stringing arrangement with the bourdon placed in the inner position of the fourth and fifth courses. Other evidence includes a painting by Sebastiano Lazzari, dated 1757, housed in the Ashmolean Museum in Oxford. It shows a guitar that is so clearly and accurately depicted that one is able to see both the stringing arrangement (with the bourdons in the inner positions) and the name of the guitar maker, Domenico Sellas.[29] This same arrangement, but with the fourth and fifth courses triple strung, is described in a later French guitar book, Michel Corrette's *Les Dons d'Apollon . . .* (Paris, 1763, p. 4). It is also clearly illustrated in Paixão Ribeiro's *Nova arte de viola . . .* (Coimba, 1789, Estampa I).[30]

Robert de Visée (*c.* 1655–*c.* 1735) was a celebrated theorbist and guitarist who also achieved considerable recognition as the colleague of such famed court musicians as François Couperin (harpsichord), Anthoine Forqueray (viola da gamba), Philibert Rebillé (flute), and Jean Féry Rebel (violin). In the company of these musicians, he not only performed at court, but also in the salons of the Duc de Bourbon, the Prince de

---

[29] Domenico Sellas was a member of the famed Venetian family of instrument makers. See John Downing, 'Notes on a Painting by Sebastiano Lazzari', *FoMRHI Quarterly*, 33 (1983), 13. For an example of a five-course guitar by Domenico Sellas, see Pl. 7.5. For a description of the Stradivarius stringing, see Patrizia Frisoli, 'The Museo Stradivariano in Cremona', *GSJ* 24 (1971), 33–50 at 40.

[30] See Tyler (1980*a*), 54–5 and Boye (1997). Also note that the *charango* of Bolivia, Argentina, and Peru; the *tiple* of Colombia; and the *jarana jarocha* of Mexico are all guitars with double courses which, to this day, use re-entrant tunings and a stringing arrangement with the lower octave placed in the inner position.

PL. 7.5. Five-course guitar by Domenico Sellas, Venice, *c.*1670. America's Shrine to
Music Museum, University of South Dakota, Vermillion. Photo: Simon Spicer

Condé, and Madame de Maintenon, Louis XIV's mistress.[31] He was already one of the illustrious chamber musicians to the king when he published his *Livre de guittarre* . . . (Paris, 1682). Dedicated to Louis, it undoubtedly represents the kind of intimate chamber music that Visée performed for him at the palace of Versailles. The music is grouped according to key, but not arranged into formal suites (as is suggested by the earlier of the two editions of his complete works).[32] Certain of the key groups contain only three pieces, others as many as thirteen; some lack preludes, while others provide two from which to choose; not all include the requisite *allemande*. Visée's book, like those of many Baroque guitar composers, seems to be offering players the materials from which to form their own suites. More than a third of the pieces, including the beautiful commemorative work on the death of Corbetta, *Tombeau de M.ʳ francisque Corbet*, can be performed either as solos or with the treble and bass parts that Visée has provided. As previously mentioned in the discussion of Granata's last three publications (1674–81),[33] this type of trio arrangement, with a plucked instrument playing what amounts to a solo while its treble and bass are reinforced by other instruments, was commonly found in French and German lute music. For Visée's pieces, employing a theorbo on the bass line can produce a stunning effect. The pieces in his final key group are especially exquisite. They use a scordatura tuning, which greatly enhances the guitar's sonority.

Visée provides little in the way of prefatory material, but what he does say is important: 'you must not forget to put an octave on the fourth course. It is very necessary'.[34] Clearly, the re-entrant tuning *without* a bourdon was still in common use, otherwise he would not have had to remind guitarists to put the octave string on the fourth course to play his music.

Visée's second guitar book, *Livre de pieces* . . . (Paris, 1686), was also dedicated to Louis XIV. As in his earlier collection, the pieces are grouped together by key, but not organized into actual suites. Also, many of the pieces have corresponding treble and bass lines for ensemble performance. This seems to have been a feature of Viseé's published work, doubtless because the king favoured such pieces and they were composed for performance by his chamber musicians. The collection opens with the group of pieces in D minor with which most guitarists are familiar. Both collections, together with many other works by Visée found in guitar and theorbo manuscripts,[35] encompass some of the finest instrumental music of the late French Baroque.

---

[31] H. Charnassé, 'Visée, Robert de', in Benoit (1992), 728–9.
[32] Strizich (1971). A new edition is Charnassé, Rebours, and Andia (1999).   [33] See pp. 74–5.
[34] 'il ne faut pas oublier une octave a la quatrieme corde, elle y est tres necessaire' (p. 6).
[35] Many of Visée's guitar pieces are contained in such manuscripts as F–Pn Rés. F. 844, Rés. 1402, Vm⁷ 675, Vmb MS 58 and Vm⁷ 6222, as well as B–Bc Littera S. 5615 (Castillon), B–Br MS II. 5551. D., and GB–Lbl Add. 31640 (Murcia), some of which are discussed later. Many of his guitar pieces also are found in versions for theorbo in such manuscripts as F–Pn Rés. 1106, Rés. 1820, and Vm⁷ 6265, to name only a few. It is not known which versions were created first. For a thematic index and concordances to the works of Visée, see Rebours (2001).

The guitar music of Visée's younger contemporary François Campion represents the last manifestation in France of the late Baroque style and, at the same time, embodies the newer *galant* or *rococo* style. Campion (*c*.1685–1747) was one of two theorbists in the orchestra of the Académie Royale de Musique from 1704 to 1719, and probably played continuo for many of the operas performed there during this period. In his treatise on continuo accompaniment, *Traité d'accompagnement et de composition*. . . (Paris, 1716), he explains the method of playing from a figured or unfigured bass, taught to him by Monsieur Maltot, the theorbist who preceded him at the Académie. Eleven years later Campion expanded the work with an *Addition au traité . . . ou est compris particulièrement le secret de l'accompagnement du théorbe, de la guitare & du luth* . . . (Paris, 1730), in which he explained in considerable detail the 'secret' method by which theorbo, guitar, and lute players can learn the art of continuo accompaniment.[36]

Campion's first collection of guitar music, *Nouvelles découvertes sur la guitarre*, was published in Paris in 1705. The 'new discoveries' referred to in the title are a series of seven scordatura tunings. The first of them, and the one he employs most, is *f′, c′c′, gg, dd′, b♭b♭*.[37] This tuning works very well for pieces in the flat keys of G minor, E flat, B flat, F, C minor, and D minor—keys which, in the normal tuning, can be awkward for the left hand. Because the music is notated in tablature, playing in this or any other scordatura tuning is as easy as playing in the normal tuning. The scordatura pieces occupy about three-quarters of the book and are followed by pieces in the normal tuning.

Campion groups his pieces according to key, thus making it easier for players to select the ones they wish to include in a suite. The pieces are the usual dance movements and preludes, as well as three pieces each labelled 'rondeau'. Most are in the scordatura tuning described above, and Campion seems to have put his best efforts into these. Many display his gift for writing pleasing melodies, his refined contrapuntal skills, frequent use of parallel thirds and sixths to vary tone colour, moderate use of strumming, and masterful use of the guitar's re-entrant tuning. Compared with the pieces in scordatura, the ones in normal tuning seem a bit dull.

Interestingly, Campion continued to work on this book for many years after it was published, making extensive manuscript additions to his personal copy and binding them into the appropriate sections of the book. He dated the latest of the additions '1731', and bequeathed this rare and fascinating document to the Académie Royale de Musique in Paris. Now preserved in the Bibliothèque nationale de France, it is classified as a manuscript (MS Vm[7] 6221). The additions include about a dozen more pieces in scordatura, an expansion of the 'chacone' found on page 39 of the 1705 book,

[36] For an excellent study of Campion's two continuo treatises, see Mason (1981). Both are available in facsimile: Geneva: Minkoff Reprint, 1976.
[37] Campion gives no nominal tunings, only tablature tuning charts in which the third course acts as the unchanging reference in each scordatura. I have assumed this course to be *gg*, and, because of the style of the music, suggest a bourdon on the fourth course, regardless of the tuning.

and about forty more pieces in the normal tuning, including such items as the *Tombeau de M.^r De Maltot*, commemorating the death of his mentor, and two extensive pieces each marked 'sonatina', which display Campion's superb contrapuntal skills (as do a series of pieces labelled 'fugue'). This is music of exceptional quality and charm.

Although the French sources of printed music for the Baroque guitar end with Campion, there are at least twenty extant manuscript sources. The earliest three, from the mid-seventeenth century, are discussed above, as is Campion's manuscript additions to his 1705 book. As expected, the Bibliothèque Nationale in Paris has a good many of the remaining ones, as have libraries in Great Britain.[38] One major source of French guitar music is found today in Oxford (GB–Ob Mus. Sch. C 94). Actually, it is two manuscripts bound together to form a source of over 500 pieces. The larger of the two, dated 18 September 1661, is a collection compiled by Henry François de Gallot entitled 'Pieces de guitarre de differendes autheures recueillis par Henry François de Gallot Escuyer S. de franlieu . . .'.[39] There are also other dates in the manuscript, the earliest being 1660 and the latest 1684. This huge and comprehensive source contains music by various members of the Gallot family, including Henry François, who is known in the manuscript as 'Gallot d'Irlande'.[40] There are also about seventy-five pieces by Corbetta copied from his 1643, 1648, 1671, and 1674 books; two pieces by the lutenist François Dufaut (*fl.* 1629–69); and about eight pieces by 'A. M.', who is most likely Angelo Michele (Bartolotti).[41]

Apparently, Henry François cast his net widely, for his manuscript also contains instructional material copied from Foscarini (*c.*1632), Carbonchi (1643),[42] and other writers who have not yet been identified. In addition, there are six trios for equal-tuned guitars, pieces for theorboed guitar,[43] and pieces for mandore. It can be surmised from the setting for guitar of the popular tune 'Over the Montaine' and the English names that appear beside the titles of several pieces (for example, 'Mr Talbot' and 'Ann Walls') that Henry François either visited or resided for a time in Restoration England. Perhaps he knew Corbetta, who was also there in the 1660s.

Another large manuscript, this one dating from *c.*1700, is found in Paris (F–Pn Vm⁷

---

[38] See the list of sources at the conclusion of this chapter.

[39] For a description of the manuscript, see Gill (1978).   [40] C. Massip, 'De Gallot', in Benoit (1992), 312.

[41] Bartolotti seems to have arrived in Paris late in 1661, where he took part in a performance of Francesco Cavalli's opera *Ercole amante* on 7 Feb. 1662 at the French court. During this period he also accompanied the Italian soprano Anna Bergerotti on the theorbo in salon recitals in the houses of the nobility. Court documents show that he was a member of Louis XIV's Cabinet du Roy. In the same year he performed in Molière's *Le Mariage forcé*, and later published his treatise on continuo playing for theorbo, *Table pour apprendre facilement à jouer le théorbe sur la basse continue* (Paris, 1669). See Henri Prunières, *L'Opéra italien en France avant Lulli* (diss., University of Paris, 1913), 277–8 and 311–13.

[42] See Ch. 6, p. 61 and n. 24 for a discussion of Carbonchi's multi-guitar tuning instructions.

[43] For information on the theorboed guitar see Ch. 6 n. 51. One of the pieces for this instrument in the De Gallot manuscript, the saraband on fo. 101^r, is based on a saraband for Spanish guitar in Médard (1676), 19. See Crawford (1997), no. 22.

675). It too is an anthology, but its compiler is anonymous. It contains a wide range of pieces, from guitar arrangements of music by Lully and Luigi Rossi, to original guitar compositions by Visée, Grenerin, Corbetta, Bartolotti, and an unknown composer 'De Valleroy'. There are also several arrangements for guitar of music by the lutenist Gautier (probably Ennemonde), including the ubiquitous *La belle homicide*, for which there are about fifty extant lute or keyboard versions in French sources alone,[44] and the equally popular *Le Canon*.[45]

A similar but smaller manuscript (F-PnVm⁷ 6222) from the same period has a large amount of music by Visée, not all of it copied from his printed books. 'M.ʳ Paisible' is mentioned as the composer of one of the minuets, and it has been possible to identify a new concordance for an allemand by Bartolotti on fo. 43ᵛ.[46]

Concordances abound in yet another large guitar manuscript preserved in Paris (F-Pn F. C. 844). This one, from the early eighteenth century, contains approximately 540 items, including arrangements of pieces by Lully, Couperin, Rameau, Campra, and other French opera and cantata composers. Music by Visée is plentiful in this source, including some second guitar parts ('contrapartie') to solos found in his printed books. This manuscript is a veritable treasure trove of the best French instrumental music by the best composers of the period, as well as popular French airs, all arranged for guitar. About 250 of its 540 items are apparently unique to this source.

Finally, mention must be made of another Paris manuscript (F-Pn F. C. 1402), which dates from *c.*1700 and was compiled by an anonymous player with an apparent fondness for Spanish music. Many of the pieces either have Spanish titles or are described as being 'Espagñole', including *Las vacas* and *Tu la tienes Pedro*. There are also a number of different versions of the *passacaille* and *chaconne*. The manuscript's Italian pieces include *Se voi Lucia amate*, *La Luchi italienne*, and *Mi volla faire una causa que negra*, as well as music copied from Corbetta's 1639, 1643, and 1648 publications. Pieces from Corbetta's 1674 book of French guitar music have also been included, and some items from Visée's two publications are found appended to certain sections, having been copied by another hand. Several of the pieces are from the reign of Louis XIII (for example, *Le berger Tirsis*, *Branle de Saint Nicolas*, and *Le Care de mole*), and there is a tablature tuning chart (fo. 192), which gives the 'Acor de guitere a l'unison', a totally re-entrant tuning.

While it is not possible to discuss all the French manuscript sources in these pages, Table 7.1 contains all known French manuscript and printed sources.

[44] See n. 5.
[45] See Goy et al. (1991), 135–8.
[46] Bartolotti's guitar music appears in GB-Ob Mus. Sch. C94, F-PnVm⁷ 675, Vm⁷ 6222, and F. C. 844, in addition to other non-French sources discussed in Ch. 8.

TABLE 7.1. *French sources of Spanish guitar music*

A. PRINTED BOOKS

1626   Briceño, Luis de, *Metodo mui facilissimo para aprender a tañer la guitarra a lo español . . .* (Paris)
        Facs. edn.: Geneva: Minkoff Reprint, 1972.

1629   Moulinié, Estienne, *Airs de cour avec la tablature de luth et de guitare . . .* (Paris)
        Facs. edn.: Béziers: Société de Musicologie de Languedoc, 1986.

1636   Mersenne, Marin, *Harmonie universelle . . .* (Paris)
        Treatise containing (*livre second, proposition XIV*) music examples by P. Millioni [1624] and a 'Monsieur Martin' found in no other source. Facs. edn.: Paris: CNRS, 1965.

1648   Mersenne, Marin, *Harmonicorum libri XII . . .* (Paris)
        Latin reworking of the above material, plus new material. Facs. edn.: Geneva: Minkoff Reprint, 1972.

1663   Martin, François, *Pièces de guitarre* [sic] *à battre et à pinser . . .* (Paris)

1671   Carré, Anthoine (Sieur de la Grange), *Livre de guitarre contenant plusieurs pieces . . .* (Paris)
        Facs. edn.: Geneva: Minkoff Reprint, 1977.

1671   Corbetta, Francesco, *La Guitarre royalle dediée au Roy de la Grande Bretagne . . .* (Paris)
        Facs. edn.: Geneva: Minkoff Reprint, 1975.

1674   Corbetta, Francesco, *La Guitarre royalle dediée au Roy* [Louis XIV] *. . .* (Paris)
        Facs. edn.: Bologna: Forni Editore, 1971; facs. edn. of partbook for the second guitar: Florence, S.P.E.S., 1983.

c.1675 Carré, Anthoine (Sieur de la Grange), *Livre de pieces de guitare de musique . . .* (Paris)
        Facs. edn.: Geneva: Minkoff Reprint, 1985.

1676   Médard, Rémy, *Pieces de guitarre . . .* (Paris)
        Facs. edn.: Geneva: Minkoff Reprint, 1988.

1680   Grenerin, Henry, *Livre de guitarre et autres pieces de musique . . .* (Paris)
        Facs. edn.: Geneva: Minkoff Reprint, 1977.

1682   Visée, Robert de, *Livre de guittarre dedié au Roy . . .* (Paris)
        Facs. edn.: Geneva: Minkoff Reprint, 1973.

1686   Visée, Robert de, *Livre de pieces pour la guittarre . . .* (Paris)
        Facs. edn.: Geneva: Minkoff Reprint, 1973.

1705   Campion, François, *Nouvelles découvertes sur la guitarre . . .* (Paris)
        Facs. edn.: Geneva: Minkoff Reprint, 1977, and New York: Performers Facsimiles, 1993.

B. MANUSCRIPTS

Location	Source	Date	Remarks
B–Lc	MS 245	early 18th c.	Anon. Includes music by Visée and others. Rebours (2001), 14
D–B	Mus. ms. 40631	late 17th c.	Anon. Small French tablature MS containing dance movements and a 'Ciachona'. RISM B/VII, 37
D–DO	Mus. ms. 1215	early 18th c.	Anon. No details available. Danner (1979), 15
D–Mzfeder-hofer	MS (no shelf no.)	c. 1670–85	20 pieces in an *angélique* MS belonging to Julien Blovin. Meyer (1994), 202
F–Pn	MS Rés. Vm7 374	early 18th c.	Anon. 'Recueil d'airs avec accompag. de guittar'. RISM B/VII, 259–60
F–Pn	MS Vm7 675	c. 1665	Anon. Contains music by Visée, Pelée, Valleroy, Grenerin, Bartolotti, et al. Goy (1991), 135–8
F–Pn	MS Vm7 6221	c. 1705–31	MS additions to Campion 1705 by the composer. RISM B/VII, 262–3. Facs. edn.: Geneva: Minkoff Reprint, 1977
F–Pn	MS Vm7 6222	c. 1700	Anon. Contains music by Visée, Paisible, Bagnolet, et al. RISM B/VII, 264
F–Pn	MS Vm7 6235	c. 1680	Anon. MS belonging to 'Madame la Comptesse du Rumain'. Accompaniments to chansons. RISM B/VII, 264
F–Pn	MS Vm7 6236	c. 1680	Anon. MS belonging to the 'Duchesse de Neufville-Villeroi'. Accompaniments to chansons. RISM B/VII, 265
F–Pn	MS Vmb. 58	mid–18th c.	Anon. 8 pieces (3 preludes, 3 minuets, 'gavotte dhinde', 'les folies d'espagne'). RISM B/VII, 266–7
F–Pn	MS Vmb. 59	c. 1690–1700	Anon. 7 pieces for voice and guitar, 1 for instrument and guitar, 1 solo (Folias). RISM B/VII, 267
F–Pn	MS Rés. Vmf 49	early 18th c.	Anon. MS titled: 'Catharina De Ryck her boeck'. Includes music by Visée. Rebours (2001), 14
F–Pn	MS F.C. Rés. 1107	mid–18th c.	Anon. 6 different settings of the Folia. RISM B/VII, 271
F–Pn	MS F.C. Rés. 1402	c. 1700	Anon. Contains music by Corbetta and Visée. Has a strong Spanish and Italian influence. RISM B/VII, 273; Yakeley and Hall (1995), 60

TABLE 7.1. *continued*

Location	Source	Date	Remarks
F–Pn	MS F.C. Rés. 1956	'1763'	Anon. 'Chansons avec la Guithare'. Accompaniments to chansons. RISM B/VII, 275
F–Pn	MS F.C. Rés. F. 844	*c.*1730–40	Anon. Contains music by Visée, Corbetta, Bartolotti, et al., with many arrangements of music by Lully, Campra, et al. RISM B/VII, 274–5
F–Pn	MS F.C. Rés. F. 1145	mid-18th c.	'Chansons et Vaudevilles avec des accompagnements de Guitarre'. Accompaniments to chansons. RISM B/VII, 275
F–Psg	MS Rés. 2344	'1649'	Anon. MS belonging to 'Monsieur Dupille'. Solos and French popular airs. RISM B/VII, 275–6; Garros and Wallon (1967), 18–20
F–Psg	MS Rés. 2349	'1649'	Anon. MS related to above. 32 solos. RISM B/VII, 276–7; Garros and Wallon (1967), 24
F–Psg	MS Rés. 2351	mid-17th c.	Anon. MS related to above. RISM B/VII, 277; Garros and Wallon (1967), 26–7
GB–Lam	(ex Spencer) (no shelf no.)	*c.*1700	Anon. Four folios. 6 pieces: 'Prelude', 'antrez', [untitled], 'menuet', '[g]igue', 'gigue'
GB–Ob	MS Mus. Sch. C. 94	*c.*1660–85	'Pieces de Guittarre de differends autheurs recueillis par Henry François de Gallot . . .'. Contains music by Corbetta, Bartolotti (?), De Gallot d'Angleterre, De Gallot cadet, De Gallot d'Irlande. Solos and pieces for 2 guitars, 3 guitars, theorboed guitar, mandore. RISM B/VII, 252; Gill (1978); Pinnell (1979)
GB–Ob	MS Mus. Sch. F. 579	*c.*1740	Anon. 73 solos, including *La marche du Prince de Bade*, *Deus variatie de les Foglie de' Spange* [sic], *Dragon Espagnol*
PL–Kj	Mus. ms. 40626	'1658'	Anon. 23 pieces in a lute MS, 5 by 'Dufresneau', 1 each by 'Gautie' and 'M^r DuFau'. Facs. edn.: Mainz: Schott, 1996. Kirsch and Meierott (1992), 348–62
US–Wc	MS M. 2. 1.T2. 17D. Case	*c.*1660–70	Anon. Accompaniments to chansons. RISM B/VII, 348–9

8

England, the Low Countries, and Scandinavia

England

Although English publishers and aristocratic amateurs showed interest in the four-course guitar and its French repertory during the mid-sixteenth century, there is little evidence that the five-course instrument was known in England before the 1640s. Of course, it is likely that the exotic instruments played by the band of Gypsies in Ben Jonson's 1621 court masque, *The Gypsies Metamorphosed*, were Spanish 'guittars'.[1] It will be recalled that guitars served a similar function at the French court during this period. However, conclusive evidence does not appear until *c.*1640–50, the approximate date of a manuscript belonging to Lady Ann Blount. Lady Ann's songbook contains a fragment of a guitar solo (GB–Llp MS 1041, fo. 91ᵛ) written in five-line French tablature with Italian-style stroke signs, which appears to be the opening bars of a simple chaconne.

Other evidence from the period includes mention of the 'gittar man' who taught Lady Francis, daughter of the Earl of Rutland, in 1643; the diarist John Evelyn's remarks in both 1651 and 1653 that a 'Madame la Varenne' (Lavaran) sang to the guitar; and Sir Peter Lely's well-known painting, *The Duet*, dated 1656, in which one of the ladies is playing a typical Spanish guitar.[2] A common spelling of the word from around the middle of the seventeenth century was 'guittar', and another 'gittar'. The directive 'for the gittar' is found beside a song with an unfigured bass in Henry Lawes's autograph manuscript (GB–Lbl Add. MS 53723, fo. 183ᵛ).

Charles II, like his French counterpart Louis XIV, took a keen interest in the Spanish guitar, an instrument he apparently played quite well. After he reclaimed the throne in 1660, the guitar was seen regularly in court masques and theatrical productions,[3] frequently in the hands of an actor playing a Spaniard, an Italian, an

---

[1] Holman (1993), 369.

[2] See Gill (1978), 79. The Lely painting is reproduced in Grunfeld (1969), 116.

[3] Restoration plays and masques in which the guitar was played by one of the characters include: John Dryden's *The Indian Emperor* (1667); Thomas Shadwell's *The Royal Shepherdess* (1669); Dryden's *An Evening's Love* (1671);

African, or a gypsy. The following stage direction from Thomas Porter's 1664 play *The Carnival* is typical: 'Enter Antonio with a guittar . . .'.

Early in his reign Charles signed an edict granting funds for the recruitment of Italian singers and musicians to perform at court and possibly to produce operas.[4] These musicians were known officially as the 'Italian Players to his Majesty'. It will be recalled that the guitarist Bartolotti was a member of the Italian ensemble employed at Queen Christina's court in Stockholm. When she abdicated in 1654, the Italians dispersed. Some went to Rome and others, including the singer-guitarist-theorbist Pietro Reggio (d. 1685), to Paris. At the French court Reggio was employed as a singer in the royal chapel. By 1664, however, he was working in London. The diarist Samuel Pepys made note of some of 'Signor Pietro's' earliest performing and teaching activities in London, describing him as 'a famous musitian, who had been long in Sweden in Queene Christina's court; he sung admirably to a guitar, and had a perfect good tenor and base [voice] . . .'.[5]

It is likely that Reggio compiled the manuscript collection of arias by Italian composers, which is found in the British Library (GB-Lbl Harl. 1501), for one of his English students. For another student he compiled the remarkable manuscript now preserved in Los Angeles (US-LAuc MS f. C. 697. M. 4), which bears his signature ('Signor Pietro Regio') on the rear flyleaf and the name of the manuscript's probable owner, 'Ann Hilton', within. The middle portion of the manuscript consists of a highly interesting collection of embellished French dance tunes and songs mainly from the era of Louis XIII. This section is not in Reggio's hand, however, and is likely to be an unrelated layer from before his time. In Reggio's hand is the anthology of Italian vocal music from the early Baroque by some of the best composers of the period.[6] The music comprises opera arias and cantatas by Giacomo Carissimi, Francesco Cavalli, Luigi Rossi, Barbara Strozzi, and Francesco Lucio. For eighteen of the twenty-nine items there is a vocal line, a figured bass line, and a 'realization' of the bass line in French tablature for the guitar.[7] These guitar parts, which must demon-

---

Shadwell's *The Humorists* (1671); Dryden's *The Assignation* (1673); John Crowne's *Calisto* (1675); Thomas D'Urfey's *The Banditti* (1686); Nahum Tate's *Dido and Aeneas* (1689 version, with music by Henry Purcell); D'Urfey's *Love for Money* (1691); Peter Motteux's *The Novelty* (1697); and John Lacey's *The Old Troop* (1698). For more details, see Price (1979), 61, 79–80, 194, 256, 266–7, and Holman (1993), 366–71.

   [4] Mabbett (1986), 244.

   [5] Ibid. 238–9, 242.

   [6] Reggio went on to become a well-known composer of theatre songs, contributing music to, amongst other productions, Thomas Shadwell's famous adaptation of Shakespeare's *The Tempest* (1674), with instrumental music by Matthew Locke (1621–77). Reggio's two publications were a treatise on vocal technique and embellishment entitled *The Art of Singing* . . . (Oxford, 1677) and a collection of musical settings of the poems of Abraham Cowley (1618–67) entitled *Songs* . . . (London, 1680, 2nd edn. 1692). His vocal treatise is described in the literature as an important document that was printed in London (rather than Oxford) in 1678 (rather than 1677), and is now lost. However, a copy of the book (Oxford, 1677) was sold at Sotheby's on 16 May 1997 for £20,700. See a facsimile of the title page in *EM* 25 (1997), 532.

   [7] This manuscript is described as having six-line Italian tablature for lute in RISM B/VII, 194–5. Reggio is not mentioned.

Ex. 8.1. Realization of the bass part to Barbara Strozzi's *Rissolvetevi o pensieri* from
US-LAuc, Music MS f C 697 M 4, p. 10

strate the manner in which Reggio played guitar accompaniments, answer the question: how did Baroque guitarists play from bass lines that frequently dip below the range of the guitar? Even on a guitar with bourdons on both the fourth and fifth courses the lowest pitch is *A*, the first space on the bass clef. Reggio's tablatures show how he dealt with each such occurrence (see Ex. 8.1).

In 1661 Charles II married the daughter of John IV of Portugal, the Infanta Catherine of Braganza. Although Catherine brought many of her household and chapel musicians with her from Portugal, they were steadily replaced by Italians, one being

Francesco Corbetta. Corbetta's letter to Charles, written in *c.*1664 when he was
ensconced in the household of the Duchess of Orleans (Charles's sister Henrietta-
Anne) in Paris, reveals that the guitarist was in need of help in a matter concerning the
ownership of an English gambling monopoly.[8] Evidently, Corbetta the entrepreneur,
guitar teacher, and social gadfly enjoyed close relationships with the kings and courtiers of France as well as England.[9] Court documents show that he made frequent
excursions between the two courts. Perhaps Charles appointed him 'Groom of the
privy chamber to the Queen' and 'Page of the backstairs to the King' in an effort to
keep him in London. His duties apparently included giving occasional guitar lessons
to Charles, his brother James, and James's daughter Anne.[10]

As previously mentioned, Corbetta published the first of his two *Guitarre royalle*
books in Paris in 1671, and dedicated it to Charles. The music it contains is entirely in
the French style, which is not surprising since Charles spent nine years in exile at the
French court and in The Hague. It is laid out in suites according to key. Each suite
begins with a prelude followed by an *allemande* and other dance movements. There are
also some separate, miscellaneous items. The titles of some of the pieces refer to political events that occurred during the Stuart monarchy and to members of the royal family. For example: *Allemande faite sur l'emprisonnement du Duc de Bouquingam*
('Allemande composed on the imprisonment of the Duke of Buckingham' in 1667 for
political intrigue); *Gavotte aymée du Duc de Montmouth* ('Gavotte loved by the Duke of
Monmouth', Charles's illegitimate son born in 1649); *Allemande sur la mort du Duc de
Glocester* ('Allemande on the death of the Duke of Gloucester', Charles's brother
Henry, who died in 1660); *Allemande cherie le Duc d'York* ('Allemande cherished by
the Duke of York', Charles's brother James, later James II); and *Sarabande Tombeau
de Madame* (Saraband in memory of Henrietta-Anne, Charles's sister, known as
'Madame', who died in 1670). There are also some vocal pieces at the end of the book,
including two duets and two trios, each with a figured bass and an intabulated guitar
accompaniment.[11] The book finishes with brief instructions on basso continuo.

Corbetta wrote two prefaces, the first in Italian and the second in French. The
Italian preface contains many biographical details not found in the French, while
the French contains the following tuning information not found in the Italian: 'I
advise you to put an octave on the fourth course *d′* because the two unisons do not in
fact make [a full] harmony.'[12] Corbetta's reminder, like Visée's eleven years later,
implies that many guitarists normally used a totally re-entrant tuning and needed to
be reminded that the music in his book requires a bourdon on the fourth course. While
Carré (1671) was the first to mention this stringing arrangement in connection with

---

[8] Mabbett (1986), 245–6.   [9] Pinnell (1980), ch. 6.   [10] Mabbett (1986), 239.
[11] One has a text, 'Filli mia s'interi', by Francesco Buti (1604–82), the librettist of Luigi Rossi's opera *Orfeo* (written and performed in Paris in 1647).
[12] Corbetta (1671), 8: 'Je vous avertis de mettre une octave à la 4.me corde de. la. re. sol. parceque les deux unissones ne composent point d'harmonie . . .'.

continuo playing, Corbetta (1671) seems to have been the first to use it for solo music as well.

In the early 1670s the Stuarts faced a growing threat from both Parliament and the populace. The fact that Charles's wife, Queen Catherine, was a Portuguese Catholic and his brother James had recently married Princess Maria of Modena, an Italian Catholic, caused fierce anti-Catholic sentiment amongst the many who feared the re-emergence of the Catholic Church in England. A terrifying development (for Catholics) occurred in March 1673 when Charles was forced by Parliament to sign the Test Act, which specified that, in addition to other oaths of allegiance, every office holder had to publicly take communion in the Church of England. Since 'office holders' included household staff, and since household staff included musicians, something approaching an exodus ensued. Corbetta left for Paris before the year was out, having been granted a privilege to publish his second *Guitarre royalle* book, this one dedicated to Louis XIV.

In England the London printer John Carr advertised music for 'Lutes, Viols, Violins, [and] Gittars . . .',[13] signifying that by 1673 the guitar was fully established, both at court and in the music rooms of the middle class. Soon after, the anti-Catholic hysteria died down somewhat, and the fact that both the Queen and Princess Maria were permitted to maintain their own chapels encouraged Catholic musicians to return to England. Corbetta was back by July 1674, when, according to court records, he was one of four guitarists involved in the preparations for the lavish production of John Crowne's masque *Calisto* (performed on 15 February 1675). The other three were a 'Mr Custom', 'Mr Deloney', and 'Mr Dellony', about whom nothing is known.[14]

Corbetta was back in Paris in 1676, but returned to London in 1677, where, according to court records, he taught Lady Anne, the daughter of James, Duke of York, to play the guitar.[15] In the same year he published *Easie Lessons on the Guittar for young Practitioners; single and some of two Parts. By Seignior Francisco . . .* (London, 1677), now lost.[16]

About three years later a truly outstanding guitar publication by another Italian musician, Nicola Matteis, appeared in England, *Le false consonanse della musica per poter' apprendere a toccar da se medesimo la chitarra sopra la parte . . .* (London, *c.* 1680). A Neapolitan, Matteis (d. 1707) apparently came to London in the early 1670s and dazzled music connoisseurs like Roger North (*c.* 1651–1734) with his virtuoso violin playing. In his writings on music North said of him: 'His profession was the violin and guittar, but withall an accomplisht musition, and I know no master fitt to be named

---

[13] Price (1979), 257.

[14] Andrew Ashbee, *Records of English Court Music*, i (Snodham, 1986), 146.

[15] Mabbett (1986), 239 and Pinnell (1980), 183.

[16] Pinnell (1980), 183. Another lost book by Corbetta seems to have been recovered in part. See above, Ch. 4.

with Corelli but him . . .'. In reference to *Le false consonanse della musica*, North wrote: 'He made another book, which was designed to teach composition, ayre, and to play from a thro-base. And his exemplars were for the Guittarre, of which instrument he was a consumate master, and had the force upon it to stand in consort against an harpsichord.'[17] Matteis used the engraved music plates from this publication for his revised edition in English, *The False Consonances of Music or Instructions for the playing a true Base upon the Guitarre . . .* (London, 1682). This important treatise provides detailed instruction and a solid foundation to guitarists wishing to acquire professional-level continuo-playing skills.[18] In addition the book contains a solo 'Preludio' and four 'Ayres for a Guitarre', two of which have an accompanying figured bass line.

Another London-based guitarist, Cesare Morelli, was born in the Spanish Netherlands (dates unknown), educated in Rome, and was in the employ of a nobleman in Lisbon before arriving in London, where he entered the service of Samuel Pepys in 1674. Morelli's duties as a musician in the Pepys household were to teach music theory, give guitar lessons to Pepys and his colleagues, and take part in the household's musical evenings. There are five manuscripts in Morelli's hand in Pepys's library, which survives intact in Cambridge. One (GB-Cmc MS 2805), entitled 'A table to the Ghitarr by Seign.: Caesare Morellj', is a continuo treatise with musical examples in French tablature and is dated 1680. The other four are collections of songs with the figured bass line realized for guitar in French tablature. One of the four (MS 2804) consists largely of Pietro Reggio's settings of poems by Abraham Cowley from Reggio's 1680 collection, transposed for a bass voice (presumably Pepys's) with guitar accompanment. The other three manuscripts (2591, 2802, and 2803) contain music by Carissimi, Cesti, Giovanni Battista Draghi, Lully, Morelli, and Stradella—all accompanied by guitar. There are English songs as well, including Pepys's own well-known setting of William Davenant's 'Beauty retire' (MS 2803, fos. 111ᵛ–112ᵛ).[19]

Finally, mention must be made of a guitar manuscript dated 1684 and 1685, now in Cambridge, Massachusetts (US-CA MS Mus. 139), which belonged first to Elizabeth Cromwell and a bit later to Mary Mathewes.[20] It contains English 'pastime' music—the sort of repertory that all middle-class young ladies were expected to learn and perform for their parents' guests. Most of the pieces are English popular tunes of the time, such as 'the morice dance', 'old Sʳ Simon the King', 'the Begger', 'black gack', 'my delight', and 'the long sarabrand'. There is also what appears to be an accompaniment to Pietro Reggio's air 'Madam why dos love torment you'.[21] The settings are all quite simple, but also rather charming. Although nothing is said about unisons and octaves, the tablature tuning chart on fo. 3 (which begins, as usual, with

---

[17] *Roger North on Music*, ed. John Wilson (London, 1959), 309 and 357.
[18] See the introduction to Tyler (1980*b*).
[19] See the facsimile of these pages in Tyler (1980*a*), 45.
[20] The MS is described in Ward (1979–81), 201–3.
[21] Published in *The Theater of Music* (London, 1685).

the tuning of the third course) results in a totally re-entrant tuning, and the pieces' many cascading scale and melodic single-line passages certainly require a stringing without bourdons if they are to ring on in a full and pleasing manner.

A virtually identical tuning chart was copied by hand into a surviving copy of John Playford's *Select Musical Ayres*... (London, 1653)[22] under the heading 'The Gitter Tuning'. Here, however, the chart actually specifies 'unisons', and the resultant tuning is, of course, totally re-entrant. So it appears as if both the totally re-entrant tuning and the modified re-entrant tuning with a bourdon on the fourth course, required for Corbetta's, Matteis's, and, probably, Reggio's music, were used by English guitarists.

For a complete list of English sources of Spanish guitar music, see Table 8.1 (pp. 135 ff.).

The Low Countries

Little guitar music survives from the Netherlands—be it the Protestant north (Holland) or the Catholic south (Flanders, the Spanish Netherlands)—from before the late seventeenth century. There are a few fragments of Italian *alfabeto* with Dutch text on the eight leaves removed from a miscellaneous manuscript album from Utrecht (B–Bc MS Littera S, no. 28. 052), dated 1613. These comprise ten short anonymous pieces with *alfabeto* letters above one horizontal line and mensural noteheads on the line, the direction of their stems indicating up or down strokes. A few of the pieces have titles, including *Marsche du Roÿ*, *Tantara, tan tarra*, and *Vroede als je mÿn jeijlehe vries*. Musically, the fragments are of little interest; however, they do confirm that the guitar and the *alfabeto* system were known in Holland in the early seventeenth century.

A manuscript from around the middle of the century (NL-DHk MS 133. K. 6) belonged to a Dutch noblewoman named Isabel van Langhenhove. It is in French guitar notation, but has Italian stroke lines rather than the expected French noteheads and stems. In this source the stroke lines are of two different lengths, the longer of the two equivalent to twice the time value of the shorter.[23] The music comprises French dance movements and arrangements of French, Italian, and Spanish songs.

By the third quarter of the century both The Hague (the seat of Dutch government) and the enormously prosperous city of Amsterdam were offering excellent work opportunities to freelance musicians. Since Holland was a republic, there was no court *per se*, but there were plenty of wealthy merchants keen to have musicians perform in their homes and teach them to play. Among the many musicians employed in this capacity was the guitarist Nicolas Derosier (*fl.* 1680–1700).

---

[22] See App. III.
[23] For a sample of this manuscript, see Wolf (1919), 203.

Some scholars have assumed that Derosier was a Frenchman;[24] however, little is known about his life and what is known suggests that he was a Dutch Protestant. His first known publication, *Douze ouvertures pour la guitare . . . op. 5 . . .* , was printed in The Hague in 1688. No copy of it has been found. An undated publication from *c.*1691, which Derosier himself referred to as 'op. 5', entitled *Ouverture, courante, sarabande, gigue etc. sur huit tons différents à 3 et 4 parties, ou l'on peut jour la guitarre avec, ou, seul sy l'on veut . . .* was published in Amsterdam. Apparently, it too is missing, although a copy had been preserved in Prague, as Paul Nettl's brief description of it attests.[25] According to Nettl, it contained seven suites for guitar solo or ensemble, and one suite for 'guitarre angelique'. The latter instrument is described by the Flemish guitarist Castillon as having eight strings more than the normal guitar. Castillon also cites Derosier's *c.*1691 publication in his remarkable manuscript (B–Bc MS 5.615), which is discussed below.

Derosier also wrote a twelve-page didactic work, *Les Principes de la guitarre . . .* (Amsterdam, 1689), in which he explains the various signs used in his French guitar notation, such as left- and right-hand fingerings, articulations, the *barré* sign, and the signs for such ornaments as the *tremblement*, *martellement*, and *miolement*. He also touches upon some of the rudiments of music, staff notation, and playing from a figured bass line. He illustrates the latter in both French tablature and Italian *alfabeto*, and then gives a series of I–IV–V–I chaconnes in six minor and six major keys and a tuning chart in tablature and staff notation that results in a re-entrant tuning in *e′* with a bourdon on the fourth course.

The success of this little book, of which there were three subsequent editions, encouraged Derosier to publish another little book, *Nouveaux principes pour la guitare . . .* , printed in Paris in 1699. According to its title page, by this date the guitarist had obtained an official appointment as 'Ordinaire de la Musique de son Altesse Electorale le Prince Palatin'. The Prince Palatine in 1699 was the Protestant duke Ernst Augustus of Brunswick [Braunschweig]–Lüneberg, whose court was in Celle, but who apparently spent a good deal of time in The Hague and Paris. This might explain how *Nouveau principes . . .* came to be published in Paris. It too is twelve pages long, and although it contains instructional material similar to that found in Derosier's earlier book, the explanations and charts in *Nouveaux principes . . .* are far more explicit. His unequivocal tuning instructions result in a re-entrant tuning in *e′* with a bourdon on the fourth course. Nevertheless, if Derosier's extant publications were all one had to judge him by, his contribution to the repertory would be slight indeed. But, as soon will be seen, there is a great deal more.

First, however, one final manuscript from Holland should be mentioned

[24] For example, H. Charnassé, in Benoit (1992), 223–4.
[25] Paul Nettl, 'Musicalia der Fürstlich Lobkowitzschen Bibliothek in Raudnitz', in *Beiträge zur böhmischen und mährischen Musikgeschichte* (Brno, 1927), 60–70.

(NL–DHgm MS 4. E. 73). This mid-eighteenth-century source belonged to Princess Anne, daughter of George II of England and wife of William IV of Orange, the effective (if not seated) ruler of the Dutch Republic. It contains French dance movements organized by key but not arranged in suites; some pieces were apparently copied from the books of Robert de Visée.[26]

From the early sixteenth century a thriving musical establishment had been maintained in Brussels, the capital of the Spanish Habsburg-ruled south Netherlands. During the early seventeenth century the Habsburg governors were the Archduke Albert Ernst and Archduchess Isabella, whose court employed many superb musicians, including the exiled English Catholics Peter Philips and John Bull, as well as the Italian guitarist Giovanni Paolo Foscarini. To judge by the works of such Flemish artists as Rombouts, Ryckaert, Coques, and Teniers, whose paintings frequently portray their subjects playing a guitar,[27] the instrument was widely used in the province throughout the seventeenth century. Regrettably, there is very little in the way of extant music sources; no printed books survive and only two manuscripts, one of which is a copy of most of the other! Fortunately, these are of exceptional interest.

Both manuscripts (B–Bc MS 5.615 and B–Br MS II. 5551. D.)[28] are in the hand of the aforementioned Jean Baptiste Ludovico de Castillon, a Flemish cleric and amateur guitarist. In the first, begun in 1730, Castillon informs us that he was inspired to take up the guitar again, after a period of neglect, upon hearing a performance by François Le Cocq. According to Castillon, Le Cocq presented him with a manuscript collection of his guitar music in 1729, and Castillon copied it, along with an anthology of pieces by the best masters of the seventeenth century ('Recueil des pieces de guitarre des meilleurs maitres du siecle dixseptieme'), into his own manuscript (5.615). Castillon describes Le Cocq as a 'Musicien jubilaire de la Chapelle Royale a Bruxelles' (a retired musician of the Chapel Royal in Brussels). Nothing further is known of Le Cocq's life, and this manuscript is the only source of his music.

Castillon's preface includes a highly detailed essay on the fundamentals of reading tablature and staff notation, as well as his opinions on many issues involving the guitar and guitarists. For example, he expresses concern that since the death of Louis XIV, 'the last [ruler] to practise it [seriously]', the guitar has been in danger of languishing. He remarks that after Corbetta dedicated his 1648 book to Albert and Isabella (actually, to Leopold Wilhelm, Archduke of Austria—Albert died in 1621), the nobility in Brussels all took up the instrument. He states that François Le Cocq taught the Electress of Bavaria (Adelaida of Savoy) to play it, and that he (Le Cocq) had played several times before the 'Archduchess[29] [of Austria], Governess of the Low Countries'.

---

[26] For details, see Turnbull (1974), 54–5.

[27] Grunfeld (1969), esp. ch. 4, reproduces a good selection of these paintings.

[28] All the music contained in B–Br II. 5551. D, and a great deal more, is also found in B–Bc MS 5.615.

[29] Maria Elisabeth (1650–1741) was the sister of Emperor Charles VI, not the daughter, as Russell (1988/9), 289 has

Castillon then speaks of the masters of the previous century: Corbetta, 'Lelio' (Colista), and Perez de Zavala (the teacher of Castillon's father *c.*1690). He says that the pieces of Gaspar Sanz and Giovanni Battista Granata are not without merit, and that Robert de Visée was famous for his connection with Louis XIV. According to Castillon, a guitarist of great skill was 'Saint Luc' (probably the Brussels-born Jacques Alexandre, 1663–1710).[30] Finally, he mentions Nicolas Derosier, whom he held in high regard. Derosier, he says, invented the 'guitarre angelique', which had eight strings more than the ordinary instrument, and he published a book for both types in 1691.[31]

In the next section of the manuscript, entitled 'Principes de la Guitarre', Castillon discusses the rudiments of music and explains the marks and signs Le Cocq uses in his tablature. After briefly discussing the fretting of the guitar and how to choose gut strings, Castillon remarks that the fourth course must be in octaves; presumably he is describing the same stringing arrangement recommended by Carré (1671) for continuo playing, and Corbetta (1671), Visée (1682), and Derosier (1689) for their solo music. He also mentions that some guitarists put an octave ('bourdon') on the fifth course as well, and that he has been experimenting for some months now with open wound strings for these two courses to make the instrument sound fuller. Fully wound strings, he says, sound too dry and hard.[32] Hence, Castillon in 1730 expressed a preference for a stringing arrangement that would not become standard until after *c.*1750, when music entered a new era and the instrument moved closer in function and design to the Classical guitar.

The entire first section of music in Castillon's manuscript is by Le Cocq and consists of French dance movements grouped according to key. One is immediately struck by the clarity and melodic appeal of this composer's music, which is comparable to the best of Visée. Indeed, the *Menuet* on page 63 *is* by Visée (1686, p. 16), and the *Vilanelle* on page 22 is very similar to one of his (F-Pn Rés. F. 844, p. 186). Of course, it is entirely possible that these two pieces were mistakenly attributed to Le Cocq by Castillon, and more important is the question: how is it possible that music of the quality of Le Cocq's never appeared in print? Perhaps it did. Perhaps, like several of Nicolas Derosier's equally splendid pieces, which Castillon includes in the second

---

written. Charles VI's daughter was Maria Theresa of Austria (1717–80).

[30] P. Vendrix, in Benoit (1992), 629–30.

[31] No copies survive.

[32] 'Et a fin de donner à cet instrument plus de son, je charge les deux octaves que je mets au quatrieme et cinquieme rang d'un fin filet de laiton ou d'argent, ce dernier en vaut mieux[.] Et pour prevenir qu'elles ne sautent en les montant au ton d'octaves necessaire, je ne les charge qu'à demi: c'est à dire qu'il reste un espace vuide à la corde, de la grosseur du dit filet ou même un peu plus, et je choisis des cordes d'une moindre grosseur. Je les prepare moi-même, à cause que celles qu'on trouve aux boutiques sont entierement chargées ou trop grosses, ce qui rend le son sec et dure. Il y a quelques mois que j'emploie cette sorte des cordes avec success et contentement, et je crois être le seul qui s'en sert . . .' (fo. 3ᵛ). See Ch. 12 for a short history of string-making.

section of his manuscript, François Le Cocq's music was copied from a printed book, no copies of which have survived. That certainly would explain how the Spanish guitarist Santiago de Murcia, who included several arrangements of Le Cocq's pieces in a manuscript collection that he probably compiled in Mexico, had access to them. (For a discussion of Murcia's music, see Ch. 10.)

All the seventeenth-century guitarists mentioned in Castillon's preface, with the exception of 'Saint Luc', are represented in the manuscript's second section of music. Of the seventy-six separate items, forty-one are by Derosier, fourteen by Corbetta, six by Visée, six by Colista, four by Perez de Zavala, two by Granata, and one by Sanz, and two pieces are anonymous. This anthology is invaluable for the large number of pieces it contains that are not found elsewhere. Most of the pieces by Corbetta are unique; only two (the *Chacone* on p. 106 and the *Gigue* on p. 108) were copied from his 1671 book. Two of Visée's six are unique (the *Sarabande* on p. 100 and the *Gigue* on p. 101), as are the two by Granata. (Sanz's *Passacaille* was copied from his Book III, pl. 3.) None of the items by Perez de Zavala, Lelio Colista, and Nicolas Derosier is found elsewhere.

Derosier's music is another happy discovery. Unlike the pieces in his printed books of 1689 and 1699, the forty-one preserved in Castillon's manuscript are uniformly outstanding, an opinion evidently shared by Castillon. That some of Derosier's pieces are dated '1691' in the manuscript all but confirms that they were copied from his, apparently lost, 1691 publication.

Lelio Colista (1629–80) was a renowned lutenist, theorbist, guitarist, and composer of trio sonatas, cantatas, and oratorios. He was born in Rome, where he worked his entire life, and where the Spanish guitarist Gaspar Sanz, who regarded him as 'the Orpheus of these times', studied with him.[33] The six pieces by Colista preserved in Castillon's manuscript are the only surviving examples of his music for guitar. They include an *Allemande* and *Sarabande* in D minor; an *Allemande*, *Courante*, and *Sarabande* in G minor; and a *Passacaille dite Mariona*. The last item, a showpiece for the Baroque guitar (see Pl. 8.1), consists of Colista's virtuoso variations on the 'Mariona', a high-spirited Spanish dance based on a I–V–vi–IV–V harmonic ground,[34] in which he ingeniously employs the instrument's distinctive idiom of cascading melodic scale passages across all five courses, and builds to a dazzling climax.[35] These precious surviving pieces by Colista, who was obviously considered a great guitarist in his day, not to mention the gems left by Derosier, Perez de Zavala, and Le Cocq that are unique to this collection, attest to the importance of Jean Baptiste Ludovico de Castillon to the repertory.[36]

[33] Gaspar Sanz, *Instruccion de musica sobre la guitarra española* . . . (Zaragoza, 1674), fo. 11ʳ.
[34] Russell (1995*a*), 30 and 146.
[35] An edition of the piece in tablature is found in Tyler (1984*b*), 30–1.
[36] At the conclusion of the music sections, Castillon also provides a brief dictionary of music terms. See Russell (1988–9), 288–9.

PL. 8.1. Conclusion of *Passacaille dite Mariona* by Lelio Colista (B–Bc MS 5. 615), p.117

For a complete list of Spanish guitar sources from the Low Countries, see Table 8.2 (pp. 137 ff.).

Scandinavia

A mere eight guitar sources of Scandinavian provenance have been recovered to date in Sweden and Denmark. The earliest (S-SK MS 493b) is from the mid-seventeenth century and contains only three guitar pieces, a *Sarabande*, *Menuette*, and a second *Menuette*, all in French tablature and anonymous. The manuscript was compiled by Gustav Düben (*c.*1628–90), a keyboard player at the Swedish court from the time of Queen Christina and hence a colleague of Bartolotti and Reggio. The repertory in the keyboard portion of the manuscript is French court music, some of it transcriptions of lute music by Gautier, Mercure, and Pinell.[37]

The four other manuscripts in Sweden also feature French repertory. The two in Norrköping (S-N 9096, 2 and 9096, 14), both dating from the late seventeenth century, belonged to the prominent De Geer family of financiers.[38] Many of the pieces in the first of the manuscripts are copied from Corbetta (1671) and Médard (1676); other pieces are arrangements for guitar of music by Lully. The second of the manuscripts is of particular interest because Médard is credited with arranging four of the pieces by Lully (for example, 'Ouverture d'Isis [1677] mise par Medard').

Lully is also represented in a manuscript preserved in Stockholm (S-Sr MS 52 S) dated 1692, which was compiled by the Swedish courtier Hedevig Mörner (1672–1753). The guitar pieces (eight in French guitar notation contained in a viola da gamba manuscript) include an arrangement of Gautier's lute piece, the inevitable *La belle homicide*. Another piece found here, and in innumerable lute, guitar, and keyboard sources, is André Campra's *Aimable vainqueur* from his opera ('tragédie lyrique') *Hésione* (1700). The rest of the manuscript includes more arrangements of Lully's music, and many anonymous French chansons and dance movements.

All the music in an enormous collection of guitar pieces found in Denmark (DK-Kk MSS 377, 1879, and 110) is by one composer and written in his own hand. The composer is Nathanael Diesel (d. 1744), lutenist at the Danish court in Copenhagen from 1736 until his death. Diesel wrote his manuscripts for the court of Christian VI,[39] where one of his duties was to teach the Princess Charlotte Amalie to play the guitar. Indeed, some of the pieces are dedicated to her. Regrettably, little else is known of Diesel's life.[40] His manuscripts, all in French guitar notation, contain solo suites, guitar duets, pieces for guitar and basso continuo, chamber music with bass and lute,

---

[37] Rudén (1981), 76.   [38] Ibid. 37.
[39] Not Frederik IV (reigned 1699–1730), as stated in Lyons (1975), 81.
[40] Lyons (1975).

secular songs with guitar, and a great many 'geistliche Gesänge', morally uplifting
devotional songs reflecting the beliefs of Christian VI, the noted Lutheran Pietist.

Stylistically, Diesel's guitar music is noticeably different from that of the Baroque
guitarists surveyed thus far. He wrote entirely in lute style; there are no strummed
chords; and his music requires bourdons on both the fourth and fifth courses. The
only discernible Baroque feature is his extensive use of ornaments on individual notes
(trills, mordents, and so on).[41] Indeed, the strong treble and bass emphasis and the
broken arpeggiated triads and Alberti basses that characterize Diesel's music are the
hallmarks of mid–eighteenth–century musical style in general. As these traits also carried on well into the Classical era, many modern guitarists may find that Diesel's music is not too far removed from that of Simon Molitor (1766–1848), Anton Diabelli
(1781–1858), Mauro Giuliani (1781–1829), and Matteo Carcassi (1792–1853). Certainly, unlike the majority of Baroque guitar music, which tends to rely greatly on the
idioms made possible by re-entrant tuning and stringing, Diesel's lute-like music can
be played on a modern guitar with little compromise or distortion of the music.

All known Scandinavian sources of Spanish guitar music are listed in Table 8.3.

[41] Ibid. 84–6.

TABLE 8.1. *English sources of Spanish guitar music*

A. PRINTED BOOKS

1671   Corbetta, Francesco, *La Guitarre royalle dediée au Roy de la Grand Bretagne . . .* (Paris)
See details in the list of French sources (Table 7.1A).

[1677]   Corbetta, Francesco, *Easie lessons on the Guitarr for young practitioners single, and some of two parts. By Seignior Francisco . . .* (London)
Ward (1979–81), 20.

*c.*1680   Matteis, Nicola, *Le false consonanse della musica per poter'apprendere a toccar da se medeimo la chitarra sopra la parte . . .* (London)
RISM B/VI², 557.

1682   Matteis, Nicola, *The False Consonances of Musick or Instructions for the playing a true Base upon the Guitarre . . .* (London)
RISM B/VI², 557. Facs. edn.: Monaco: Éditions Chanterelle S.A., 1980; Tyler 1980*b*.

B. MANUSCRIPTS

Location	Source	Date	Remarks
GB–Cmc	MS 2591	'1693'	'Songs & other compositions light, grave and sacred, for a single voice . . . with a thorough-base on yᵉ guitar by Cesare Morelli'. Italian and English songs with Morelli's accompaniments in French notation; *alfabeto* chart; continuo instructions; and several preludes. This and the following four MSS prepared by Morelli for Samuel Pepys. Latham (1989), 13–14
GB–Cmc	MS 2802	*c.*1693	'Liber I: Voice & Ghittarre by Sigʳ Cesare Morelli'. English, French, Italian, and Latin songs (as above), but also with figured bass. Latham (1989), 15–16
GB–Cmc	MS 2803	*c.*1693	'Liber II: Songs sett by Sigʳ Pietro Reggio &c.'. Reggio's printed 1680 songbook with appended MS of English and Latin songs for voice, figured bass, and guitar (as above). Latham (1989), 16
GB–Cmc	MS 2804	*c.*1693	'Liber III: Songs, & Operas of Sigʳ Pietro. & Sigʳ Baptist'. English songs copied from Reggio 1680 (transposed), and French songs by Lully from various stage works, all accompanied as above. Latham (1989), 16–17

TABLE 8.1. *continued*

Location	Source	Date	Remarks
GB–Cmc	MS 2805	'1680'	'A table to the Guitarr by Seign^r: Caesare Morellj. 1680'. Charts and instructional material with *alfabeto* and French guitar notation. Latham (1989), 17
GB–En	MS 9452 (Panmure MS 5)	mid-17th c.	Lute MS with two fragments of guitar music in French tablature. RISM B/VII, 103–4
GB–Hu	MS DDHO/20/2	mid-17th c.	Flute partbook to 'Walsingham' consorts dated 1588 with a later fragment of a piece for 5-course guitar in French guitar notation. Ward (1979–81), 203
GB–Llp	MS 1041	*c.*1640–50	'Ann Blount songbook' with one fragment of French notation on fo. 91^v. Facs. edn.: New York: Garland Publishing, 1987: *English Song 1600–1675*, vol. 11
GB–Ob	MS Mus. Sch. C 94	*c.*1660–85	See details in the list of French sources (Table 7.1B)
GB–Ob	MS Mus. Sch. F 572	late 17th c.	Anon. A few pieces in French notation in a viola da gamba MS. RISM B/VII), 255
US–CA	MS Mus. 139	'1684/5'	MS belonging to Elizabeth Cromwell and later Mary Mathewes. Solo versions of English and French dances and popular songs. Ward (1979–81), 201–3
US–LAuc	MS f. C. 697. M. 4	*c.*1665–75	MS of opera arias and cantatas by Luigi Rossi, Barbara Strozzi, Francesco Cavalli, Giacomo Carissimi, and Francesco Lucio, most with figured bass realized for guitar in French notation. Described inaccurately in RISM B/VII, 194–5
US–R	MS Vault ML 96. m. 435	*c.*1680–5	MS copy of Nicola Matteis, *Le false consonanse* . . . (London, *c.*1680). Possible holograph. Ward (1979–81), 20

TABLE 8.2. *Sources of Spanish guitar music in the Low Countries*

A. PRINTED BOOKS

[1688]   Derosier, Nicolas, *Douze ouvertures pour la guitare . . . op. 5 . . .* (The Hague).
         See Danner (1979), 10. Possibly a bibliographical 'ghost'.

1689   Derosier, Nicolas, *Les Principes de la guitarre . . .* (Paris)
         See Danner (1979), 10. Other edns.: Amsterdam, *c.*1690 (RISM B/VI²; Facs. edn.: Bologna: Forni
         Editore, 1975); Amsterdam, 1696; Amsterdam, 1699.

[1691]   Derosier, Nicolas, *Ouverture, courante, sarabande, gigue ect. sur huit tons differents à 3 et 4
         parties, ou l'on peut jour la guitarre avec, ou, seul sy l'on veut . . .* (Amsterdam)
         Seven suites for solo guitar or guitar with other instruments and one suite for 'Guitarre angelique'. Nettl
         (1927), 60–1.

1699   Derosier, Nicolas, *Nouveaux principes pour la guitare . . .* (Paris)

B. MANUSCRIPTS

Location	Source	Date	Remarks
B-Bc	MS Littera S, No. 5.615	1730/39	'Recueil des pieces de guitare . . .'. Compositions by François Le Cocq and an international anthology of solos by other guitarists compiled by Jean de Castillon in Brussels. RISM B/VII, 53–4; Esses (1992), 133–4. Facs. edn.: Brussels: Éditions Culture et Civilisation, 1979
B-Bc	MS Littera S, No. 28.052	'1613'	From an album belonging to 'Adr. Ger. Zuezerenge' (Utrecht). Eight leaves of anon. pieces in *alfabeto*. One has text: 'Vroede als jeij mijn . . .'. Not listed in RISM
B-Br	MS II. 5551.D	*c.*1730–40	A second MS of music by François Le Cocq and others, compiled by Castillon; similar to the one in B–Bc. RISM B/VII, 66 gives an inaccurate description
NL-DHgm	MS 4. E. 73	mid-18th c.	Anon. MS belonging to Princess Anne, eldest daughter of George II of England. RISM B/VII), 83–4
NL-DHk	MS 133. K.6	mid-17th c.	Anon. MS belonging to Isabel van Langenhove. Solos in French guitar notation; French and Spanish songs. RISM B/VII), 86–7

TABLE 8.3. *Scandinavian sources of Spanish guitar music*

Location	Source	Date	Remarks
DK-Kk	MS Gl. Kgl. Saml. 377, 2°	*c.*1736–45	Collection of solos, songs, and chamber music for guitar in French guitar notation by Nathaniel Diesel. RISM B/VII, 143–5
DK-Kk	MS Gl. Kgl. Saml. 1879, 4°	*c.*1736–45	Guitar solos by Nathaniel Diesel. RISM B/VII, 145–6
DK-Kk	MS Ny. Kgl. Saml. 110, 2°	*c.*1736–45	Collection of guitar solos and duets in French guitar tablature by Nathaniel Diesel. RISM B/VII, 146–8
S-N	MS Finsp. Nr. 9096, 2	late 17th c.	Anon. French notation. French dance movements, some copied from Corbetta and Médard (1676). Formerly in the library of the De Geer family. Rudén (1981), 38–9
S-N	MS Finsp. Nr. 9096, 14	late 17th c.	Anon. French notation. Arrangements of three overtures and one song by Lully, apparently arranged by Médard. Formerly in the library of the De Geer family. RISM B/VII, 241; Rudén (1981), 39
S-SK	MS 468	'1692'	Eight guitar pieces in French notation in a viola da gamba MS belonging to Hedvig Mörner (1672–1753). French dance movements and arrangements of music by Lully and Gautier. RISM B/VII, 320; Rudén (1981), 44
S-SK	MS 493b	'1659'	Three anon. pieces (*Sarabande, Menuette, Menuette*) in French notation in a keyboard MS belonging to Gustaf Düben. RISM B/VII, 321; Rudén (1981), 43
S-Sr	MS Ericsberg- arkivet Nr. 52 S	*c.*1710	Anon. MS in French notation belonging to A. M. Lewenhaupt(?). Contains French dance movements and songs, some by Lully, Dubut, and Gautier. RISM B/VII), 328; Rudén (1981), 41–2

9

Germany and the Austrian Empire

In the early seventeenth century the Spanish guitar was virtually unknown at the courts of Protestant north Germany, Catholic south Germany, Austria, and her Bohemian possessions.[1] In the north the earliest mention of the guitar apparently refers only to the four-course instrument. The source of this citation is Michael Praetorius (*c.*1572–1621), and it appears in his famous encyclopedic music treatise of 1614–19, *Syntagma musicum: . . . tomus secundus de organographia . . .* (Wolfenbüttel, 1618/19).

As Praetorius acknowledges, the basis of this work was the published material, in particular the numerous Italian treatises and music collections available to him at the court in Wolfenbüttel, where he served as *Kapellmeister*. Indeed, one of the reasons he published the work was to introduce and promote in the German-speaking lands the new approach to musical composition that was evolving in Italy in the age of Giovanni Gabrieli and Claudio Monteverdi. Yet, oddly, Praetorius seems to have had little direct knowledge of the five-course guitar, which, as we have seen, flourished in Italy at precisely this time. He presents two tunings, both for the four-course guitar, without giving details of stringing (see Ex. 9.1). Clearly, his tuning information is for a guitar with a bourdon on the fourth course, and not the re-entrant four-course guitar tuning of Cerreto (1601). His first tuning is a fourth lower than the second, and it seems to suggest a considerably larger instrument than the one we have encountered in the Spanish, French, English, and Italian sources. He does not cite the source(s) of his information, and it is possible he was unaware that there were two distinct types of guitar, that one had four courses and the other five, and that the latter was larger than the former. Indeed, he appears to have given as his first tuning the pitches of the top four courses of a five-course guitar tuned to *d'*, as found in two contemporaneous five-course guitar sources, Sanseverino (1620) and the 'Barbera manuscript'.

The suspicion that Praetorius had no first-hand knowledge of guitars grows stronger when, elsewhere in the book, he states: 'The Quinterna or Chiterna (his terms for guitar) is an instrument with four courses which are tuned like the very earliest lutes', that 'it has however not a rounded back, but is completely flat, quite like a bandora, and hardly two or three fingers in depth . . . Some have five courses, and, in Italy, the charlatans and mountebanks (a reference to *commedia dell'arte* characters),

---

[1] By Bohemia is meant the historic ethnic regions of Moravia and Bohemia, now the Czech Republic.

Ex. 9.1. Tuning chart for the four-course guitar from
Michael Praetorius, *Syntagma musicum* (1619)

who are like our comedians and clowns, strum them, singing their *Villanellen* and
other foolish songs. Nevertheless, good singers can sing fine and lovely songs with it'.[2]

Not until the mid-seventeenth century is there firm evidence that the Spanish guitar was known and used in north Germany: a manuscript (PL-Kj MS 40142) in
French guitar notation, signed by its owner, the 'Freiherr DE Döremberg', and dated
1652. This modest but interesting source was copied by two scribes. The first entered
unattributed pieces, which, from their titles, appear to be French and are written in
French guitar notation, yet are very reminiscent of Corbetta's Italian-style music from
his 1648 book. One of the untitled pieces (fo. 5) is a version of the well-known Ballo di
Mantova, while an attempt at notating Italian *repicci* is evident in a series of eleven
consecutive folias.[3]

The second scribe entered vastly different music, and in a much neater hand. It consists of a series of twelve pieces—a prelude, six sarabands,[4] a 'Ballet', an *allemande*,
and three *courantes* (one, the traditional *L'Avignonne*), all attributed to 'Bellony',
about whom nothing is known. The music is written in the French lute style (with no
strummed chords), and Bellony was probably the arranger, since the 'Sarrabande de
Bellony' (fo. 23) is actually a guitar version of a lute saraband by the Parisian lutenist
Jean Mercure (*fl.* 1641–7), who worked at both the English court of Charles I and,
later, the French court.[5] The next 'Sarrabande de Bellony' is an arrangement of
another lute piece, this one anonymous, which is found in the manuscript PL-Kj Mus.

---

[2] 'Quinterna oder Chiterna, ist ein Instrument mit vier Choren/ welche gleich wie die allereltester erste
Lauten . . . gestimpt werden: Hat aber keinen runden Bauch/ sondern ist fast wie ein Bandoer gantz glatt/ kaum
zween oder drey Finger hoch . . .

Etlich haben 5. Chorsaetten/ und brauchens in Italia die Ziarlatini und Salt'in banco (das sind beyn uns fast wie die
Comoedianten unnd Possenreisser) nur zum schrumpen; Darein sie Villanellen und andere naerrische Lumpenlieder
singen.

Es koennen aber nichts desto weniger auch andere feine anmuthige Cantiunculae, und liebliche Lieder von eim
guten Senger und Musico Vocali darein musicirt werden' (p. 53).

[3] Three more appear later in the manuscript, and all fourteen were probably intended to be performed in succession.

[4] The one on fo. 22 is given in modern edition and tablature in Wolf (1919), 170.

[5] See P. Vendrix, 'Mercure (les)', in Benoit (1992), 452–3. The lute piece is no. 16, p. 92 in *Œuvres des Mercure*, ed.
M. Rollin and J.-M. Vaccaro (Corpus des Luthistes Français; Paris: CNRS, 1977).

ms. 40626, no. 69. It also has two additional lute and two guitar concordances.[6] A side-by-side examination of the lute versions and Bellony's guitar versions reveals how skilful he was as an arranger.

There is only one printed source of guitar music that is of German provenance: *Musicalische Gemüths-Ergötzung* . . . (Dresden, 1689) by Jakob Kremberg (*c.*1650–*c.*1718), a musician in the service of the Elector of Saxony. This collection of songs, some with verses written by Kremberg himself, has parts in French tablature for lute, *angelique* (a type of theorbo with the open strings tuned stepwise, diatonically, like a harp; not to be confused with the *guitarre angelique*), viola da gamba (to be played in a chordal style), and guitar. Each of the tablature parts incorporates the melody (treble) and bass lines together with the inner harmonic voicings appropriate to each of the instruments. Consequently, the pieces can be performed either as solos for any of the instruments, or as songs with one or more of the instruments playing a kind of continuo accompaniment, or even as ensemble pieces for all or any combination of the four instruments—the permutations are endless. Kremberg specifies bourdons on both the fourth and fifth courses of the guitar, and requires a tuning of *d'*. As a source for the study of late seventeenth-century north German performance practice, this book is well worth investigating.[7]

It is difficult to pin down exactly when the Spanish guitar was first introduced to Bavaria and the Habsburg domains of Austria, Hungary, and Bohemia. We know that the copy of Foscarini's Books 1 to 4 in Prague has an engraved dedication to the Bohemian nobleman 'Veneslao di Michna . . . Conte di Watzinowa . . .' (Václav Michna, Count of Vacinov), dated 25 April 1638 in Rome; therefore, we know that at least one guitar publication reached Bohemia when the Count returned from Rome. From around this same early date comes a manuscript belonging to Johann Sebastian von Halwil (b. *c.*1610), written during his student days in Rome, Vienna, and elsewhere (A-K MS L81).[8] It contains French lute music and nineteen pieces for Spanish guitar in *alfabeto* notation and Italian mixed tablature. It also contains a chart explaining the *alfabeto* letters headed 'Musikalisches Alphabeth'. The music consists of Italian popular pieces, *passacaglie*, *ciaccone*, *gagliarde*, and two *preludi*, one of which ('Praeludio D.ni Sebastiani de Halwyl quod ipsemet descripsit') was apparently written by Halwil himself. Overall, the music is comparable to Foscarini's better pieces. Italian mixed tablature is also found in a manuscript dated 1648 from Schloss Annenberg in the south Tyrol (A-I la MS 533), which belonged to the Countess Marie-Catharine-Ursula de Montfort. The repertory comprises Italian songs and French dance movements, including the *Courante la Reyne* and *Schabotte*.[9]

---

[6] Goy (1996), 13.   [7] Wolf (1919), 128–9 contains a sample of Kremberg's music.

[8] Coelho (1995a), 92–5 believes that the lute pieces in French tablature are from *c.*1630–58, and that the lute and guitar pieces in Italian tablature were copied in Rome *c.*1638.

[9] See the list of concordances prepared by Robert Spencer for the facsimile edition of *Albrecht Werl's Lutebook* (D-Mbs Mus. ms. 21646) (Geneva: Minkoff Reprints, 1990), nos. 37 and 58.

Another mid-century manuscript, this one in French lute tablature, is possibly of Bohemian provenance (US-R MS Vault ML 96. L. 973). It contains thirty-seven pieces for guitar and thirty-eight for the French mandore[10] (not for lute, as some have assumed, and not for mandora, the Germanic bass lute of the late Baroque).[11] The guitar pieces have Italian titles, such as *Preludio*, *Corrente*, *Pavana*, *Ciacona*, *Furioso*, and *Moresca*; a few French titles, including *Les enfarines* and *Ballet*; and one German, a setting of *Clorys lass dich nit verdrissen*. The music for the last is actually a saraband by the French lutenist Germain Pinnel (d. 1661).[12] The French lute tablature has small Italian stroke signs on the bottom line of the five-line stave.

In Bavaria is a manuscript from *c.*1660 (D-Mbs MS 1522), which includes a mixture of anonymous Italian and French pieces, some in *alfabeto* notation and some in Italian mixed tablature. It belonged to the Electress of Bavaria, Adelaida of Savoy (1636–76), whose tastes apparently shaped the artistic and musical life of the Munich court. Adelaida promoted concerts, performances of ballet, and, eventually, opera productions. As the 14-year-old Princess of Savoy, she married Ferdinand Maria, the Elector of Bavaria, and shared his reign from 1654. An energetic patroness of the arts, she brought to Munich the sort of music and spectacle she had enjoyed during her childhood at the Savoy court in Turin. The music in her guitar manuscript reflects her mixed heritage—French on her mother's side (her mother was the sister of Louis XIII), and Italian on her father's (he was Vittorio Amadeo I of Savoy).

Adelaida's interest in the guitar apparently continued throughout her life. It will be recalled that Castillon, in the preface to his manuscript (B-Bc MS 5.615), revealed that Francois Le Cocq had been her guitar teacher. Since Adelaida died in 1676 and Le Cocq did not retire until 1729, her lessons with him must have taken place quite late in her life and quite early in his career. Adelaida's husband seems to have shared her interest in the guitar. As previously mentioned, Giovanni Battista Granata's *Novi capricci armonici...* (Bologna, 1674) is dedicated to Ferdinand Maria, Duke of Bavaria and Imperial Elector.

The Imperial court in Vienna was fully immersed in Italian culture during the reign of Emperor Leopold I (1658–1705). Italian was the official language at court, and many Italian musicians were employed in the *Hofmusik*, including the celebrated opera composer Antonio Cesti (1623–69). Another of the Emperor's musicians was the court theorbist Orazio Clementi, who was born in Padua in *c.*1637 and worked in Vienna from 1663 until his death in 1708. Clementi wrote a little guitar manuscript

[10] This manuscript is listed twice in RISM B/VII, once on pp. 47–8 as being in Bloomington, library of Paul Nettl, and again, on p. 304, as being in US-R. It is not in Bloomington but Rochester and, judging by the description, RISM has confused it with another manuscript, also in Rochester and also for mandore (US-R M. 125. FL. XVII). A description of the latter, with many inaccuracies, appears in RISM B/VII on p. 301.

[11] For information on the French mandore, see Tyler and Sparks (1989), 7–10 and Tyler (2000c); and for details on the Mandora, see Tyler (2000d) and the present book, App. III.

[12] A modern edition of the lute piece is no. 60 in *Œuvres de Pinel*, ed. M. Rollin and J.-M. Vaccaro (Corpus des Luthistes Français; Paris: CNRS, 1982).

(A-Wn MS 10248) for Leopold, a noted composer and player of several instruments. Clementi's music is written in French lute tablature with *alfabeto* letters to indicate full chords; this is actually a quite sensible style of notation. The music includes three *ciaccone*, two of them marked 'battuta' (strummed), and four pieces marked 'Passa-gallo', one in the strummed style and the others in the mixed lute and strummed style. The music contained in this humble manuscript could not be further removed from Leopold's own body of work, which includes oratorios, masses, stage works, madrigals, and sonatas. Now we know how the Emperor-composer spent some of his leisure moments.[13]

In other regions of Austria the French style was influential. Austro-Bohemian lutenists such as Johann Peyer (d. *c.*1677), Ferdinand Hinterleithner (1659–1710), and Count Jan Anton Losy (1650–1721) found inspiration in the works of contemporary French lutenists, and between 1650 and 1720 they developed their own distinctive style. It is in this context that the guitar music in a recently recovered manuscript (A-KLse MS I 38) should be considered. Dated 1686, it is from Schloss Ebenthal near Klagenfurt in the southern region of Carinthia. It was copied by Johann Vogl for Maria Anna von Sinzendorff and contains forty-seven pieces for guitar and twenty-eight for lute, all notated in French lute tablature.[14] The guitar music is mainly French; twelve of the pieces were copied from Médard's book of 1676, while seven others are the expected arrangements of pieces by Lully, most of which have concordances in French manuscripts containing similar versions (F-Pn Rés. F. 844 and Vm^7 675, and GB-Ob MS C. 94). In addition to the French pieces for guitar, there are two by the aristocratic Austrian and Bohemian lutenists Christoph Franz von Wolkenstein-Rodenegg (d. 1707) and the aforementioned Count Jan Anton Losy. Both pieces are arrangements for guitar of their respective lute solos, and once again it is fascinating to discover how music that was conceived for a large, eleven- to fourteen-course French or German lute could be arranged for an instrument with a much narrower compass and a radically different technical idiom.

Count Losy's music also appears in other guitar manuscripts, including two in Prague that originated at the castle in Raudnitz (Roudnice), seat of the noble Lobkowitz family (CZ-Pnm MS X. L. b. 209, CZ-Pu MS II. Kk 77). The first of these contains eleven of his pieces, in addition to an 'Allemande amoureuse de Mons. Corbett fait a Naple' (composed by Corbetta in Naples), and a saraband by an unknown composer, 'Melau'. The second manuscript contains forty-four of Losy's pieces, among other, anonymous items.[15] There is no direct evidence that Losy actually played or composed for the guitar, but surely, like most lutenists residing in the cosmopolitan centres of Vienna and Prague, he had knowledge of the instrument.

---

[13] See the description and discussion of this manuscript in Koczirz (1933).

[14] See Crawford and Goy (1997).

[15] A modern edition transcribed for classical guitar of all the pieces by Losy in both MSS is found in Jan Antonín Losy, *Pièces de guitare*, ed. J. Pohanska (Prague: Editio Supraphon, 1958/1979).

And the fact that only seven items in the three guitar sources containing music by him are known to be arrangements of his lute music, while the remaining forty-nine guitar pieces have no known lute concordances, certainly suggests that at least some of the forty-nine are original guitar compositions by this highly accomplished composer.[16]

There is one final source from this region of Europe that is worth mentioning—an anonymous manuscript, now in Vienna (A-Wn MS S. M. 9659) but originally from Bad Aussee near Salzburg. It encompasses ninety-two dance movements notated in French lute tablature, with the occasional use of *alfabeto* notation within the staff, and composed in the fully evolved Austrian *galant* lute style of the 1720s. The melodic content is clearly etched, and the composer's excellent idiomatic writing for a guitar with bourdons on both the fourth and fifth courses suggests that this sizeable collection could prove to be a source of pure delight for modern guitarists seeking repertory from this period.[17] Interestingly, the tuning chart provided in the manuscript indicates (in tablature and staff notation) two different tuning options: the first in *g′* (a minor third higher than a modern guitar), and the second a semitone lower in *f♯′*.[18] Although these tunings seem to imply that a smaller instrument is intended, since the music is in tablature it can be played on a guitar of any size.

All known German and Austrian sources of Spanish guitar music are listed in Table 9.1, and Bohemian sources in Table 9.2.

[16] This supposition runs contrary to other scholarly opinion, e.g. Emil Vogl, 'The Lute Music of Johann Anton Losy', *JLSA* 14 (1981), 7–10.

[17] A selection of these pieces is found in modern edition: *Ausgewählte Werke aus der Ausseer Gitarretabulature des 18. Jahrhunderts*, ed. J. Klima (Graz: Akademische Druck u. Verlagsanstalt, 1958).

[18] For other evidence of the *f♯′* tuning, see the description of the Portuguese manuscript (P-Cug MS 97) in Ch. 10.

TABLE 9.1. *German and Austrian sources of Spanish guitar music*

A. PRINTED BOOK

1686   Kremberg, Jacob, *Musicalische Gemüths-Ergötzung, oder, Arien . . . auf der Lauthe, Angelique, Viola di Gamba, und Chitarra . . .* (Dresden)
            Vocal music with French tablature in scordatura tunings for guitar and the above-named instruments.

B. MANUSCRIPTS

Location	Source	Date	Remarks
A-Ila	MS Nr. 533	'1648'	Anon. MS belonging to Maria Catherine Ursula, Comptesse de Montfort. Italian mixed tablature and *alfabeto*. Solos; French and Italian songs. RISM B/VII), 135–6; Goy (1996), 14
A-KLse	Hs. I. 38	'1686'	Anon. MS belonging to Maria Anna von Sinzendorff; copyist, Johann Vogl. Guitar and lute MS in French lute tablature. Several pieces copied from Médard (1676) and arrangements of music by Lully, Wolkenstein-Rodenegg, and Losy. Crawford and Goy (1997). Facs. edn.: Munich: Tree Edition, 1997
A-KR	MS L 81	*c.*1630–58	Anon. MS for lute and guitar belonging to Johann Sebastian Halwil. Guitar section, *c.*1638, in *alfabeto* and Italian mixed tablature. Coelho (1995), 92–5
A-Wn	MS Suppl. Mus. 9659	early 18th c.	Anon. MS from Bad Aussee in French notation, some with *alfabeto*. French and Italian dance movements and some local Austrian titles. RISM B/VII, 357–8
D-B	Mus. Ms. 40160	*c.*1640	One leaf of anon. music in French notation; formerly in the library of the Von Dörnberg family, Kassel. See PL-Kj 40142. RISM B/VI, 28
D-B	Mus. Ms. 40631	late 17th c.	Anon. French notation. RISM B/VII, 37
D-DO	Mus. Ms. 1215	early 18th c.	Anon. French notation. Danner (1979), 15
D-Mbs	Ms. Mus. 1522	*c.*1660	Anon. MS belonging to Adelaida di Savoya, Electress of Bavaria. Italian mixed tablature and *alfabeto*. 50 guitar solos and Italian songs. RISM B/VII, 222–3

TABLE 9.1. *continued*

Location	Source	Date	Remarks
D–W	MS Cod. Guelf. 302 Blank.	early 18th c.	Anon. MS belonging to Christine Luise von Braunschweig-Lüneburg. French notation; contains 40 French dance movements (some by Visée) and Italian popular pieces. Not in RISM B/VII
PL–Kj	Mus. ms. 40142	'1652'	Anon. MS in French notation; formerly in the library of the Von Dörnberg family, Kassel. See D–B 40160. Mostly French preludes, folias, and other dance movements, some by 'Bellony'. Kirsch and Meierott (1992), 54–62
PL–Kj	Mus. ms. 40267	*c.*1700	Six pieces in French notation in a cithrinchen MS: *Menuet, Aria von deinen Küssen . . ., Sarabande, Aria Verhengniss treibstu denn; Bourree, Ich ruff zu Dir Herr Jesu Christ.* The pieces could possibly be for a cithrinchen tuned and played like a guitar. Kirsch and Meierott (1992), 214–41; Tyler (2000*e*)
PL–Wn	Ms. Mus. 2088	*c.*1765	No details available. Boetticher (1979), 202

TABLE 9.2. *Bohemian sources of Spanish guitar music*

Location	Source	Date	Remarks
CZ–Bm	MS D. 189	early 18th c.	Anon. MS for mandora (colachon) and guitar in French notation and *alfabeto*. Solos and German songs; one mandora piece by Losy. RISM B/VII, 51–2; Tyler (2000*d*)
CZ–P dobrovsky	MS b. 2	*c.*1690–1700	Anon. MS in French notation and *alfabeto*; formerly in the library of the Grafen von Nostitz family. RISM B/VII, 286
CZ–Pnm	MS II. L. a. 1	late 17th c.	Two anon. pieces added in French notation to Kremberg (1689); formerly in the Lobkowitz library. RISM B/VII, 287
CZ–Pnm	MS X. L. b. 207	early 18th c.	Anon. MS partbooks for violin(?) and guitar in French notation; formerly in the Lobkowitz library. RISM B/VII, 288
CZ–Pnm	MS X. L. b. 208	early 18th c.	Anon. MS partbooks for violin(?) and guitar in French notation; formerly in the Lobkowitz library. RISM B/VII, 289
CZ–Pnm	MS X. L. b. 209	early 18th c.	Anon. MS in French notation, containing, in part, music by Logy, Melau, and Corbetta; formerly in the Lobkowitz library. RISM B/VII, 289
CZ–Pnm	MS X. L. b. 211	early 18th c.	Anon. MS in French notation, containing pieces by Corbetta and 'Fr. Günther' (Ginter); formerly in the Lobkowitz library. RISM B/VII, 289–90
CZ–Pu	MS II. Kk. 75	early 18th c.	Anon. MS in French notation containing 50 anon. suites; formerly in the Lobkowitz library. RISM B/VII, 294
CZ–Pu	MS II. Kk. 76a & b	early 18th c.	Anon. MS in French notation; formerly in the Lobkowitz library. Guitar parts related to MS 76b for violin(?). RISM B/VII, 295
CZ–Pu	MS II. Kk. 77	early 18th c.	'Pieces composée [*sic*] par le Compte Logis'. MS in French notation; formerly in the Lobkowitz library. Arrangements of pieces by Logy, Mouton, and others. RISM B/VII, 295
US–R	MS Vault ML 96. L. 973	mid-17th c.	Anon. MS in French notation for mandore and guitar. Italian titles: 'Preludio', 'aria', 'Spannioleta', 'Furioso', etc.; and French dance movements. RISM B/VII, 47–8 gives location as Bloomington in the library of Paul Nettl. Tyler (2000*c*)

10

Spain, Portugal, and the New World

The history of composed music and instruction for the Spanish guitar in Spain begins in the year 1596 with a modest tutor on chord playing by Juan Carlos Amat (*c.* 1572–1642).[1] Amat was Catalan, a prominent medical doctor in the town of Monistrol near Barcelona, who also wrote a book on medicine in 1623 and a popular book of 400 Catalan aphorisms in 1636.[2] No copies of the original 1596 edition of his guitar tutor survive. The earliest extant edition, published in Lérida in 1626, is entitled *Guitarra española de cinco ordenes la qual enseña de templar, y tañer rasgado todos los puntos . . .* (The Spanish Guitar of Five Courses, which teaches tuning and all the chords for playing in strummed fashion). Widely known within Spain and Portugal, this book was added to, plagiarized, and paraphrased in many later editions, the last of which appeared in around 1819![3]

In the first chapter of his own 1626 edition Amat explains the tuning and stringing of the instrument, which he describes as having a single first and bourdons on the fourth and fifth courses. In Spain, unlike Italy and most of Europe, this stringing arrangement, which was closely associated with the *rasgueado*, or strummed style of playing, would become the one most commonly used. Amat then explains how to use his *cifras* system, which consists of twelve different numbered chords in major keys, marked *n* ('naturales'), and twelve in minor keys, marked *b* ('b mollados'). A chord signified by *1^n* equals E major, *2^n* equals A major; while *1^b* equals E minor, *2^b* equals A minor, and so on. Amat arranges his sequence of chords so that they progress in a circle of fifths.[4] This harmonic approach, while familiar to modern readers, was unheard of in 1596. All music theory books of the time expounded the traditional modal system for both liturgical chant and polyphonic composition. What the guitar *cifras* system represented was written-down insight into the performance practice of the untrained

---

[1] Many modern writers cite 1586 as its publication date, basing this on the date given in the revised and expanded edition (Barcelona, 1639) produced by Padre Leonardo de San Martín. However, the evidence suggests that a printing error was made. In his prefatory letter San Martín gives Amat's age as 67, which means he would have been 14 years old in 1586. The earliest surviving edition (1626), as well as the reprints of 1627, 1640, and 1674, all contain the three letters of approval for the book's first edition that are clearly dated 1596.

[2] Esses (1992), 118.

[3] Amat himself wrote nine chapters. All additional chapters were written by anonymous authors, primarily from the 18th c. See Hall (1980).

[4] Extensive discussion of Amat, his chord system, and the bibliographical complexities involving his book can be found in Hall (1980).

street musician, engaged in the type of traditional, spontaneous music-making which, in sound and style, probably carries on today, little changed, in the folk and popular music of the western hemisphere, particularly Latin America.[5]

Luis de Briceño's *Metodo . . .* (Paris, 1626) was discussed briefly in the chapter dealing with Spanish guitar music in France (Ch. 7). Briceño's method of notating chords is closer in concept to the Neapolitan *alfabeto* system than Amat's in that one number or symbol stands for one specific chord shape. Moreover, unlike Amat's circle of fifths, Briceño's sequence of chord shapes is virtually random. Briceño uses only sixteen chords, which are represented by the numbers one to nine and seven additional letters and symbols. His book contains a wealth of Spanish song texts with his style of *cifras* notation (later known as Castilian *cifras*, as opposed to Amat's Catalan). Among the texts is one for Lope de Vega's wild and wonderful 'Vida bona, vida bona, esta vieja la chacona', with, of course, the chords of the *chacona* for accompaniment.[6] This and other popular Spanish grounds are found throughout the book; and although Briceño's rhythmic strumming notation is rather vague, much of his music can be understood and performed through comparison with other examples of the same basic material.[7]

Nicolao Doizi de Velasco's *Nuevo modo de cifrar para tañer la guitarra . . .* (Naples, 1640) is a treatise and manual for guitarists on transposition and how it is notated. When his book was published, Doizi, a Portuguese, was employed by Philip IV's brother Ferdinando, who was then Viceroy of Naples. Not long after and until his death in *c.*1659 he was in the service of the King of Spain himself.[8] Doizi's treatise is remarkable: using Italian *alfabeto* as his starting point, he puts forward a highly sophisticated chord notation system encompassing chord inversions and dissonances for each pitch degree of an octave scale: nineteen in all for each degree. This can be accomplished, he says, because, unlike keyboard instruments, the guitar is fretted in equal temperament, a feature he praises. This comprehensive transposition capability of the guitar is essential for playing in ensemble, he says, and is especially important for accompanying singers. Unfortunately, Doizi's chord notation is very complicated and difficult to memorize, and for that reason, one surmises, no one else seems to have used it.[9]

Not a single collection of solo guitar music was published in Spain before 1674—unless the incomplete engraved tablature book sold at auction in Sotheby's (London) on 20 November 1991 is Corbetta's lost book, *Guitarra española, y sus diferencias de*

---

[5] For a thorough discussion of all *cifras* systems and their sources, see Yakeley and Hall (1995).

[6] It is translated and discussed in Walker (1968), 315–16. For further information on some of Briceño's pieces, see also Baron (1977), 32.

[7] Yakeley and Hall (1995), 31–40 provides some solutions to Briceño's notation.

[8] Esses (1992), 119–21.

[9] See Pennington (1981), 125–6, 263–78 and Esses (1992), 111–21, 143, and 159–61.

PL. 10.1. Page possibly from Francesco Corbetta, *Guitarra española* . . . (n.p., *c.*1650)

sones, which he dedicated to Philip IV (see Pl. 10.1).[10] Cited in an eighteenth-century edition of Nicolás Antonio (d. 1684), *Bibliotheca hispana nova sive Hispanorum scriptorum . . . notitia* (Madrid, 1783),[11] this newly recovered source lacks a title page and preface; however, sixty-two of its eighty-four pages of engraved music are reprinted from Corbetta's Italian publication of 1648, with the page numbers altered and some of the Italian words re-engraved in Spanish. The remaining pages seem to be the work of at least two different engravers, and contain settings of such typical Spanish pieces as the *Mariona* and *Pavana*,[12] along with a 'Brand', two 'alemandas' and a 'Sarabanda'. The last four items are in Italian mixed tablature and are quite similar in style to his 1648 pieces, while the first two items are written in a predominantly *punteado* (lute) style with no *alfabeto* chords. Corbetta was in Brussels, capital of the Spanish-ruled Netherlands, for the 1648 publication of his Italian guitar book. Perhaps he visited Spain afterwards, taking with him the plates for that book together with the newly engraved Spanish additions. It is known that he travelled a great deal in an effort to secure a court position, and, while it is also known that such a position was not on the cards for him in Spain, the information he gives in the Italian preface to his 1671 *Guitarre royalle* certainly suggests that he may have gone there for that purpose in around 1650.

[10] Esses (1992), 139. As I write, neither the name of the present owner nor the book's location is known.
[11] Vol. i. 416. See Esses (1992), 139.
[12] The Spanish Pavanas is the Italian Pavaniglia, which was assimilated into Spanish culture during the 16th c.

One of the earliest Spanish manuscript sources of solo guitar music survives from the late seventeenth century; however, it is not from Spain but from Spanish Colonial Mexico. The manuscript (MEX-M Códice Saldívar No. 2) is entitled 'Metodo de Citara' (Method for Cittern) by Sebastian de Aguirre.[13] Along with the pieces for cittern, there are twelve for the 'vihuela de cinco órdenes'. (By the mid-seventeenth century, the term 'vihuela' no longer referred to the lute-like instrument of the Renaissance, but to the guitar.)[14] The guitar pieces include an unascribed *Sarabandas* from Sanz's 1674 book, six *Pasacalles*, and other pieces entitled *Tono, Marisapalos, Canario agaitado, Jacaras*, and *Minue*. One additional *Pasacalle* with its *Diferensia* (variation) is for a four-course instrument. This manuscript is important because it very well may contain the earliest manifestation of written-out music that originated in the New World.[15]

Evidence of guitar playing elsewhere in the New World is found in a manuscript miscellany (RA-BA Rojas Museum) from *c.*1670–1703. It was copied in Peru by Gregorio de Zuola, a Franciscan friar, who provides an Italian *alfabeto* chart and, for some of the letters, the corresponding Castilian *cifras*. Significantly, Father Gregorio also gives the traditional names of the chords, for example, 'cruzado', 'cruzadillo', 'patilla', 'guzmanillo', 'bacas', 'rebayas', and 'tendido',[16] which probably pre-date any of the written systems. It seems the guitar was as much a part of everyday life in the New World as it was in the homeland.

Meanwhile, a Spanish priest in the city of Zaragoza produced the first collection of Spanish guitar music to be published in Spain. The priest, of course, was Gaspar Sanz (*fl.* 1674–97), whose book, which also includes a comprehensive guitar tutor, is entitled *Instruccion de musica sobre la guitarra española . . .* (Zaragoza, 1674). Sanz received approval to publish the book from the chapel master of the Holy Metropolitan Church of Zaragoza and the organist of the Holy Church of Our Lady del Pilar in the same city. He had sought, and may have acquired, the patronage of 'Juan de Austria' (1629–70), the Vicar General of Aragon, to whom the book is dedicated and whose engraved portrait appears in it.

[13] This MS is in a private library. I have been unable to examine it personally and am relying on the published descriptions in Stevenson (1968), 234–5 and, especially, Russell (1995*b*), 13–14, 21–4, and 37–8. Russell seems unaware that much of the music in the Aguirre MS is for a Spanish cittern similar to the one described by Minguet y Yrol (*c.*1752–74) on p. 71 of the facsimile edition (see Table 10.1). He conjectures that the 'citara' is a small Mexican guitar that is known today as a 'requinto jarrocho'. However, judging by the MS pages that he reproduces on pp. 37–8, the music requires a particular interval pattern that is identical both to Minguet's chord chart for 'citara' (cittern) and the chord chart and music found in another Spanish cittern MS from the same period that is listed in a 1974 London auction catalogue (see Tyler (1974), 20 and Tyler (2000*a*), 883), but is not the interval pattern of a 'requinto jarrocho'. Further evidence that the intended instrument is a cittern appears on another of the pages reproduced by Russell: a drawing of a typical cittern fingerboard with twenty-two frets, including some that do not extend all the way across. This same number of frets and fret pattern are found on many surviving citterns, and, indeed, are unique to citterns. (See L. P. Grijp, 'Fret Patterns of the Cittern', *GSJ* 34 (1981), 62–97 and Budasz (2001), 40–4.)

[14] The term was also used throughout the 18th c. to mean guitar. See Ch. 11.

[15] For example, titles of some of the cittern pieces include *Panema, Portorrico de los Negros, El Guasteco, Puerto rico de la Puebla*, and *Gallarda portugueza*.   [16] Esses (1992), 157–9; Yakeley and Hall (1995), 31 and 60.

Sanz's book is remarkable in many ways. First, he engraved all the music plates himself. This was probably necessary because there was virtually no music printing in Spain at this time, and it is unlikely that any local printer would have possessed either the music font or the skill to use it.[17] Also remarkable is the sheer quantity of information and instruction Sanz provides: before the music begins there are instructions for tuning, chord formation, right- and left-hand technique, ornaments, and metre; after the music there is a detailed treatise on accompanying using figured bass, followed by a few more music examples and *passacalles*. In his 'Prologo' Sanz informs us that he went to Italy to study music with organists and guitarists in Naples and Rome and that he was quite familiar with the guitar music of Foscarini, Kapsperger, Pellegrini, Granata, and Corbetta. (He mentions also a 'Lorenzo Fardino', about whom nothing is known.) He states that he learned much from Lelio Colista[18] (whose music, it will be recalled, was discussed in relation to the 'Castillon' MS in Brussels). Next Sanz deals with tuning and stringing, providing the information that the guitar masters in Rome used a totally re-entrant tuning, while in Spain they used either a bourdon on the fourth and fifth courses, or even two bourdons on each of those courses. The bourdons, Sanz says, are good for people who play noisy, popular music ('música ruidosa') and for playing from the bass (that is, basso continuo). He then states his reasons for preferring a totally re-entrant tuning for the performance of sophisticated solo music:

But if anyone wishes to play in the plucking manner with grace and sweetness, and use *campanelas* (which is the modern method now used in composing), the *bordones* do not come out well, but only the thin strings, both in the *quartas* and *quintas*, as I have experienced a good deal. The reason is, that if there is a *bordón* it impedes the making of trills . . . and slurs . . . and other gallantries of the left hand, because one string is thick and the other thin, and the hand cannot press evenly and control one thick string as it can two thin ones. Furthermore, if with *bordones* you form the letter or chord E [i.e. a D minor chord] . . . , the open fifth course produces the interval of a fourth [below] in the bass . . . and will confuse the principal bass, and will be imperfect according to the teaching of counterpoint.[19]

The music in the 1674 edition begins with *alfabeto* solos of the most familiar Spanish and Italian harmonic grounds (Villano, Jacaras, Dance de las Hachas, Jacara de la Costa, Españoleta, Rugero, Granduque de Florencia, Baile de Mantua, La Taran-

---

[17] The portrait of Juan de Austria and the later (3rd edn., 1675) illustrations of hands fingering the sequence of chords were the work of the Flemish engraver Jean Blavet.

[18] Sanz (1674), fos. 5ᵛ–7 in the facsimile reprint of the third edition (Zaragoza, 1966).

[19] Translated in Esses (1992), 146. 'pero si alguno quiera puntear con primor, y dulçura, y usar de las campanelas, que es el modo moderno con que aora se compone, no salen bien los bordones, sino solo cuerdas delgadas, assi en las quartas, como en las quintas, como tengo grande experiencia; y es la razon, porque para hazer los trinos, y extrasinos, y demas galanterias de mano izquierda, si ay bordon impide, por ser la una cuerda gruessa, y la otra la delgada, y no poder la mano pissar con igualdad, y sugetar tambien una cuerda recia, como dos delgadas; y à mas desto, que con bordones, si hazes la letra. o punto E, que es *De lasolre*, en la musica sale la Quinta vacante en Quarta baxo, y confunde el principal baxo, y le dà algo de imperfeccion, conforme el contrapunto enseña.' Sanz (1674), fo. 8ʳ.

tella, and so on). These are followed by similar dances, *passacalles*, and preludes, some in *punteado* style and others in Italian mixed tablature. The music is good, but shows only a glimmer of the brilliance to come.

For the second edition, published the very next year, Sanz added a *libro segundo* consisting of twelve new settings of popular grounds in *punteado* style. The music is more complex and shows a greater awareness and skill in Sanz's use of the special guitar idiom of cascading scales ('campanelas'). Apart from the two well-known *Canarios*, it also contains the *Pavanas* (the Italian *Pavaniglia* ground). In modern editions of this piece usually only the first two of Sanz's three variations on the ground are included, presumably because the third uses *campanelas* throughout. In Sanz's tablature hardly any two consecutive scale notes are on the same course; so, if an editor is transcribing it into staff notation for a guitar with bourdons, that third variation, with its apparent leaping sevenths and the like, will look odd, to say the least. Even if the notes that Sanz wrote are transcribed in the correct octave, played on a modern guitar with bourdons they will not sound as he intended—like little bells ringing or reverberating, bell- or harp-like, one into the other—and for the reasons he stated (see Ex. 10.1).

For the third edition of his book, published later in the same year (1675), Sanz added a *libro tercero* to the contents of the first and second editions.[20] It consists entirely of *Passacalles*—thirteen of them in various keys. His exquisite and ingenious variations on this four-bar harmonic pattern are among the gems of the Spanish guitar repertory. Indeed, after their publication variations over grounds became the hallmark of the repertory and the primary means of expression for the fine Spanish guitar composers who followed.

The guitar, as we know, traditionally accompanied Spanish song, and a scattering of examples can be found in Spanish sources in the form of song texts with *cifras*, or songs in staff notation with *cifras*;[21] but there is only one extensive source, the truly remarkable manuscript collection (GB-Cfm MS Mus. 727) by José Marín (1619–99). This collection comprises fifty-one songs for solo voice with a simple, effective, fully written-out guitar accompaniment in *punteado* style using Italian tablature.[22] Marín was a singer who began his career as an ordained priest, and was employed as a tenor in the Royal Chapel in Madrid from 1644 until 1649. In 1656 he was accused and convicted of robbery and even suspected of murder. Apparently, he was imprisoned, tortured, and banished from Madrid; but having been a highly accomplished composer and performer, and being associated with composers of theatrical music, he was welcomed back to the royal court when the scandal died down.[23] Marín's songs to the guitar and arrangements of the songs of other composers have great charm and

---

[20] Sanz, who knew the music of Foscarini, apparently emulated his style of cumulative music publishing.

[21] For further information, see Yakeley and Hall (1995).

[22] A modern edition with both the tablature and its transcription is *José Marín: 51 Tonos*, ed. A. Lázaro (Heidelberg: Chanterelle Verlag, 1997; Mel Bay Publications for North America).

[23] For information on Marín, see Stein (1993), 301–5 and Yakeley (1999), 16–26.

convey a wide range of moods and sentiments. Some of his material originated in theatrical productions, including a text by Lope de Vega, 'Al son de los arroyuelos' from *La Dorotea* (1632).[24]

Another priest, Lucas Ruiz de Ribayaz, published his guitar book *Luz y norte musical . . .* (Madrid, 1677) on his return from the Spanish colony of Peru, where he was in the service of the viceroy. Ruiz de Ribayaz's book deals with the rudiments of mensural notation and tablature for guitar and harp, and includes music for both instruments. The guitar music consists mainly of pieces by Gaspar Sanz that have been 'reworked' by Ruiz de Ribayaz—which is to say, he eliminated all the difficult sections and, because his book is intended for a guitar with bourdons on the two lower courses, the *campanelas* as well. To make matters worse, his Italian tablature is full of errors. Apparently, his book was the first attempt by a seventeenth-century Spanish printer to typeset music in tablature.[25] It makes one appreciate even more Sanz's remarkable achievement as both composer and engraver.

A number of guitar manuscripts from the end of the seventeenth century and beginning of the eighteenth are well worth examining. One is a collection for the 'Biguela hordinaria' by Antonio de Santa Cruz (E-Mn MS 2209).[26] Santa Cruz's manuscript consists mainly of sets of variations on Spanish harmonic grounds. Although he includes an *alfabeto* chart at the beginning and describes the 'keys' of some of the pieces by means of *alfabeto* letters (for example, the 'Jacaras sobra la E' on fo. 3), his tablature contains no *alfabeto* notation; the music is entirely in *punteado* style. Moreover, unlike Sanz, Santa Cruz includes not a single overtly 'foreign' piece. As his manuscript appears to be from the very end of the seventeenth century, this may reflect the growing hostility towards the French presence and French culture at the court of Carlos II. Indeed, much to the horror of the Spanish people, Carlos, whose sad reign was finally nearing an end and who had failed to produce an heir, bequeathed the Spanish throne to Philippe d'Anjou of the French Bourbon dynasty rather than to a Spanish Habsburg.

Whether Santa Cruz was being deliberately nationalistic in his choice of musical material or not, his *diferencias* on the Jacara, Mariona, Canario, Villano, Pavana, Pasacalle, and other Spanish grounds are of a remarkably high standard and technically quite demanding. His variations contain passagework that requires shifts up to the twelfth fret. Unfortunately, his notation is problematical in that the rhythm signs are rather vague and idiosyncratic; however, most of the problems can be solved by comparing his settings with some of the many extant versions of the same thematic material. Once this is done, one cannot help but be impressed by the quality of his music, which stands with the best of the Spanish guitar repertory.[27]

---

[24] Stein (1993), 363.   [25] See Esses (1992), 124–5; Strizich (1974); and Yakeley and Hall (1995), 33–4 and 50.
[26] In the 17th and 18th cc. the term 'Biguela hordinaria' (common vihuela) no longer referred to the six-course lute-like instrument from the 16th c., but to the guitar.
[27] See Esses (1992), 127–9, 173. Vol. ii of Esses contains transcriptions of twenty-three of the manuscript's twenty-

Ex. 10.1. Final section of Gaspar Sanz's *Pavanas* (1674)

[★] If an octave string is used on the third course then the upper *g'* will sound.

Three little-known manuscripts of Portuguese provenance (P-Cug MS 97, P-Lcg, and P-Ln F. R. C. Ne. 1) for 'viola' (the Portuguese term for five-course guitar) are also of great interest, and two are connected with the royal court.[28] Portugal had won its independence from Spain in 1640 during the reign of John IV, and by the early

eight items, which provide a useful basis for understanding Santa Cruz's rhythmic intentions. Esses does not reproduce Santa Cruz's tablature.

[28] I am grateful to Rogério Budasz, whose Ph.D. dissertation (Budasz, 2001), in part, concerns these manuscripts, for kindly sharing his knowledge of them with me.

eighteenth century was not only benefiting once more from the natural resources of its far-flung colonial empire but had established a court culture quite different from that of its former rulers. In this context it is interesting to contrast the Spanish sources of the time, which consist primarily of well-known dance grounds and variations, with the first of the 'viola' manuscripts (P-Cug MS 97), dating from the early eighteenth century, which opens with thirty-three free-form pieces labeled 'Fantasia'. Not that there are no dance grounds in the manuscript. Indeed, along with the fantasias are variations on Spanish dances, other pieces comprising variations on what appear to be Portuguese popular grounds (for example, 'Rojão', 'Magana', 'Maricota', and 'Marinheira'), and still others with apparent connections to the Portuguese colony of Brazil and other territories in the New World. These include such pieces as 'Cubanco', 'Meya dança', 'Cumbé', and 'Arromba', the last of which appears to be the forerunner of the rhumba.

While composers' names abound in this large 115-folio manuscript, regrettably most of them are still just names, such as Monteyro (6 pieces), Silva (37 pieces), Gomes (6), Fra João (5), Çofalo (1), and Pepe Licete (5). A couple of others are a bit more familiar: Abreu (11 pieces) and [Deniz de] Barros (19). And Marques (12 pieces), identified in another of the manuscripts (P-Lcg) as 'Antonio Marques [1639–1709], tocador da capella rea' (musician of the royal chapel), is the well-known Portuguese writer and composer Antonio Marques Lésbio (of Lisbon), master of the royal chamber musicians from 1668.

The music is in Italian *punteado*-style tablature, with only rare indications of strummed chords. Frustratingly, it is all but devoid of rhythm signs; and although many of the pieces can be reconstructed by referring to other sources of the same basic material, some are unique and thus difficult (though not impossible) to transcribe.[29] One of the manuscript's many interesting sections is headed 'Peces de Viola Italianas e Francesas' (Italian and French pieces for the guitar). It consists of several items from earlier printed sources of guitar, lute, and keyboard music, such as the *Alemanda* (fo. 92^r) from Corbetta's 1643 book (p. 47), as well as a piece entitled *Bayletto del Corbetto* (fo. 93^r), which has not been found in Corbetta's surviving works. Another piece, *Outra Alemanda* (fo. 92^v), is found in a Spanish source (E-Mn MS 811, no. 16) as *Alemanda del Corbera*, but is actually an *alemanda* copied from Domenico Pellegrini's 1650 book (p. 49). A comparison between Pellegrini's piece and the manuscript's version of it provides an excellent, if baffling, illustration of how the Portuguese scribes dealt with music that was originally in Italian mixed tablature. In this instance, the scribe eliminated all the *alfabeto* letters and wrote the strummed chords out in Italian lute tablature. That alone would not present a problem; however, he also elimi-

---

[29] Budasz has convincingly transcribed much of the material in this and the other two Portuguese MSS, despite their lack of rhythm signs. These sources contain some highly original music that is worth exploring. See Budasz (2001), 186–403.

nated all Pellegrini's original stroke signs for the strummed chords, and all his other rhythmic indications as well!

Another section of this huge collection contains pieces that employ five different scordatura tunings. Interestingly, at the end of the section is an *alfabeto* chart—even though no *alfabeto* notation is used for any of the music. There is also a simple tuning chart in tablature (for the regular tuning only), a chart comparing the tuning of the 'viola' to that of the 'machinho', and a table that shows what chord shapes the latter plays in order to match the harmonies of the 'viola' when the two instruments play together.[30] From this table it is apparent that the Portuguese *machinho* is a smaller five-course guitar tuned to f', one tone higher than the 'standard' Spanish guitar.[31]

Yet another section of the manuscript comprises thirteen pieces in tablature for a five-course *bandurra*, a treble-range instrument related to the guitar, which is tuned, beginning with the first course: $a'' a'' - e'' e'' - b' b' - f\sharp' f\sharp' - c\sharp' c\sharp'$.[32] The second manuscript (P-Lcg) also has a section of pieces for bandurra, as well as a *Minuete* (fo. 26[v]) for two guitars. In fact, both contain similar material, including several of the same pieces.[33] The third of the manuscripts (P-Ln F. R. C. Ne. 1) is from a slightly later period, *c*.1750, and, while it has some music in common with the two earlier ones, primarily contains examples of the later-style minuet. One of the minuets, entitled *Minuete de Escarlate*, is probably an arrangement of a keyboard piece by Domenico Scarlatti (1685–1757), who was head of the royal chapel in Lisbon between 1719 and 1728. Some of the others are by composers named 'Cain', 'Varan', and 'Jorze'. There is also a sonata by 'Corely', which is an intabulation of Corelli's Op. 5 No. 7 (for violin and basso continuo).

Although these manuscripts contain a preponderance of Portuguese material that sets them apart from contemporaneous Spanish sources, they also have much thematic material in common. Francisco Guerau's 1694 publication *Poema harmonico, compuesto de varias cifras por el temple de la guitarra española* . . . (Harmonic Poem, comprising tablature for the tuning of the Spanish guitar), for example, consists entirely of sets of variations on some of the same Spanish grounds found in the Portuguese manuscripts. He includes 39 sets of variations on the Jacara, 29 on the Jacara de la Costa, 12 on the Marizapolos, eight on the Españoleta, 12 on the Pavana, 14 on the Gallarda, 12 on the Folia, 18 on the Mariona, three on the Canario, and 13 on the Villano. There are also thirty sets of variations on the Pasacalle.

---

[30] The charts are reprinted in Budasz (2001), 32.

[31] This specific pitch has been encountered previously in connection with an Austrian manuscript (A-Wn MS 9659), the so-called 'Ausseer' tablature from Bad Aussee near Salzburg. The Italian term 'chitarriglia' may refer to the smaller guitar that used this tuning.

[32] For further information about the instrument, see Pablo Minguet y Yrol, *Reglas . . . par a tañer la bandurria . . .* (Madrid, *c*.1752–74), facs. edn., Geneva: Minkoff Reprint, 1981, 91–8.

[33] The first manuscript ends with forty-three dance pieces for 'Rebeca' (violin) in Italian four-line tablature with bowing indications throughout.

Guerau's tablature is entirely in *punteado* style and seems to require two bourdons. His writing is very lute-like and avoids any 'foreign' stylistic effects, such as *campanelas*. His conservative style and nationalistic repertory are interesting considering that his book is dedicated to the aforementioned Carlos II, who was married to Marie Louise of France, niece of Louis XIV, and whose court was strongly influenced by French (and Italian) style. However, as Guerau (1649–1722) informs us in his preface, he had served in the royal chapel for thirty-five years, and thus began his tenure during the reign of a far more conventional Spanish Habsburg, Philip IV.[34]

Guerau's music is rich in certain types of embellishment, including slurred passagework (*Extrasinos*) and individual ornaments such as the *Trino* or *Aleado* (trill) and *Mordente* (lower mordent), which he discusses at the beginning of the book. These ornaments are an intrinsic part of Guerau's musical style, and to perform one of his pieces without them is tantamount to performing only half the piece. Of course, to play his music *with* the ornaments is quite technically demanding; however, as today's virtuoso guitarists would soon realize, it includes some of the finest music in the Spanish guitar repertory.

It is now time to return briefly to Amat, since other later Spanish and Portuguese publications are actually plagiarisms of his 1596 chord book. These include Andres de Sotos's *Arte para aprender . . . la guitarra* (Madrid, 1760 and 1764) and the almost literal translation into Portuguese by João Leite Pita de Roche in his publication *Liçam instrumental da viola portugueza . . .* (Lisbon, 1752).[35] Still others, such as Pablo Minguet y Yrol's *Reglas, y advertencias generales par tañer la guitarra . . .* (Madrid, [1752]) are compilations of material from the books of Amat, Ruiz de Ribayaz, Sanz, and Santiago de Murcia.[36]

Murcia (*c.* 1682–*c.* 1740) was arguably the most brilliant of all the Spanish guitarists. Furthermore, as he states in his book *Resumen de acompañar la parte con la guitarra . . .* (Antwerp, dated 1714, but issued in 1717), he had been the guitar teacher of the late Queen Maria Luisa Gabriela of Savoy (d. 1714), consort of Philip V of Spain (Carlos II's Bourbon successor), and was thus clearly a member of the musical establishment at the Madrid court. Yet, hardly anything is known about him. Craig Russell, who has convincingly pieced together every shred of information concerning Murcia's life, shows that he was probably the son of Gabriel de Murcia, luthier ('Guitarrero') to the royal chapel; that he may also have been related to the composer Juan Hidalgo; and that he received his musical training in the chapel choir under Francisco Guerau and the composer Antonio Literes (1673–1747).[37]

---

[34] Guerau was also a priest, singer, and composer of vocal music, who was probably active in the same court circles as Juan Hidalgo (*c.* 1616–85) and José Marín (1619–99). See Stein (1993), 301 and 305 and Parets i Serra (2000).

[35] Yakeley and Hall (1995), 57 and Esses (1992), 140.

[36] Esses (1992), 136–39.

[37] Russell (1995*a*), ch. 4.

As the title of his book indicates, Murcia's *Resumen...*[38] opens with an important treatise on continuo playing. Almost as extensive as Matteis's *False consonances...* (London, 1682), it offers instruction on how to realize a figured bass line on guitar, an explanation of the traditional modes and cadential formulas, instruction on reading from G and C clefs, and superb examples of bass realizations in various metres. The treatises of Murcia and Matteis should be the starting point for all Baroque guitarists who intend to play the instrument professionally.[39]

Despite the probability that Guerau was his guitar teacher, Murcia's music could not be more dissimilar. For a start, much of it consists of his arrangements for guitar of the most fashionable dance music performed at the Spanish court—French dance music! *Resumen...* includes fifty-nine *contredances* culled from contemporary Parisian publications—the sort of dances that drew bitter opposition from the conservative Spanish clergy, who considered them immoral.[40] The *contredances* are followed by twenty-five minuets; these, too, are from various collections of French dance music. Like Guerau he also presents his own variations on such traditional Spanish grounds as the Folias, Marizapolos, Las Sombras, and Marsellas, among others. However, while Guerau's idiom is virtually lute-like (for example, strummed chords are exceedingly rare and the notes of his scale passages move from course to adjacent course), Murcia's makes full use of Italian Baroque guitar technique, including strummed chords and cascading scale passages, the notes of which are distributed across non-adjacent courses. Although he does not indicate his tuning and stringing preferences, his mixed tablature strongly indicates that, like Sanz, he did not use a bourdon on the fifth course. Murcia ends his book with three original suites in different keys, the first having five movements, Preludio, Allemanda, Giga, and Zarabanda Despacio, and the remaining ones four, Alemanda, Correnta, Zarabanda Despacio, and Giga. Perhaps the happy blend of French *galant* tunefulness, Italian technique, and Spanish inventiveness that defines his music is also what makes it such a pleasure to listen to and perform.

It was in Mexico that Murcia's last and finest work was discovered: two substantial manuscripts (MEX-M Códice Saldívar No. 4 and GB-Lbl Add. MS 31640) that form a massive, two-part compendium of high-calibre guitar music. The first of the manuscripts now lacks its title page, but the second is entitled 'Passacalles y obras de

---

[38] 'Summary of Accompanying from a figured bass on the Guitar'.

[39] Russell (1981) contains a translation and complete transcription of Murcia's book. Murcia's contemporaries evidently thought his continuo instructions were quite important, since E-Mn MS 881 is a copy of it in its entirety, while both E-G MS B-25 and E-Mn MS 1233 include large portions of it, and Sanz's continuo treatise as well. In addition Minguet y Yrol (*Reglas* of 1752) plagiarizes much of Murcia, while Vargas y Guzman ('Explicacion para tocar la guitara...' [MS], 1776) bases much of his work on Murcia's. See below, Ch. 11.

[40] See Russell (1981), 145–51. The French dance publications include Louis Pecour, *Recueil de dances...* (Paris, 1700), from which Murcia transcribed every single item; Raoul-Auger Feuillet, *Recueil de contradances...* (Paris, 1706); and Pecour, *Noveau recueil...* (Paris, 1712).

guitarra . . .' and is dated 1732.[41] Both manuscripts are in Murcia's own hand and contain an extraordinary range of instrumental genres, including, among others, suites, battle pieces, and Spanish, French, and Mexican dances with *diferencias*. Fortunately, Murcia's music has received the attention of scholars over the years, with the result that his printed book and GB–Lbl Add. MS 31640 are available both in facsimile and in reliable modern editions that include Murcia's own tablature.[42] Michael Lorimer was the first to study Códice Saldívar No. 4 in detail and to recognize that it was an important manuscript by Murcia. There are now two facsimile editions and a reliable transcription of that work as well.[43]

As alluded to previously, Murcia's enormous skill as an arranger of French dance music is demonstrated in his guitar book of 1714;[44] however, as the second of his two Mexican manuscripts, 'Passacalles y obras de guitarra . . .' ('obras', in this case, meaning suites) reveals, he was also an excellent compiler, editor, and arranger of the works of other guitarists. Several of the movements in his suites are Murcia's arrangements in the normal *e'* tuning of scordatura pieces from François Campion's 1705 book. Other movements are by Visée (1682), Corbetta (1648 and 1671), and Le Cocq (pieces that are also found in the Castillon manuscript). Some have been slightly altered by Murcia. Creating suites comprised of movements written by several composers was a common practice in the Baroque, and many of Murcia's open with one of his own preludes, followed by movements by the composers named above. For unknown reasons Murcia does not name them in either this source or his printed book. Yet, unquestionably, his own compositions—the highly imaginative *Passacalles*, the *diferencias* on Spanish dances and grounds in the first of his two Mexican manuscripts (Códice Saldívar No. 4), the suites in his 1714 publication, and the outstanding preludes in his 1732 manuscript—shine as brightly as theirs, and in many instances outshine them.

It is fitting that the Spanish repertory for the Baroque guitar ends so splendidly with the works of Sanz, Santa Cruz, Guerau, and Murcia, for, as will be seen in Part III, Spanish musicians and *guitarreros* would soon lead the way to a new era for the guitar and its music.

---

[41] The heading of the table of contents on fo. 2 indicates that the second MS is, indeed, the second book (*L.° 2.°*). According to Russell (1995*a*), 133 and 134, the *Passacalles* . . . was found and purchased in Puebla, Mexico, by the British collector Julian Marshall, who sold it in 1881 to the British Museum. The first manuscript was found in 1943 in Léon, Guanajuato, by Gabriel Saldívar, and remains in private hands in Mexico City.

[42] For example, E. M. Lowenfeld, 'Santiago de Murcia's Thorough-Bass Treatise for Baroque Guitar (1714)' (Master's thesis, City University of New York, 1974); Hall (1983) and Russell (1981).

[43] The manuscript was first produced in facsimile as a labour of love by the guitarist Michael Lorimer, *Saldívar Codex No. 4, Vol. 1* (Santa Barbara: Michael Lorimer, 1987). Russell (1995) i and ii is a comprehensive study of its contents, plus a facsimile and transcription.

[44] It also includes his arrangements for guitar of movements from various of the violin sonatas in Corelli's Op. 5.

TABLE 10.1. *Sources of Spanish guitar music in Spain, Portugal, and the New World to* c.*1750*

A. PRINTED BOOKS

1626   Amat, Juan Carlos [y], *Guitarra española de cinco ordenes* . . . (Lérida)

> Not listed in RISM. Later edn. of a lost 1596 print. Further edns. of the 1626 print are dated 1627, 1640,
> 1674. The Barcelona print of 1639 is an edn. of the original 1596 print, which mistakenly gives 1586 as its
> date in the preface. All other edns. are posthumous 18th-c. publications with anonymous additions,
> which usually include the 'Tractat brev' in Catalan and additional material on the 'vandola'. Last known
> edn.: Valencia, 1819. Facs. edn. of a *c.*1761 edn. Monaco: Éditions Chanterelle S.A., 1980.

1626   Briceño, Luis de, *Metodo mui facilissimo para aprender a tañer la guitarra a lo español* . . .
            (Paris)

> Facs. edn.: Geneva: Minkoff Reprint, 1972.

1640   Doizi de Velasco, Nicolao, *Nuevo modo de cifra para tañer la guitarra* . . . (Naples)

*c.*1650   [Corbetta, Francesco, *Guitarra española y sus diferencias de sones*]

> Lost, but survives in part, perhaps, in the anon. print sold in London at Sotheby's, 20 Nov. 1991.

1674   Sanz, Gaspar, *Instruccion de musica sobre la guitarra española* . . . [and] *Documentos, y
            advertencias generales* . . . (Zaragoza)

> The first section is Sanz's 'Libro primo', although not indicated as such in this edn. This, and a second
> edn. of 1675, contain neither the engraved plates nor the chart showing the left-hand fingering of *alfabeto*
> chords.

1675   Sanz, Gaspar, *Instruccion de musica sobre la guitarra española* . . . (Zaragoza)

> Third edn., to which he added his *Libro segundo*.

1675   Sanz, Gaspar, *Instruccion de musica sobre la guitarra española* . . . (Zaragoza)

> Fourth edn., to which he added his *Tercer libro*. Fifth and sixth edns. were also published in 1675; and
> seventh and eighth edns. in 1697. (Facs. edn. of a composite of the third and eighth edns.: Zaragoza:
> Institución 'Ferdinando el Católico' de la Excelentíssima Disputación Provincial, 1966)

1676   Ruiz de Ribayaz, Lucas, *Luz y norte musical para caminar por las cifras de la guitarra
            española* . . . (Madrid)

> Facs. edn.: Geneva: Minkoff Reprint, 1976.

1694   Guerau, Francisco, *Poema harmonico, compuesto de varias cifras por el temple de la guitarra
            española* . . . (Madrid)

> Facs. edns.: London: Tecla Editions, 1977 and Madrid: Editorial Alpuerto S.A., 2000.

1714   Murcia, Santiago de, *Resumen de acompañar la parte con la guitarra* . . . [Antwerp]

> Facs. edn.: Monaco: Éditions Chanterelle S.A., 1980.

1752   Pita de Roche, João Liete, *Liçam instrumental da viola portugueza ou de ninfas, de cinco
            ordens* . . . (Lisbon)

> Portugese translation of Amat.

1752   Minguet y Yrol, Pablo, *Reglas y advertencias generales para tañer la guitarra, tiple, y vandola,
            con variedad de sones* . . . (Madrid)

> One of several pamphlets for various instruments issued by Minguet in *c.*1752–74 that were sold either
> separately or under the collective title *Reglas y advertencias generales que enseñan el modo de tañer todos los
> instrumentos mejores* . . . Facs. edn. of the latter: Geneva: Minkoff Reprint, 1981.

[1760]   Sotos, Andres de, *Arte para aprender con facilidad, y sin maestro, á templar y tañer rasgado la
            guitarra de cinco órdenes* . . . [Madrid]

> Another edn.: 1764. Facs. edn.: Valencia: Librerías 'Paris-Valencia', n.d.

TABLE 10.1. *continued*

B. MANUSCRIPTS

Location	Source	Date	Remarks
B-Bc	MS Littera S. no. 5.615	1730–9	Anthology that includes four pieces by D. Michel Perez de Zavala and one by Gaspar Sanz. (For details, see Table 8.2.)
E-Bc	MS M. 165	c.1700 (1995), 59	Anon. guitar tutor. Booklet bound in a miscellany. Catalan *cifras*. Yakeley and Hall
E-Bc	MS M. 691/2(4)	c.1720	Anon. MS of mixed tablature. One 'preludio', one 'correnta', nine 'minuetos', three 'sarabandas'. Also some Catalan *cifras*. Pennington (1981), 119–21; Esses (1992), 133
E-Bbc	MS 759/7	c.1700	Anon. Melodic line with *alfabeto*. Stein (1987), 366
E-GRu	MS caja B-25	c.1716	Theoretical material compiled by Manuel Valero from the works of Sanz and Murcia. This in turn copied by Joseph Trapero (1763) in E-Mn MS M. 1233. Esses (1992), 141–2, 770
E-Mn	MS M. 811	'1705'	'Libro de diferentes cifras de guitara escojidas de los mejores autores . . .'. Anon. compilation from the works of Murcia (1714), Pellegrini (1650), Sanz (1674), and many others. RISM B/VII, 201–2; Pennington (1981), 98–9; Esses (1992), 129–31, 168–9, 174
E-Mn	MS M. 881	'1726'	Anon. MS copy of Murcia 1714, 5–56. Castilian *cifras* have been added to his *alfabeto* chart. Esses (1992), 140; Yakeley and Hall (1995), 60
E-Mn	MS M. 1233	'1763'	Copy by Joseph Trapero of E-GRu MS B-25, which, in turn, is theoretical material copied from Sanz (1674) and Murcia (1714). RISM B/VII, 202–3; Pennington (1981), 112–13; Esses (1992), 142
E-Mn	MS M. 2209	c.1699	'Livro donde se veran pazacalles . . . para biguela hordinaria . . .' by Antonio de Santa Cruz. Punteado tablature collection of *passacalles* and *diferencias* on Spanish themes. RISM B/VII, 203; Esses (1992), 127–9, 173
E-Mn	MS M. 2618	'1659'	Violin MS in Italian tablature by 'Gaspar', which includes written instructions on tuning a guitar from the notes of a violin. Pennington (1981), 115–19

Location	Source	Date	Remarks
E-Mn	MS M. 5917	*c.*1680	'Arte de la guitarra . . .' by Joseph Guerrero. Four folios of basic chord and tuning information (damaged) in a miscellany. Includes traditional chord names and Castilian *cifras*. RISM B/VII, 204; Esses (1992), 157; Yakeley and Hall (1995), 60
GB-Cfm	MS Mus. 727	late 17th c.	Spanish songs with *punteado* guitar accompaniments by José Marín. RISM B/VII, 70–1
GB-Lbl	Add. MS 31640	'1732'	'Passacalles y obras de guitarra . . .' by Santiago de Murcia. Volume ii to MEX-M Códice Saldívar No. 4. RISM B/VII, 182–3; Russell (1981); Hall (1983); Esses (1992), 135–6. Facs. edn.: Monaco: Éditions Chanterelle, 1979
MEX-Mn	MS 1560	mid-18th c.	Anon. guitar and violin MS that includes music copied from Murcia (1714) and Corelli, Op. 5. RISM B/VII, 208 confuses this with MEX-M Saldívar No. 4; Pennington (1981), 103–10; Hall (1983), App. III a and b.
MEX-Msaldívar	Códice Saldívar No. 2	late 17th c.	'Metodo de citara' by Sebastian de Aguirre. Pieces for 'vihuela de cinco ordenes' (fos. 31–7) in a cittern MS. Stevenson (1968), 234–5; RISM B/VII, 208; Russell (1995), 13–14, 21–4
MEX-Msaldívar	Códice Saldívar No. 4	*c.*1732	MS of mixed tablature by Santiago de Murcia. Companion volume to GB-Lbl Add. MS 31640. Russell (1995). Facs. edns.: Santa Barbara: Michael Lorimer, 1987 and Russell (1995)
P-Cug	M. M. 97	early 18th c.	'Cifras de viola por varios autores' compiled by Joseph Carneyro Tavares Lamacense. MS of *punteado* tablature that includes music by Portugese composers (e.g. Antonio Marques), an anthology of pieces from French and Italian guitar books (e.g. Corbetta, 1643 and Pellegrini, 1650), pieces in scordatura, tuning instructions for a 'Machinho', tablature pieces for 'Bandurra', and a tablature section for 'Rebeca'. Danner (1979), 15
P-Lcg	[no shelf no.]	early 18th c.	Anon. MS of *punteado* tablature containing repertory similar to that of P-Cug MS97. Includes a treatise and section of pieces notated in 'Cifras Aritmeticas', a duet for two 'violas', and a section of tablature for 'Bandurra'. No literature

TABLE 10.1. *continued*

Location	Source	Date	Remarks
P-Ln	F.C.R. MS Ne. 1	mid 18th c.	Anon. MS of *punteado* tablature that includes arrangements of pieces by Lully, Campra, and Corelli. French and Portuguese/Spanish dance pieces. Azevedo (1987). Facs. edn.: Lisbon: Instituto Português do Património Cultural, 1987
RA-BArm	[no shelf no.]	*c.* 1670–1709	'Libro de varias curiosidades'. A miscellany by the Franciscan friar Gregorio de Zuola, written in Peru. Contains an *alfabeto* chart corresponding to nine Castilian *cifras* and 14 traditional chord names. Esses (1992), 157–9; Yakeley and Hall (1995), 31 and 60. *Note*: Yakeley and Hall (1995) cites further vocal sources with *cifras*. These range from single loose sheets to items found in various *cancioneros*.

A Brief Guide to Reading and Interpreting Baroque Guitar Tablatures

A. Tablature Notation

1. Italian Tablature

The Italian tablature system was used by Italian as well as Spanish composers. The five-line staff below represents the five courses of the guitar (the first four lines for the four-course instrument), and the numbers placed on or between the lines represent the frets to be fingered: i.e. 0 = open string, 1 = first fret, 2 = second fret, 3 = third fret, etc. For the tenth, eleventh, and twelfth frets, x, ii, and 12 are used:

Ex. App. 1.1

The same transcribed as for modern guitar.

The rhythm signs, usually ordinary, free-standing mensural notes, are placed above the staff over particular numbers and indicate when each note or chord, represented by the numbers, begins. The duration of any individual note depends on how long the left-hand finger can remain holding it before another note must be played. It is assumed that bass notes will be held for as long as possible. The value of any given rhythm sign remains valid until a new rhythm sign appears:

Ex. App. 1.2

Ex. App. 1.2 *continued*

For the right hand, the only notation signs are single dots under individual notes. These are found chiefly in running scale passages and signal that the note is to be played with the index finger. In later seventeenth-century music, two dots under a note mean that the middle finger is to be used.

Only five- (and four-) course guitar tablature is illustrated here; however, the same system and principles apply to lute tablatures. Simply add a sixth line to represent a sixth course, etc.

2. *French Tablature*

This system differs from the Italian in the following ways:

(*a*) While the courses of the guitar are still indicated by five (or four) lines, in the French tablature system they are in reverse order:

1st course _____

2nd course _____

3rd course _____

4th course _____

5th course _____

(*b*) Instead of numbers to indicate the frets, letters are used: a = open string, b = first fret, c = second fret, d = third fret, etc. Note that the letter 'j' was not yet used:

Ex. App. 1.3

(*c*) Rhythm signs are often represented by the following symbols or flags:

Ex. App. 1.4

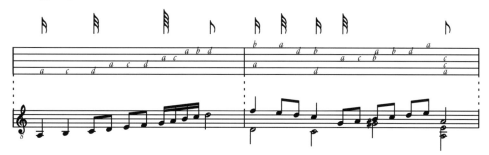

Hence, the music in the second example above looks like this in French-style tablature:

Ex. App. 1.5

As with the Italian system, the value of the rhythm sign remains in force for all subsequent notes until a new sign appears.

Knowledge of the foregoing information is sufficient to cope with the majority of *punteado* tablatures found in the repertory of sixteenth-century Italian-, Spanish-, and French-style four-course guitar music. However, tablatures for seventeenth- and eighteenth-century five-course guitar music require a familiarity with some additional signs for ornaments and idiomatic effects. These are discussed below under the heading 'Ornaments'. But first, familiarity with another important form of notation, created especially for the guitar, is necessary.

3. The Alfabeto System

There were a few chord systems in use during the early seventeenth century, but the Italian *alfabeto* system was the most widespread, and many fine composers employed it, either alone or mixed in with the *punteado*-style tablature described above. In this system a specific letter or symbol signifies a specific chord:

Ex. App. 1.6

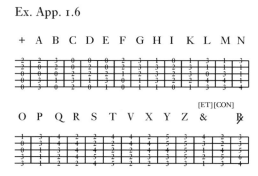

Of course, the *alfabeto* letters have no relationship whatever to the actual harmonic name of the chord; they are merely symbols. Notice that some of the chords use the same finger pattern, but in a higher position. That caused some authors of *alfabeto* books to use a modified *alfabeto* system in which a number over the basic chord pattern shows the position that the fingers must be shifted to in order to play the same chord in the higher position. Here, for example, are chords in the third and fifth positions:

Ex. App. 1.7

G3 G5 H3 H5 M3 M5 N3 N5

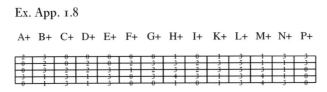

Further refinements to the *alfabeto* system include Foscarini's 'alfabeto dissonante', in which the basic chord is changed to include a dissonance or suspension:

Ex. App. 1.8

A+ B+ C+ D+ E+ F+ G+ H+ I+ K+ L+ M+ N+ P+

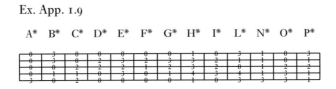

Calvi's 'alfabeto falso' involves a different arrangement of dissonances:

Ex. App. 1.9

A* B* C* D* E* F* G* H* I* L* N* O* P*

So does Ricci's 'lettere tagliate':

Ex. App. 1.10

A^t C^t D^t E^t

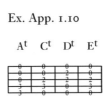

And Millioni calls different inversions and positions of the same basic chord 'lettere false'.

Some *alfabeto* diagrams merely present the frets to be fingered and leave the remaining tablature lines blank. The blank lines simply mean that those strings are to be played open. With only a few exceptions, the *alfabeto* chord involves all five courses, which are strummed in a variety of ways. The occasional exceptions to the rule are discussed below. The *alfabeto* system should be memorized (at least to the letter 'I').

The usual method used for indicating rhythmic strumming shows a single horizontal line with the *alfabeto* letters placed either above or below it. The line normally was divided up into bar-like segments, and short vertical lines were used to indicate an up stroke or down stroke. A line hanging down from the horizontal line meant the chord was to be strummed with the right hand travelling in the direction of the floor, striking the fifth to the first courses in that order. A line sticking up from the horizontal line meant that the chord was to be strummed with the right hand travelling upwards, striking the first to the fifth courses in that order.

For music written entirely in *alfabeto* notation, the right hand should be positioned near the place where the neck and the body of the instrument meet, as several of the early writers have recommended. A time signature appears at the beginning of such pieces as follows: 3 = triple metre; c or ¢ = duple metre. Frequently, mensural notes are found above the horizontal line over the appropriate letter to indicate the rhythmic values of the chord(s). To illustrate, here is an *Aria detta del Gran Duca* from Sanseverino's 1620 book:

Ex. App. 1.11

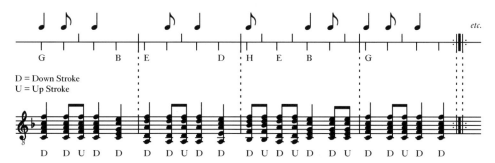

(*Note*: The inversions of the chords will be different, of course, with different stringing arrangements. Sanseverino uses bourdons.) For an introduction to *alfabeto* solo music, the publications of Sanseverino (1620) and Calvi (1646) are recommended for the relative clarity with which the music is presented. A considerable number of books containing *alfabeto* solos are included in Table 6.2. A few are available in facsimile editions.

Although the basic *alfabeto* system indicated above was by far the most common, certain writers personalized it by altering one or two small details. For this reason, when working with facsimile editions of the early guitar books, avoid confusion by always studying the composer's own *alfabeto* diagram (generally found at the beginning of the book) before proceeding to the music. Foscarini's *alfabeto* chart from page 1 of the *c.*1632 edition of his book is shown in Pl. App. I.1.

Other contemporary systems of chord notation, using numbers for symbols, seem to have been Spanish in both origin and usage: the 'Castilian' system used by Briceño and Ribayaz, and the 'Catalan' system used by Amat and Minguet. As very few books and manuscripts employ these systems, the contemporary diagrams shown in Pls. App. I.2 and App. I.3 should provide an adequate explanation of them. The Castilian system is beautifully illustrated by Briceño in his 1626 book. Note that Briceño presents the chords ('puntos') in French tablature and places the numbers and other signs above their respective chords. Amat's 'Catalan' system

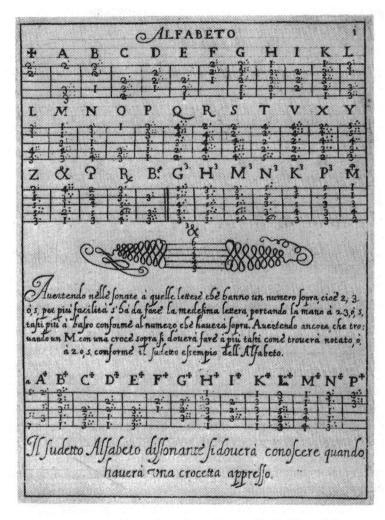

PL. App. I.1. *Alfabeto* chart from Giovanni Paolo Foscarini,
I quatro libri della chitarra spagnola (*c.*1632), p. 1 of the engraved plates

Pl. App. I.2. *Cifras* chart from Luis de Briceño, *Metodo mui facilissimo* (Paris, 1626), fo. 4ᵛ

is given in Minguet's 1774 book, in which twelve different numbered chords in major keys, marked *n* ('naturales'), and twelve in minor keys, marked *b* ('b mollados'), are illustrated. A chord indicated by *1ⁿ* equals E major, *2ⁿ* equals A major; while *1ᵇ* equals E minor, *2ᵇ* equals A minor, and so on (see Pl. App. I.3).

4. Mixed Tablatures

In mixed tablature, chords are not written out in full (as in lute-style tablature), but are each represented by an *alfabeto* symbol, which appears within the tablature staff. The lines indicating stroke direction appear directly below the *alfabeto* symbol (or a bit after it), and the mensural noteheads indicating the rhythm, as previously noted, appear above the staff:

Ex. App. 1.12

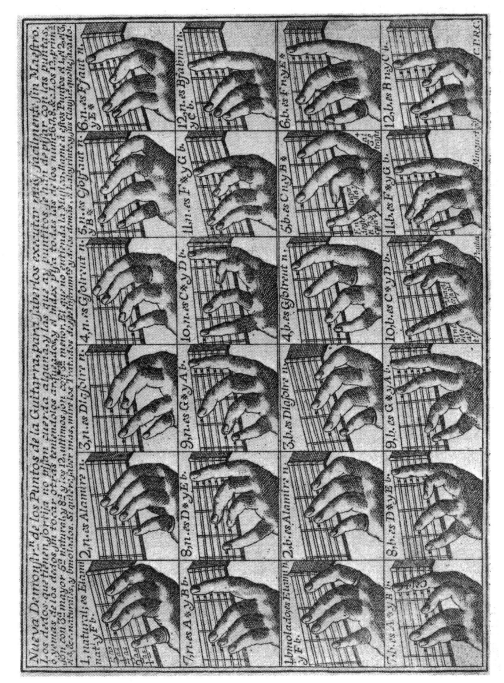

Pl. App. I.3.   *Cifras* chart from Pablo Minguet y Yrol, *Reglas y advertencias* (Madrid, 1774), pl. 2–2

Only chords that do not fit within the 'standard' *alfabeto* system are written out in full. Unlike *alfabeto* chords, the fully written-out ones should be played using only the specific notes indicated. Occasionally, one encounters the following example, which should be interpreted as a struck chord employing only the following four notes:

Ex. App. 1.13

As an illustration of mixed tablature style, here is a section from a *Ciaccona* by Francesco Corbetta from his 1648 collection:

Ex. App. 1.14

Mixed tablatures appeared less frequently towards the end of the seventeenth century in Italy, and French guitar publications generally omitted *alfabeto* notation from their tablatures and used fully written-out chords in French-style lute tablature. In some French tablatures, such as Visée's, the mensural noteheads served both their normal rhythmic function and, when placed inside the staff, also indicated the stroke direction. For example, when the tail of the notehead hangs down, the chord that appears just before it receives a full down stroke for the time value indicated by the notehead. If the tail points upwards, an up stroke is required for that time value. Be sure to distinguish between noteheads within the staff and noteheads above.

In French guitar tablatures, common chords are often written with only the fingered notes on the staff and the remaining lines left blank. When a down or up stroke is also indicated, it is assumed that the blank lines are to be played as open strings. For example:

Ex. App. 1.15

There are instances when a strummed chord requires only four or three courses, however. In such cases, generally a dot will be found on the line or lines, which are *not* to be played:

Ex. App. 1.16

Of course, the strum must be executed with care, so the right-hand fingers do not strike any unwanted courses. And, when no dots appear on the lines, it is up to the player to decide whether to eliminate any of the courses from the strummed chord.

Before going on to a discussion of ornamentation, one additional point concerning the *alfabeto* symbols in Italian mixed tablature should be mentioned. Sometimes a single note is found above the staff after a full *alfabeto* chord. This note has a stroke sign (usually for an up stroke) beneath it. Most of the time this can be interpreted as a single note to be plucked with an up stroke of the index finger of the right hand (as though there were a dot instead of a stroke sign beneath the note). Occasionally, however, it means that the composer wants the entire previous chord to be strummed again, this time with the additional note added to the fabric of the chord:

Ex. App. 1.17

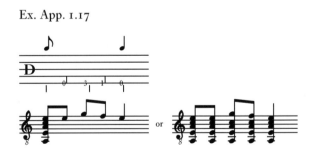

The early writers are rarely clear on these points, and, once again, it is the responsibility of the player to decide what the composer had in mind and how to play the passage.

B. The Ornaments

No ornament signs are found in the sixteenth-century guitar sources; however, that does not mean that ornaments (in the form of graces, i.e. trills and mordents) were not played during this period. The reason music in printed books contained no ornament signs probably has something to do with the technical difficulties involved in the typesetting, because later, when music books were engraved, these problems were eliminated. Of course, the main type of ornamentation during the sixteenth century was running passagework, which is found in abundance, fully written out, in the tablatures. As for single ornaments, we know that during this period trills and mordents were used very often in lute music—for some commentators, such as Bermudo writing in 1555, too often! And since the two instruments shared a great deal of musical material during this period, the lute sources provide useful information on this type of ornamentation.

From the beginning of the seventeenth century the guitar books provide us with this sort of information, and a whole range of new (and old) ornaments are described (though perhaps not as carefully as we would like). The following are ornaments used in the guitar's two basic playing styles.

1. Battente (Rasgueado) *Style*

(*a*) *Trillo*

This ornament, described in different ways by various seventeenth-century guitarists, is a series of rapid down and upstrokes:

The trillo is made with the finger called the index, touching all the strings downwards and upwards with rapidity . . . (Abatessa, 1627, fo. 3ʳ)

. . . when the player has had practice in moving his hand well and has learned the fingerboard of the guitar, and learned all the chords, it will then be necessary to vary the [right] hand with different kinds of *trillo* and *repicco*. And concerning the way of trilling is the advice that with the thumb and the middle finger [respectively] one makes the strokes. For example: A ⊤⊥, which is made with a downward stroke with the thumb and then an up stroke [with the thumb] and similarly with the middle finger [for the succeeding stroke sign]. This is the technique of this percussive ornament if a *trillo* is needed. Note further that the *trillo* is also made with the index finger dividing the stroke signs into four parts, i.e. into four quavers if there is a minim. The first down, the second up, the third down, and the fourth up. But all of these should be made with a speed corresponding to the tempo of the piece. (Foscarini, *c.*1630, fo. 4ʳ)

Foscarini advocates playing two strokes to every one that is printed, and gives the player the option of when to use the *trillo*. One style of executing these strokes is given by Ricci (1677, 13): 'The four strokes should be bound together in a winding fashion like a wheel. . .'.

(b) Repicco

The *repicco* is similar to the *trillo*, but often much more intricate and hence more rhythmically charged.

> To play a *repicco* one plays four strokes, i.e. two down and two up. The first down is played with the middle finger, the second down with the thumb, the third up is played with the thumb and the fourth up with the index, playing however only the first course. A *repicco* lasts for two [printed] strokes [⊤⊥]. (Pico, 1608, 9)

This is the basic four-stroke pattern, which, like that of the *trillo*, doubles the number of printed strokes in the same amount of time. These two ornaments are very different in terms of their sound and stresses, however, because the *repicco* brings the thumb into play:

> The *repicco* is made with [two] fingers: the index or middle and the thumb, which touches all the strings downwards and returns rapidly upward. (Abatessa, 1627, fo. 3ᵛ)

Abatessa does not give away much here, but there is a possibility that what he is actually describing is a variation on the four-stroke pattern—that is, a three-stroke pattern: thumb down, thumb up, index (or middle) up.

Foscarini describes the three principal stroke patterns for playing 'picchi' and 'repicchi' on the guitar:

> Firstly. Wanting to play a pattern such as this for example: **B** ⊤⊥, you let the two fingers, middle and index, brush softly [downwards] and follow with the thumb, making the sound of the stroke [⊤] in three consecutive blows in the same amount of time as the stroke. For the upstroke, you should do the opposite: the thumb begins up, followed by the index and middle.
>
> The second way: having played the above, then make quickly and simply with all four fingers [a, m, i, p] one stroke [⊤] and repeat the pattern as above. You should use this style in slow pieces such as *Toccate, passi e mezi, Arie di Firenze* etc.
>
> The third way will be, in playing this, for example **C** ⊤⊤⊥, you should brush downward with the middle finger, the thumb following and the index quickly makes the same motion, upwards and downwards, making the strings sound many times repeated, adding with the index and middle fingers, i.e. so that the index will brush the strings in downward motion and the middle finger goes up. This method will sort itself out pleasantly by ear. (Foscarini, *c.*1630, fo. 4ʳ⁻ᵛ)

Foscarini is not very clear in his descriptions, but his 'first' way seems to require a triplet for each printed stroke; 'the second way' requires four notes per stroke; and 'the third way' appears to be a description of a continuous roll, such as might be used today by Flamenco guitarists.

In his 1671 book Corbetta provides two even more complicated versions of the *repicco*. The music is for a guitar with a bourdon on the fourth course only:

Ex. App. 1.18

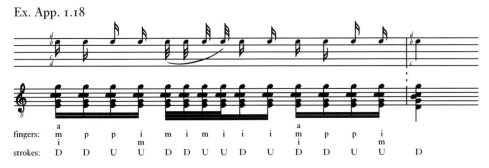

He comments:

You will see the example of a *repicco* in a *Ciaccona* [p. 72] where the note with the extended stem is played with the thumb. Having begun first with the fingers, the thumb then plays the same and this is repeated as upbeats. Notice that the four tied beats indicate that one must play the first note with the middle finger, and the next with the index, and so again as up strokes, all at a faster speed, and then continue with the fingers and thumb [pattern]. (Corbetta, 1671, 3)

In the next *Ciaccona* [p. 75] you will see another *repicco* [marked, 'Batterie'] . . . Where you see six quaver strokes play four of them from the third course downwards, and moving the hand, play the next two strokes on the other two courses, the first and second, without touching the other [third, fourth, and fifth] ones. After changing the chord, play in the same way for the other six [quavers]. And changing the chord at the next four, hit the first quaver loudly, and the other three softly. Do the same on changing the chords at the other [groups of four] until the [pattern of the] first six begins again. Where you find an *f* this means play the first of the four strokes loudly, and in this way you will achieve a beautiful *repicco*. (Corbetta, 1671, 3)

Ex. App. 1.19

2. *Pizzicato* (Punteado) *Style*

In seventeenth-century guitar tablature, the general term for an ornament applied to a single note is *tremolo* in Italian, *agrémen* in French, and *habilidade* or *afecto* in Spanish. Each of those terms is defined as a short melodic formula gracing a single note. In other words, the term *tremolo*, for example, does not necessarily refer to a specific ornament. Therefore, when a *tremolo* sign appears under a particular note in the tablature, it often means that the player should apply an ornament to that note, be it a trill, a mordent, an appoggiatura, a slur, vibrato, or an arpeggio—whichever one judges to be appropriate to the particular musical passage. Some guitarists might be surprised to find the slur and vibrato on the list; however, they were regarded as ornaments by early guitarists and not, as they are today, an integral part of guitar technique.

(*a*) Trill (Italian: *trillo* or *tremolo*; Spanish: *trino* or *aleado*; French: *tremblement*)

Despite their frequent use of trills, seventeenth-century guitar composers rarely tell us how to play them; neither it seems, is there any consensus among them as to what sign to use to indicate that a trill is to be played:

This is the sign for the *trillo* ⸜ . Where it is found on a line, one ought to trill [*trillar*] that string . . . (Bartolotti, 1640, fo. 2ᵛ)

The letter *t*, above or below the course, indicates the *trillo* which is played with the most convenient finger of the left hand for as long as appropriate to the note so marked. (Anonymous, *Conserto vago*, 1645, p. 3)

The sign **T•** means the *tremolo*, which is made with the little finger on the first course in the chords C and E [of the *alfabeto*]. In the B it is made with the same finger on the fourth course. In the F chord it is made with the third finger on the third course. In the I chord it is made on the second course with the same finger, etc. (Calvi, 1646, p. 6)

You will also find a small line with two little dots like this: ⁊ called *trino* or *aleado*. The Italians mark it with a T and two little dots. It is executed with the left hand by placing a convenient finger at the fret so marked with a number. Strike the course with another finger of the same hand without stopping, one or two frets higher, depending upon the key. (Guerau, 1684, fo. 5ᵛ)

The importance of reading the technical information given by the guitar composers in the prefaces of their books before playing their music cannot be stressed enough. Here, for example, are the various signs they use to indicate the trill:

T	Granata, 1674; Sanz (*trino*), 1674
T•	Corbetta (*tremolo*), 1643; Calvi (*tremolo*), 1646; Granata (*tremolo*), 1646; Pellegrini (*tremolo*), 1650
.T.	Foscarini (*tremolo*), *c.*1630 (T• or .T. could mean the involvement of one or two frets, respectively, i.e. a half or a whole step of the scale)
t	*Conserto vago* (*trillo*), 1645; Corrette (*tremblement*), 1763
⁊	Bartolotti (*trillo*), 1640; Corbetta (*tremolo*), 1648; Guerau (*trino* or *aleado*), 1684
•	Valdambrini (*trillo*), 1646
)	Visée (*tremblement*), 1682
x	Corbetta (*tremolo/tremblement*), 1671 and (*tremblement*), 1674; Campion (*tremblement*), 1705

Notice that Granata gives different signs in his books of 1646 and 1674, while Corbetta changes both the sign and the term for it in almost every book. Clearly, the prefatory material of one guitar book can only be applied to the music in that book, and it cannot be assumed that the same information will apply to the music in another book—even if both books are by the same composer!

(*b*) Mordent (Italian: *mordente*; Spanish: *mordente*; French: *martellement*, *pincé*)

There is far less confusion surrounding the use of the mordent than the trill; however, signs for the mordent do vary from source to source:

✶	Bartolotti (*mordente*), *c.*1655; Visée (*martellement*), 1682
‿	Sanz *(mordente)*, 1674
)	Corbetta (*martellement*), 1674; Guerau (*mordente*), 1694; Campion (*martellement*), 1705; Murcia (*mordente*), 1714
v or +	Corrette (*martellement*, *pincé*), 1763

Notice that two of these signs have been used by several guitar composers to indicate the trill! It is perhaps worth restating the importance of reading each composer's preface before coming to any conclusions about the meaning of his ornament signs.

The mordent is normally played:

Ex. App. 1.20

Bartolotti provides the following example in his guitar book of *c.*1655:

Ex. App. 1.21

'Modo per far il mordente'

(*c*) Appoggiatura (Italian: *appoggiatura, per appogiar le corde*; Spanish: *apoyamento, esmorsata, ligadura*; French: *cheute, petite chute*)

There are two types of appoggiatura, the ascending and the descending, and various signs are used to indicate when to play them:

Descending:	T	Pesori, *c.*1650
	x	Corbetta (*tremolo* or *tremblement*), 1671
	‿	Sanz (*esmorsata*), 1674
Ascending:	d̲	Bartolotti (*per appogiar le corde*), *c.*1655; Campion (*petite chute*), 1705
	d⌢	Corbetta (*cheute*), 1671
	b‿	Visée (*cheute*), 1682
	‿	Sanz (*apoyamento*), 1674

Notice that Sanz uses the same sign for the appoggiatura as he does for the mordent, and the same sign for both the descending and ascending appoggiatura. This usage is explained, more or less, in his preface.

Bartolotti (*c.*1655, fo. 3ʳ) notates the ascending appoggiatura like this:

Ex. App. 1.22

'Modo per appogiar le corde'

Corbetta (1671, p. 9) gives both types; the ascending he calls 'cheute', and the descending, like the trill in several of his books, he calls 'tremolo' or 'tremblement':

Ex. App. 1.23

Gaspar Sanz also has a specific name for each type: *esmorsata* for the descending, and *apoyamento* for the ascending.

(*d*) Slur (Italian: *strascino*; Spanish: *extrasino*; French: *tirade*, *cheute*)

Slurs are executed with the left hand after plucking only the initial note with the right— exactly as modern guitarists are taught to play them—and are notated with curved lines above and below the tablature notes, thus:

Ex. App. 1.24

Because the sound of slurred notes is so different from ones that are individually plucked, it is not surprising that the early guitarists and lutenists considered slurs to be ornamental devices.

Occasionally one encounters a large slur mark involving more than one course. Presumably, the intention was for the player to divide the large slur into more than one, as in the following:

Ex. App. 1.25

It should be noted that slurs are absent from sixteenth-century tablatures, be they for lute or guitar, in printed books *and* manuscripts. Apparently, slur marks first appeared in Girolamo Kapsperger's engraved publication *Libro primo d'intavolatura di chitarrone* (1604). The first guitar source containing slurs was probably Foscarini's *c.*1630 publication. It might be reasonable to propose, therefore, that slurs not be used for the sixteenth-century guitar repertory.

In seventeenth-century guitar music, slurs are used to produce some rather interesting rhythmic effects. Groupings of slurs tend to be quite irregular, often extending over bar lines. Naturally, the first note of a slur grouping, being the only one that is plucked, is stronger than the others, and this produces rhythmic stresses in all parts of the bar. To illustrate, here is a portion of a *Chiacona* by Corbetta (1648, p. 29):

Ex. App. 1.26

Rhythmic variety is characteristic of all guitar music of the period, so one should not be tempted to regularize the slur patterns, as so many modern editors have done.

(*e*)Vibrato (Italian: *acento, accento; trillo, tremolo sforzato*; Spanish: *temblor*; French: *miolement, miaullement, plainte, flatement*)

The signs for vibrato are:

⋊⋉   Foscarini, *c.*1630; Bartolotti, 1640 (*trillo, sforzato*); Corbetta, 1643 and 1648 (*tremolo sforzato*); Corbetta, 1671 (*acento* or *flatement*); Sanz, 1674 (*temblor*); Visée, 1682 (*miolement*); Guerau, 1694 (*temblor*); Campion, 1705 (*miaulement*); Corrette, 1763 (*plainte*)

ſſ   Pellegrini, 1650 (*tremolo sforzato*)

Vibrato was used primarily on higher pitched notes; only occasionally was it used in the bass. As the Italian term 'accento' implies, it was used to accent and emphasize specific notes, usually the highest one in a phrase. Vibrato was described as being suitable for the vihuela as early as 1557 by Luis Venegas de Henestrosa (*Libro de cifra nueva para tecla, harpa y vihuela*). Lutenists first mention it in the early seventeenth century. Foscarini was the first to describe it for the guitar:

A sharp sign being placed under a number: ⋊⋉ . . ., you should separate the [thumb of the left] hand from the guitar, putting the most convenient finger at the number shown, and shake the hand back and forth. This will produce, as far as possible, a sustaining, bit by bit, of the sound of the string. (Foscarini, *c.*1630, fo. 3[r])

Note his instruction to free the left hand from the neck. The same advice is given by several other guitar composers and suggests a quite strong vibrato. Others, however, make no mention of the freeing of the hand:

This sign: ⋊⋉ like a double tremolo is called *Accento*. It is made by shaking the [left] hand with the finger fixed on the note of the course to which [the sign] is put. (Corbetta, 1671, p. 3)

This sign: ⋊⋉ indicates *temblor*. It is performed by plucking the string with the right hand and then moving the left hand from side to side without lifting the finger from the fret. (Guerau, 1694, fo. 4[v]) (*f*) Arpeggio (Italian: *arpeggio*; Spanish: *harpeado*; French: *arpège*)

The signs for the arpeggio are:

   ƒ: *Conserto vago*, 1645; Valdambrini, 1646; Bartolotti, *c.*1655; Sanz, 1674
   :/: Roncalli, 1692
   ·/· Pellegrini, 1650; Matteis, 1682

   Arpeggiated chords belong more to the seventeenth and eighteenth centuries than to the sixteenth, since lute and guitar music was largely contrapuntal in style until the early seventeenth century. Beginning in the early seventeenth century, chords of long duration were often arpeggiated, or broken up into individual notes, sometimes in a quite elaborate manner. The first clear-cut instruction for playing this ornament on the guitar is by Valdambrini, who, before explaining how it is played, mentions that he is following the method of Girolamo Kapsperger:

The sign for *arpegiare* is this ⸉. It is made by touching the course separately, with the first note played with the thumb, the second note with the index, the highest note with the middle finger, and the other with the index. For example:

Ex. App. 1.27

   . . . reiterating the pattern four times in order to last for the duration [of the note] written above. (Valdambrini, 1646, p. 2)

This is an unusual pattern for arpeggiation, and is clearly derived from chitarrone (or theorbo) technique, of which Kapsperger was an important exponent. For the chitarrone, the first two courses are tuned an octave lower than that of a lute; hence the third course becomes the highest and the one on which the melody line is most often played. Since Valdambrini tunes his guitar with the lowest pitch that of the third course, the last note in his example of the arpeggio ends at the bottom of the chord!

Other writers indicate the patterns given below:

Ex. App. 1.28

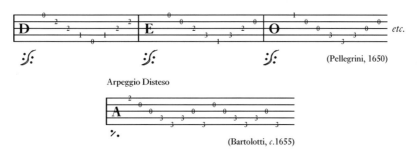

Arpeggio Disteso

(Pellegrini, 1650)

(Bartolotti, *c.*1655)

Gaspar Sanz discussed arpeggios, but did not notate any with the signs he provides in his preface. However, he does include a piece that is completely written out in arpeggiated style— 'Preludio o capricho arpeado'. Actually, from the manner in which they are treated in the guitar books, the implication is that ornamental arpeggios can be played at long-held chords, even in the absence of a sign, and at the discretion of the player.

Sources of Specific Information on the Tuning and Stringing of the Five-Course Guitar

1. Completely re-entrant (no bourdons)

D-W MS Guelf. 302	No pitch given; tune from 3rd course. See Table 9.1.
E-Mn MS 2618	*e′* tuning; written instructions (on tuning from a violin) imply no bourdons. See RISM B/VII, 37.
F-Pn MS Rés. 1402	No pitch given; tune from 3rd course. See Table 7.1.
F-Pn MS Vmc 59	No pitch given; tune from 5th course. See Table 6.4.
GB-Ge	No pitch given; tune from 3rd course. MS addition to J. Playford, *Select Musical Ayres . . .* (London, 1653). Tablature tuning chart for 'Gitter'. See Ch. 8.
GB-Och Mus. MS 1187	*d′* and *e′* tunings; no bourdons for the *d′* tuning, but a bourdon on the 4th for the *e′*. James Talbot's MS (*c.*1695). See Gill (1960), 67–9.
F-Psg MS 2344	*a′* tuning; tune from 3rd course. See Table 7.1.
F-Psg MS 2349	No pitch given; tune from 3rd course. See Table 7.1.
I-Bc MS AA/360	*e′* tuning; octave *g′* on 3rd course. See Table 6.4.
I-MOe MS Campori 1612	*e′* tuning; tune from 5th course; octave *g′* on 3rd. See Table 6.4.
Pl-Kj MS 40626	*e′* tuning. See Table 7.1.
US-CA MS Mus. 139	No pitch given; tune from 3rd course. See Table 8.1.
Abatessa (1635, etc.)	No pitch given; written instructions are vague, but imply no bourdons and an upper octave on the 3rd course. See Table 6.2.
Briceño (1626)	No pitch given; tune from 3rd course. See Table 10.1.
Campion (1730)	*e′* tuning. François Campion, *Addition au traité d'accompagnement . . .* (Paris, 1730). See Russell (1995), i. 78–9.
Carré (1671)	*d′* tuning; tune from 3rd course; bourdon on 4th for continuo. See Table 7.1.
Corbetta (1671)	*e′* tuning; implies that re-entrant tuning is common, but advises putting a bourdon on 4th. See Table 7.1.
Costanzo (1627)	No pitch given; written instructions are vague, but imply no bourdons. See Table 6.2.
Grassineau, J.	(1740) No tuning given, but describes bourdon on 4th. *A Musical Dictionary* (London, 1740), 90.

Kircher (1650)	*d´* tuning. See Grunfeld (1969), 65.
Mersenne (1636 & 1648)	*d´* tuning; tune from 3rd course. *e´* tuning in 1648. See Table 7.1.
Monte (*c.*1625)	No pitch given; written instructions are vague, but imply no bourdons. See Table 6.2.
Nassarre (1724)	No pitch given; describes stringing without bourdons and with one on the 4th course. Pablo Nasarre, *Escuela música . . .* (Zaragoza, 1724). See Russell (1995), i. 80–1.
Sanz (1674, etc.)	*e´* tuning; tune from 3rd course; discusses bourdons, but recommends re-entrant. See Table 10.1.
Valdambrini (1646)	*e´* tuning; tune from 5th course. See Table 6.3.
Velasco (1640)	No tuning given. Mentions re-entrant, but recommends bourdons on 4th and 5th. See Table 10.1.

2. *Bourdon on the fourth course only*

B–Bc MS 5.615	*e´* tuning; mentions bourdon on 5th as well. See Table 8.1.
GB–Och Mus. MS 1187	See above.
Carré (1671)	(See above). Earliest mention of this stringing.
Corbetta (1671)	See above.
Derosier (1689 & 1699)	*e´* tuning. See Table 8.1.
Grassineau (1740)	See above.
Nassarre (1724)	See above.
Viseé (1682)	*e´* tuning. See Table 7.1.

3. *Bourdons on the fourth and fifth courses*

A–Wn MS 9659	*f♯´* or *g´* tuning; tune from 3rd course. See Table 8.1.
B–Bc MS 5.615	See above.
E–GRu MS B–25	No pitch given; tune from 3rd course. See Table 10.1.
F–Psg MS 1070	No pitch given; tune from 5th course. P. Trichet, *Traité des instruments . . .* (*c.*1640). See Lesure (1957), 156.
I–Fc MS C. F. 83	*d´* tuning. See Table 6.1.
I–Fr MS 2774	*d´* tuning. See Table 6.4.
Amat 1626 (etc.)	*e´* tuning; tune from 3rd course. See Table 10.1.
De Sotos [1760]	*e´* tuning; tune from 3rd course. See Table 10.1.
Foscarini (1629, etc.)	No pitch given; tune from 5th course. See Table 6.3.
Kremberg (1686)	*d´* tuning. See Table 8.1.
Minguet y Yrol (1752)	*e´* tuning. See Table 10.1.
Montesardo (1606)	No pitch given; tune from 5th course. See Table 6.2.
Ribayaz (1676)	No pitch given; tune from 3rd course. See Table 10.1.

Sanseverino (1620, etc.)	*d'* tuning; tune from 5th course. See Table 6.2.
Sanz (1674, etc.)	See above.
Velasco (1640)	See above.

4. *Miscellaneous sources*

D–B Mus. MS 40631	*d'* tuning; no information on bourdons. See Table 8.1.
F–Psg MS 1070	No pitch given; describes bourdon on 5th only. Pierre Trichet: *Traité des instruments . . .* (MS *c.*1640). See Lesure (1957), 156.
I–Fn MS XIX 143	*e'* tuning; no information on bourdons. See Table 6.4.

Note: All other sources are ambiguous concerning tuning and stringing.

APPENDIX III

The Mandora

As regards function and tuning, there seems to be a rather strong connection between the late eighteenth-century guitar and the mandora, a type of bass lute also known as the calichon and gallichon (and the many variant spellings of the latter two names). The mandora was developed during the late seventeenth and early eighteenth centuries by makers and players in Germany, Austria, and Bohemia as an instrument for both basso continuo accompaniment and solo performance.

Earlier, German musicians had adopted the 11-course French D minor-tuned lute and developed it into a 13-course instrument. It inspired a large, excellent solo repertory, but was quite ineffective as a continuo instrument. The principal plucked continuo instruments throughout much of the Baroque era were, of course, the Italian-style archlute and theorbo; and until the late seventeenth–early eighteenth century the music had bass lines that were easily realized with those instruments' standard 13- to 14-course tunings, even though a portion of their respective bass ranges relied on off-the-fingerboard open diapasons.

With the rise of the *galant* and later musical styles, however, archlute and theorbo players found themselves at a critical disadvantage. The bass lines of these newer styles had much wider ranges and were more active; their frequent chromatic changes were awkward to negotiate on these large and suddenly quite ungainly instruments. While the plain gut diapasons could be pre-set for required flats or sharps, according to the key of a particular piece, they could not be changed as required during a performance.

What eighteenth-century composers, music directors, and plucked-string players wanted was a lute-type instrument on which the full bass range could be played with complete chromatic flexibility and ease of handling, and with a tuning that allowed for plenty of melodic possibilities. What Germanic instrument makers and players came up with was a smaller, simpler, almost Renaissance-style lute, with six to eight courses, all of them over the fingerboard, at the pitch level of a viola da gamba, and with the tuning intervals of the top five strings of the guitar: the mandora.

In the sixteenth and seventeenth centuries 'mandora' was a neo-Latin term used by theorists in reference to certain plucked instruments from antiquity. An early seventeenth-century instrument, the tiny French mandore was a type of treble lute with its own unique tuning and distinctive repertory; by the end of the seventeenth century it had become obsolete. In the late sixteenth century the Italians also developed a tiny, high-pitched lute-type instrument, but gave it a different tuning. They called it 'mandola' or, occasionally, 'mandora', and later, 'mandolino'. (See Tyler and Sparks 1989). However, these instruments, though gut-strung and played with the right-hand fingers, have nothing whatever to do with the later, larger, Germanic bass-range mandora.

The term 'calichon', which has many variant spellings, frequently was used instead of 'mandora', and clearly derives from the Italian term 'colascione', an Italian development of a Middle Eastern instrument (the saz). The colascione has two or three courses and a very long neck, and was used by the Italians as an exotic, lute-type folk instrument. Although the colascione and calichon have been linked by modern writers (perhaps because they have similar sounding names), the eighteenth-century German instrument is not related to the earlier Italian folk instrument.

The mandora/calichon does indeed look very much like a simple Renaissance lute. It has a vaulted back constructed of separate ribs, a flat soundboard with a rosette, and a wooden bridge, which acts as a stringholder, glued to the soundboard. However, its neck, like that of a guitar, is often long enough for ten to twelve tied gut frets, whereas the neck of a Renaissance lute has only seven or eight. The mandora's pegbox is either straight and set at a sharp angle, like a lute pegbox, or slightly curving and set at a shallow angle. The five to eight gut courses (six being most common) are either single or, particularly on instruments made by Italian makers, double. On the German-made instruments the first (highest pitch) course is usually single (a *chanterelle*, or melody string), often having its own separate raised peg holder attached to the pegbox.

The instrument's numerous music sources in tablature reveal that the highest five courses (which are the main fingered ones) have the same left-hand patterns as the top five strings of both the Baroque and the modern guitar. The sixth course was sometimes tuned to $E\natural$ (or flat), or to D. Johann Mattheson (*Das neu-eröffnete Orchestre*, 1713, p. 277) gives a tuning for the 'Calichon' of $D-G-c-f-a-d'$, a pattern later used, at a tone higher, by J. G. Albrechtsberger (*Gründliche Anweisung zur Composition*, 1790) and others. Albrechtsberger gives a tuning for the mandora that is identical with that of the modern guitar ($E-A-d-g-b-e'$), with the addition of D and C' for a seventh and an eighth course respectively. This pitch tuning is actually found as early as 1756 in A. Mayr's tutor for mandora (I-Tr). For details of the manuscript, see P. Prosser, 'Uno sconosciuto metodo manoscritto (1756): considerazione sull'identificatione della mandora nell XVIII secolo', in M. Tiella and R. Romano (eds.), *Strumenti per Mozart* (Rovereto, 1991).

The vibrating string lengths of surviving Germanic mandoras are normally only 62–72 cm; however, low pitches could be used effectively on these relatively short string lengths, because the mandora seems to have been one of the first instruments specifically designed to take advantage of the period's newest advance in string technology: gut with wire-wrapped strings. These strings were quite similar to modern cello or violin strings, and, therefore, enabled the instrument to produce the volume and resonance required for the continuo accompaniment of vocal and instrumental ensembles.

A fair number of mandoras from the mid-eighteenth century survive more or less in their original condition (although until recently it was thought that they had been modified in a later period to make them more guitar-like). In the latter part of the century an Italian-style design, developed by makers in Venice and, particularly, Milan, became popular. Well-known instrument makers such as the Landolfo, Monzino, and Presbler families produced late-period mandoras that were smaller bodied and had the curved pegboxes usually associated with Italian mandolin construction. They had even shorter string lengths (55–65 cm) than the Germanic models. These Italian instruments were tuned $E-A-d-g-b-e'$, with the overall configuration of the modern guitar. They were used throughout the nineteenth century, usually with double courses, and well into the twentieth with single strings. Today, one frequently encounters these 'guitar-lutes' in the older music and antique shops.

Playing the mandora involves the same right-hand finger style technique as for all eighteenth-century lute-type instruments, and, because of the tuning intervals of its upper five courses, a left-hand technique similar to that of the eighteenth-century guitar (see Ch. 13). Music for the mandora is notated either in French-style lute tablature or in staff notation. For solo music it appears mostly in tablature; for continuo in vocal music as single-line parts in bass clef; and for chamber music as single-line parts in bass clef, changing to treble clef for obbligato passages. There are also fully written-out vocal accompaniments in treble clef. As in modern guitar notation, the treble clef is meant to sound an octave lower than written.

The lute-like mandora, then, was the first instrument specifically designed to cope with the demands of the new musical styles. The instrument and its tuning were developed long before the guitar was finally compelled to become a bass-range instrument capable of doing precisely what the mandora had been invented to do—accompany the voice with complete chromatic flexibility in the new arpeggiated style. Indeed, by the end of the eighteenth century the music for these two competing instruments was virtually interchangeable. In addition to the fully written-out vocal accompaniments, the mandora's quite sizeable repertory includes solos and chamber music that can be readily played on the modern guitar without any distortion of the music. I strongly urge classical guitarists to investigate what could turn out to be a new and gratifying source of repertory.

For further details, see Tyler (2000*d*) and D. Gill, 'Alternative Lutes: The Identity of 18th-Century Mandores and Gallichones', *The Lute*, 26/2 (1986), 51–60.

PART III

THE ORIGINS OF
THE CLASSICAL GUITAR

11

1750–69: The Emergence of the Six-Course Guitar

Spain, Portugal, and South America

When Philip V (the newly crowned Bourbon king) entered Madrid with his entourage in 1701, he brought with him all manner of international influences into the Spanish capital. French was soon being spoken at court to a far greater extent than before, and the Italian musical style became strongly favoured (not just in royal circles but also by the fashion-conscious Spanish middle classes), while national expression was generally held in low esteem and was even regarded with suspicion as a potential focus of Spanish resistance to foreign domination. By mid-century the publication of new Spanish music had been largely suppressed (the court repeatedly forbade the establishment of a dedicated music press, so most eighteenth-century Spanish music existed only in manuscript form), and the guitar had all but vanished from fashionable middle-class theatres, where it had formerly been used to accompany short pieces such as *entremeses*.

The natural home of the guitar at this time was in the humbler parts of Spanish society: the bar, the street, and the barber's shop. In Madrid it was particularly associated with the poor but glamorous figures of the *majo* and *maja* (men and women who lived on the margins of society, playing, singing, and dancing in the streets at night), and the guitar and bandurria were an essential accompaniment to drinking sessions, not just for the lower classes but also for dissident artists and intellectuals, such as the young Francisco Goya. Bars usually had a guitar hanging on the wall, ready for use by customers, and the instrument's day-to-day existence was inextricably interwoven with semi-improvised songs, and popular dances such as the fandango. This seductive dance with guitar accompaniment (in 3/4 time, using the Phrygian mode) was strongly disapproved of by polite society, partly for moral reasons (because it supposedly encouraged licentiousness, and because impromptu performances often ended in public brawls), but also because Spain's foreign rulers recognized that such rousing music had the potential to foster a potentially destabilizing sense of nationalism.

When played in the street or in the noisy environment of a Spanish bar, the guitar was usually strummed forcefully, a style that had been known since the seventeenth century as *música ruidosa* ('noisy music')[1] and was widely regarded by foreign guitarists as being rather crude and uncouth. In their desire to produce strong bass notes when strumming, Spanish guitarists often preferred to string the fourth and fifth courses of their instruments with two *bordones* (bass strings, usually made from plain gut), as this extract from *Reglas y advertencias generales para tañer la guitarra* by Pablo Minguet y Yrol (Madrid, 1752, one of the few music books published in Spain at this time), makes clear:

In tuning there is variety, because in Italy they string [the guitar] with delicate strings, without any *bordón*, neither on the fourth course, nor the fifth. In Spain it is the contrary; some use two *bordones* on the fourth course, and another two on the fifth; or at least, as is more common, one *bordón* on each course. These two styles of stringing are both good, for different effects: for he who wishes to use the guitar to play *musica ruidosa* is better off with *bordones* than without them; whereas if someone wishes to pluck [*puntear*] with perfection and sweetness, two *bordones* will not speak well: and therefore the aficionado can choose whichever style he prefers of the two, according to the way that he wishes to play. (*regla segunda*)

Minguet y Yrol's information about Italian tuning was actually somewhat behind the times, because by the mid-eighteenth century the simple, melodic, *galant* style of composition that had begun in Italy was becoming popular throughout Europe, and the guitar was increasingly being used to provide delicate arpeggiated accompaniments to songs. This style of playing required clear bass notes on the first beat of each bar, and by about 1750 virtually all guitarists were therefore stringing their instruments with at least one *bordón* on the fourth and fifth courses, turning what had often been a purely treble instrument into one that now possessed both a treble and a bass range. Nevertheless, guitarists on the Iberian peninsula were alone in frequently choosing to use two *bordones*, and this desire to produce strong bass notes in their forceful strummed accompaniments may also explain why the sixth course first came to be added in Spain, long before it appeared in the rest of Europe.

We have already noted the dearth of published music in eighteenth-century Spain. Apart from the book by Minguet y Yrol (which, as noted, borrowed heavily from Gaspar Sanz's 1674 instructions for the five-course guitar), the only other guitar work of note published during these years was by Andre de Sotos, *Arte para aprender con facilidad y sin maestro a templar y tañer rasgado la guitarra* (Madrid, 1760). This too was based on a much earlier book for five-course guitar (Juan Carlos Amat's *Guitarra española de cinco órdenes*, originally published in Barcelona in 1596). Concentrating on

---

[1] The term *música ruidosa* was used by Sanz in his *Instrucción de música sobre la guitarra española* (Zaragoza, 1674), and later by Pablo Minguet y Yrol in the second rule of his *Reglas y advertencias generales para tañer la guitarra* (Madrid, 1752). The latter author was not a guitar specialist, and his work is very heavily indebted to Sanz, Amat, and other sources, which is why some of the information in it was already out of date at the time of its publication.

these two anachronistic guitar works, few modern scholars seem to have spotted the early emergence of a sixth course on Spanish guitars. However, ample evidence of the widespread existence of six-course guitars can be found, both from surviving instruments of the period and from the numerous 'for sale' advertisements that appeared in Spanish newspapers, especially in the capital.[2] The earliest reference to a six-course guitar appeared in a Madrid newspaper in 1760, where mention was made of a 'vihuela' (a word used interchangeably with 'guitarra' in everyday Spanish parlance from the mid-seventeenth century onwards, the Renaissance vihuela having fallen into disuse and long been forgotten), which was described as having six courses ('6 órdenes') and being 'good for accompanying': 'En la calle de Atocha, casa del Granadino, se vende una vihuela de 6 órdenes, hecha de su misma mano, buena para acompañar . . .' (*Diario noticioso universal*, 3 June 1760). However, this instrument made by 'el Granadino' was by no means the earliest Spanish guitar with more than five courses, because the Gemeentemuseum in The Hague has a large guitar bearing the label 'Francisco Sanguino, me fecit. En Sevilla año de 1759' (Pl. 11.1). It is not possible to say exactly how many strings this instrument originally had, because it has been modified since its original manufacture, but it undoubtedly had at least six courses (possibly seven or eight), with a vibrating string length of 670 mm. Sanguino lived in Seville during the second half of the eighteenth century and was widely recognized as a fine maker of violins and guitars. The latter are some of the best guitars of the period, and this 1759 instrument is the oldest known example of a guitar with a fan-strutting system beneath the soundboard (or table), having three fan struts and two diagonal bars. This is similar to the pattern adopted by (and widely attributed to) Antonio de Torres in the mid-nineteenth century, but Sanguino seems to have created it a century earlier, thus paving the way for the development of lightly built guitars with thin soundboards, higher string tension, and an improved treble response. Two other similar guitars by Sanguino are still in existence—one in the Museu de la Música, Barcelona (no. 48, also dated 1759), and one in the Central Museum of Musical Culture, Moscow (dated 1767)—and all have some form of fan strutting.[3]

Few of the advertisements in the Madrid newspapers during the 1760s specified the number of courses, but it seems probable that the five-course guitar initially remained the more common type, and that the new six-course instrument was sufficiently unusual to merit a specific description whenever it made an appearance. Thus the following extracts (just two of the many which appeared during that decade) probably refer to five-course guitars, although that is not explicitly stated:

[2] The quotations from Madrid newspapers that follow can be found, along with many others, in an important and informative article by Beryl Kenyon de Pascual, 'Ventas de instrumentos musicales en Madrid durante la segunda mitad del s. XVIII (parte II)', *RdMc* 6 (1983), 299–308. In it she remarks that 'una proporción relativamente elevada de los anuncios, aproximadamente el 35%, se utilizó la palabra *vihuela* por guitarra'.

[3] I am grateful to Alex Timmerman for providing me with information about Sanguino's guitars.

Two Portuguese vihuelas for sale, new, made in Lisbon by one of the best makers, which can be used to accompany or to pluck [*puntear*] . . . (*Diario noticioso universal*, 29 July 1760)

The person who wants to buy a guitar and a *tiple* [small treble guitar], smooth and graceful, well shaped and of superb wood, made by the celebrated and famous *guitarrero* [guitar maker] Sanguino, el Sevillano, good to pluck [*puntear*], strum [*rasguear*], and play however one wants, with a rare and exquisite sound, should go to the *guitarrero* who has his new premises in la Fuente de Moros . . . (*Diario noticioso universal*, 15 Sept. 1762)

The words 'vihuela' and 'guitarra' were synonymous in eighteenth-century Spain, but in neighbouring Portugal the related word 'viola'[4] gradually usurped the meaning of 'guitarra'. During the seventeenth century the two terms had been used interchangeably by the Portuguese,[5] but by the mid-eighteenth century 'viola' had become the preferred term for several regional types of five-course guitar, while (as we shall later see) 'guitarra' came to be used to describe a new and altogether different instrument. As well as the typical five-course Baroque guitar, one Portuguese variant from this period is of particular interest to us: the *viola toeira*, which was (and still is) played in the north of the country, especially in the area around Coimbra. The distinctive feature of this type of guitar is that it had twelve strings but only five courses. The top three courses were double-strung in unison, but the fourth and fifth courses were triple-strung (with one thick *bordão* and two thin strings tuned at the octave), and the entire instrument could be fitted with either gut or metal strings.

The guitar was also an integral part of life in the Spanish and Portuguese colonies in South America. All classes relied on it for entertainment, and the guitar suffered somewhat less from the social stigma that so adversely affected it in Spain, presumably because it reminded settlers of their mother country. Antoine Joseph Pernety, a French traveller who journeyed there in 1763 and 1764, noted that, among the respectable classes in Montevideo:

the women are as much at ease in their homes as in France. They receive company very graciously, and they themselves never need an invitation to sing, to dance, to play the harp, or guitar, or lute, or mandoline. They are more pleasing in it than our French counterparts . . . During the morning, the women remain seated on a stool, and at the back of the room, they have under their feet, first a reed mat over the paved floor, then on top of the mat wild animal skins or tiger furs. There they play the guitar or some other instrument accompanying themselves with their voice, or they drink their *mate* while their negresses prepare dinner in their apartment.[6]

---

[4] Although most music dictionaries state that the Portuguese word for the guitar is 'violão', that term has only been generally used in Brazilian Portuguese. In Portugal 'viola' was and is the preferred term.

[5] For more information, see Ernesto Veiga de Oliveira, *Instrumentos populares tradicionais portugueses* (Lisbon, 1982), 186.

[6] Pernety (1770), 277 and 283.

PL. 11.1. Guitar bearing the label 'Francesco Sanguino, me fecit.
En Sevilla año de 1759' (NB. This is not the original head).
Courtesy of the Gemeente-museum, The Hague

However, the guitar was also found in lowly *pulperías* (shops that sold rum and tobacco) throughout South America, where the fandango was typically played and danced. Richard Pinnell has described in fascinating detail how the church, police, and city councils in Uruguay, Chile, and Argentina repeatedly tried to stamp out the dance, which was believed to lead to drunkenness, brawling, indiscriminate fornication, and even manslaughter.[7] Guitar playing in public was sometimes banned after nightfall, because of certain persons 'going around the streets at odd hours of the night with the guitar singing indecent verses', and attempts to suppress the fandango (and other dances with guitar accompaniment) were made by the church in Buenos Aires, which passed a resolution:

> to exterminate from among the people those dances commonly called fandangos, and to see that there be all due moderation in the other festival dances . . . in order that the fandangos be stopped inasmuch as they are merely entertainments of the vulgar, ordinary class . . . (Buenos Aires, 13 May 1754, signed by ten members of the city council)[8]

France

Although the eighteenth century was a period of massive economic decline for France (largely due to royal extravagance and a series of disastrous wars), the wealthy and titled continued to lead lives of rare elegance and grace. Music and opera were eagerly patronized by the privileged strata of French society, and this in turn encouraged musicians from throughout Europe (especially from Italy, which at this time was not a united country but simply a collection of poor and disparate regions) to seek their fortune in Paris and in France's second city of Lyons. The simple Italian melodic style that they brought with them gradually became fashionable among Parisians (who termed it *style galant*), and by mid-century it was steadily superseding the grander traditions of the French Baroque. This popularity increased dramatically after 1752, when an Italian opera company created a sensation in Paris with their performances of Pergolesi's *La serva padrona*. Although this *opera buffa* had been composed some years earlier, the freshness and directness of its music overwhelmed the public, and influential French figures were soon actively championing the Italian style. The philosopher Jean-Jacques Rousseau argued strongly in favour of it, stating that a musical performance should 'at one time carry only one melody to the ear and one idea to the soul', and he even composed an opera of his own, *Le Devin du village*, to show how the new style could be applied to the French language.

As a result of this popularity, France experienced an unprecedented influx of Italian musicians during the 1750s and 1760s. These were chiefly opera composers and sing-

[7] Pinnell (1993). [8] Quoted ibid. 327.

ers who worked at both the Comédie-Italienne and the Opéra, but in their wake came many instrumentalists, including a number of guitarists. They mostly settled in Paris and Lyons, earning their living by teaching, performing, and composing music for their instrument, and their presence quickly helped to revive interest in the five-course guitar, which had fallen out of fashion in France during the previous twenty years. The most significant of these Italian guitarists was Giacomo Merchi from Brescia, who was to have a profound influence upon the way the guitar developed in France over the next few decades.

As we shall see, these Italian guitarists all specialized in the gut-strung guitar, but we should briefly note the popularity in Italy (especially in the south) of the *chitarra battente*. This wire-strung guitar was widely used there to accompany songs and dances, and its classic form seems to have been perfected in Naples in about 1740, at the same time as the Neapolitan mandoline, with which it shares many features. The chitarra battente had a vaulted back, a distinctive inward bend in the soundboard (at bridge level), five courses of wire strings (usually pairs, but sometimes triplets, attached not to the bridge but to pegs at the bottom of the instrument), and fixed metal or bone frets. It was played with a plectrum, usually in a strumming style, and was capable of producing a loud and forceful accompaniment. However, it was never widely played outside Italy, although other southern European countries also have a long history of metal-strung guitars (notably Portugal, where wire-strung regional guitars have been in constant use since at least the seventeenth century).

Although the gut-strung guitar was too quiet to be heard adequately in the great Parisian theatres or at the Concert Spirituel, arpeggiated guitar chords offered the perfect accompaniment for simple melodies when they were performed in either a domestic setting or alfresco; and, as Paris was the unrivalled centre of European music publishing during the eighteenth century, it is not surprising to find a large quantity of airs with guitar being printed there during this period. The great *Encyclopédie* of Diderot and D'Alembert was already noting in 1757 that 'some amateurs have given the guitar a rebirth, and have at the same time reawakened our taste for vaudevilles, pastorales, and brunettes',[9] and the increasing number of songs with guitar accompaniment that were published from 1760 onwards testify to its renewed popularity.[10] Many of these songs were transcriptions of the latest fashionable airs from productions at the Opéra-Comique, while others were composed specifically with the guitar in mind. The market for both types expanded steadily throughout the second half of the eighteenth century, and the ability to sing a chanson to one's own accompaniment became an important social accomplishment for men and women who wished to

---

[9] *Encyclopédie* (1757), ii. 1011. A brunette was a type of popular love song, with lyrics usually addressed to a brown-haired girl.

[10] A selected list of these songs can be found in App. V.

display their artistic refinement, or simply to defend themselves against boredom and world-weariness.

Guitars in mid-eighteenth-century France were not very different in appearance and stringing from those being made fifty years earlier. Some makers were beginning to favour a simple, open soundhole, rather than a traditional ornate rose, but many features of the Baroque guitar remained unaltered. Typically, French guitars of this period had a fingerboard that lay flush with the soundboard, ten wooden tuning pegs, five double courses (with one *bourdon* and one octave string on the fourth and fifth courses), and ten gut frets tied around the neck at semitone intervals. Although metal-wound *bourdons* had been available for many decades,[11] French guitarists at this time seem to have preferred to use traditional plain gut bass strings, for the following reasons:

Wound *bourdons* have two inconveniences. One is of wearing through and cutting into the [gut] frets; the other greater problem is that of dominating the other strings too much, and of causing the final overall sound to be lost, through the long duration of the *bourdons*, especially in *batteries*. It is in full chords where they can sound well, because they produce the fundamental notes; but as these full chords do not occur very often, it is better to keep to the simple *bourdons*, at least if one only wants to pluck the strings.[12]

Neither had the system of notation yet changed, with tablature still being the standard way of writing guitar music. The *Encyclopédie* of 1757 discusses tablature at some length—'this method, although ancient, is conserved for this instrument through the ease which it gives to the gracefulness of the hand, the arrangement of the fingers, the beauty of sound, harmony, and the facility in execution'—but does not even mention the possibility of using staff notation. However, the fashionable new *galant* style of simple melodic writing (and in particular the guitar's recently acquired role of providing arpeggiated chordal accompaniments to well-known songs) was already pulling the instrument into the musical mainstream; and in the same year that the *Encyclopédie* was defending the continued use of tablature, Merchi published his *Quatro duetti a due chitarre e sei minuetti a solo con variationi . . . op. 3* (Paris), using standard staff notation (part of Duetto IV is reproduced in App. VIII). The duets were marked as also being suitable for accompaniment by a violin (something that would have been impossible had they been written in tablature), and the notation is mostly indistinguishable from violin writing, except that the guitar sounds an octave lower than written. It should be observed that for several decades after staff notation was introduced, guitarists made little or no attempt to distinguish between different voices on a single stave, or to indicate precise duration when notes of differing lengths were struck simultaneously. The player's grasp of harmony was expected to be sufficient to

---

[11] See the opening of Ch. 12 for a brief history of guitar string making.
[12] *Encyclopédie* (1757), ii. 1012.

inform him or her when a bass note should be left to resonate and when it should be stopped.

Although this use of staff notation for the guitar probably began among musicians in Italy, Merchi was the first to use it in a Paris guitar publication, and later took full credit for its introduction by claiming that it was he who 'withdrew the guitar from the servitude which it had relative to tablature' (Merchi (1777), 2). Earlier, in his *Le Guide des écoliers de guitarre, œuvre VII* of 1761, he had already forcefully stated his reasons for rejecting tablature:

I believe that it is an abuse, and I shall prove it by the following reasons. Those who only know tablature cannot truly play, and accompany only by routine and without balance. Those who use tablature successfully were good musicians before they learned it, and had no need of it. These reasons have led me to suppress its use in this work. If someone objects that it is necessary to mark the [left hand] positions, I would respond that the violin, the cello, etc. never use tablature, and that the guitar has less need [to do so] than them because it has frets. As with other instruments, all that is necessary for success is the application of a good method; I have neglected nothing to render mine easy, clear, and agreeable.[13]

Giacomo Merchi had settled in Paris in 1753, after touring France and Germany with his brother, Joseph Bernard, in the early 1750s, performing duets on two *colascioni* (Italian long-necked lutes, each with only two strings). Their abilities on those instruments were undoubtedly remarkable, as these contemporary reports testify:

13 June 1753, Versailles . . . At the end of the concert, two Italians played on an unusual instrument; it was a type of guitar with a very long neck. This instrument is called the *calichonchini*; it has two strings, tuned a fourth apart; it has two octaves; the strings are plucked with a small piece of tree bark, shaped to a point. They played a piece of music which was a dialogue in duo form; they got the best from their instrument, and played it most agreeably; their execution was prodigious.[14]

The Merchi brothers played a concerto of their own composition on the *calasoncini*: this is a two-string instrument, tuned to d and a, and consequently very limited; but the extraordinary manner in which the two Italian musicians played it is astonishing and agreeable. (*Mercure de France*, June 1753, pt. 2, 163, reviewing their appearance at the Concert Spirituel)

The *Journal de Paris* (1754, p. 175) lists Merchi as a *maître* of calascione, guitar, and of the newly invented Neapolitan mandoline, which was also becoming fashionable in Paris at this time and for which he later published a number of instrumental pieces. However, the guitar clearly became his favoured instrument after he settled in Paris, and most of the approximately thirty-eight volumes of music that he published over the next few decades were for guitar: mostly songs with guitar accompaniment, guitar

[13] Merchi (1761), 4.   [14] Duc de Luynes (1860; repr. 1970), 157–8.

duets (the best of which are well worthy of serious study), or guitar solos.[15] Although not a full treatise on guitar playing, his *Guide des écoliers de guitarre* of 1761 gives us a good deal of contemporary information about the instrument and its technique. Like all other guitarists in France at this time, Merchi advocated the use of five courses (a single *chanterelle*, unison second and third courses, and octave stringing on the fourth and fifth courses), and he also recommended using the right-hand thumb to pluck all notes on the third, fourth, and fifth courses, the first and second fingers being reserved for the top two courses only.[16] This short work ends with a set of thirty variations on *Folia da Spagna*, during which Merchi uses the melody's simple chord sequence as a means of teaching students some of the many different right-hand arpeggio patterns that guitarists habitually use when accompanying. (See Pl. 11.2.)

A year later saw the publication of *Les Dons d'Apollon, méthode pour apprendre facilement à jouer de la guitarre* by Michel Corrette (Paris, 1762). Born in Rouen in 1707 but working throughout his adult life in Paris, Corrette was an educated composer and organist who produced an impressive output of orchestral and choral music throughout his lifetime. He also published treatises for many instruments (including violin, cello, flute, and mandoline), and, although he does not seem to have been a guitar specialist, his comments are especially valuable as they reflect the attitudes of the musical establishment in France at this time rather than those of the frequently introspective (and regrettably self-obsessed) world of the guitar.

Corrette used both tablature and staff notation in his *méthode*, recognizing that the latter system was becoming the standard way of notating new music, but rightly stressing that it was still essential to be able to read the former system if one wished to play guitar music from the seventeenth and early eighteenth centuries by past masters such as Visée and Derosier.[17] He mentions that the guitar used to be tuned to a lower pitch, but points out that 'a higher pitch makes the instrument more brilliant', and he recommends the use of the best gut strings, which came from Rome, Florence, Naples, or Lyons. He also suggests that the *bourdon* on the fourth course should be open-wound (with thin metal wire), and that the *bourdon* for the fifth course should be close-wound, or alternatively that wound silk strings 'in the Chinese manner' should be used to increase the sonority of the basses.[18]

Intriguingly, Corrette also discusses a type of five-course guitar with twelve strings, known in France as the 'guitarre à la Rodrigo'.[19] This is in fact the traditional Portuguese viola toeira, identical to the type played in Coimbra, except that Corrette recommends two *bourdons* and one octave string on the lower courses, whereas the Portuguese typically used one *bordão* and two octave strings. Corrette does not give

---

[15] A full list of Merchi's compositions is given in App. VII.
[16] Merchi (1761), 1–2. A full discussion of 18th-c. technique can be found in Ch. 14.
[17] Corrette (1762), 15.
[18] Ibid. 22. The opening of Ch. 12 gives fuller details of close-wound and open-wound strings.
[19] Corrette (1762) 4.

PL. 11.2. Opening theme and variations, 8, 13, and 28 from
Giacomo Merchi's *Folia da Spagna*

the origin of the instrument's popular French name, but it may well have had some connection with the Portuguese guitarist Rodrigo António de Meneses, who is known to have toured Europe as a concert performer during the 1760s and who subsequently enjoyed great success in Germany, especially in the city of Leipzig in 1766.[20]

Although many volumes of songs with guitar accompaniment were published in Paris during the 1760s, most of the composers remain obscure to the point of virtual anonymity. Besides Merchi (who was by far the most sophisticated guitarist of his generation in Paris), only two—Mignard and Mlle Cherbourg—produced any instrumental music,[21] and the accompaniments to the hundreds of individual songs that appeared are usually straightforward arpeggiated affairs, providing a simple harmonic cushion for the voice and set in keys that would cause little trouble, even to a performer of modest abilities. In her *IIe Recueil de chansons avec accompagnement de guitarre par musique et par tablature* . . . (Paris, 1761), Mlle Genty was still providing guitar parts written in both tablature and staff notation; but the battle to preserve the old system was quickly lost in Paris, with works such as the *Premier recueil d'airs choisis, avec accompagnement de guitarre . . . par Mr. Godard* (Paris, 1762) using only the new form of notation. The appearance of volumes of songs such as *Le Festin de l'Amour* (1765) and *Les Projets de l'Amour* (1765), both of which included accompaniments that could be played by 'harpe, guitarre, mandoline, violons, ou clavecin et basse', necessitated the use of staff notation and further helped to hasten the demise of tablature.

Instrument-making in mid-eighteenth-century Paris was based in the streets around the rue de la Pelleterie, where a total of sixty-five *maîtres* and their apprentices (each of whom studied for six years) between them made all types of musical instruments. Among the makers of stringed instruments, Joseph Gaffino was one of the most prominent during the 1750s, selling guitars and 'excellent strings from Naples, Rome, Florence, and Lyon, and all sorts of wound strings' from his workshop in the rue des Prouvaires. In 1769 Georges Cousineau was sworn into the Corporation of Instrument Makers in Paris, and opened a large and successful workshop opposite the Colonade du Louvre. Cousineau himself made only harps, but his workers manufactured guitars and a wide variety of other stringed instruments, although guitars were also imported directly from Spain. His shop also sold 'English guitars', but, as we shall shortly see, these instruments had a completely different origin from the authentic guitar, with little in common except for a shared name.[22]

Although smaller and less affluent than Paris, Lyons lay much closer to Italy; it was therefore an attractive destination for Italian musicians who wished to try their luck abroad, as well as an important stopping-off point for touring performers from other

[20] João de Freitas Branco (1959), 218.
[21] See App. V for a list of instrumental music, and a selected list of songs.
[22] Pierre (1893), 51, and Vannes (1951) (entry 'Cousineau').

parts of France. The city's regular Concert de l'Académie des Beaux-Arts (and the more intimate, smaller-scale concerts known as *séances*) were enticing showcases for ambitious young singers, many of whom accompanied themselves on the guitar. M. Godard spent some time in Lyons in 1761, announcing himself as a 'musicien ordinaire de l'Académie royale de musique de Paris' and advertising several concerts at which he promised to perform 'many ariettes and little airs which he will sing while accompanying himself on the guitar'.[23] Two singer-guitarists who performed at the Concert de l'Académie in 1765 were Warin (a *basse-taille* who had made his debut at the Paris Opéra in 1762) and Itasse (a composer and *haute-contre*), while another, unnamed singer gave a *séance* at the Académie des Beaux-Arts on 25 July 1774, singing 'many ariettes with guitar accompaniment'.[24] The orchestra at the Concert de l'Académie des Beaux-Arts is even said to have included a guitar in its continuo section (together with lutes, theorbos, and a harpsichord), and a list of the orchestra's *pensionnaires* from the 1760s included 'the guitarist Latour, employed at the Comédie and at the Concert'.[25]

No more is known about Latour, but Warin stayed in the city for some time thereafter, teaching the guitar, as did Itasse, who took up residence in the rue Ecorcheboeuf and advertised himself thus: 'M. Itasse, of the Académies royales de musique de France et de l'Académie des Beaux-Arts de Lyon, informs the public that he is starting to give, at his house and in town, lessons in guitar and in *musique pour le goût du chant*.'[26] Other professors of the guitar during these years included Ferré (a 'musicien ordinaire de M. Le Prince de Monaco' who taught singing, guitar, and pardessus de viole),[27] and Tauseany, who arrived in Lyons towards the end of 1765 and began to teach lute, guitar, mandoline, and pardessus de viole.[28] The singer Nicolas Suin (of the Lyons Comédie theatre) was a guitarist too, and in 1768 published a *Recueil d'airs choisis pour la guitarre avec accompagnement de violin*, as well as offering for sale a number of stringed instruments from Paris, including a pedal harp, a guitar, two mandolines, and a violin.[29]

Compared with Paris, publishing in Lyons was a very small-scale affair, but music issued in the capital—such as *Les Soirées de Paris, XVIIIe livre de guitarre contenant des airs d'opéra comique avec des accompagnemens d'un nouveau goût, des préludes et des ritournelles par Mr. Merchi, op. XXII* (*c*.1766–70)—was often marked as also being available at 'Lyon, Castaud', the name of one of the largest lutheries and music sellers in the city. Castaud made a wide variety of instruments, including guitars, and also

[23] *Petites affiches de Lyon*, 7 Oct. 1761.
[24] Vallas (1932), 337 and 331.
[25] Vallas (1908), 10 and Vallas (1932), 336.
[26] *Petites affiches de Lyon*, 1765, quoted by Vallas (1932), 337.
[27] *Petites affiches de Lyon*, 12 Jan. 1763.
[28] *Les affiches, annonces, et avis divers de Lyon*, 28 Dec. 1765.
[29] Ibid. 16 June and 21 Sept. 1768.

stocked printed guitar music, Spanish guitars, and Italian gut strings, as did the rival firm of Serrière.[30] Another luthier called Mériotte (who came from Paris but had been based in Lyons since 1757) boasted an even wider variety of plucked instruments, including lutes, archlutes, mandolines, guitars, and 'guitarres à la Rodrigue'.[31]

Britain

During the first half of the eighteenth century, the five-course, gut-strung guitar steadily lost the status and the popularity it had enjoyed in Britain (above all in England) during the seventeenth century, when it had been a favourite instrument at the court of King Charles II. It had virtually disappeared altogether from the popular English consciousness by the middle of the eighteenth century, and was clearly regarded by the writer James Grassineau as something that now belonged purely to southern Europe:

GUITARRA. A musical instrument of the string kind, with five double rows of strings, of which those that are bass are in the middle; unless it be one for the burden, an octave lower than the fourth. This instrument was first used in *Spain*, and by the *Italians* it has the particular denomination of *Spagnuola* given it: it is found in *Italy* and other countries, but more frequently in *Spain*.[32]

Its oblivion in Britain was due in large measure to the growing popularity of a rival plucked instrument, nowadays commonly referred to as the 'English guittar' (or simply 'guittar').[33] This was, strictly speaking, not a guitar at all but a kind of cittern that became fashionable in London about 1755, although some sources suggest that it first appeared a little earlier in Scotland.[34] It had six courses of metal strings (usually with single stringing on the two lowest courses, and the top four courses doubled in unison), was tuned to a simple chord of C major ($c - e - g \, g - c' c' - e' e' - g' g'$), and was plucked with the fingertips of the right hand. Another distinctive feature found on many English guittars was the watch-key tuning mechanism at the top of the neck to which the strings were attached, which made tuning the metal strings easier than

---

[30] *Petites affiches de Lyon*, 10 Dec. 1767.

[31] Ibid. 11 July 1770.

[32] Grassineau (1740), 90.

[33] Coggin (1987), 205, whose article provides a useful introduction to the instrument's repertoire and technique, notes that the term 'English guittar' was not used in Britain until 1781. However, the name 'guitarre Anglaise' was apparently being used in Paris before that date (by instrument sellers such as Cousineau) to distinguish the imported English guitar from other types of plucked string instrument, such as the standard 'guitarre espagnole' and the 'guitarre à la Rodrigue'.

[34] For example, Baines (1966), 42–3, although a tutor published by Bremner in 1758 says the instrument was 'but lately introduced'. It may initially have been imported from Germany *c.*1740–50, but it soon established itself as a particularly English (and Scottish) instrument. Recent research by James Tyler and by the Scottish musician Rob MacKillop suggests that the guittar was probably imported to Britain from Germany, and first became popular among Scottish musicians such as James Oswald, who then introduced it to England in the 1750s.

when simple wooden pegs were fitted. Although it was initially popular with men, the guittar soon came to be regarded chiefly as an essential accoutrement for fashion-conscious English and Scottish ladies of the middle class and aristocracy. They used it primarily to play melodic lines rather than to provide chordal accompaniments, and for a while, among musical dilettantes, the instrument even threatened the domestic pre-eminence of keyboard instruments. Almost every English-language reference to a 'guittar' (or 'guitar') written during the second half of the eighteenth century relates to this type of instrument, the term 'Spanish guitar' generally being used on those comparatively rare occasions when the gut-strung variety was under discussion.

No sooner had the English guittar gained widespread popularity than serious musicians began to attack it, dismissing it as a superficial instrument, unworthy of serious study. As early as 1757 Dr John Brown was deriding it as 'a trifling instrument in itself, and generally now taught in the most ignorant and trifling manner';[35] but its importance during the second half of the eighteenth century should not be underestimated. Its metal strings gave it a greater volume of sound than could be produced by the gut-strung guitar, and the single strings on the fifth and sixth courses produced true bass notes, not the somewhat ambiguous pitch that inevitably resulted from octave stringing. Some superb English guittars were made during the 1760s (especially by John Preston of London); and although much of the instrument's repertoire is rather trivial, some fine works were composed for it, including a sonata for violin and guittar by Johann Christian Bach, music by the eminent Italian violinist Francesco Geminiani, and several works by the Scottish composer and publisher James Oswald.

When Giacomo Merchi visited London in 1766 to perform at Hickford's Rooms, he played 'on the calisoncino and the Spanish guitar',[36] but even he could not ignore the popularity of the English guittar when composing for an English audience. By 1770 he had published at least four volumes of music in London, including *Twelve divertimentos for two guitars or a guitar and violin*, and the many close-position six-note C major chords these pieces contain (and the absence of any bass notes below *c*) make it clear that he wrote these pieces with the English guittar in mind. The instrument even achieved some popularity in Paris, as did a related eight-string German variant known as the 'guitarre Allemande'. References to both these types of cittern can be found in advertisements for Parisian music shops from the 1760s onwards; l'Abbé Joseph Carpentier composed a number of works for a cittern-like instrument that he called the 'cythre' or 'cytre', while Corrette (near the end of his *Nouvelle méthode de mandoline*) describes the 'cistre', which, despite its different tuning, is also clearly a relative of the English guittar: 'Presently in Paris one plays it like the guitar, that is to say one

---

[35] Brown (1757), ii. 77
[36] Elkin (1955), 45–6. Merchi also performed 'several pieces on a new instrument invented by him called the Liutino Moderno'.

plucks the strings with the right hand . . . the cistre is mounted with strings of white and yellow brass, and the basses with wound silk strings, which one plucks with the thumb.'[37] He also states that this instrument has eighteen frets, and gives three possible tunings for three types of cistre: one with seven double courses (*e–a–d′–e′–a′–c♯′–e′*), one with six courses (*a–d′–e′–a′–c♯′–e′*), and one with five courses (*a–e′–a′–c♯′–e′*).

[37] Corrette (1772), 42.

12

1770–89: The First Six-String Guitars

A Short History of String-Making

The subject of string-making has received little or no attention in most histories of the guitar, yet the development of the instrument cannot be fully appreciated without an understanding of the innovations that were taking place at the same time in the manufacture of musical strings. The luthier and the string-maker have always been dependent upon each other's skills, and the following paragraphs offer a concise summary of the ways in which they have influenced each other. This necessitates briefly stepping back in time to investigate the way that strings were made in earlier periods, but the detour is worthwhile because it will allow us to see how modifications in string manufacture came to affect the development of the guitar in the second half of the eighteenth century.

Gut strings (made from the dried and twisted intestines of sheep, and then stretched over a resonating chamber) have been in use for thousands of years. They seem to have been first developed by the ancient Egyptians, but their use subsequently spread throughout Arab and Western cultures; and by the sixteenth century gut and silk strings (the latter probably of Chinese invention, made by twisting numerous silk fibres together) were being produced in many European cities. Gut is not a naturally dense material, and so was more suitable for the manufacture of treble rather than bass strings (or *bourdons*); but in the second half of the sixteenth century makers developed various treatments that substantially increased the specific weight or flexibility of gut and allowed the production of more resonant bass strings. However, these thick plain gut *bourdons* were still less powerful than treble strings of the same length, so players of plucked instruments either used them together with a thinner octave string for greater emphasis (as was customary on the fourth and fifth courses of the guitar), or adopted the theorbo principle by fitting a second pegbox above the main one, thus accommodating a number of unfretted bass courses with a much longer vibrating length.

A significant development in string-making occurred in the mid-seventeenth century, with the invention of strings that were overspun with fine metal wire, a process that increased the overall density of the string, thereby producing deeper and more powerful bass notes for a given vibrating length. The earliest reference to this technique dates from England in 1659 and can be found in the manuscript *Ephemerides* by

Samuel Hartlib: 'Goretsky hath an invention of lute strings covered with silver wyer, or strings which make a most admirable musick. Mr Boyle. . . . String of guts done about with silver wyer makes a very sweet musick, being of Goretsky's invention.'[1]

A few years later, an advertisement at the end of the 1664 edition of John Playford's viol treatise *An Introduction to the Skill of Musick* mentions strings that were made from metal wound on a silk core,[2] and by the end of the seventeenth century wound bass strings were becoming common throughout Europe, especially on bowed instruments. Violinists, who had hitherto used four plain gut strings, now began to fit a close-wound fourth string (that is, a gut or silk string completely overwound with wire, so that the core is not visible beneath), and many French violinists also preferred a *demifilé* or open-wound third string (that is, a string partially covered with wire, so that much of the core can still be seen). The increased density of these strings also allowed luthiers to redesign the larger bowed instruments with a shorter scale length, a modification that (for example) made possible the transformation of the large, unwieldly bass violin into the smaller, more agile violoncello.

Guitarists, however, were at first unimpressed with the possibilities offered by metal-wound strings. For centuries the guitar had been an instrument made from the simplest and most natural of materials (wood and gut), and the introduction of metal was initially resisted, not least because the extra 'zing'[3] the wire covering imparted to the bass notes completely altered the timbre of the guitar's lower register compared with its middle and upper range. As we saw in Chapter 11, the author of the 'guitar' entry in the *Encyclopédie* of 1757 complained of two disadvantages with metal-wound strings—one practical (the metal winding gradually cut into the gut frets) and one musical (metal-wound strings were so powerful that they tended to dominate the other courses)—and for most of the eighteenth century the majority of guitarists continued to use plain gut strings on all courses.

Nevertheless, some players eventually began to detect benefits in the new strings. As early as 1730, in the preface to the *Recueil de pièces de guitarre* by François le Cocq (Brussels, Conservatoire, MS 5615), the copyist Jean Baptiste Ludovico de Castillon had stated that he preferred to use gut *bourdons* open wound with metal, although he seems to have been a lone voice among guitarists at this time. But after the middle of the century, when the guitar was increasingly being used to provide arpeggiated accompaniments to songs (a style of playing that required strong, clear bass notes), more players started to believe that the advantages of metal-wound strings outweighed the disadvantages. It may even be that the growing popularity of the metal-

[1] Quoted in Peruffo (1997), 158–9. Robert Spencer has suggested that this information was probably passed to Hartlib by the celebrated chemist Robert Boyle, but further information about Goretsky is lacking.

[2] This was first noted by Robert Spencer in a review in *MT* (Dec. 1970).

[3] This is the onomatopoeic and (I hope) self-explanatory term used by Ephraim Segerman—an acknowledged expert on the manufacture of historical strings—to describe the brighter, brassier sound of metal-wound strings, as opposed to the more dulcet tone of a plain gut *bourdon*.

strung English guittar (and other forms of cittern that became fashionable in parts of Europe during this period) gradually persuaded guitarists that they too needed to produce bass notes with more 'zing'. Whatever the reason, Corrette (Paris, 1762) was the first musician to advocate the use of metal wound on silk 'in the Chinese manner' on the fourth and fifth courses of the guitar to improve their sonority, and references to the use of metal-wound strings on the guitar's lower courses steadily multiply as one moves towards the end of the eighteenth century, above all in France.

Although strings were manufactured in many countries, it was generally acknowledged in this period that those made in Italy (above all in Naples) were of the highest quality, and music shops throughout Europe proudly advertised that they kept a stock of Italian strings as well as locally manufactured ones. The consistency and durability of thin Italian gut strings was unrivalled, principally because the best makers used only the guts of very young animals (twisting three strands together for a violin *chanterelle*, and just two for the top string of a mandoline), but they wisely hid this trade secret from their foreign competitors, who continued to use the guts of older animals, with inferior results. Wound guitar strings, however, were not articles of general international commerce for most of the eighteenth century, the metal windings usually being added locally, either by the retailer or by the player (Jean Baptiste Ludovico de Castillon mentioned that he added the windings himself). This restricted availability may further explain why they only gradually came into general use.

Because plain gut strings were manufactured principally for violinists, eighteenth-century guitar methods usually refer to the violin when recommending which strings to use. For example, many methods state that violin first strings should be used for the guitar's third course, so it is important to have an idea of the approximate thicknesses involved. According to Mimmo Peruffo, typical diameters for the violin's three upper strings in the mid-eighteenth century were 0.70 mm (1st), 0.90 mm (2nd), and 1.10 mm (3rd).[4] Five-course guitars had a much longer string length than violins and, to avoid excessive string breakages, were generally tuned to a lower pitch than standard orchestral instruments. Segerman estimates that in the first part of the eighteenth century the guitar's treble strings were proportionally thicker (and therefore at a higher tension) than the plain gut *bourdons*,[5] but as the century progressed the quest for increased volume led to several modifications. During the period 1770–89 more wooden bars began to be fitted beneath the soundboard of the guitar to improve treble response, the thickness of the plain gut *bourdons* (and therefore their tension) gradually increased, and wound *bourdons* were more frequently used in order to add power and 'zing' to the bass notes.

[4] Peruffo (1997), 173–81. This Italian scholar has examined data from all surviving sources, and estimates that the diameters in use in the 18th c. were about 15 per cent thicker than the standard 'Baroque violin strings' offered for sale nowadays. The widely held idea that the Baroque violin had very thin, low-tension strings therefore seems to be an erroneous one (arising from misinterpretations by scholars in the early 20th c.).

[5] Information provided to me by Ephraim Segerman in Aug.–Sept. 1999.

Spain, South America, and Portugal

In Spain, during the period 1770–89, the six-course guitar steadily began to supersede the old five-course instrument, a trend reflected in the 'for sale' columns of Madrid's newspapers, such as this advertisement for a six-course guitar made by Francisco Sanguino: 'Whoever wants to buy a six-course guitar made by the famous Sanguino of Seville should go to see maestro [Antonio de] Medina, who lives facing the Corral de la Cruz . . .' (*Diario noticioso universal*, 11 Sept. 1772.) Many of the best instruments were being made in the cities of the far south, especially in Seville, where Sanguino worked, and Cádiz, where the *guitarrero* Juan Pagés (whose instruments would later be praised by no less an authority than Fernando Sor) was just beginning his career. These makers and their contemporaries became celebrated as 'the Andalusian School', but Madrid had some fine luthiers too, including another of Sor's favoured makers, Lorenzo Alonso, one of whose six-course guitars is worthy of special mention (Pl. 12.1). Inscribed *Por Lorenzo Alonso en Madrid año de 1786*, it looks at first sight like a conventional (though well-made and richly ornamented) instrument, with a two-piece spruce soundboard, maple ribs and back, and twelve ebony tuning pegs for six double courses; but closer investigation reveals that it also has, unusually, a sunken rose in the soundhole, and a miniature psaltery with ten sympathetic wire strings inside the body. This psaltery could be removed through an opening in the instrument's tail, and the sympathetic strings were presumably intended to improve the resonance of the guitar's six main courses.[6] Rafael Vallejo Baza of Granada also made a psaltery-guitar *c*.1789 (although his design has no rose, and the sympathetic strings are mounted externally),[7] and a few years later an advertisement in the *Diario de Madrid* (8 Aug. 1795) offered for sale 'una vihuela asalteriada'.

Instruments made by these *guitarreros* were sold not just in Spain but throughout Europe (where the best Spanish guitars were highly prized), and Spanish intellectuals like Goya saw the guitar as an integral part of their national culture. Indeed, in a letter he sent to a friend in 1784, the artist listed it among the necessities of life, rather than a luxury: 'I do not require much in the way of furniture for my house, for I think that with a print of Our Lady of Pilar, a table, five chairs, a frying pan, a cask of wine, and a tiple guitar, a roasting spit and an oil lamp, all else is superfluous.'[8] But in Spain the guitar was still regarded primarily as an instrument for the accompaniment of national dances and songs, rather than as a vehicle for solo performance, and fashionable Madrid society remained generally dismissive of national culture. Its musical tastes

---

[6] This instrument, which is currently in a private collection in Spain, is described in detail in Libin (1992).

[7] This instrument is housed in the Victoria and Albert Museum, London.

[8] Goya, letter to Martin Zapater, July 1784, quoted in Grunfeld (1969), 139–40.

PL. 12.1. Guitar bearing the label 'Por Lorenzo Alonso
en Madrid año de 1786'
Photo: Stewart Pollens. Reproduced by
courtesy of Laurence Libin

were still dominated by the Italian style, and advertisements from the capital's newspapers suggest that one of the most popular plucked instruments among the Spanish
middle classes at this time was the metal-strung Neapolitan mandoline, which was
then in vogue in many European countries.[9] Another instrument that was introduced
into Madrid in the late 1780s was the English guittar, sometimes played with the
fingers of the right hand and sometimes plucked by means of a mechanism operated
by six small keys. Somewhat resembling a toy piano, this curious box (of British
design) was attached to the strings between the rose and the bridge, thus avoiding
damage to delicate fingertips and nails, but also severely reducing the English guittar's
value as a serious musical instrument.[10]

   We have already noted that Spain's foreign rulers forbade the establishment of a
dedicated music press throughout the eighteenth century, and no Spanish tutors or
compositions from the 1770s or 1780s have survived, either in published or manuscript form. The now-lost *Obra para guitarra de seis órdenes* by Antonio Ballasteros
(Spain, 1780)[11] is given by many historians as the earliest-known work for six-course
guitar, but they have overlooked a Mexican guitar manual written four years earlier,
*Explicación para tocar la guitara de punteado, por música o sifra y reglas útiles para
acompañar la parte del bajo dividida en dos tratados por Dⁿ Juan Antonio Vargas y
Guzmán. Profesor de este ynstrumento en la Ciudad de Veracruz Año de 1776.* Vargas y
Guzmán had been resident in Cádiz as recently as 1773, so it is not surprising that he is
familiar with the work of the best European authorities (especially with seventeenth-
and early eighteenth-century Spanish sources), and he teaches in some detail the art of
performing on the guitar from a figured bass. He tells us that the guitar with which he
is familiar has twelve frets and six double courses, although he mentions that some
instruments have only five courses and that others have seven. His method is
intended to teach the *punteado* (plucked) style, and he therefore recommends that
octave stringing should be used on the fourth, fifth, and sixth courses; but he also
states that when the guitar is used as an accompanying instrument (especially in large
ensembles), the fourth, fifth, and sixth courses should each be tuned in unison rather
than in octaves.[12] He presents his music in both staff notation and tablature (Pl. 12.2),
but notes that 'the day of ciphers is over' and that players can only expect to excel as
musicians if they are familiar with the treble clef.

---

  [9] When commenting on Mozart's *Don Giovanni* (which is set in Seville), scholars have frequently suggested that
the aria 'Deh, vieni alla finestra' ought (for the sake of authenticity) to be accompanied by a Spanish bandurria, and not
by a Neapolitan mandoline. However, at the time of the opera's composition (1787), it seems that a Spanish nobleman
would have been at least as likely to have played the Italian instrument as his native bandurria.

  [10] This mechanism is described in more detail later in this chapter.

  [11] This Spanish work by Ballasteros has a suspiciously ghostly presence in the history of the guitar. There are many
references to it, but I have been unable to locate it, or even to establish whether it was a published work or a manuscript.
The work (*3 piezas y 4 minués*) was first listed in the *Gazeta de Madrid*, 3 Nov. 1780, but is now lost.

  [12] Vargas y Guzmán (1776), 21–7. This two-part manuscript manual from the city of Veracruz, Mexico, is now
housed in the Newberry Library, Chicago (Case MS VMT 582 V29e).

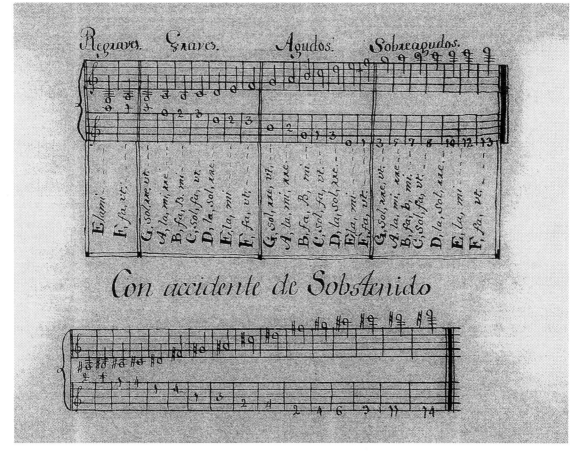

PL. 12.2. The correspondence between tablature and staff notation, from a
Mexican manuscript by Vargas y Guzmán (1776), 50. Veracruz, Mexico

Vargas y Guzmán also informs us that the second course of his guitar is mounted
with the top (*e*) strings of a violin (most European guitarists used this string for their
third course) and that his third course uses a pair of violin second (*a*) strings. He even
gives us the popular names used by guitarists to denote some of their strings: the lowest strings are *bordones* or *entorchados*, the octave string (if used) on the sixth course is
the *sextillo*, and the upper note on the fourth course is the *requinta*.[13] Gut strings were
being made locally throughout the Spanish and Portuguese colonies in South America
at this time by artisans who had brought their skills with them from the Old World,

---

[13] Vargas y Guzmán (1776), 23–4. Stevenson (1979) gives a summary of the manuscript's history and contents. The
term *entorchado* seems to have been applied to metal-wound bass strings, while *bordone* was used for thick plain gut
strings.

although the best strings were imported from Europe. They were expensive items (two sets could cost as much as a new guitar), and were generally sold in *pulperías* (bars, which doubled as general stores) because few towns had yet developed to the point where their economies could support a specialist music shop. From 1785 onwards, references to metal-wound bass strings can be found in inventories from the Buenos Aires Customs Office, relating to shipments of over-spun and plain guitar strings to Montevideo and other cities in the region.[14]

In central Portugal the viola toeira remained the popular form of five-course guitar, and a tutor was finally published for it in Coimbra in 1789. In the prologue to his *Nova arte de viola*, Manoel da Paixão Ribeiro (who was not a professional musician, but a professor of Latin at the university) laments the absence of expert guitar teachers in his city, and says that his book (aimed primarily at women, who were more interested than men in the instrument) is intended to rectify that problem. He first explains how to tie gut frets around the fingerboard, but also says that metal or silver frets can be used. Then he shows the tuning of the viola toeira (Pl. 12.3), with its distinctive triple stringing on the fourth and fifth courses (the thinner octave strings on the outside, so that the thumb strikes them slightly before it plucks the silver-covered *bordão*), and says that the instrument can be mounted either with gut or metal strings. He explains the traditional method of detecting a good gut string and spotting a bad one (by stretching it between both hands, plucking it with a finger, and ensuring that the entire length vibrates as a single string), but says that one doesn't need to be so careful when buying metal strings, because they are all good. At the back of the book are two plates containing a series of twenty-four diagrams using the 'Catalan' system to depict left-hand positions for all twelve major and twelve minor chords, in first or second position. These diagrams are clearly copied from the plate in Minguet y Yrol's *Reglas y advertencias* (Madrid, 1760), which, as mentioned above, was in turn derived from Juan Carlos Amat's *Guitarra española de cinco órdenes* originally published in Barcelona in 1596. Although Manoel da Paixão Ribeiro refers to his instrument simply as the viola (rather than the viola toeira), he indicates the origins of its popular name when he mentions that the strings used on the third course 'are commonly known as toeiras'.[15]

---

[14] Pinnell (1991), 188–96 gives further details of the manufacture of (and trade in) guitar strings in the Plata region.

[15] In Portuguese, *toeira* means (among other things) 'a loud sound'.

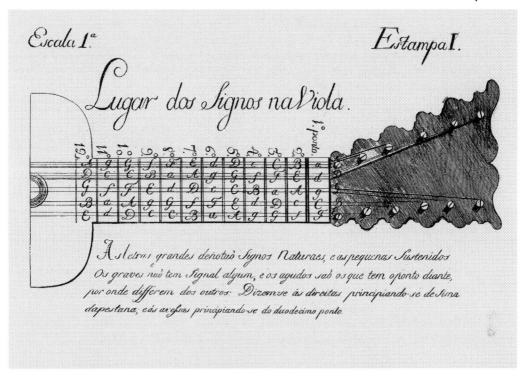

PL. 12.3. Tuning of the viola toeira, from *Nova arte de viola* by
Manoel da Paixão Ribeiro (Coimbra, 1789), Estampa I

Italy

During his tour of Italy in 1770 the English musician Charles Burney frequently observed the guitar being played by street musicians, and he recorded the scenes in his
journal:

Venice . . . upon the *Piazza di S. Marco*, I heard a great number of vagrant musicians, some in
bands, accompanying one or two voices; sometimes a single voice and guitar; and sometimes
two or three guitars together. Indeed it is not to be wondered at, that the street-music here is
generally neglected, as people are almost stunned with it at every corner; but, however, in jus-
tice to the taste and discernment of the Italians, it must be allowed, that when they do admire,
it is something excellent.[16]

[16] Burney (1771), i. 114.

Naples . . . A little before Christmas, musicians of this sort [itinerant street musicians] come from Calabria to Naples, and *their* music is wholly different from this: they usually sing with a guitar and violin, not on the shoulder, but hanging down. Paesiello had introduced some of this music into his comic opera, which was now in run. Signor Piccini promised to procure me some of these wild national melodies.[17]

Burney's descriptions do not state how many strings (or courses) these instruments possessed, and he may well have been describing the five-course, metal-strung *chitarra battente*, whose powerful tone was well suited to alfresco playing; but we do know that two significant changes were starting to take place in Italy at this time. First, some players began to abandon the use of courses and mount their instruments with just five single strings. The use of a single *chanterelle* had, of course, been common for centuries (because it was notoriously difficult to find a pair of very thin gut strings with reliable intonation), but the practice was now sometimes being adopted through- out the entire instrument, for reasons pointed out by the Italian Giacomo Merchi (writing in Paris):

I shall use this foreword to say a word about my manner of stringing the guitar with single strings. It is easier to find five true strings, than a larger number; single strings are easier to put in tune, and to pluck cleanly; moreover, they render pure, strong, and smooth sounds, approaching those of the harp; above all, if one uses slightly thicker strings.[18]

Although Merchi does not explicitly state that he used metal-wound fourth and fifth strings rather than plain gut *bourdons*, it seems probable that he did so. For centuries guitarists had found that a plain gut string did not produce sufficiently powerful bass notes by itself (which was why they either used two *bourdons* together, or paired a thick *bourdon* with a thin octave string), but the increasing availability of metal-wound strings meant that it was now possible to produce forceful low notes with plenty of 'zing', without the necessity of doubling. We know that Merchi was still using double courses in 1761 (when his *Le Guide des écoliers de guitarre, œuvre VII* recommended a single *chanterelle*, and octave-stringing on the fourth and fifth courses), so both the tonal power and the availability of metal-wound bass strings had presumably improved during the intervening years. Illustrations in late eighteenth-century method books show that players who favoured single strings simply left five of the ten tuning pegs on their five-course guitars empty, and (despite some speculation by modern writers) there is no convincing evidence that five-string guitars were ever built as a distinct type. A late eighteenth-century Italian five-string guitar in the Victoria and Albert Museum in London is sometimes cited as evidence that a separate instrument did indeed exist, but the head on this guitar is clearly a nine- teenth-century replacement.

---

[17] Burney (1771), 255.   [18] Merchi (1777), 2.

The second significant change was that a new form of guitar with six single strings was gradually coming into use in parts of Italy, and was known there as the *chitarra francese*. One of the earliest references to this new instrument can be found in a manuscript (*c*.1770–80; in Glasgow, Euing Music Library) by Francesco Conti, entitled *L'accordo della Mandola è l'istesso della Chitarra alla francese SCOLA del Leutino, osîa Mandolino alla Genovese*; an illustration[19] shows the tuning of the *mandolino alla genovese* to be $e-a-d'-g'-b'-e'$, and the accompanying text states that this tuning is identical to that of the chitarra alla francese. This statement cannot be literally true, because the little Genoese mandolin is tuned an octave higher than the much bigger guitar, and it also has six double courses, but the wording of the manuscript does suggest that a guitar with six strings had been introduced into Italy at some point prior to 1780.[20]

Although the name 'chitarra francese' translates as 'French guitar', it seems to have been a general term used by Italians (especially in the South) to distinguish the new and initially unfamiliar instrument from the traditional chitarra battente (which continued to be widely played), and it is by no means certain where the first six-string (as opposed to six-course) guitar was designed. We shall examine the earliest French six-string guitars shortly, but the first two Italian examples of which I am aware were both made in Naples, both dating from 1785 and both built by members of the city's two leading families of luthiers: one by Antonio Vinaccia,[21] and the other by Giovanni Battista Fabricatore.[22] This latter instrument has several features that soon became standard on six-string guitars, including metal frets, a flat (rather than vaulted) back, wider upper and lower bouts, with the body's curves being further accentuated by a narrower waist, and a slightly shorter string length than had been the case on many five-course guitars.

Like Spain, Italy did not possess an active music publishing industry during the eighteenth century, and, although there was a thriving trade in the copying of manuscripts, little Italian guitar music from this period has survived. We can therefore learn much more about the instrument at this time by consulting French sources, many of whose authors were well informed about developments in guitar construction and stringing that were taking place throughout Europe. However, before we move on, we

[19] Reproduced in Tyler and Sparks (1989), 140.

[20] It could well be argued that this Conti MS implies that the chitarra francese had six courses rather than six single strings. However, six-course gut-strung guitars never became popular outside the Iberian peninsula, and (as we shall see) subsequent usage of the term in Italy suggests overwhelmingly that the defining characteristic of the chitarra francese was its six single strings.

[21] Illustrated in *Carl Claudius' Samling af gamle Musikinstrumenter* (Copenhagen, 1931), no. 172, p. 147.

[22] This instrument, which is in a private collection, is described and illustrated in Timmerman (1994), 72–3. In Sept. 2001 I chanced upon a six-string Italian guitar at a recently opened exhibition in the city museum, Évora, Portugal, with a label reading 'Gaetano Vinaccia, Napoles, anno 1779'. However, Thomas F. Heck has recently drawn my attention to the work of Leopoldo Franciolini (1844–1920), a notorious Italian dealer in (and forger of) musical instruments. Franciolini inserted fake labels into many old instruments (including guitars which he then attributed to the Fabricatore and Vinaccia families), and some of these have since been purchased by unsuspecting museums and private collectors, so a label alone should not be taken as proof of authenticity.

should briefly note the existence in Italy of a young guitarist called Federico Moretti, who, according to his own later recollections, played a guitar with seven single strings. In 1786–7 Moretti first formulated (and privately circulated) a set of principles for guitar-playing, which he subsequently published in Naples (in 1792), after discovering that manuscript copies had begun to appear in other Italian cities, usually with other authors' names on them. Moretti later recalled that his instructions for the guitar had been first 'published in the year of 1792, adapted for the five-course guitar [*guitarra de cinco órdenes*], because at that time the one with six was not [widely] known in Italy.'[23]

No printed copy of that 1792 edition has survived, but Moretti's own manuscript has. It contains a tuning chart that clearly shows five single strings, and the author says that he is writing for 'the five-string guitar [*chitarra a cinque corde*]', but acknowledges that some people play the six-string guitar.[24] Until a printed copy of the 1792 edition is located, we cannot be sure whether the published form of this work was primarily intended for the five-course or the five-string instrument, but Moretti's use of the apparently contradictory terms *guitarra de cinco órdenes* and *chitarra a cinque corde* to describe the same work suggests that he was not greatly concerned which type the reader preferred. Furthermore, his words remind us that despite the experiments with a sixth string that had been taking place among pioneering luthiers and players, the majority of ordinary Italian guitarists in the early 1790s still regarded five strings (or five courses) as the norm.

France

The first French attempts to build an instrument with six (or more) single strings centred not on the guitar but on a newly designed relative, known nowadays as the lyre-guitar but originally called the 'lyre' or the 'lyre nouvelle' (Pl. 12.4). This neo-classical hybrid combined the fretted neck of a guitar with the stylized body of an ancient Greek lyre; and although the result was ungainly (one might even say kitsch), it undoubtedly played a significant part in the transformation of the guitar in France from five courses to six single strings—albeit that this transformation took place very slowly, over a period of several decades.

Exactly when and where the lyre-guitar made its first appearance in French musical life is uncertain (although *c.*1780 in Paris appears the likeliest date and place). It seems to have had single strings from the outset, usually plain gut for the trebles and metal-wound on silk for the basses. There is a surviving six-string lyre-guitar which, according to its label, was made by Lupot of Orleans in 1778,[25] but doubts have been

---

[23] Moretti (1799), 1 n.
[24] Ibid. and Moretti (1792), *prefazione*.
[25] New York Metropolitan Museum, 2590.

PL. 12.4. A late depiction of a 'lyre nouvelle', and of the hand positions on the guitar, taken from the *Nouvelle méthode de lyre ou guitarre à six cordes* by Lemoine (Paris, 1810), 2

expressed about its authenticity, and the earliest reliable date for an extant instrument is a nine-string model from 1785 made by Charles of Marseilles.[26] 1785 is also the year in which a sixth string is first documented in a French guitar publication: in the *Étrennes de Polymnie* (Paris, 1785, p. 148), an anonymous song accompaniment calls for a 'guitarre portant une corde de plus', and a low G is notated in the accompaniment. The wording clearly implies a single extra string (rather than another course), and the lyre-guitar could possibly have been the intended instrument. However, the composer could also have been referring to one of the new six-string Neapolitan models (imported from Italy), or perhaps to a five-course guitar that had been fitted with an extra (unfretted) bass string running alongside the neck. Several of these modified five-course French guitars from the 1780s have been located by Alex Timmerman, and the extra string (apparently tuned to *G*) was clearly an attempt to enable the performer to play a more satisfactory bass line.

However, both the instrument made by Charles and the request for a sixth string in the *Étrennes de Polymnie* were well ahead of their time in France, at least as far as the capital was concerned. A few six-string guitars were being made by the late 1780s in southern French cities near the Italian border (such as Marseille), but it was not until 1800 that the lyre-guitar (by now standardized with six single strings and tuned like a conventional guitar) started to become a truly fashionable instrument in Paris. And, as we shall see, 1800 was also the year in which French publishers of guitar music began regularly to issue arrangements that could be played either on a five-course or a six-string instrument.

French makers experimented with other single-string, guitar-related designs during the 1770s and 1780s, almost always in an attempt to extend the bass register downwards. An *arpi-guitare* made by Pacquet of Marseille in 1784[27] fitted a seven-string guitar neck to a harp-like soundbox. The *bissex* (literally 'twice six' strings), designed in Paris by Van Hecke and built by J. Henri Nadermann *c*.1773, combined six fretted strings with six free bass strings, the result somewhat resembling a lute with a malformed head.[28] And in 1784 (or 1785) Caron of Versailles built a *guitare décacorde*[29] with six gut strings and four extra basses, two pegboxes, an oval body, and a lever that could raise all the strings by a semitone. Yet, despite the comparatively limited possibilities of its bass register, the five-course guitar remained the overwhelmingly popular choice among lovers of plucked instruments, its simplicity and perfection of form standing in sharp contrast to the ugliness and awkwardness of these other inventions.

It is important to state clearly and unequivocally here that the five-course instrument continued to be the dominant type of guitar in Paris until the beginning of the nineteenth century. Almost no French guitar music published prior to 1800 required a

---

[26] Yale University, reproduced in Baines (1966), nos. 313 and 314.
[27] Brussels, Conservatoire royal, 3177.
[28] See Tyler and Sparks (1989), 138 for further details.
[29] Yale University, reproduced in Baines (1966), nos. 322 and 323.

sixth string, and a detailed consultation of primary sources reveals that (despite asser-
tions to the contrary by several modern-day writers) the five-string guitar did *not*
displace the five-course instrument there during the last quarter of the eighteenth
century. We have already noted that Merchi (writing in Paris in 1777) enthused about
'my manner of stringing the guitar with single strings', and a number of other guitarists also made clear their preference for five single strings. However, many Parisian
players advocated the use of five courses, French luthiers built large numbers of five-
course instruments throughout the 1780s and 1790s, and the pros and cons of single
and double stringing were still being discussed in Paris in the early nineteenth century—all of which flatly contradicts the statement by one writer that 'there are no
French sources of instruments or music for a five-course guitar after 1773,[30] and by
another that 'most French guitar music of the true Classical period [*c*.1740–90] was
composed for this [five-string] type of instrument'.[31]

One enthusiast for the five-course instrument was Antoine Bailleux, a violin professor, composer of symphonies, and publisher whose list included music by Boccherini and Haydn. In 1773 he issued his own *Méthode de guitare par musique et tablature*
(Paris), in which he described a guitar with ten frets and nine strings, grouped in five
courses and tuned *A a – d d′– g′ g′– b′ b′– e′*. He tells us that the right thumb is used to
pluck the fourth and fifth courses, while the index, middle, and ring fingers pluck the
top three courses. His use of the ring finger was somewhat ahead of its time (Merchi,
for example, recommended using only the thumb, index, and middle fingers, and it
was not until the early nineteenth century that the ring finger was fully incorporated
into guitar technique), but he also provided his music examples in old-fashioned
tablature, alongside the newer treble-clef notation (sounding an octave lower than
written), which had by now become the standard form of notation. The book contains
several minuets for guitar and violin, and also includes a set of simple solo variations
on the *Folies d'Espagne*, a sixteen-bar Renaissance theme that (in a modified form) had
become a favourite among French guitarists at this time, not least because it was a simple and convenient way of teaching repeated right-hand arpeggio patterns.

Bailleux was writing four years before Merchi recommended the use of single
strings; but four years after Merchi's publication Pierre Joseph Baillon (a *maître
ordinaire de la musique du duc d'Aiguillon*) spoke equally strongly in favour of five
courses. On page 3 of his *Nouvelle méthode de guitarre selon le sistème des meilleurs*

---

[30] Cox (1978), 21. On pp. 20–1 of this Ph.D. dissertation the author divides published Parisian methods of the late
18th and early 19th cc. into 'five-course guitar' (under which he lists only Bailleux) and 'five-string guitar' (which
includes tutors by Baillon, Doisy, and others). I have examined the various Parisian methods from this period in some
detail, and am utterly mystified as to how (for example) the clear instructions in the tutor by Alberti could have been
overlooked, or how Baillon's tutor of 1781 could have been included in a list of methods *exclusively* for the five-string
guitar, when its author praises at considerable length the advantages of double stringing and heavily criticizes the use of
single strings. I would therefore advise readers of this otherwise useful dissertation to treat these lists with some scep-
ticism.

[31] Savino (1997), 197–9. See also previous note.

auteurs (Paris, 1781) he states that the best method of stringing the guitar is with a single *chanterelle* and four double courses. The *chanterelle*, seconds, and thirds should all be of gut (each course a little thicker than the previous one), while the fourth and fifth courses should be fully wound on silk, and each accompanied by an octave gut string. On the lower courses the octave strings should be placed on the outside, so that the thumb strikes the upper note before the lower one. He then gives us the reasons why he does not like single stringing, or the use of two *bourdons* tuned in unison:

Not all the masters adopt the two octaves that ought to accompany the fourth and fifth strings. Some prefer single wound strings,[32] others think it is better to double them. I do not blame any of them, but I observe that I am here following the system of MM Rodrigue, Patoir, Vidal, l'Abbé Espagnol, and that this is how it is strung in Spain and Italy. It is doubtless not without good reason that the great masters have preferred the two octaves. Besides I have observed that if the two octaves are an inconvenience, then two wound strings are a greater one. These strings being of equal thickness, it is well-nigh impossible for the thumb to strike both. If only one is struck, then the second becomes useless, if they are both touched, then they mutually interfere with each other in their vibrations. If one only puts one string on the guitar, the sound is weak and does not produce a harmony as agreeable as when it is accompanied by an octave. The distortion [*feraillement*] that is attributed to the two octaves is only caused by bad strings, old ones, or badly chosen ones, or badly adjusted or worn frets, or by the manner in which these strings are plucked. One avoids this distortion by striking the strings with the thumb without following through downwards, in such a way that the two strings are made to vibrate equally.[33]

Baillon's book contains a number of pieces for violin and guitar, including a lengthy setting of *Les folies d'Espagnes* (in which the violin repeats the upper melody while the guitar plays twenty-four variations), a spirited, imitative *Chasse de M^r. De Lagarde* (reproduced in App. VIII), and several songs. He also includes a short prelude in each of the twenty-four major and minor keys. Unusually, he says that the strings of the guitar should be tuned to standard orchestral pitch. For centuries most guitarists had generally tuned to a suitable string tension rather than to an exact pitch (to avoid excessive breakages of their thin gut *chanterelles*), only raising their strings to orchestral pitch when required to play with other instruments. However, the author clearly wanted the guitar to conform to the musical standards of his day, so that it could be accepted by serious musicians, and he lamented: 'If all the masters were in agreement on the manner of composing for the guitar, as they are for all the instruments of the orchestra, one would soon see it take its place in a concert; and it would not be difficult to write a method that would attract everyone.'[34]

Another guitarist who preferred five courses was the Italian Francesco Alberti. Born in Faenza in about 1750, he came to Paris in 1783, settled there as a guitar profes-

[32] This could well be a reference to Merchi, in which case it confirms our earlier supposition that he used metal-wound fourth and fifth strings.   [33] Baillon (1781), 3.   [34] Ibid. 2.

sor and composer, and was still active in the city in 1796. He composed many songs with guitar accompaniment, and his instrumental works include *Trois duos pour violon et guittare, œuvre quatrième*, and a *Nouvelle méthode de guitarre dans laquelle on y trouve différentes variations, une sonate, 12 menuets et 6 ariettes* (Paris, 1786). In this latter work he states that the guitar should always be fitted with a single *chanterelle* and four double courses, the fourth and fifth courses being in octaves, and he does not even mention the possibility of using single strings.[35] This method includes some attractive songs and duets, notably a charming *gigue* for two guitars (reproduced in App. VIII).

We shall return to the five-course versus five-string debate in the next chapter, but, before moving on, we should note that the arguments offered for and against by French guitarists of this period tend to be somewhat exaggerated. Those who favoured single strings claimed that the use of unison and octave pairs caused serious problems of intonation (because the pairs were seldom completely accurate throughout their entire length); yet guitarists and lutenists had coped with such difficulties for centuries without finding them insurmountably challenging. On the other hand, enthusiasts for the five-course guitar saw no inconsistency in using a single *chanterelle* on their top course; and while Baillon considered the sound of a single bass string to be weak and lacking in sonority, Merchi thought that it gave 'pure, strong, and smooth sounds, approaching those of the harp'. As is often the case in debates, it seems that the advocates on one side of the argument tried to justify their own view by attacking the perceived weaknesses of the rival position; and although developments in string and instrument manufacture (and the desire to produce forceful, clear, and unambiguous bass notes) eventually led to the triumph of the six-string guitar in the early nineteenth century, the five-course versus five-string debate was never conclusively decided one way or the other.

Parisian sources from the 1770s and 1780s contain the names of many dozens of musicians who taught, played, and composed for the guitar, and we can concern ourselves here only with the most significant. The *Tablettes de renommée des musiciens* (Paris, 1785) listed Merchi as a *maître de guitare & de mandoline*, said that he was well known for his sonatas, *recueils d'airs variés*, and guitar methods, and noted that he was a resident of the rue Saint-Thomas du Louvre. The same work also included an entry for another prominent guitarist: 'VIDAL, one of the most celebrated and skilful masters of the guitar in Europe, has written a method for this instrument, and many duos, sonatas, and *recueils d'airs*, with variations in an educated style, worthy of being performed by the greatest masters.'[36] B. Vidal began teaching the guitar in Paris in the late 1770s, and over the next twenty years published at least eight volumes of predominantly instrumental music for the guitar (many of them with violin accompaniment),

---

[35] Alberti (1786), 2. A selected list of his instrumental music (and of his songs with guitar accompaniment) can be found in App. IV.

[36] *Tablettes de renommée des musiciens* (Paris, 1785).

as well as several collections of airs and ariettes with the guitar accompanying the voice. Shortly before 1780 his method for the guitar appeared, in which (like Baillon, Bailleux, and Alberti) he stated that the guitar should be mounted with a single *chanterelle*, and pairs on the other four courses (unisons on the second and third courses, octaves on the fourth and fifth courses).[37] Vidal was the only guitarist ever to perform at the prestigious Concert Spirituel, which was held in Paris on days of religious significance, when opera was considered unsuitable. He appeared there in 1776, but the vast Halle des Cents Suisses was not an ideal venue for a delicate plucked instrument, which is presumably why no other guitarists followed his example. Vidal was also the editor of the *Journal de guitarre composé de sonates, de pièces d'airs arrangés d'ariettes et romances avec accompagnement de guitarre et violon ad libitum*, which was published each month in Paris between 1786 and 1787 and included pieces by himself and by many other composers.

A longer-lasting guitar periodical was the *Journal de guitarre, ou choix d'airs nouveaux de tous les caractères avec préludes, accompagnements, airs variés, &c . . . pincé et doigté marqués pour l'instruction . . . par Mr. Porro*, which was published annually between approximately 1784 and 1797. Pierre-Jean Porre, who was born in Provence in 1750, Italianized his surname to Porro and moved in 1783 to Paris, where he became influential not only as a composer of some thirty-seven works (mostly for guitar) but also as a publisher. Among his early instrumental works is a *Collection de préludes et caprices dans tous les tons pour l'étude de la guitare* (1789), while his *Journal* included many of his own songs as well as those by established composers such as Haydn and Rousseau (all with Porro's own guitar accompaniments).

Cousineau remained one of the most important guitar makers and sellers in the capital, being singled out by the *Tablettes de renommée des musiciens* (in its list of *luthiers ou facteurs d'instrumens de musique à cordes*) as 'one of the most famous makers of harps and guitars'. Two other significant Parisian luthiers were J. Henri Nadermann (whose workshop in the rue d'Argenteuil had more success with harps and guitars than with the doomed bissex), and Jacques Pierre Michelot, who worked in the rue St-Honoré and developed a 'guitare en bateau' (literally 'a guitar in a boat'), which he claimed would reflect the sound of the instrument in a more focused way. A comparatively rare maker in the north of the country was Gérard J. Delplanque, a luthier from Lille whose guitars included one (made in 1775) with elaborate ivory marquetry, encrusted with shells and mother-of-pearl. In the south, we have already observed that Marseille had become an important centre for guitar construction, but we should not forget Lyons, where Bracht and Pierre Kettenhoven were both making and selling a wide range of guitars.

---

[37] Spencer (1981), Introduction.

England, Germany, and Austria

The English guittar remained the most popular plucked instrument in Britain during this period, as the large number of printed works for it attest. As well as original music by composers such as Tommaso Giordani (*Six Solos for a Guitar . . . and one Trio for a Guitar, Violin, and Bass*, c.1780) and Felice de Giardini (*Six Trios for the Guittar, Violin, and Piano Forte*, c.1775), countless pirated transcriptions of popular tunes appeared.[38] Many of these were issued by Robert Bremner, an Edinburgh music publisher who had a particular interest in the English guittar, having written a set of *Instructions for the Guitar* in 1758 and having also published several of Merchi's compositions for the instrument.

The English guittar was usually fitted with plain metal treble strings, and lower strings of metal wound on silk.[39] This gave the instrument a more forceful tone than the traditional gut-strung 'Spanish guitar', but thin metal strings can also cause callousing and nail breakages on the fingers of the right hand, something that would have dismayed the fashion-conscious ladies who were the English guittar's chief enthusiasts. One solution to this problem was arrived at by Claus of London, who patented a keyed guittar in 1783, with six small felted hammers (operated by six small pianoforte-like keys) emerging through the rose to strike the strings. Another mechanism (invented at about the same time and performing a similar function) was the externally mounted 'Smith's Patent Box', which was clamped to the body of the instrument by means of wooden arms.[40] These inventions (both of which simply required the player to fret a note with a left-hand finger, then depress the appropriate key with a right-hand finger) enjoyed a brief popularity and doubtless improved the state of the nation's manicure, but they also increased the perception of the English guittar as a toy rather than a serious musical instrument. And, when a newer, more powerful version of the 'Spanish guitar' was reintroduced to Britain in the next decade, it soon began to eclipse the English instrument.

In Germany and Austria, the cittern and lute were still the most popular plucked instruments during the 1770s and 1780s, but the guitar was gradually being

---

[38] The British Library contains hundreds of two-page, loose-leaf publications for the English guittar, originally issued by various publishers on a monthly or fortnightly basis. Transcriptions of music by major British composers of the period such as Thomas Arne and Samuel Arnold are prominently featured, but it seems unlikely that these celebrated musicians had any direct connection with the instrument.

[39] Players of plucked instruments generally preferred strings that were metal-wound on silk rather than on gut. Ephraim Segerman has suggested to me that this is because the tensile strength and pitch of gut varies considerably, depending on humidity (leading to frequent string breakages), whereas silk is much less susceptible to atmospheric changes. Silk became more widely available (and cheaper) in Europe as the 18th c. progressed, which probably explains why most references to metal-wound guitar strings from 1760 onwards suggest using silk fibres for the core, rather than gut.

[40] Illustrations of both of these devices can be found in Baines (1966), nos. 256 and 254.

introduced there during the late 1780s, although it did not start to become truly popular until the next decade. Unfamiliarity with what was happening elsewhere in Europe
led a violin maker from Weimar, Jacob Augustus Otto, to claim erroneously that he was
the first luthier to add a sixth string to the guitar (at some point after 1788):

I must take the opportunity here to observe that, originally, the guitar had only five strings. The
late Herr Naumann, Kapellmeister at Dresden, ordered the first guitar with the sixth or low
E-string, which I at once made for him. Since that time the instrument has always been made
with six strings, for which improvement admirers have to thank Herr Naumann.[41]

While Otto's claim may have been true within Germany, it clearly had no wider application, because (as we have seen) guitars in Spain had had a sixth course tuned to E
since the end of the 1750s, and the six-string guitar was known in France and Italy
from (at the latest) 1785. Indeed, it seems probable that the composer Johann Gottleib
Naumann (who had studied in Italy) was simply asking Otto to build him an instrument similar to the ones already being made elsewhere in Europe, and which he had
perhaps already encountered. However, Otto's statement is interesting for another
reason, because he tells us that when the guitar was first introduced into Germany, it
had five strings, not five courses—an observation borne out by other sources.

Lastly, we should note an encounter that took place in 1771 in Vienna between
Charles Burney and the Portuguese Abate António da Costa. In the following passage
Burney tells us how the Abate played a guitar with 'three strings to each tone' and had
invented a method of ensuring that each string on it was individually in tune at each
fret. Given the description, and the nationality of the Abate, it seems probable that
this was a specially adapted type of viola toeira:

This Abate is an extraordinary musician . . . He wanted very much to correct the imperfections
of the finger-board of his guittar, which being strung with catgut and having three strings to
each tone, he found it frequently happen, that these strings, though perfectly in unison, when
open, were out of tune when stopped, and this at some of the frets more than others . . . this he
effected in the following manner: he placed longitudinally, under the upper covering, or
veneer, as many rows of catgut strings as there were strings upon his instrument; then cutting
through the ebony at each fret, and laying these under strings open he placed under them little
moveable bits of ebony, which rendered the chords upon his instrument equally perfect in all
keys. He can, at pleasure, take off this finger board laterally; and as his modulation is very
learned and extraneous, this expedient was the more necessary.[42]

---

[41] Quoted from Turnbull (1974), 63–4. The 'Guitar' article in *NGII* (x. 563) incorrectly dates this claim as relating
to 'some point after 1688'.
[42] Burney (1771), ii. 97–8.

13

1790 to the Early 1800s:
The Triumph of the Six-String Guitar

Spain and Portugal

By 1790 the six-course guitar had become the most common form of the instrument in Spain. Most Spanish makers were now building only this type of guitar, and the numerous advertisements in the Madrid press throughout the decade reflect this change:

Whoever wants to buy an excellent six-course vihuela with a beautiful sound, made by Francisco Sanguino of Seville . . . (*Diario de Madrid*, 16 Apr. 1790)

Whoever wants to buy a six-course vihuela from Seville, with its case, very sonorous, come to the last house on the calle de Hortaleza . . . (*Diario de Madrid*, 9 Aug. 1792)

For sale, a six-course guitar made by [Joseph] Egea, with its corresponding case . . . (*Diario de Madrid*, 18 Apr. 1797)

For sale, an excellent six-course guitar with its case, made by Lorenzo Alonso . . . (*Diario de Madrid*, 13 Sept. 1798)

Whoever wants to buy an exquisite six-course Valencian guitar, made by Sanguino . . . (*Diario de Madrid*, 1 Oct. 1799)

Older five-course Spanish guitars were still being played and traded, but even some of these began to be modified to accommodate an extra course. This was not difficult to do, because (for the sake of symmetry) the head of a five-course instrument usually had two rows of five tuning pegs, but only nine strings were fitted to them (because of the preference for a single *chanterelle*). Therefore, if a single hole for an extra tuning peg was drilled between the two rows (and the bridge and the zero fret were adjusted to squeeze six courses into the space previously occupied by five), it became possible to fit eleven strings onto what had hitherto been a five-course instrument. The Portuguese viola toeira was even easier to convert, as it already had twelve tuning pegs, owing to the triple stringing on its lower courses. Museums contain many guitars that have clearly been modified to accommodate a different number of strings than was originally envisaged by the maker, which is why it is unwise to reach conclusions about stringing practices from a study of surviving instruments without also consulting written sources from the period.

Madrid was a thriving artistic centre in the final decades of the eighteenth century; and even though the French Revolution threw much of Europe into political turmoil during the 1790s, its initial consequences for Spain were beneficial. Nationalist aspirations everywhere were given a new legitimacy by the Revolution's philosophy of liberty and equality, and the Spanish middle classes (who had previously valued only foreign music and art) began to rediscover their own national cultural identity. Italian opera still thrived, but a renewed vigour was injected into native forms of music drama (notably the zarzuela and tonadilla); indigenous dance forms such as the fandango and bolero were adopted by serious composers; and the guitar, for so long ignored and disdained by fashionable Spanish society, became recognized once again as a legitimate instrument of national expression. Furthermore, restrictions on printing were gradually being relaxed. After a century in which very little new Spanish guitar music had been published, 1799 saw the appearance of four didactic works for guitar: published methods by Fernando Ferandiere, Federico Moretti, and Antonio Abreu, and a manuscript treatise by Juan Manuel García Rubio.

In his *Arte de tocar la guitarra española por música* (Madrid, 1799), Fernando Ferandiere describes the standard Spanish guitar of his day, telling us that it had seventeen frets and six courses, with octave stringing on the sixth course (a thin *sextillo* and a thick *sexto*) and unison pairs on the other courses, except for the first course (*primas*) where 'experience has shown that it is better to have only one'.[1] Although he does not explicitly state that the lower strings are metal-wound, he implies as much by initially discussing the three lower courses, then mentioning that 'the first two gut strings are called *terceras*; they are tuned in unison and called G'. He instructs players to use 'at least three fingers of the right hand, without any more nail than is necessary to strike the string', and to place the right hand:

very close to the soundhole, because this is where a sweet and agreeable tone is obtained; and not next to the bridge, which is where it is commonly strummed and played in barber-style; for here I am not talking about that school of playing, but rather showing that our guitar is capable of taking its turn with all the instruments that are accepted in an orchestra; for as against one single defect that it has (which is, having little volume and sustaining power), it has many other capabilities, such as: slurs, slides, chords, singing well, a large range, different registers, and the ability to imitate other instruments, such as flutes, trumpets, bassoons, etc.; the ability to accompany the voice, as if it were a pianoforte; and finally, it is an instrument that does not

---

[1] Ferandiere (1799), 2–3.

need the support of any other; so that it deserves the name, not of guitar, but of a whole keyboard held in one's hand.[2]

He advises pupils to learn to play in all the keys, and not to use a capotasto or *cejuela* (a device placed flat across all the strings at a particular fret in order to raise their pitch) except in cases of necessity, because they ought to be able to play exactly what is written. He also laments that there is much ignorance about the guitar, because people have hitherto regarded it as a luxury instrument rather than an essential one, and teachers have not dedicated themselves to studying it. However, he tells us that he has devoted himself to this task, and 'I am one of those who have discovered most about it [although] I know that there still remains much to discover, and that others will discover more as time goes by.'[3]

Ferandiere had studied the guitar with a Cistercian monk called Father Basilio (born Miguel García), who was organist at the Cistercian convent in Madrid. Padre Basilio was also a guitar teacher, and his pupils included not only Ferandiere, Moretti, and the celebrated nineteenth-century virtuoso Dionisio Aguado, but also many of the most important figures at the Madrid royal court, such as Queen Maria Luisa and Charles IV's chief minister, Manuel de Godoy. It is often stated that Padre Basilio was directly responsible for reviving the *punteado* (plucked) style in Spain, which is not strictly true, because we have already seen from advertisements in Madrid's *Diario noticioso universal* that guitars were being described in the 1760s as 'good to pluck [*puntear*], strum [*rasguear*] and play however one wants', and the 1776 method written by the Spaniard Vargas y Guzmán was entirely devoted to the *punteado* style. However, Basilio undoubtedly helped to make the instrument fashionable again in the capital, by emphasizing its potential as a solo, polyphonic instrument; and he can legitimately be seen as the founder of an important school of playing that continued into the mid-nineteenth century.

Basilio played with his nails, and taught Ferandiere and Aguado to do the same. Furthermore, in addition to his importance as a teacher, his playing of the fandango had a profound effect on the greatest composer in Spain at this time, the Italian Luigi Boccherini. Born in Lucca, Boccherini had lived in Madrid since 1769 and for a long time enjoyed royal patronage as he composed his finest works, most notably symphonies, string quintets, and piano quintets. However, his sources of income dried up in 1798, which is probably why he began accepting commissions in that year from an amateur guitarist, the Marquis de Benavente:

The marquis excelled on the guitar, an instrument dear to all good Spaniards. He asked Boccherini to provide a guitar part for his own use in those compositions which he liked, in exchange for one hundred francs for each quartet, quintet, or symphony. Several other rich amateurs acted in a similar manner, which prompted Boccherini, not to compose, as many

---

[2] Ferandiere (1799), 4–5.   [3] Ibid. 6.

believed, but *to arrange* with a guitar part a rather large number of chosen pieces from among his works.[4]

In December 1798 Boccherini wrote to his publisher Ignaz Pleyel that he had completed 'six quintets with guitar obbligato' by adapting some of his piano quintets, and a few months later he informed Pleyel that two mutual friends 'have heard almost the whole of the piano opus in the house of the Marquis de Benavente here (transcribed by me for the guitar for the sole use of the Marquis)'.[5] In all, he adapted twelve quintets, of which only eight have survived (Gérard catalogue nos. 445–50, 451, and 453), including one that has been nicknamed the 'Fandango' quintet (G. 448) because of its rousing final movement. Although Boccherini had long claimed to dislike Spanish dance forms, he was greatly impressed by Padre Basilio's skill on the guitar, and the manuscript of the quintet Op. 40 No. 2 is marked 'quintet imitating the fandango played by Padre Basilio on the guitar'. Another memorable movement also has strong Spanish overtones: 'La ritirata di Madrid' (from G. 453), a march-like theme with twelve variations that graphically portray a military night-watch approaching, passing by, and disappearing into the night.

Although a six-string instrument is commonly employed nowadays when performing these eight quintets for guitar and strings, there can be little doubt that a six-course guitar was originally used, and players who wish to give an authentic performance should adopt the standard late eighteenth-century Madrid tuning recommended above by Ferandiere, with octave stringing on the sixth course, a single first string, and unison stringing on the four inner courses. Ferandiere wrote a great deal of chamber music with guitar, including forty quartets for guitar, violin, viola, and basso, eighteen quintets for two guitars, two violins, and basso, and six concertos for guitar and full orchestra (sadly, none of these appears to have survived), and he was presumably also familiar with Boccherini's quintets. Indeed, he probably had Boccherini in mind when he wrote about the way that 'some people' use the guitar to accompany other instruments: 'The more famous composers Haydn and Pleyel will not risk composing a guitar quartet, nor a quintet with two guitars, simply because they do not know the instrument; unless they were to do what some people have done, namely to write not guitar quartets or quintets, but quartets and quintets with guitar accompaniment.'[6]

Players should be careful as to which modern editions of these quintets they consult, because several were re-edited in the early 1920s by Heinrich Albert and published by Zimmermann. Albert was a pioneer in the dissemination of late eighteenth- and early nineteenth-century guitar chamber music, but his editions are woefully unreliable; a comparison of his published version of G. 448 with a surviving manuscript

---

[4] Louis Picquot (1851), quoted in Ophee (1998), 10.
[5] Fink (1993), 5.
[6] Ferandiere (1799), 24.

reveals that he greatly simplified the guitar part, moving passages down an octave, giving difficult guitar phrases to the strings, and suggesting that the most challenging parts of the fandango could be omitted altogether. Unfortunately, G. 451 and G. 453 only survive in his version, but his edition of G. 448 is best avoided.[7]

In about 1795 Federico Moretti moved from Italy to Madrid (where he served in the Royal Walloon Guards of the Queen of Spain), and he published there a new and expanded two-part Spanish version of his 1792 work, the *Principios para tocar la guitarra de seis órdenes* . . . and *Elementos generales de la música* . . . (Madrid, 1799). He tells us that he would never have dared to present his *Principios* to a nation with such a close affinity for the guitar (and in a language that was foreign to him) had not the Queen herself encouraged him to do so and lent her name to the work by becoming its dedicatee. In a footnote, he mentions that:

Although I use the guitar of seven single strings [*guitarra de siete órdenes sencillos*] it seemed to me to be more opportune to accommodate these principles to the six-course guitar, that being the one that is generally played in Spain; this same reason obliged me to publish them in Italy in the year of 1792 adapted for the five-course guitar [*guitarra de cinco órdenes*]; because at that time the one with six was not [widely] known in Italy.[8]

However, the Italian Moretti would only bow so far to Spanish custom, and he recommended to his Spanish readers that they should try playing with single strings, rather than courses:

The French and Italians use single strings on their guitars, and by this means are able to tune more quickly, and the strings last longer before becoming false, because it is very difficult to find equal strings that have exactly the same pitch. I follow this system, and I give the same counsel to those who wish to apply themselves to this instrument, having known its great usefulness.[9]

As we shall see, Moretti was overstating his case a little here. Even as late as 1799 many French players still preferred double courses to single strings; despite his protestations, it was to take several more decades (and the efforts of the next generation of Spanish virtuosos) for single strings to become standard in Spain, so fond were ordinary Spanish guitarists of the sounds of their five-course and six-course instruments. However, by 1799 the six-single-string *chitarra francese* had become the chosen form among the generation of Italian virtuosos who were then perfecting their technique before emigrating in the early part of the nineteenth century to Europe's major cities, where they did so much to popularize the guitar as a solo instrument.

Before Moretti, guitar music had been written either in tablature or in staff notation, without any attempt to separate the different parts and without precise indications of the full duration of all notes. Many years later both Aguado and Sor paid

---

[7] Ophee (1998), 41–9 gives more details of the brutal surgery that G. 448 underwent at Albert's hands.
[8] Moretti (1799), 1 n.   [9] Ibid. 2.

homage to Moretti as the first guitar composer to distinguish between the various voices in his compositions:

The genre of music and the manner of writing it underwent a great change some time ago: one finally came to give each note its full value, and to write with precision everything that it was possible to play. D. Fédérico *Moretti* was the first who began to present in his written music the progress of the two parts, one the melody, the other the arpeggio accompaniment.[10]

At that time, I still had not heard tell about M. Frédéric Moretti. I heard one of his accompaniments played by one of his friends; and the progress of the bass, as well as the harmonic parts which I could distinguish there, gave me a high idea of his merit; I regarded him as the torch that serves to light up the lost path for guitarists.[11]

Despite his undoubted skill as a performer, Moretti advised guitarists to concentrate mainly on learning the art of accompaniment, because in his opinion the guitar was more suited to this than to the execution of florid solo instrumental music. Even when well performed, he said, the difficulty of playing a satisfactory bass line at the same time as executing rapid sequences of notes in high positions led to an overall sound that was too dry; and he advised players to follow the example of French and Italian guitarists, who (according to him) gave the melodic lines to violins, violas, and flutes, and used their instruments to perform the bass and the harmony. Moretti eventually modified his opinions about the guitar's suitability for solo instrumental music (his later compositions include a formidable *Fantasia variazioni e coda per chitarra sola, sul tema del Rondo della Cenerentola . . . dedicate all'esimio dilettante Il sig.r D.n Dionisio Aguado dal suo amico il cavaliere D. Federico Moretti*, published in Madrid in 1820), but it was left to the next generation of guitarists—Sor, Aguado, and their contemporaries—to explore more fully the solo possibilities of the six-string and six-course guitar.

Although various forms of guitar tablature persisted in Spain to the very end of the eighteenth century, all four of the didactic works that were written in 1799 primarily used the treble-clef notation that had already become standard in Italy and France, reflecting the move among educated Spanish guitarists away from the strumming of chords and towards the plucking of two or more individual parts. Juan Manuel García Rubio taught this new, more delicate approach in his *Arte, reglas armónicas para aprehender a templar y puntear la guitarra española de seis órdenes* (MS, dated 12 March 1799, and apparently written in Madrid). He uses staff notation, talks of the 'modern style', and (like Ferandiere) describes the standard instrument as having six courses (the lowest course in octaves) and seventeen frets. His tutor does not give us much further information about guitar technique, most of it being concerned with teaching the pupil to read not just the G clef, but also the C clef in various positions.

Antonio Abreu (a Portuguese guitarist of great renown who had settled in Madrid)

[10] Aguado (1826), p. iv.   [11] Sor (1830), 3 n.

is customarily credited with being the author of the *Escuela para tocar con perfección la guitarra de cinco y seis órdenes* (Salamanca, 1799). However, any reader of this fascinating little book soon becomes aware that much of it was written by Victor Prieto, the organist at the Royal Monastery in Salamanca. Prieto was an avowed admirer of the great guitarist's skills, and the resulting book is a mixture of Abreu's ideas and of Prieto's own thoughts. After giving us a somewhat fanciful history of music in general and of the guitar in particular, Abreu and Prieto tell their readers that they should use violin strings from Madrid for the upper courses, that a thin violin first string makes a good guitar second string, and that a normal violin first is suitable for the guitar's third strings. As for the three lowest courses, they say that they should all be strung in octaves when playing *punteado*, or with unison *bordones* when playing the bass part in an orchestral ensemble. They also give advice on how to trim the right-hand nails with scissors, then polish them with sandpaper so that they will not catch on the strings, and they seem unimpressed by those who prefer to play with the fingertips.

Despite the sophistication of the text, Abreu and Prieto give us only very simple musical examples, using tablature and an elementary form of staff notation. Abreu's apparent unfamiliarity with notation explains why Aguado later included him among a number of late eighteenth-century guitarists whose skill could not be fully appreciated from a perusal of their surviving work:

They did not know how to write with exactitude they things that they were playing with such success. One can see the proof of this in the compositions that remain to us by Laporta, Ferandiere, Arizpacochaga, Abrèu, my teacher Padre Basilio, and others; one scarcely recognizes the great performing talent of these skilful teachers, although one can perceive that they had divined a part of the character of the instrument: but one is far from recapturing on paper what one had been used to hearing from them.[12]

Moretti laid the foundations of a more precise form of guitar notation in Spain, but it was the Catalan Fernando Sor (1778–1839) who perfected the art of part-writing on the instrument. Although he had studied the guitar as a child, Sor was also an accomplished pianist, violinist, and singer, and during the early part of his career regarded himself principally as a composer of orchestral music. His approach to part-writing on the guitar was, therefore, far more rigorous than might have been the case had he been a 'mere' guitarist. Many decades later (and speaking about himself in the third person), he recalled in the *Encyclopédie pittoresque de la musique* how he had first encountered Moretti's music in Barcelona during the late 1790s:

He [Sor] understood the merit of certain instrumental effects; but deprived of the piano, he had not yet dreamed of trying to reproduce on the guitar the effects which so pleased him. At this time, he heard the brother of General Solano playing on the guitar a piece in which one could distinguish a melody and an accompaniment. The composer of the piece was Moretti,

[12] Aguado (1826), p. iv.

an officer in the Walloon Guards, who was the first to understand the true nature of the guitar. Moretti's music gave Sor a new direction, and with a little work and by applying his knowledge of harmony, he soon came to compose and perform music in several real parts. Guitarists asked him for his compositions, but then they changed the note values, in order to write—so they said—according to the true nature of the guitar.[13]

In the same work Sor tells us that he composed a good deal of guitar music during the first decade of the nineteenth century, when he was living successively in Madrid, Barcelona, Málaga, Jerez, and Valencia.[14] Little of it appeared in print until after 1813 (following his lifelong exile from his homeland, which resulted from his support for the French during the 1808–14 Peninsular War), but we know that some major works were written in Spain, including the Grand Solo Op. 14, and possibly also his Op. 7, published by Ignaz Pleyel (to whom it was dedicated) as *Fantasie pour la guitarre* (Paris, 1814). This work represents Sor's most rigorous attempt to notate guitar music with complete accuracy, first by using two staves, and secondly by writing each note at its correct octave. In the foreword to this piece he attacked the deficiencies of standard notation, saying that 'I only employ the G clef when the instrument has to play the notes that lie within its range', and the entire *Fantasie* was printed on two staves, mostly using the bass and alto clefs. But although the result was admirably clear and musicianly, guitarists who had learned to read only from a single treble clef (with octave transposition) would have found it extremely difficult to sight read, and later editions of the same piece appeared in conventional guitar notation, a system that (despite its cramped appearance, excessive use of leger lines, and other manifest imperfections) has survived more or less unaltered into our own day.

Moretti's influence must also have guided the young Sor in his decision to use six single strings on his guitar rather than six courses, and several Spanish luthiers too were beginning to follow the Italian's example. No Spanish maker seems to have built a six-string guitar during the eighteenth century, but they are found with increasing regularity throughout the first decade of the nineteenth century. The first signed and dated Spanish six-string guitar of which I am aware was made by Agustín Caro of Granada in 1803, and has several features that came to be increasingly common in nineteenth-century guitar construction: internal fan strutting, harmonic bars above and below the soundhole, a raised fingerboard, and metal frets. However, it also preserved some traditional features, such as a *golpeador* (a tapping plate on the table below the top string, often fitted to Spanish guitars to protect the wood when the player used it for percussive effects), and wooden tuning pegs (machine heads being a rare feature on Spanish guitars before about 1820).[15]

---

[13] Ledhuy (1835), 164, reproduced in Jeffery (1977).

[14] Jeffery (1977) contains a detailed biography of Sor's life and work, including a reproduction of the Ledhuy article.

[15] An illustration and description can be found in *La guitarra española* (1991), 133–4. The same catalogue also

Within a few years other Andalusian makers were also making six-string guitars, as were luthiers in Madrid and Catalonia, but it would be incorrect to assume that the six-string guitar immediately replaced the six-course instrument in Spain. Six-course instruments continued to be built, such as a fine example by Joan Matabosch of Barcelona dated 1815,[16] and many musicians throughout the first third of the nineteenth century remarked on the persistence of six-course instruments throughout Spain. In the French edition of Aguado's *Méthode complète pour la guitarre* (Paris, 1826), the author mentions guitars with double stringing, and a footnote from the translator, François de Fossa, adds that they are 'still in use in Spain'.[17] And later in the same work Aguado (who had initially written his method for Spanish readers) gives a lengthy explanation of why he considers single strings to be better than courses, which clearly implies that many Spanish guitarists had not yet been convinced:

I have said that I prefer the guitar with single strings and I have very good reasons for this: 1. it is difficult to find two strings that keep in unison from one end of the fingerboard to the other; 2. as it is customary, on double-stringed guitars, to leave the *chanterelle* single, in passing from this string to the others one perceives an unevenness in the sounds; 3. it is still customary to pair the sixth string with a thin string that gives the octave: a ridiculous custom which prevents one hearing the bass notes; 4. if one has difficulties to conquer when there is only a single string to touch, one will have plenty more trouble when one has to touch two strings; 5. it is an error to imagine that one obtains more sound with double strings, except on open strings, because the sound is produced by the duration of vibrations, and it is much easier to obtain them from one string than from two; 6. finally, double courses are an obstacle to agility, and increase the difficulty of keeping in tune.[18]

Another footnote from de Fossa adds that 'one must not forget that M. Aguado writes in Spain, where double strings are still in use'. And a decade later the British writer George Hogarth was still noting that 'the Spanish guitar is constructed with double strings, which are tuned in unisons, with the exception of the lowest pair, which are in octaves'.[19] So, while Aguado and Sor (who both spent significant parts of their adult lives in other countries) may have followed Moretti's example and adopted single strings at the start of the nineteenth century, it was a very long time indeed before the six-string instrument became the dominant form throughout their native land. This may in part have been because the six-course instrument was louder when rhythmical *rasgueado* passages were being played, and this somewhat jaundiced view from a

includes an anonymous guitar from the Madrid school, listed as 'c. 1800', but there is no direct proof that quite such an early date is warranted.

[16] Museu de la Música, Barcelona, no. 447. Although it has six courses in the old style, this instrument also has several modern features, notably a raised fingerboard with eighteen metal frets.

[17] Aguado (1826), 3. De Fossa was a fine guitarist in his own right, and is believed to be the first person to have described the production of artificial harmonics on the guitar. It is also thanks to him that many of Boccherini's guitar quintets have survived. The composer's original manuscripts are lost, but de Fossa fortunately made copies of them in Madrid, in 1811.

[18] Aguado (1826), 31.   [19] Hogarth (1836), 85.

Frenchman of the merits of the average Spanish guitarist certainly suggests that charm and delicacy were not always the main priorities of the typical Iberian player:

People assure us that it is to the Spanish that we owe the guitar. I do not counterbalance that opinion: but I venture to assert that that country is not the one which improved that instrument. In general, playing the guitar the Spanish way is not the most agreeable way. Usually, they make it boil, seeing that they only perform on the instrument by passing and repassing the thumb over the strings, without discretion, without variety, and without principles. Would one say that it is in Italy that the instrument is at its perfection? Will not all agree that the Italians sacrifice the instrument to their voices? They sing, singing in a divine way, they possess an abundance of perception in the musical art, for perceiving that a heavy accompaniment cannot marry with the embellishments of their singing, they accompany themselves with strums or *batteries*, judiciously applied. But it is only in France that this instrument has all of its charm, its grace, its purity, and its tenderness.[20]

English guittars were still being bought and sold in Madrid throughout the 1790s, but it was in northern Portugal that they truly began to permeate the national culture. The city of Porto had long been home to wealthy British families who managed the wine trade along the Douro, and they seem to have been the first to introduce this instrument to Portuguese society. By 1795 it had become sufficiently popular there for António da Silva Leite to publish his *Estudo de guitarra, em que se expoem o meio mais fácil para aprender a tocar este instrumento*, and it presumably sold well, because a second edition appeared in 1796. In it the author spoke of the history of the instrument, which has since become known throughout Portugal as the guitarra portuguesa:

The guitarra, which, so it is said, had its origin in Great Britain, is an instrument that, through its harmony and smoothness has been accepted by many people, who find it capable of substituting for some instruments of greater volume, like the harpsichord and others; and sufficient for entertaining a gathering, avoiding the inconvenience that the invitation of an orchestra could cause, they adopted it, perfecting themselves in playing with great skill: and I (seeing that the Portuguese nation has also adopted it, and has pledged itself to playing it with the greatest perfection, desiring to contribute to the instruction of my fellow countrymen, with the little means that I possess, and there not being any treatise that speaks of this matter) composed the present little work, and added the rules to it, that seemed to me most appropriate and necessary to learn to play with perfection the aforesaid instrument.[21]

He gives the conventional eighteenth-century English tuning for the *guitarra* ($c-e-g$ $g-c'c'-e'e'-g'g'$), and tells us that the best guitarras at the time were being made by Mr Simpson of England, adding that 'in this city of Porto is Luis Cardoso Soares Sevilhano, who today is little inferior to the aforementioned Simpson'. He explains which strings to use ('the first courses ought to be *carrinho no. 8*, and not *no. 7* as many wish . . .'),[22] and concludes the book with a number of little duets for two guitarras,

---

[20] Gatayes (*c*.1807), 2–3.   [21] Silva Leite (1795), 25.
[22] Traditional Portuguese music shops (such as the one run by António Duarte, Rua Mouzinho da Silveira 165–67,

including a short but attractive *Tocata do Sr. Francisco Gerardo*. Portuguese makers initially copied the style of the English guittar, sometimes using the watch-key tuning mechanism, but often fitting simpler wooden pegs instead. However, during the nineteenth and early twentieth centuries, they began to redesign the guitarra, fitting a distinctive (and more durable) fan-shaped screw-tuning mechanism, and developing new tunings. They also began to pluck the strings with picks attached to the right-hand fingers, and the hard, zither-like sound they produced (accompanied by the *viola*, or six-string guitar) became an integral part of the melancholy folk music known as the *fado*. However, Silva Leite's *Estudo de guitarra* confirms that at the end of the eighteenth century this most Portuguese of instruments was identical in all respects to the English guittar.

Britain

While the popularity of the English guittar was growing in Portugal during the 1790s, it was declining in Britain. Music for the instrument was still being published until the early nineteenth century (especially in Scotland), but its days as a fashionable accoutrement for ladies were largely over, and its role in domestic music-making was eventually usurped by the Spanish guitar. It is often stated that the Spanish guitar did not reappear in England until 1815, when Fernando Sor came to live in London (staying until 1823 and impressing the public with his remarkable playing),[23] but it had in fact been quietly growing in popularity there over the previous thirty years, as we shall now see.

The English luthier John Preston was making fine Spanish guitars throughout the 1780s (presumably having identified a small but lucrative market for such instruments); and the revival of the Spanish guitar in Britain was given a further impetus by the arrival of Francesco Chabran, a musician from Piedmont who settled in London *c.*1782 and adopted the more English Christian name of Felice or Felix. He worked mostly as a violinist, but advertised himself in 1795 as 'teacher of the violin, pianoforte, Lyre, and Spanish Guitar, of 15, Standgate Street, Lambeth',[24] and in the same year published his *Compleat Instructions for the Spanish Guitar . . . by F. Chabran, teacher of the Spanish & Pianoforte Guitar & Violin'.*[25] In this little book he recommends the use of five single strings, tells us that 'the tone of the *Spanish Guitar* is much

Porto) still sell strings in this way, by cutting the desired length from numbered *carrinhos* or reels. The guitarra and various regional types of viola have been in continuous use in Portugal since at least the 18th c., and the strings appear to have altered little during that time (apart from the introduction of high-tensile steel for the thinnest diameters).

[23] Jeffery (1977), 39–74 gives a full account of Sor's English period.
[24] On copies of his *Six Favourite Songs and Rondos*, which was published in that year. Button (1989), 4–7 gives further biographical details.
[25] London, 1795. The pianoforte guitar was another name for the English guittar when fitted with one of the keyed plucking mechanisms (such as 'Smith's Patent Box') described earlier.

like the Harp, very harmonious, is esteemed the most complete accompaniment to the female voice, and is capable of producing all the desired beauties of harmony', and includes a setting of the *Folies d'Espagne* and a fandango.

By 1800 the instrument was becoming sufficiently well known for a song about it (by the composer Samuel Arnold) to be published in Dublin.[26] The song, *The Spanish Guitar*, was not intended to be accompanied by the instrument in question, but the lyric did conjure up a typically Iberian scenario:

> A lady in fair Seville city,
> Who once fell in love very deep,
> On her Spanish guitar play'd a ditty,
> A ditty that lulled her old Guardian to sleep.
> With a hoo lira lira . . .

In 1806 the composer Thomas Bolton published a *Collection of Airs, Marches, Dances, Pollacas and Quick Steps* for the pianoforte, featuring *ad libitum* parts for several instruments, including the guitar. This includes a G major chord that could only be played on a six-string guitar, thus indicating that the extra string was by now being adopted in Britain.[27] The Italian Filippo Verini established himself in London *c.*1809 as a teacher of (and performer on) the Spanish guitar; and in 1813 Chabran published the first British six-string guitar method, *A New Tutor for the Harp and Spanish Guitar* (London), in the preface of which he claimed: 'The Spanish Guitar in regard to power and brilliancy of tone is little inferior to the Pedal Harp, and as an accompaniment to the Voice, surpassing all instruments of a similar kind.' Three years later he published *A Complete Set of Instructions for the Spanish Guitar*, the first publication of an English tutor written exclusively for the six-string instrument.

At about this time Edward Light was trying to interest the British public in a rival instrument of his own invention, the Harp-Lute-Guitar. Several different versions were built, all of them combining a fretted neck (of English guittar proportions) with free-standing bass strings, and in his *Tutor with a Tablature for the Harp–Lute–Guitar* (London, *c.*1810) Light listed what he claimed were the many advantages of his new design:

The Harp-Lute-Guitar, so call'd from the structure of it, partaking partly of the Harp, partly of the Lute, and partly of the Guitar. This little Instrument is confessedly greatly superior to any other of its size and kind, the Inventor gives this short account, to shew wherein it differs from, and particularly excels others—First, by containing a greater number of Strings, which not only renders it more easy to play on, but the Tones also more perfect by having the more open Notes . . . Lastly, by way of observation, many attempts have been made to introduce portable Instruments for Ladies accommodation, such as the English Guitar, Spanish Guitar,

---

[26] *The Spanish Guitar: A Favourite New Song* (Dublin, 1800). Treble and bass only. Copy in British Library, H.1652.ww.8   [27] Button (1989), 3.

Mandola, Mandoline, and latterly the Lyre and the Lute, the Inventor of the Harp-Lute disdaining to depreciate the merits of other Men's productions, will therefore here decline making comparisons. (p. 1)

However, as with the attempts made by Parisian luthiers in the 1770s and 1780s to extend the range (such as the arpi-guitare, the bissex, and the guitare décacorde), the sheer awkwardness and ungainliness of the resulting instrument outweighed any musical benefits it might have possessed; despite some vigorous marketing by its inventor, it never became more than a musical curiosity.

The Peninsular War of 1808–14 (in which the British, Spanish, and Portuguese fought against the French and eventually drove them out of Iberia) also had a significant effect on the guitar's popularity in Britain, as *The Giulianiad* (a guitar magazine published in London in 1833) later recalled:

Mixing, as did our warriors, with the people of Spain and Portugal; and domesticated as many of them were, and are to this day, with the families of those countries, it was only natural that they should have discovered the immense influence which the guitar there possessed, and have felt themselves, the witching power of its fascination . . . How delightful must be the associations connected with this instrument to those who first heard its sound, and learnt its touch, amid the danger and terror of warfare, now that they can recall to their memories those days of chivalry and romance, by their own peaceful hearths in old England! (p. 18)

1815 saw the arrival in London not just of the Spaniard Sor, but also of the Italian Giuseppe Anelli, whose concerts had previously attracted widespread acclaim in Turin and Paris. Both of these virtuosos undoubtedly increased the popularity of the six-string guitar in Britain, but they were by no means the sole cause.

Italy

Anelli was just one of a large number of young Italian players of the new six-string guitar who followed Moretti's example and emigrated to various European capitals during the early nineteenth century, pursuing wealth and fleeing poverty. But unlike Moretti, who was a professional soldier, these younger Italians had to earn their living from music by teaching, composing, and performing, all of which further helped to popularize the six-string instrument. Anelli's abilities as a performer can be gauged from this review of a concert he gave in Turin in 1809, which included what may well be the earliest performance of a concerto for six-string guitar (the lost concertos by the Spaniard Ferandiere were, of course, written for a six-course instrument):

Anelli's success yesterday evening was most complete; everyone was delighted by his astonishing performance on the guitar, and by his peculiar manner of singing. He sings with great taste and expression; and his voice coupled with the affecting sounds of his guitar produced an uncommon sensation through a crowded house which encored him several times. But his performance on the guitar was still more surprising; of the powers of this instrument no one had formed an idea until Signor Anelli evidently proved it to be one which possesses the capability of producing the greatest effects. He really plays the guitar in a style never heard before, and his concert on it, of his own compositions, which was accompanied by a grand orchestra has excited general admiration and was received with enthusiasm. We have heard since that in consequence of his brilliant success, Signor Anelli has been engaged to remain with her Royal Highness the Princess Paoline Borghesi who was delighted at the signor's performance.[28]

It is beyond the scope of this book to look in detail at the careers of nineteenth-century players, but we should briefly list the most famous of these peripatetic virtuosos, who usually toured Europe for several years before adopting a new city. The most celebrated Italian guitarist was Mauro Giuliani from Bisceglie (Puglia), who moved to Vienna in about 1806; but Paris also proved a popular destination during the early nineteenth century, attracting the Neapolitan Ferdinando Carulli, Filippo Gragnani from Livorno, Francesco Molino from Ivrea, and the Florentine Matteo Carcassi. These players (and their Spanish contemporaries) composed a huge amount of music for six-string guitar and also wrote a great deal of didactic material, and their various methods (mostly published in Paris) form the basis of what is nowadays considered to be classical guitar technique.

We have already noted that Italians called this new six-string instrument the chitarra francese, and that name frequently occurs in Italian documents from the late eighteenth and early nineteenth centuries (although players who emigrated to other parts of Europe usually called it simply the guitar). The Robert Spencer collection, for example, contains a folder of manuscripts (originally from Padua) of songs and instrumental music with chitarra francese: one piece is dated 1799 and is entitled *Un tema con sei variazioni per chitarra francese di Gregorio Trentin*; another is called *Nun 2 Duetti e A Cavatine ridotti per chitarra francese e dal sig.r Matteo Bevilacqua*;[29] while a third is *Duetto con chitarra Francese Obligat ho verduto una civetta del Sig. Luigi Caruso*. Elsewhere, the manuscript of an early nineteenth-century guitar concerto by Giuseppe Malerbi is entitled *Concerto [con] chitarra franc.se obbligata con strumenti . . .*,[30] and a piece for guitar and Genoese mandoline by the great Niccolò Paganini[31] is headed *Serenata p. L'amandolino e chitarra francese*. All of these works require a low E string for the performance of the guitar part.

At this time Naples was undoubtedly the most important Italian city for the manufacture of guitars (including the traditional chitarra battente), and it is unsurprising to discover that many of the earliest performers on the new six-single-string guitar

---

[28] *Moniteur des Alpes*, quoted ibid. 13–14.

[29] Heck (1995), 23 states that Bevilacqua emigrated to Vienna *c*.1800. The handwriting in this folder of manuscripts is almost illegible in places, so these titles are only an approximation.

[30] This manuscript is preserved at the Biblioteca Comunale 'F. Trisi' at Lugo, in the Malerbi Holdings, MS A 431.

[31] MS in I-Gl.

(including Moretti, Giuliani, and Carulli) had been born and raised within the Neapolitan kingdom. However, very little guitar music was published there, so, although we know a good deal about guitarists who toured throughout Europe and had their works printed abroad, we shall probably never learn much about those who remained within the city. Nevertheless, these observations made in 1805 by the Naples correspondent for a German music magazine give us some idea of the guitar's pre-eminence in the city at that time:

In closing, a word about a secondary matter. The cultivation of instrumental music is, as a rule, subsidiary here. And no instrument is so cultivated as—the guitar. Furthermore, it is a fact that there are good composers here for this little creature, and first-rate virtuosos, in a more elevated sense than one would expect for the guitar. In order to meet the demands of the amateurs, there are countless teachers, and two workshops that construct guitars of all types. It is already well known that there are several concerns here that manufacture the best strings in the world and export them to every nation.[32]

France

We have already seen that the custom of using pairs of strings lasted well into the nineteenth century in Spain, and the same is true, to a lesser extent, in France. Many Parisian guitar teachers were recommending five single strings by the 1790s, but five courses were still commonly encountered there, the fourth and fifth courses being tuned either in octaves or in unison. As late as 1801 the Parisian guitarist Charles Doisy was noting in his *Principes généraux de la guitare* (Paris), in a section entitled 'Manner of Stringing the Guitar', that:

This is arbitrary. Some prefer double strings, others single strings. Whichever it be, one ordinarily only has five . . . The A and the D are called BOURDONS. Some people fit two A and two D strings; of which one is of [wound] silk, the other of gut, tuned at the octave; the G and B strings are in unison; the E single. With some others, the two A and two D strings, in silk, are tuned in unison; the two G and two B strings are also in unison, the E single. These two manners are good. As for me, I adopted willingly the single strings on which the sounds leave more purely, the difficulty of pairing double strings is eliminated, and which take much less time to tune. (pp. 9–10)

The three guitar methods published in Paris (*c*.1790, *c*.1802, and 1810) by the guitarist and violinist Antoine Lemoine neatly illustrate the way in which single stringing in France gradually moved from being an option during the last decade of the eighteenth century to being the norm by the end of the first decade of the nineteenth. In his *Nouvelle méthode courte et facile pour la guitarre à l'usage des commençans* (Paris, *c*.1790)

[32] *Allgemeine musikalische Zeitung* (1805), 569–70.

he acknowledged that five courses were favoured by many French players and, having discussed his preferred method of single stringing, added: 'This manner serves for tuning the guitar fitted with single strings; one can use it for tuning the double-strung guitar, observing that the strings that accompany the fifth and fourth strings are tuned an octave higher, and those that accompany the third and second strings are tuned at the unison' (p. 4). He repeats this advice in the second, expanded edition of his *Nouvelle méthode courte et facile pour la guitarre à l'usage des commençans* (Paris, *c*.1802); but by the time he published his *Nouvelle méthode de lyre ou guitarre à six cordes* (Paris, 1810), he was more direct about the reasons for his dissatisfaction with double stringing. However, his antagonistic remarks make it clear that the double-strung instrument was still being used in France well into the nineteenth century:

Many people fit the guitar with double strings: but this method is subject to great inconvenience. 1. It is extremely difficult to find two strings of equal thickness and above all perfectly in tune. 2. One never attacks the two strings well together, the result of this is that whichever one is attacked first is more out of tune than the other; note that the first, being plucked with more force, is more prone to sinking in pitch than the second: and the instrument then is never in tune; this produces also a sort of beating between the two strings, which becomes very disagreeable to the ear: in general, the guitar fitted with single strings is far more agreeable to the ear; seeing that the basses are heard much more clearly: the double-strung guitar is tolerable only in solo pieces, like the sonata, moreover it is necessary to use a lot of force in the right hand to avoid hearing the beating [*chaudronnement*] produced by the unison of the two strings. (p. 2)

These complaints about the problems of double stringing were obviously exaggerated, because players had for centuries been coping with the potential problems of intonation and distortion; modern enthusiasts for the Baroque guitar and lute still find that only double stringing can produce the sonority they seek. However (as with the remarks of Doisy and Aguado observed earlier), Lemoine's complaints demonstrate that many guitarists of the early nineteenth century were expecting their instruments to produce different sounds from those preferred by previous generations, and the clear and unambiguous bass notes these players now sought were best obtained from single, metal-wound, high-tension silk strings.

In his *c*.1802 method Lemoine described himself as 'professeur de guitarre et de lyre', and the latter instrument had by then become very fashionable in Paris. We noted earlier that the *lyre nouvelle* (or lyre-guitar) was already in existence by 1780, but it initially failed to capture the public imagination, and very little music was published for it during the 1780s and 1790s. However, several makers persevered with the instrument, and the six-single-string lyre eventually achieved popularity in Paris some twenty years later, enjoying a brief heyday there throughout the first decade of the nineteenth century. Most of the surviving lyres were made between 1800 and 1810, and much of the guitar music published in Paris during that decade (especially songs with guitar accompaniment) was marked 'de guitarre ou lyre' or 'arrangé pour la lyre ou guitarre' and could be played on either a five-course or six-string instrument.

Given that the first documented appearance of a sixth string in a Parisian guitar publication was in 1785 (the *Étrennes de Polymnie*, which called for a 'guitarre portant une corde de plus'), and that six-string guitars were being made in Marseille by the late 1780s, it is surprising to note that the six-string guitar made little impact on musical life in the French capital until the middle of the first decade of the nineteenth century. This was partly because the popularity of the lyre initially prevented the six-string guitar from establishing itself there, and partly because French players in general (and Parisian players in particular) continued to regard the five-course guitar (whether single or double-strung) as a perfect form which could not be improved upon. Parisian luthiers such as Nicolas François Fourier were still making five-course instruments during the 1790s,[33] as were provincial makers such as Lamblin of Ghent[34] (although the traditional curved and ribbed back had by now been replaced by a flat two-piece back), and many French players were downright contemptuous of attempts to increase the number of strings:

I won't speak about those who use 6, 7, 8 and sometimes 9 strings. These are nothing more than whims, that consequently do not have rules. Nevertheless, as some use six strings, above all on guitars in the form of a lyre, one can see in this regard what I have to say on page 70 . . . One has lately seen some people, wanting to imitate certain famous Spaniards, putting on six strings; others seven, eight, and even nine. For this they changed and changed again the form, many times: but this did not captivate. One [returned to] the simplicity, which is one of the great merits of the guitar. Some Italians have also fitted six strings, even double strings, and sometimes even triple. There are others who use brass strings. But what difference is there in the playing?[35]

Doisy was unenthusiastic about the lyre, regarding it merely as 'a guitar in disguise' that only looked graceful when vertical (a position in which it was impossible to play), and as an instrument suitable 'only for strumming some mediocre accompaniments'. Its popularity among Parisian amateurs during the early years of the nineteenth century should not be underestimated, but, despite its neoclassical appeal, it eventually proved to be too awkward and impractical to compete with the six-string guitar, which shared its tuning but not its physical and aesthetic disadvantages. Writing in about 1807, the Parisian guitarist Guillaume-Pierre-Antoine Gatayes sarcastically commented upon the recent rise of the lyre, and correctly predicted its imminent replacement by the six-string guitar:

---

[33] There is a fine five-course guitar by him, dated 1791, in The Hague, Gemeentemuseum, EC 362-'33.
[34] The Conservatoire Royal de Musique in Brussels has a five-course guitar by Lamblin, dated 1795 (no. 2909).
[35] Doisy (1801), 10 and 70.

... the guitar had only five strings. A sixth one has been added, which renders the instrument entirely different from what it was, as much for the way of being played, as for the name and shape; the name because one no longer said a GUITAR, but a LYRE: the shape, because it really had the shape of the lyre with which Orpheus is represented. It was wished that that shape could render ideal the harmony of that instrument; but it gave only grace; during a certain period, that seductive lyre found itself in the homes of all of OUR LITTLE GEN-TLEMEN, and in the boudoirs. Good taste and reason have finally replaced it. I mean that the guitar has reappeared with a sixth string, which in truth gives more difficulties to the instrument; but also more possibilities in harmony and melody. One still says today THE SIX-STRING GUITAR; but after a little while one will call it merely the guitar, and the lyre will still be an 'ideal' instrument, until an ingenious imagination finds the means of rendering it a 'real' instrument.[36]

By 1810, when Lemoine published his *Nouvelle méthode de lyre ou guitarre à six cordes*, five-string and five-course guitars were gradually disappearing in Paris, and the lyre's fortunes were also entering into terminal decline as the six-string guitar became the generally accepted form. However, all these instruments had co-existed there during the previous decade, and between 1800 and 1810 concerted attempts were made by composers and publishers to notate guitar music so that it could be played on either five or six strings and therefore appeal to a wider market. This was commonly done by making *A* the lowest written note, but indicating with a figure 8 those bass notes which could be moved down an octave by players of the lyre or six-string guitar. This system usually worked well enough with simple arpeggiated song accompaniments, but could be most unsatisfactory at times, as Ex. 13.1 demonstrates.

Although the use of tablature had long ceased in France, both Doisy and Lemoine considered it to be important for guitarists to understand how the old system had worked. In his 1810 *Méthode* Lemoine briefly discusses guitar music from the seventeenth and eighteenth centuries and notates a few pieces in tablature, while Doisy remarks that 'it seems that today it [tablature] is entirely abolished. Although I am not

Ex. 13.1. Antoine–Marcel Lemoine, *Nouvelle méthode de lyre ou guitarre à six cordes* (1810)

[36] Gatayes (*c.*1807), quoted by Cox (1978), 37.

PL. 13.1. Minuet by Charles Doisy (1810)

trying to revive it, I dare say that I do not however believe it to be totally useless.' He then goes on to suggest that tablature would be a good way to notate harmonics on the five-string guitar, because the five lines of the staff could equally well be interpreted as five strings, so that one bar could be written in staff notation, followed by a bar of harmonics in tablature, then back to staff notation (see Pl. 13.1). The eventual triumph of the six-string guitar meant that his system was never widely adopted, but it was not without merit; and two centuries later a modified form might yet be of benefit to modern-day guitarists, who have still singularly failed to agree amongst themselves upon a single, clear, intuitive, and easily read method of notating harmonics.

Many of the players, teachers, and composers whom we have already encountered remained active in Paris during this period, including Francesco Alberti, who published several sets of variations for solo guitar during the 1790s, and Pierre Porro, who published *Six sonates pour la guitare avec accompagnement de violon . . . œuvre XI* (*c.* 1790), followed by about twenty-five sonatas for solo guitar, several sets of duos for two guitars, dozens of chamber works for guitar with flute and violin, and two concertos for guitar with small orchestra (most of these works appeared during the first decades of the nineteenth century). Porro ran his own publishing house in Paris, which was chiefly dedicated to the guitar, and he published not only his own music but also works for guitar by his contemporaries, such as Charles Lintant, a violinist from Grenoble who moved to Paris and devoted himself to the guitar in the late 1790s. Porro published Lintant's *Trois grandes sonates pour guitare et violon*, but his name is most commonly encountered on early nineteenth-century song arrangements, which are frequently marked 'accompagnement de guitare ou lyre par Lintant'.

Porro also published several pieces for solo guitar by l'Abbé François Guichard, a musician and singer in Notre-Dame cathedral, who lost his ecclesiastical position after the 1789 revolution and turned to the guitar. Like Lintant, Guichard composed guitar accompaniments for many songs; but perhaps the most prolific French guitarist in this field was Jean-Baptiste Phillis, who arranged dozens of chansons and romances during the late eighteenth and early nineteenth centuries, as well as writing two *méthodes* for the guitar and a good deal of instrumental music. His best arrangements, such as *Les Remords de David* (reproduced in App. VIII),[37] go far beyond the mere provision of simple arpeggio accompaniments and use the full resources of the five-course guitar to contribute a recitative-like drama to the music. Porro and Gatayes also composed song accompaniments, and special mention should be made too of Henri Montan Berton who (using the pseudonym 'Borghesi') wrote an accompaniment to a *Ronde provençale* in 1803 that required a lyre or guitar with a sixth string tuned down to *C* (see Ex. 13.2). As far as I am aware, this is the earliest example of a *scordatura* tuning on the new six-string instrument.[38]

During the early years of the Revolution developments in instrument-making in Italy and Spain seem to have had little effect on French guitarists, particularly on those in Paris. Inventories of instruments seized by officials from unlucky victims of *la terreur* (1793–4) included dozens of guitars made by French luthiers such as Michelot and Cousineau, but very few foreign guitars;[39] and in Paris during the early years of the nineteenth century only the lyre challenged the dominance of the traditional five-course and five-string instruments. It was not until 1808, with the arrival in Paris of the flamboyant Neapolitan Carulli, that a new approach to guitar playing and manufacture was established, and the six-string guitar finally triumphed in the French capital. We cannot concern ourselves here with the subsequent development of the instrument, but we should briefly note the work of René François Lacote, the first great Parisian maker of six-string guitars and one of the first French luthiers to add machine heads to his instruments (from about 1820 onwards). And although Sor, Carulli, and Carcassi are the three guitarists who are usually credited with establishing the supremacy of the six-string guitar in the French capital, we should not move on without also acknowledging the influence of Giuseppe (Joseph) Anelli, a performer who has long been forgotten, but who was considered unrivalled in Paris (where he lived between 1813 and 1815) by no less an authority than the great musicologist François-Joseph Fétis:

We regretted that the sounds Sor drew from the guitar were not sufficiently cultivated; it appeared to us that he had neglected to study this essential part of an instrument, in its nature not very harmonious. Joseph Anelli, on the contrary has felt that the great charm of the guitar principally consists in producing good sounds, and we must confess the tones he draws from

---

[37] Copy in GB–Lbl (B.362.a.)   [38] Copy in GB–Lbl (E.1717.p.)   [39] Bruni (1890).

Ex. 13.2. *Ronde provençale* by Henri Montan Berton (1803)

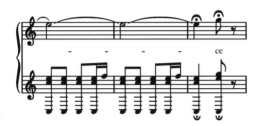

his instrument surpass in quality all that we have heard. They are at once clear, sonorous, mellow, and at the same time so powerful, that one would think the tone of a harp were added to the sympathetic sounds of the guitar. It appears that having been accustomed to play concerts accompanied by a grand orchestra Signor Anelli has acquired that powerful quality of sound in which he has been so eminently successful. In his brilliant execution he seems quite easy; the position and holding of the instrument is very elegant, and he executes with great precision the most difficult passages without any apparent exertion, which proves him to have studied upon a plan the parts of which act together in perfect uniformity with the system, without distracting or contradicting its operations. His hands are also evidently well disposed upon the guitar, particularly his right hand which assumes a position entirely different from other professors, which induces us to believe that it has the greatest influence upon the quality of sounds he draws from his instrument.[40]

Germany, Austria, and Russia

Because the guitar was seldom played in Germany and Austria until the final years of the eighteenth century, musicians there did not share the convictions held by French guitarists such as Doisy as to the perfection of the five-course instrument. They were

---

[40] Fétis, *The Courier*, quoted by Button (1989), 15, who was in turn quoting from a *Singing Academy Prospectus* by Joseph Anelli (Bristol, 1825), 17–18.

quick to adopt the new six-single-string guitar when it first appeared, and it became the accepted form in those countries from the early 1790s onwards, initially being used simply to accompany songs. As far as I am aware, the first music for the six-string guitar to be published in Germany dates from 1795: the *Sei ariette italiane con parole allemande per l'arpa, o piano-forte o guitarra . . . dal sigr. Giuseppe Millico* (Bonn: N. Simrock), the guitar part of which contains numerous G7 chords with a low G in the bass.[41] The first guitar method to be published exclusively for the six-string guitar also appeared in Germany: the *Kurze Anweisung zum Guitarrespielen by Heinrich Christian Bergmann* (Halle: Hendel, 1802).[42] A significant German figure was Christian Gottlieb Scheidler, who began his career as lutenist at the court of the Elector of Mainz before moving to Frankfurt towards the end of the eighteenth century, where he became a celebrated guitar teacher. Scheidler wrote a number of attractive pieces, including the *Duo pour guitarre et violon* in D major, which remains a favourite amongst student guitarists. Also of interest are his two sonatas for guitar, both of which require a sixth string tuned to *G*.[43]

Italian players of the six-string guitar began arriving in Vienna at the very beginning of the nineteenth century. Matteo Bevilacqua emigrated there in about 1800, as did the Brescian Bartholomeo Bortolazzi, who also excelled as a mandoline virtuoso (his concert performances on that instrument usually being accompanied on the guitar by his son). Bortolazzi published a good deal of instrumental music in Vienna, almost all of it for mandoline and guitar, his *6 variations sur une pièce d'Alcine* (1802) and *6 thèmes variés*, Op. 16 (1803) being among the earliest.[44] But the most significant guitarist in the city (prior to the arrival of Mauro Giuliani in 1806) was Simon Molitor, a German who became a civil servant in the Austrian War Office. He composed dozens of solo sonatas, duets, and trios from the late 1790s onwards, and showed an awareness of part-writing that was noticeably absent from the compositions of many of his contemporaries. Writing *c.* 1811, he recalled the way in which the guitar had developed during the final decades of the eighteenth century, and how it had first become popular in Germany and Austria:

[41] Copy in GB-Lbl (E.64). At first glance the chord shapes suggest that the music was probably intended for a guitar with a sixth string tuned to E. However, the use of a sixth string tuned to G was by no means unknown in Germany at the end of the 18 c., and was even remarked upon by Heinrich Koch in his *Musikalisches Lexicon* (Frankfurt-am-Main, 1802), 707–8.

[42] Cox (1978), 3.

[43] The original copy of the *Duo pour guitarre et violon* (written for five-string guitar) is in the Austrian National Library, Vienna (Kaldeck Collection, MS 41.988). This duo, and the two aforementioned guitar sonatas (now housed in the Royal Swedish Academy of Music in Stockholm) have been published in facsimile by Éditions Chanterelle (Monaco, 1979 and 1981). Scheidler is believed to have published two guitar sonatas in 1793, but the clear two-part notation of the pieces reproduced by Éditions Chanterelle would be most unusual for such an early date, and suggests to me that these are probably not the same works. Rather, I suspect that these two republished works date from 1812 and 1813 (years in which Scheidler is also known to have published guitar sonatas), and that no copies of the 1793 sonatas have yet been located.

[44] Tyler and Sparks (1989), 100–2.

Our ordinary guitar notation was being introduced then; the awkward double courses were done away with; guitar methods appeared, as did compositions for the guitar. But we were not yet free from old and limited styles that went against the most elementary rules of harmony, often more than once in a single measure. People were satisfied if [the guitar] was only vaguely consonant with the song. In such circumstances, some eighteen or twenty years ago, guitar-playing sneaked its way into Austria and Germany, where earlier it had been very rarely seen. Public taste made the instrument fashionable, to be sure, but the way in which it was generally handled could not remove the prejudice that connoisseurs had formed against it when it first appeared. A second substantial improvement of the guitar was made then, by adding the sixth string, namely the low E, which was soon in general use here . . .[45]

Following the example of Molitor, a number of Viennese musicians began to write for the guitar, mostly composing simple chamber music in which the guitar was used primarily to accompany melodic instruments. Three of the most prolific composers were: Leonard von Call, whose instrumental pieces were being published as early as 1803 (his *Variations*, Op. 8 for violin or mandoline and guitar appeared in that year); the Bohemian Wenzel Matiegka, one of whose compositions (a trio for violin or flute, viola, and guitar) was subsequently adapted by Franz Schubert (who turned it into a quartet by adding a cello part); and Anton Diabelli, an important music publisher whose clientele included Schubert and Beethoven. A lively school of Austro–German chamber music with guitar was already flourishing in the early nineteenth century, several years before Giuliani's arrival in Vienna. However, until the great Italian virtuoso settled there, the guitar was seen primarily as a simple and charming instrument for amateurs, as this contemporary extract makes clear:

Isn't it true that it can be found in the home of every even only moderately modern, attractive, affectionate, flirtatious, playful, pretty, exuberant, mischievous or even innocent, demure, respectable woman? And that every day new songs, choruses, romances, duets, trios, solos, sonatas, potpourris, chansons, contredanses, anglaises, waltzes, minuets, allemandes, and rondos, yes even concertos, are created, written, composed, produced, and arranged for guitar?[46]

The career of Giuliani has already been extensively covered by other authors (notably Thomas F. Heck), but we should briefly note the mesmerizing effect he had on Viennese guitarists and public alike when he settled there in 1806. Molitor was one of many who unreservedly sang his praises, and observed that (like Moretti and Sor in

---

[45] Molitor and Klinger (*c*.1811), 7. A longer version of this passage from Molitor is quoted by Heck in his excellent 1995 study of the life and work of Giuliani. However, on p. 33 Heck misinterprets a section in which Molitor talks about the 'French guitar', and draws from it the erroneous conclusion 'that the *chitarra francese* ("French guitar") was known to be a "five-stringed"—not five-course—guitar some 18–20 years earlier, i.e. around 1790'. In fact, Molitor clearly describes the 'French guitar' as a guitar with five courses (he speaks about the 'fünften Chors'), not five strings, and furthermore he does not suggest that it existed *c*.1790. Rather, he seems to be discussing a period several centuries earlier, when the four-course guitar first acquired a fifth course, and when it still 'lagged far behind the much more perfect lute and mandora'.

[46] Werder and Schneider, 1804, quoted by Grunfeld (1969), 169.

Spain) his method of notation was clearer and more musical than the earlier systems had been:

Then Herr Mauro Giuliani, a Neapolitan, came to us—a man who had been led early in the right direction through a correct sense of harmony, and who, as an accomplished virtuoso, combined with the most correct performance the greatest perfection of technique and of taste. He began writing in the new manner here, and during his extended stay he has already presented us with a series of charming compositions that may all be regarded as models of good style. Through his teaching and the competition he has aroused among teachers and lovers of the instrument, he has formed for us so many outstanding amateurs that there could scarcely be another place where authentic guitar-playing is so widely practised as here in our Vienna.[47]

By the end of the eighteenth century, itinerant guitarists were popularizing the instrument throughout Europe, including St Petersburg, home of the Russian royal court. An Italian guitarist called Santi is known to have been there in about 1794, in the service of Count Platon Zoubof, and to have been involved in the Count's various amorous liaisons (which included an affair with Catherine II).[48] But, more significantly for us, Jean-Baptiste Hainglaise settled there during the first half of the 1790s and published a large number of songs with guitar accompaniment, including *6 ariettes pour la guittarre* (1796), and the *Journal d'airs italiens, français, et russes, avec accompagnement de guitarre*, which appeared weekly between 1796 and 1798. Announcing its publication, a note in the *Gazette de S. Petersbourg* (25 July 1796) stated:

Journal d'Airs Italiens, Français, et Russes, avec accompagnement de Guitarre ... under this title, from this day, will appear, every Monday of each week, a folio, well engraved and printed by Gerstenberg & Dittmar, in the Grande Morskaya, no. 122. We shall make every effort to satisfy lovers of this instrument by procuring for them attractive, easy, and agreeable airs by different composers. *Monsieur le Maître* [Hainglaise], who has made the accompaniments, is well known for his works in this genre. The subscription price for twelve months is 25 roubles. In the provinces and in Moscow, 30 roubles, postage paid ... the first number that will appear is an ariette by Righini.

A few years later, Andrey Osipovich Sychra (or Sichra) published his *Journal pour la guitare à 7 cordes pour l'année 1802* (Moscow). Sychra was a virtuoso from Vilna who subsequently wrote a method for the same instrument which was published in St Petersburg in 1817. His small seven-string guitar was very different from the one favoured by Moretti (being tuned $D - G - B - d - g - b - d'$ and having a detachable neck for ease of transportation), and it became a favoured instrument among gypsies during the nineteenth century. Another early Russian tutor for this instrument, the *Méthode facil pour apprendre à pincer la guitare à sept cordes sans maître*, was published

---

[47] Molitor and Klinger (*c.*1811), 10.
[48] Mooser (1948–51), 678.

by Ignatz von Held in 1798.[49] Napoleon Coste (one of Sor's most famous pupils) also played and composed for a seven-string guitar; but despite the enthusiasm of various performers throughout the late eighteenth and early nineteenth centuries, no type of seven-string guitar ever achieved widespread popularity outside Russia.[50]

[49] Bobri (1956), 26, and Timofeyev (2000).

[50] Although, during the twentieth century, a form of seven-string guitar was used by a number of Brazilian musicians.

14

The Guitar 1750–*c*.1800:
Practical Information

The Instrument

As we have seen during the three previous chapters, the guitar evolved very differently in Spain, Italy, and France during this period, and performers whose primary interest is complete authenticity should ideally either concentrate on the music from one of those countries or else have three instruments at their disposal. Most surviving guitars from the eighteenth century are now in museums or private collections, and (although original examples in a playable condition are still occasionally offered for sale in auction houses) the majority of players will need to acquire modern reproductions. The following paragraphs summarize the main differences between typical Spanish, Italian, and French (especially Parisian) guitars of the late eighteenth century, give some measurements of typical instruments, and suggest detailed sources that can serve as a starting point for luthiers intending to build modern reproductions.[1]

The typical Spanish guitar of the late eighteenth century (Pl. 14.1) is a six-course instrument with wooden tuning pegs, internal fan strutting (usually three, but sometimes as many as seven), an open soundhole decorated with marquetry, a fairly wide neck that joins the body at the twelfth fret (a width of 58–60 mm at this point is common), a fingerboard that lies flush with the table, up to seventeen metal frets (those above the twelfth fret being laid directly into the table), a body with a fairly narrow waist, and a rosewood bridge without a saddle, to which the strings are tied. The string length (or diapason) of guitars made by Juan Pagés of Cádiz during the 1790s is slightly longer than on a modern-day instrument (averaging about 660 mm), and an instrument made by Joseph Martínez of Málaga *c*.1792 has a string length of 668 mm; but guitars from Madrid were usually a little shorter, and one made by Lorenzo

---

[1] Many of the measurements given in this section are taken from Baines (1966), Timmerman (1994), and *La guitarra española* (1991). The two last sources contain very detailed measurements of several guitars from this period, including drawings of the various internal strutting systems.

Pl. 14.1. A six-course Spanish guitar, made by Josef Benedid (Cádiz, 1794).
Photo: Alex Timmerman. Reproduced by courtesy of Roland Broux

Alonso in 1786 has a diapason of just 615 mm.[2] Tied gut frets were gradually abandoned in favour of metal frets after 1750. The raised fingerboard does not seem to have become a feature of Spanish guitar-making until the early nineteenth century, at about the same time that luthiers in that country began making guitars with six single strings.

[2] Further details and illustrations of all these instruments can be found in *La guitarra española* (1991), 115–24.

The typical Italian guitar of the late eighteenth century (Pl. 14.2) is an instrument with six single strings, wooden tuning pegs, several internal strengthening struts that run across the table at right angles to the strings (but no fan strutting), a somewhat narrow, extended fingerboard (usually between 52 mm and 54 mm in width at the twelfth fret), with seventeen metal frets (often silver), and a bridge (sometimes with a very low saddle) to which the strings are either tied or secured by pins (a feature borrowed from harp construction). The string length is often quite short, such as an example made in 1785 by Giovanni Battista Fabricatore in Naples, which has a vibrating length of just 624 mm. A notable feature of Italian instruments at this time is their tightly constricted waist, which further accentuates the guitar's distinctive figure-of-8 shape.[3] The five-course, metal-strung chitarra battente was also widely played in Italy, but does not seem to have been used as a solo instrument.

By contrast, the typical French guitar of the late eighteenth century (Pl. 14.3) still shares many similarities with the instruments that were being made at the beginning of the century. It is designed for five courses (although some players preferred to use five single strings), the body narrows only slightly at the waist, it has internal strengthening struts running across the table at right angles to the strings (but no fan strutting), wooden tuning pegs, a neck that usually joins the body at about the eleventh fret (the exact point seems to have been unimportant to most French luthiers, but the width at this junction was usually about 52 mm), a fingerboard that lies flush with the table, and a tied bridge without a saddle. Tied gut frets survived much longer in France than in Spain or Italy, and as late as 1801 Doisy was telling his readers that 'there are ordinarily twelve frets placed along the neck, of which ten are silver, brass, or ivory, but more commonly gut'.[4] This suggests that many of the five-course instruments in regular use at the start of the nineteenth century were quite old, because all French guitars built after 1780 seem to have been fitted with metal frets.

The string length of a guitar built in 1791 by Nicolas François Fourier in Paris is 646 mm, although Doisy argued that the length between nut and saddle should not exceed twenty-four *pouces* (about 610 mm), because otherwise it became difficult to tune the instrument to standard pitch. By the beginning of the nineteenth century orchestral pitch in France and Italy had risen close to the modern level, and it has been calculated that guitars with a string length above about 650 mm would have suffered an unacceptably high frequency of string breakages if they had tried to tune to standard pitch.[5] The shorter string length of the new Italian six-string guitar made it ideal for performers who wished to play at orchestral pitch, and this factor undoubtedly helped it to replace the old five-course model as the most popular form of guitar in France during the early nineteenth century. Indeed, the Neapolitan Carulli made this point

---

[3] Further details and illustrations of Italian instruments of this period can be found in Turnbull (1974), pl. 36 a–c, Timmerman (1994), 72–3, and Baines (1966), 48.

[4] Doisy (1801), 9.   [5] Figures given to me by Ephraim Segerman in Aug. 1999.

PL. 14.2. A six-string Italian guitar by
Giovanni Battista Fabricatore (Naples,
1791). Reproduced by courtesy of the
Stockholm Music Museum

PL. 14.3. A five-course French guitar by
George Cousineau (Paris, *c*.1795).
Photo: Alex Timmerman. Reproduced
by courtesy of Taro Takeuchi

explicitly in his Paris *méthode* of 1810, when he stated that 'The guitars that were made until now were of an extremely large size, their diapason too long, preventing them from tuning to the pitch of the other instruments . . . Today, the dimensions of the guitars are smaller; they have a diapason which can easily be tuned to the other instruments'.[6]

Strings

In 1750 almost all guitarists appear to have used plain gut strings on their instruments. During the second half of the eighteenth century, wound bass strings became increasingly common, and the gradual change to single stringing seems inextricably bound up with their growing popularity. The wire was preferably wound around silk, but sometimes it was spun over a gut core, and this development allowed players to produce more powerful bass notes, without the need for octave stringing. However, despite this development, we have already seen that it took many decades for courses to give way to single stringing, and I shall briefly summarize the different forms of stringing that were standard in Spain, Italy, and France during the 1790s.

The late eighteenth-century Spanish guitar was typically fitted with six courses. If we follow the advice given in the various Spanish tutors of 1799, then when playing *punteado* style we should use thick violin first strings for the guitar's third course, thin violin first strings for the guitar's second course, and an even thinner string for the guitar's single *prima*. As to the lower three courses, opinions differed. Abreu and Ferandiere agree that the lowest course should be tuned in octaves (with one wound *sexto* and a thin gut *sextillo*), but Ferandiere thought that the fifth and fourth courses should be in unison, whereas Abreu strung them in octaves. However, Abreu added that, for accompanying other instruments, all three lower courses should be in unison to emphasize the bass—exactly the same suggestion that the Spaniard Vargas y Guzmán had made in his Mexican guitar tutor of 1776.

The late eighteenth-century Italian guitar was typically fitted with six single strings, the top three of gut, the lower three of metal wound on silk. There is little direct information about the precise diameters that were initially used, but the shorter string length of Italian instruments certainly allowed players to fit much thicker strings than had hitherto been possible and to tune them to a higher pitch. Writing as one of the first Italian virtuosos of the early nineteenth century, Carulli (1810, p. 2) contrasted old guitars ('their very thin strings floated, the instrument distorted, and one drew from them a sound that was disagreeable and weak') with the new powerful Italian instruments he was playing ('they are fitted with strings of the same thickness as those of a violin, and one draws from them very agreeable sounds, strong enough to

[6] Carulli (1810), 2.

accompany the voice or the most resonant instrument'). Carulli seems to be saying that instead of using a violin first string as the second or third string of a guitar (as French and Spanish guitarists did, usually tuning it slightly below standard pitch), Italians used it as the first string and then raised it to orchestral pitch! This suggests that the string tension on late eighteenth- and early nineteenth-century Italian six-string guitars was considerably higher than on present-day classical guitars (which have much greater resonance than late eighteenth- and early nineteenth-century Italian instruments), something which research carried out by Ephraim Segerman would seem to confirm.[7]

We have already seen that throughout the last quarter of the eighteenth century French guitarists were divided as to whether the guitar should be tuned with five single strings or five courses. Those who used pairs of strings (such as Bailleux, Baillon, Alberti, and Vidal) preferred octave stringing on the fourth and fifth courses, but Merchi's championing of single stringing in 1777 also won converts in Paris (such as Lemoine and Doisy) over the next few decades. Merchi initially used only 'slightly thicker strings' on his guitar, and the lightly built French instruments of this period could certainly not have supported the stress of the high-tension stringing that players such as Carulli expected their Italian instruments to withstand. It should also be remembered that most French guitarists of the eighteenth century fitted their instruments with low-tension strings (gut for the upper courses, metal wound on silk for the *bourdons*) and tuned them below standard pitch. Indeed, as late as 1810 Lemoine was noting that the guitar and lyre 'are generally tuned a semitone below the ordinary pitch of the orchestra' (1810, p. 4). And at the beginning of the nineteenth century many French guitarists were still essentially playing on the delicate, low-tension, five-course instrument that we nowadays refer to as the 'Baroque guitar', rather than the high-powered, single-string Italian model that was about to replace it.

Playing Positions

1. The lower part of the body of the guitar must rest on the right thigh. 2. The left arm must be high, in a semicircle, and at least six inches from the body. 3. The fingerboard, instead of resting in the palm of the hand, ought to be supported by the semicircle that the index finger forms with the thumb. 4. The fingers of the left hand have to be arched over the strings, because in this way you hold the hand in a more elegant position, and have the fingers better prepared to press down on the strings. 5. The right arm rests naturally on the upper end part of the body of

---

[7] In *FoMRHI Quarterly*, 67 (Apr. 1992), Comm. 1096, 41–2 and *The Strad* (Mar. 1988), 201, Segerman examined guitar strings belonging to the poet Percy Bysshe Shelley, and analysed a letter from Nicolò Paganini concerning the diameters of strings (apparently guitar strings). The information from both these sources seems to confirm Carulli's statement, and suggests that stringing on late 18th- and early 19th-c. Italian guitars was considerably heavier than is the case today.

the guitar, in a way that the mid-point between the elbow and the wrist is the point of support. 6. The right hand will be correct if it is held almost horizontally with the strings, in which position it happens that the fingers can pluck more easily, and the nails do not inconvenience, because otherwise it will be impossible to pluck with sweetness and harmony. 7. The little and ring fingers of the same hand ought to rest on the table of the guitar in the space between the bridge and the soundhole or rose, close to the first string and nearer to the bridge than to the rose. The player who accustoms himself to positioning the guitar in this way will hold the body elegantly and naturally, and will play with less effort and without tiredness because he is in his natural position.[8]

Although the guitar and its tuning varied considerably from one country to another during this period, there was general agreement about the best way of holding the instrument and about how to position the hands. The sitting position was universally favoured for serious playing, with some sources (such as Alberti) suggesting that the right foot should rest on a small object, so that the right leg is slightly raised.[9] However, the standing position was often adopted for serenading, with a ribbon tied to both ends of the guitar and worn around the neck. Many eighteenth-century instruments were fitted with a strap button, and Corrette points out that players use a ribbon and adopt the standing position 'principally when one goes to sigh beneath the window of some beauty, as is still the custom in Italy and in Spain'.[10]

Placing the little finger of the right hand (or the ring finger, and sometimes both) on the table of the instrument had been standard practice since the days of Renaissance lutenists, and no eighteenth-century sources attempt to dissuade the player from this custom. Corrette (1762), Merchi (1777), and Baillon (1781) all recommended this position. Although it is extremely awkward to play in this way on a modern instrument with a high bridge, one should remember that the strings on eighteenth-century guitars (especially French and Spanish ones) lay much closer to the table than is the case nowadays. The practice continued well into the nineteenth century, but influential authorities such as Fernando Sor argued against it, and the standard right-hand position gradually changed to the freer position in use today.

Although the word *tirando* was not used, the surface stroke (in which a right-hand finger brushes the string rather than playing downwards into the instrument) was the standard method of plucking. *Apoyando* (rest stroke) does not seem to have been used until the nineteenth century, which is not surprising, because it is well-nigh impossible to perform the rest stroke when the little finger is resting on the table, and in any case it would not have produced a satisfactory tone on double-course instruments with low bridges and low-tension strings. Bailleux (1773) and Lemoine (*c*.1802) were amongst the few writers to recommend plucking the strings with the ring finger, most

---

[8] Moretti (1799), 1–2.
[9] Alberti (1786), 2. However, the frontispiece of this tutor depicts a player using a cittern-like instrument, with his left leg crossed over his right. Nowadays, of course, the conventional position requires the player to place his or her left foot on a small stool.   [10] Corrette (1762), 2.

preferring to use just the thumb, index, and middle fingers. Various methods of indicating right-hand fingering were employed, but one of the most common was the convention used by Baillon (1781) and Lemoine (*c*.1802). In this system the thumb is indicated by ، , the index finger by . , the middle finger by .. , and the ring finger (if used) by ... , as in Pl. 14.4.

One area of disagreement was the vexed question of whether to use nails or fingertips to pluck the strings. In the eighteenth century a clear preference for nails can be detected amongst the Spanish, with players such as Abreu (1799), Ferandiere (1799), and Moretti (1799) recommending the use of a small amount of nail in each stroke. By contrast, French and Italian sources usually made no mention of nails, thereby implying the use of the fingertips. Merchi (1777, p. 5) specifically warned 'take care not to pluck with the nails; they produce dry and ungrateful sounds', and the nineteenth-century Italian virtuoso Matteo Carcassi agreed: 'to obtain a full sound . . . it is necessary to pluck with the fingertips, avoiding contact between the nails and the strings' (Carcassi, 1836, p. 8). This national distinction became somewhat clouded during the early nineteenth century, mainly because the great Spanish guitarist Fernando Sor, after he had been exiled from his native land, also argued strongly against the use of nails. However, other Spanish players of the period (such as Aguado) believed that they improved the sound quality, and the use of nails has been a feature of most (though by no means all) Spanish guitar-playing from the eighteenth century until our own.

The recommended position for the left hand was little different from that of a modern guitarist, with the fingers running parallel to the frets, and the thumb placed beneath the neck between the first and second frets (when playing in first position). However, one unusual technique favoured by late eighteenth- and early nineteenth-century Italian guitarists was the occasional use of the thumb to fret notes on the sixth string, something which was not difficult to do on their narrow-necked instruments, although it is extremely awkward on a modern guitar. This left-hand technique had been introduced into Paris in the 1760s by Italian mandolinists such as Giovanni Battista Gervasio (who indicated it with + placed below the note),[11] and it was widely copied by the first generation of Italian six-string guitar virtuosos, such as Carulli, who settled in that city. He also used + to indicate bass notes that were to be stopped with the left-hand thumb, although other Italian guitarists, such as Giuliani, preferred the term *col pollice* (with the thumb). A misunderstanding of this simple procedure has led one modern writer to claim that Giuliani (who was also a cellist) wanted players to use a distinctive cello technique when he wrote *7ᵐᵒ tasto col pollice* above certain passages:

[11] See Tyler and Sparks (1989), 113.

Ces signes ,,, désignent les notes qu'il faut pincer avec le poulce. un point.
désigne le premier doigt. deux points .. désignent le second doigt, trois
points ... désignent le troisième doigt. celui-ci s'emploie rarement .
La liaison___ désigne qu'il faut tenir la note de la basse pendant toute la
durée du même accord .

PL. 14.4. Indication of right-hand fingering, from Pierre Joseph Baillon (1781)

The technique involves moving the left-hand thumb from its customary position behind the neck, under and around to the front of the guitar (fingerboard side), where it is used to stop one or more strings in an upper position. It is something we can only imagine a 'cellist attempting on the guitar, since it is so foreign to what the guitar tutors of the time usually taught by way of technique, or to how we handle the guitar today.[12]

Such a strange technique was indeed foreign to guitar tutors of the time; and imaginative though this modern theory is, the extract from Giuliani's music shown in Pl. 14.5 can be played much more easily on a narrow-necked instrument by simply allowing the left-hand thumb to creep up from the back of the neck and fret the sixth string from behind, while the fingers fret notes on the treble strings, in exactly the manner favoured by Carulli and several of his Italian contemporaries.

[12] Heck (1995), 27–8.

PL. 14.5. *Variations*, Op. 6, var. viii, by Mauro Giuliani

Specialist Techniques and Ornamentation

The following pages look briefly at some of the many techniques and ornaments that were a typical part of guitar-playing in the late eighteenth century, above all in France. As far as is possible, I shall allow the guitarists to describe them in their own words, and have therefore concentrated on those authors (such as Merchi and Alberti) who give the clearest and most concise definitions. While some of the ornaments can also be performed on a modern guitar, others are only effective on an instrument with low-tension strings, which is why some had disappeared from standard guitar technique (or else had been modified) by the time that Sor, Carcassi, and other players of the new six-string high-tension guitar were publishing their methods in the early nineteenth century.

Tirade

The *tirade* derives its name from the action of the left-hand fingers, which execute this technique by pulling the notes (*tirant les notes*):

> The *tirade* is performed by the left hand, pulling the notes one after another without the assistance of the right hand [Pl. 14.6(*a*)]. One can also perform the *tirade* differently; because with the force of the fingers one can descend diatonically from the *g*, third finger on the chanterelle, down to the *C*, third finger on the fifth string, without the assistance of the right hand [Pl. 14.6(*b*)]. One can go right down to the *A*, if this does not form a dissonance to the ear.[13]

Chûte

The *chûte* was a favourite ornament of Renaissance lutenists, and also derives its name from the action of the fingers. In this case, it is so called because the fingers fall onto the strings to produce the required sounds (*chûte* is the French word for a fall):

> The *chûte* is formed by two, three, or four ascending notes tied together (or flowing together), so one only plucks the first one. The *chûte* formed from two notes like e and f is performed in this way: one plucks the open e string, then one intercepts the vibration of this e by putting the first finger on the string and pressing strongly against the fingerboard which produces the f [Pl. 14.7(*a*)] . . . the *chûtes* formed from three or four notes [Pl. 14.7(*b*)] are subject to the same principles established above; but it is necessary to pay attention to the following rules. After having plucked the first of the three or four notes, one must make the fingers fall successively and rapidly like little hammers onto the appropriate frets for the notes indicated; observing that one must press down firmly as they fall, in order that the vibration is conserved and communicated from one note to the next, and that each sound is heard clearly. The observation of this last rule is essential, because if one puts the fingers down flat, the *chûtes* will only give muted sounds.[14]

Martellement

This three-note ornament is equivalent to the mordent, was indicated by + placed above a note, and was used to decorate simple melodic passages:

> The *martellement* is composed of a *chûte* where the second note becomes the first note of a *tirade*, like f, g, f [Pl. 14.8]. The *martellement* is performed thus: one plucks the first f with the right hand, and then one leaves the left-hand finger on the fret that gives this f until after the rapid execution of the *chûte* and *tirade*, f, g, f.[15]

[13] Alberti (1786), 5.   [14] Merchi (1777), 11–13.   [15] Ibid. 18.

(a)

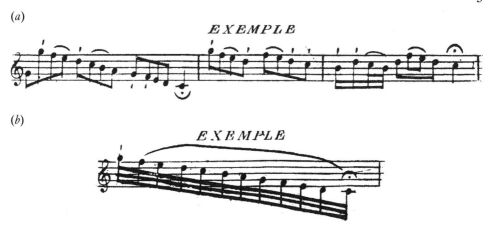

(b)

PL. 14.6. *Tirade* from Francesco Alberti (1786)

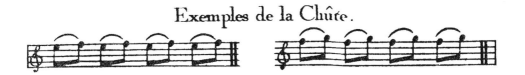

PL. 14.7. *Chûte* from Giacomo Merchi (1777)

PL. 14.8. *Martellement* from Merchi (1777)

(a)

(b)

(c)

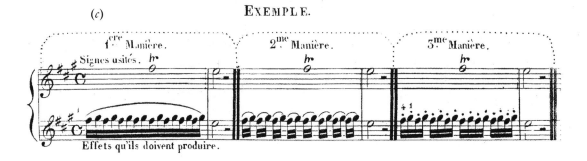

PL. 14.9. (*a*) *Cadence* in E major from Baillon (1781); (*b*) *Exemples du trill* from
Merchi (1777); (*c*) *Exemples du trill* from Ferdinando Carulli (1825)

Trill or *Cadence*

To perform the *cadence* [Pl. 14.9(*a*)], it is necessary to pluck the note above the one on which the *cadence* is marked, and to perform the beats with the finger of the left hand; and afterwards to pluck [with the right hand] the note that terminates the cadence.[16]

The *trill* or *cadence* is a succession of *martellements* [Pl. 14.9(*b*)] or of alternative rapid *chûtes* and *tirades*, like f, g, f, g, many times. The *trill* is performed in this way: as with the *martellement*, one only plucks the first f, and one leaves the left-hand finger on the fret which gives this f until after the rapid execution of many alterntive *chûtes* and *tirades*. Make sure that you allow the finger to fall perpendicularly on the fret for each *chûte* and pull the string towards the palm of the hand with each *tirade*.[17]

Lastly, although Carulli wrote the passage shown in Pl. 14.9(*c*) in the mid-1820s (well after the end of our chosen period), it is interesting to note the three ways he describes of performing a trill, especially the third method, which is identical to the two-string trill made famous in the 1950s and 1960s by Alexandre Lagoya and Ida Presti:

One can play the *cadence* in three ways on the guitar. 1. By plucking the note only once, and binding [*coulant*] it as many times as necessary with the other note. 2. By plucking the note every time that one binds it with the upper note. 3. By preparing the two notes on two different strings with the left hand, and plucking them with two different fingers of the right hand.[18]

Frémissement

So that the string can tremble, it is necessary to push down forcefully with one of the fingers of the left hand on one of the frets, above all on one of those furthest from the nut, and you will hear a very agreeable sound. You ought to use the index and middle fingers, these being stronger than the others. If you can get the effect with the other fingers, so much the better [Pl. 14.10].[19]

Alberti's description of the *frémissement* is identical to the modern vibrato, and was also known during the eighteenth century as the *son filé* or *son flaté*. Merchi (1777, pp. 22–3) also describes the *double son filé*, where two notes (usually on adjacent strings) are both vibrated by rocking the left hand rapidly to and fro while the fingertips stay in the same place on the strings.

Plainte

The *plainte* is made by sliding a finger of the left hand along the string from one fret to the next, that is to say advancing it to the note on which you wish to make the *plainte* [Pl. 14.11].[20]

---

[16] Baillon (1781), 9.   [17] Merchi (1777), 18.   [18] Carulli (1825), 51.
[19] Alberti (1786), 6.   [20] Bailleux (1773), 9.

PL. 14.10. *Frémissement* from Alberti (1786)

PL. 14.11. *Plainte* from Antoine Bailleux (1773)

PL. 14.12. *Glissades* and *Double glissades* from Merchi (1777)

The *plainte* usually involved an ascending slide of a semitone (an interval that emphasized its plaintive, yearning quality). Merchi (1777, pp. 20–1) called this technique a *glissade*, and used it for intervals of up to a major third. He also described the *double glissade* (which involved sliding two notes simultaneously, usually a third or a sixth apart), said that the *glissade* could descend as well as ascend, and indicated the direction with a straight diagonal line between the notes (see Pl. 14.12).

Harmonics

Harmonic sounds are made by putting the finger of the left hand on a string, not onto the fingerboard but above the fret.[21] For this effect it is necessary to pluck the string with one of the right-hand fingers, and lightly lift the left-hand finger. One will find it easier to produce true sounds on the thicker strings, the little ones not having enough substance to produce a consistent sound. The truest sounds that one can find are in the middle of the string, above all at the mid-point of the instrument [Pl. 14.13].[22]

Barré

The half-barré and full-barré (made by placing the index finger across several or all of the strings) are so well known to guitarists that they scarcely need to be mentioned here, but one Iberian technique favoured by Abreu (1799, p. 78) deserves brief discussion. Having described the standard *zegilla* (or *cejuela*, as the barré was also known in Spanish), he then mentions a technique that he calls *zegilla ladeada o torcida* ('a twisted barré'), which involves the index finger lying diagonally across the strings, so that treble notes can be stopped at one fret and a bass note at another, all with the index finger. This unusual technique is also required in the performance of some of the works of the nineteenth-century Italian guitarist Luigi Legnani.

Batteries

Batteries are simply continuous arpeggios, where all the notes are detached and measured. To play them well, it is necessary to have recourse to the *Guide des écoliers de guitarre*, which contains thirty variations on the *Folies d'Espagne* [see above, Pl. 11.2], full of the most frequently used *batteries*. It is necessary to learn the first variation in block chords, then execute on the same chords (without moving the [left-hand] fingers differently) the different *batteries* indicated, and understand the diverse sounds they produce, above all on the lowest strings.[23]

---

[21] Only natural harmonics were written about during the 18th c. Artificial harmonics may also have been in use, but it was not until the 19th c. that François de Fossa first described how to produce them.

[22] Alberti (1786), 8.

[23] Merchi (1777), 8.

PL. 14.13. *Ah vous dirai-je Maman, en sons harmoniques* from Alberti (1786)

(*a*)

(*b*)

PL. 14.14. *Roulades* from Baillon (1781): (*a*) ascending; (*b*) descending

Roulades

To play ascending *roulades*, it is necessary to pluck the first note on each string and make the others with the left hand, by quickly putting the successive fingers in place [Pl. 14.14(*a*)]. To play descending *roulades*, it is sufficient to pluck the first note; all the others are made by the left hand [Pl. 14.14(*b*)].[24]

[24] Baillon (1781), 9.

Guitar Music Published
in Paris, 1750–*c*.1800

Appendices IV–VII contain published and manuscript guitar music, most of it from Paris, and all of it dating from between 1750 and *c*.1800. Although I believe them to be the most comprehensive lists of guitar music from this period yet assembled, I would not claim that any of the four lists is likely to be complete; as I have not been able personally to examine every listed item, I have in some cases had to rely on the accuracy of library catalogue entries (with all their attendant perils). Dates have been given wherever possible, but these have not always been obtainable, so it is possible that a few of the pieces listed may have been published slightly after the end of our chosen period. Standard RISM location symbols are also given for surviving copies. Any editorial comments will be found in square brackets.

Appendix IV, arranged alphabetically by composer, concentrates on instrumental music from Paris (together with those methods and songbooks that contain instrumental music), as these are likely to be of the most immediate interest to guitarists.

Albanese, Egide-Joseph-Ignace-Antoine, *Les Amusements de Melpomène ou IVe recueil d'airs mêlés d'accompagnement de violon, de guitare et des pièces de guitarre par Mrs. Albanese et Cardon* (*c*.1768–70). F-Pn; F-Pa; US-Cn; GB-Lbl. RISM A 566. [GB-Lbl catalogue gives date as 1775.]

Alberti, Francesco, *Nouvelle méthode de guitare dans laquelle on y trouve différentes variations, une sonate, 12 menuets et 6 ariettes . . .* (1786). F-Pn. RISM A 663.

—— *Trois duos* [*F, D, A*] *pour violon et guittare. Œuvre quatrième.* GB-Lbl. RISM AA 663a.

Bailleux, Antoine, *Méthode de guitare par musique et tablature* (1773). [facs. repr. Geneva: Minkoff, 1980].

Baillon, Pierre Joseph, *Nouvelle méthode de guitarre selon le sistème des meilleurs auteurs* (1781). [facs. repr. Geneva: Minkoff, 1977].

Bouleron, *Trio pour la guitarre ou recueil de morceaux choisis mis en trio pour une guitarre, un violon et un alto* (1772). F-Pn; F-Pa.

Carpentier, Joseph, *Ier Recueil de menuets, allemandes etc. entremélés d'airs agréables à chanter . . . arrangés exprès pour le cytre ou guitthare allemande qui peuvent néantmoins s'exécuter sur la guitthare espagnolle et sur la mandore . . .* (1770). F-Pn; F-Pm; F-Psg.

—— *2e Recueil de menuets, allemandes etc. avec des variations entremélés d'airs agréables à chanter . . . arrangés exprès pour le cythre, ou guitthare allemande qui peuvent néantmoins s'exécuter sur la mandore et sur la guitthare espagnolle . . .* (1770). F-Pn; F-Pm; F-Psg.

Carpentier, Joseph, *IIIe Recueil de menuets, allemandes, et contredances, avec vingt et une variations des Folies d'Espagne, touttes en pincés différents, et d'un genre nouveau, entremêlés d'ariettes avec leurs accompagnements pour le cythre, ou guitthare allemande, qui peuvent néantmoins s'exécuter sur la Mandore et sur la guitthare espagnolle* . . . (1771). F-Pn; F-Pm; F-Psg.

Cherbourg, Mlle, *Premier recueil de chansons avec accompagnement de guitarre et six menuets en duo pour deux guitarres* (c.1765). F-Pn. RISM C 2016.

Doisy, Charles, *Principes généraux de la guitare* (1801). F-Pn [facs. repr. Geneva: Minkoff, 1977].

Felix, J. S., *Recueil d'airs et ariettes choisies avec accompagnement de guitarre ou mandore* . . . *Œuvre 2e* . . . *suivi de sonates pour la guitarre avec accompagnement de violon* (c.1770). F-Pn.

Gaude, *Vingt-quatre variations pour la flûte traversière accompagnée de la guitarre* . . . *op. 1* (c.1788). F-Pn.

Guichard, François, *N^o I. Petits airs arrangés pour une gitarre seule par Mr. l'abbé Guichard* . . . (c.1780). F-Pn. RISM G 5027.

Lemoine, Antoine-Marcel, *N^o [1] Pot pourri d'airs connus arrangés pour la guitarre avec accompagnement de flûte ou violon* . . . (c.1800). F-Pn. RISM L 1878.

—— *Nouvelle méthode courte et facile pour la guitarre à l'usage des commençans* (c.1790). GB-Lam, ex-Spencer.

—— *Nouvelle méthode courte et facile pour la guitarre à l'usage des commençans* (c.1802). D-DEsa, F-Pn. RISM LL 1879a. [facs. repr. Geneva: Minkoff, 1980].

—— *Nouvelle méthode de lyre ou guitarre à six cordes* (1810). GB-Lbl; F-Pn; D-Mmb. RISM L 1879.

Lintant, *Trois sonates progressives pour la guitarre avec accompagnement d'alto.* HR-Zs. RISM LL 2567a.

—— *Dix airs variés pour guitare ou lyre.* S-Skma. RISM L 2568.

Merchi, Giacomo, *Quatro duetti a due chitarre e sei minuetti a solo con variationi* . . . *Li duetti possono essere anche acompagnamenti dal violino opera tersa* (c.1757). GB-Lbl; F-Pn. RISM M 2284. [facs. repr. Florence: S.P.E.S., 1981].

—— *Sei trio a due violini e basso* . . . *opera V* (c.1760). GB-Lbl; S-Skma. RISM M 2286.

—— *Le Guide des écoliers de guitare ou préludes aussi agréables qu'utiles, sur tous les modes, les positions et les arpégemens avec des airs et des variations* . . . *V^e livre de guitare, œuvre VIIe* (1761). F-Pc. RISM M 2287. [facs. repr. Geneva: Minkoff, 1981].

—— *Sei duetti a chitarra e violino con sordina del signor Merchi, IXth. Livre de guitare, œuvre XII* (c.1764). [facs. repr. Florence: S.P.E.S., 1981].

—— *XVIe livre de guitare contenant des airs, romances et vaudevilles avec des accompagnemens, préludes et ritournelles* . . . *œuvre XXe* (1768). RISM M 2295.

—— *Les Soirées de Paris, XVIIIe livre de guitare contenant des airs d'opéra comique avec des accompagnemens d'un nouveau goût, des préludes et des ritournelles par Mr. Merchi* . . . *œuvre XXIIe* (c.1770). F-Pn. RISM M 2298.

—— *XXe livre de guitare contenant des airs d'opéra comique. Avec des accompagnements d'un nouveau goût, des préludes et des ritournelles* . . . *œuvre XXIVe* (1770). F-Pn. RISM M 2299.

—— *XXIe livre de guitare, contenant des airs connus [à 1 v.] avec des accompagnements faciles, des préludes et des ritournelles* . . . *œuvre XXVe* (c.1777). F-Pn. [facs. repr. Florence: S.P.E.S., 1981].

—— *Sei duetti a chitarra e violino con sordina o a due chitarre, XXIXᵉ livre de guitarre, œuvre XXXIIIᵉ* (*c.*1777). GB-Ckc. RISM M 2300.

—— *Traité des agrémens de la musique exécutés sur la guitare . . . œuvre XXXVᵉ* (1777). F-G. RISM M 2301. [facs. repr. Geneva: Minkoff, 1981].

—— *XXXIVᵉ livre de guitarre, contenant des airs d'opéra et opéra comique et autres de societez. Avec des accompagnements, des préludes et des ritournelles . . . œuvre XXXVIᵉ* (1780). F-Pn. RISM M 2302.

Mignard, *Duo pour la guitarre . . .* (1766). F-Pn. RISM M 2713.

Phillis, Jean-Baptiste, *Ah! vous dirai-je Maman. Avec 12 variations pour la guittare.* D-DÜk. RISM P 2006.

—— *Étude nouvelle pour la guitare ou lyre dans les tons les plus usités, majeurs et mineurs, ou l'on démontre les difficultés, les agréments et les positions du démanchement.* DK-Kk. RISM P 2007.

—— *Nouvelle méthode pour la lyre ou guitare à six cordes . . . œuvre 6.* I-Mc. RISM P 2008.

Porro, Pierre, *Nouvelles étrennes de guitarre ou recueil des plus jolies romances et couplets qui aient paru dans l'année 1784, suivis d'une sonate et de plusieurs pièces pour la guitarre seule, mis en musique et arrangés expressément pour cet instrument . . . œuvre IVᵉ* (1785). F-Pn; US-NYp. RISM P 5149. [facs. repr. Florence: S.P.E.S., 1982].

—— *Journal de guitarre, ou choix d'airs nouveaux de tous les caractères avec préludes, accompagnements, airs variés, &c . . . pincé et doigté marqués pour l'instruction . . . par Mr. Porro . . . 12 cahiers et les étrennes de guitarre* (1788). F-Pc [incomplete, only 43 pp.], US-NYp. RISM P 5150. [facs. repr. Florence: S.P.E.S., 1982].

—— *Six sonates pour la guitare avec accompagnement de violon . . . par Mr. Porro. Œuvre XI* (*c.*1788–1794/6). GB-Lam, ex-Spencer [facs. repr. Monaco: Éditions Chanterelle, 1981].

—— *Collection de préludes et caprices dans tous les tons pour l'étude de la guitare* (1789). F-Pn. [facs. repr. Florence: S.P.E.S., 1982].

Ritter, *Huit sonates* [C, F, C, B♭, G, C, d, G] *pour la guitarre avec un violon . . . opera II.* CH-Bu. RISM R 1751.

Tissier, Mr, *IVᵉ recueil d'ariettes d'opéra comiques et autres avec accompagnement de guitarre et autres airs connus par la guitare seule par Mr. Tissier . . . Œuvre 8ᵉ . . .* (*c.*1780). B-Bc.

Trille Labarre, *Étrennes de guitarre ou recueil des plus jolies romances et couplets qui aient paru dans l'année 1787, suivis d'une sonate avec accompagnement de violon obligé et de plusieurs autres pièces . . . par Mr. Trille Labarre. Œuvre IIᵉ* (1788). F-Pn.

Vallain, Mr, *Airs choisis arrangés en trio et dialogués pour guitare, violon, et alto par Mr. Vallain. Œuvre 3ᵉ. Ces airs sont tirés de Chimène, d'Armide, de l'Olympiade, de la Frascatana, du Barbier de Séville, mis en musique par Paisiello, de Roland, de Blaise et Babet, de Richard coeur de Lion et de l'Epreuve villageoise. On y peut joindre la partie du Chant en observant les ritournelles telles qu'elles sont dans la partition* (1787). F-Pn.

Vidal, B., *Les soirées espagnoles ou choix d'ariettes d'opéra-comiques et autres avec accompagnement de guittare, menuets et allemandes* (1776 and/or 1782). CH-Zz; F-Pn [both copies incomplete]. RISM V 1446.

—— *Méthode de guitare* (*c.*1778). [A copy is believed to have been in GB-Lam, ex-Spencer, but I have so far been unable to locate it.]

Vidal, B., *Recueil d'airs avec accompagnement de guitare et clavecin, entremêlés de petits morceaux et airs variés et d'une sonate avec accompagnement de basse . . . œuvre XVIII (c.1782).* GB-Lbl; F-Pn. RISM V 1447.

—— *Recueil d'airs d'opéra comiques, menuets et contredanses avec des variations arrangés pour la guitarre . . . par Mr. Vidal. Œuvre 18 et 2ᵉ Recueil d'airs variés (1782).* F-Pn. RISM V 1443.

—— *Recueil d'ariettes, d'opéra comiques, et autres . . . avec accompagnement de guitare, plusieurs airs variés, et trois duo pour guitare et violon, ou deux guitarre.* CH-N. RISM V 1445.

—— *Journal de guitarre composée de sonates, de pièces d'airs arrangés d'ariettes et romances avec accompagnement de guitare et violon ad libitum séparés du journal dédié . . . par Mr. Vidal* (1786–7) [monthly]. CH-Bu (2ᵉ année); F-Pc (2ᵉ année incomplète). RISM V 1442.

—— *Pot-pourri en trio concertant pour guitare et deux violons (1787).* F-Pn. RISM V 1441.

—— *4ᵉ Recueil de menuets, allemandes, ronde, gavotte et autres airs arrangés pour la guitarre . . . Œuvre [32] (c.1788).* F-Pn. RISM V 1452.

—— *Six sonates pour la guitarre avec accompagnement de violon . . . IVᵉ œuvre de sonate (1788).* F-Pn. RISM V 1437.

—— *Six sonates pour la guitarre avec accompagnement de violon . . . 2ᵉ livre de sonates (c.1790).* F-Pn.

—— *Six duos concertants pour guitarre et violon . . . VIIᵉ œuvre de duos (c.1792).* F-Pn [guitar part only]. RISM V 1438.

—— *Recueil d'airs et romances avec accompagnement de guitare formant les premiers leçons, No. 1* (1795). GB-Lbl. RISM V 1449.

—— *Recueil de pièces et airs variés, suites des premières leçons nouvellement composées pour la guitare (c.1800).* F-Pn. RISM V 1450.

Recueil (various authors), *Le Festin de l'Amour à 4 parties, voix seule, harpe, guitarre, mandoline, violons, ou clavecin et basse* (1765); *Les Projets de l'Amour avec les mêmes accompagnements* (1765). [no copies located].

—— *Journal de guitare.* S-Skma.

APPENDIX V

Selected List of Songs with Guitar Accompaniment Published in Paris, 1750–*c*.1800

(including Songbooks and Methods containing Instrumental Music)

This list is selective, partly because a comprehensive catalogue of the thousands of song arrangements with guitar accompaniments that appeared in that city during this period would be of limited value, partly because many of the composers had no direct connection with the instrument, and also because most of the songs have nothing more than a simple arpeggiated accompaniment. Therefore, this list itemizes only those songs composed and/or arranged by known guitarists of the period, and excludes those which have already appeared in Appendix IV. Even so, its considerable length bears eloquent testimony to the great popularity of the guitar in France during the second half of the eighteenth century.

Albanese, Egide–Joseph–Ignace–Antoine, *Comment voulez vous qu'on vous aime* [*Air*] . . . *avec accompagnement de guithare par Mr Guichard* (1779). GB-Lbl. RISM A 588.
—— *La Comtesse de Saulx. Romance . . . avec accompagnement de guithare par Mr Tissier* (1779). GB-Lbl. RISM A 589.
—— *Depuis plus de six mois. La consolation bachique. Chanson nouvelle, avec accompt. de guitare par Mr. Alberti.* GB-Lbl. RISM AA 590a.
—— *Je le tiens ce nid de fauvettes. Idylle de M. Berquin. Accompagnement de guittare de Mr. Comien.* US-PHu. RISM AA 591c.
—— *Le connais tu ma chère Éléonore. Ariette, avec accompagnement de guithare, par Mr. Comine.* US-PHu. RISM AA 592b.
Alberti, Francesco, *Ici tout rend hommage. Couplets nouveaux sur La Redoute chinoise. Air de Colinette à la cour. Col accompagnamento di guittarre* (1782). US-PHalbrecht. RISM AA 660g.
—— *Air nouveau (Oiseaux de ce bocage) avec accompagnement de guitare . . . no. 29* (*c*.1786). F-Pn; F-Pc. RISM A 662.
—— *Romance par M . . . accomp^t de guitare . . . no. 33* (*c*.1786). F-Pn.
—— *L'amant infidelle ou les regrets superflus. Romance . . . avec accompagnement de guitare.* D-DÜk. RISM A 659.
—— *Les Charmes de Colin. Chanson nouvelle . . . avec accompagnement de guitare.* GB-Lbl. RISM A 660.

Alberti, Francesco, *La Maladie amoureuse. Ariette nouvelle avec accompt. de guitare.* GB–Lbl. RISM A 661.

—— *La Bonne Chère et le bon vin. Chanson de table. Avec accompagnement de guitare.* GB–Lbl. RISM AA 659a.

—— *Le Cœur me bat, je n'en puis plus. Cloris pénitente. Romance nouvelle avec accompagnement de guitare. Air de Confiteor.* GB–Lbl. AA 660a.

—— *Colin a des yeux charmants. Les charmes de Colin. Chanson nouvelle avec accompagnement de guitare.* GB–Lbl. RISM AA 660b.

—— *Dans un bois solitaire. La fille prudente. Chanson nouvelle avec accompagnement de guitharre.* GB–Lbl. RISM AA 660d.

—— *Dans un bois je vis l'autre jour. La villageoise instruite. Romance nouvelle avec accompagnement de guitare.* GB–Lbl. RISM AA 660e.

—— *Déjà dans la plaine. L'amour délicat . . . avec accompagnement de guitare.* GB–Lbl. RISM AA 660f.

—— *Pourquoi belle Adelaide. Romance, accompagnement de guitare . . . No. 33.* F–Pn. RISM AA 662a.

—— *Un Berger quand on l'écoute. Ariette nouvelle. Avec accompagnement de guitare.* GB–Lbl. RISM AA 662b.

Bérard, Jean-Baptiste, *Premier recueil d'airs choisis avec accompagnement de guitarre dédié à Mme la Comtesse d'Egmont par M. Bérard . . . (1764).* F–Pn.

Berton, Henri Montan, *Blondelette joliette. Barcarole d'Aline . . . accompagnement de guitare par Borghesi.* S–Skma. RISM B 2193.

—— *Email des prés. Romance du Délire . . . avec accompagnement de guitarre par Lemoine.* F–Pc. RISM B 2245

—— *Jouer toujours, changer d'amour. Air du Délire . . . avec accompagnement de guitarre par Lemoine.* F–Pc. B 2246.

—— *Ah', ah', qu'il me tarde. Air . . . accompagnement de lyre ou guitare par M*ʳ* Meissonnier.* S–Skma. RISM B 2252. [This song, and all others by Berton marked 'de guitare ou lyre', probably date from between *c.*1800 and 1805.]

—— *Souvent il veut me. Romance chantée . . . accompagnement de guitare ou lyre par Lintant.* S–Skma. RISM B 2261.

—— *Infortuné j'ai commandé. Romance . . . arrangée pour guitarre par Lemoine.* S–Skma. RISM B 2280.

—— *Mon cœur s'ouvroit. Couplets . . . avec accompagnement de guitare ou lyre par Borghese.* S–Skma. B 2323.

—— *En affaires comme en voyages. Air . . . avec accompagnement de guitare ou lyre par Borghese.* B–Bc; S–Skma. RISM B 2349.

—— *Tu m'aimeras toute la vie. Duo . . . chanté par M*ᵈᵉ* Gavaudan et Baptiste . . . accompagnement de guitarre par Borghese.* US–PHu. RISM BB 2221a.

—— *Un Soir après mainte folie le etc. Air . . . accompagnement de lyre ou guitare par M*ʳ* Meissonier.* D–Kll. RISM BB 2255b.

—— *Duo (Quand une belle est infidèle) . . . arrangé pour la lyre ou guitare par Lami.* US–PHu. RISM BB 2270b.

—— *Canon à trois voix (Je vous adore aimable inconnue)* . . . *arrangé pour lyre ou guitare par Lami*. US-PHu. RISM BB 2270d.

—— *Romance (Ah qu'il est beau)* . . . *arrangée pour lyre ou guitare par Lami*. US-Cum, US-PHu. RISM BB 2271a.

—— *Rondeau (Ah grand Dieu se peut-il)* . . . *accompagnement de lyre ou guitarre par Lami*. US-PHu. RISM BB 2272a.

—— *Venez venez aimable Stéphanie. Duo* . . . *avec accompagnement de lyre ou guitarre par Lami*. US-PHu. RISM BB 2286b.

—— *Ah parois a mes yeux aimable objet. Duo* . . . *avec accompagnement de guitare ou lyre par Borghese*. US-PHu. RISM BB 2318a.

—— *Oh, soubrette si jolie. Duo* . . . *avec accompagnement de guitare ou lyre par Borghese*. US-PHu. RISM BB 2327a.

—— *Ronde provençale* [by 'Borghesi', a pseudonym for Berton; uses 6th string tuned down to *C*]. GB-Lbl.

Borghese, Antonio, *Douze petits airs connus, arr. pour guitarre ou lyre*. CZ-Pnm. RISM B 3691.

Bouleron, *Recueil d'airs choisis avec accompagnement de guitarre* . . . *Gravé par le Sr Huguet* (1768). F-Pn. RISM B 3809.

Boyer (or Boyé), *Suite des soirées de la Comédie italienne, contenant les airs chantés sur ce théâtre et autres. Avec accompagnement de guitarre par M. Boyé* . . . (*c.* 1783). GB-Lbl (suite 1–3); US-Wc (suite 1–11). RISM BB 4180a.

Corbelin, *Recueil hebdomadaire d'airs d'opéra comique et autres, avec accompagnement de guittarre, dédié à la Reine par M. Corbelin, élève de M. Patouart fils* (*c.*1777). F-Pa.

Demignaux, Jacques Antoine, *Nouveau recueil d'airs avec accompagnement de guittare*. F-Pc, US-Cn. RISM D 1618 [and RISM DD 1618a].

—— *Nouveau recueil d'airs accompagnement de guittare* (1770). F-Pn.

Denis, Pietro, *Les IV saisons européennes. Second recueil contenant les meilleurs morceaux de chant avec leurs parties d'accompagnements, qui ont été donnés l'année dernière sur les théâtres d'Italie, d'Allemagne, d'Angleterre et de Paris et notamment sur le théâtre de la comédie italienne avec des parties d'accompagnements faits pour les différens instrumens comme harpe, guitarre, mandoline, violon et flute. Terminé par le commencement d'un traité de composition musicale le meilleur qui ait encore paru* . . . *par le Sr. Pietro Denis* (1774). B-Bc.

Domnich, Heinrich, *Ces bois épais. Romance* . . . *arrangée pour guitare ou lyre par Lintant*. S-Skma. RISM D 3369.

—— *Charmant ruisseau* . . . *accompagnement de lyre ou guitare par Lemoine*. US-PHu. RISM DD 3370a.

Felix, J. S., *Ariette avec accompagnement de violon et de guitarre, paroles et musique par M. Felix, amateur* (*Journal de Musique*, 1773, no. 5, pp. 2–5).

G***, Mr, *Le Petit Polisson, ou Veni mecum. 1er livre de chansons, rondes nouvelles etc.* [*avec ou sans accomp. de guitare*] *composé par Mr. G***, autheur de la Luronicomanie*. F-Pn.

Gatayes, Guillaume, *L'Absence, romance, paroles de Mme P.xxx Accompagnement de guitare* . . . (*c.*1800). F-Pn.

—— *Avis aux amans, avec accompagnement de guitare* . . . (*c.*1800). F-Pn.

—— *Romance, A la tourterelle, paroles de M. Boucher, musique et accompagnement de guitarre* . . . (*c.*1800). F-Pn.

Gaveaux, Pierre, *Vaudeville de l'amour filial ou des deux Suisses avec accompagnement de guitarre* (*c.*1793). F–Pn.

—— *Vaudeville des deux hermites. Avec accompagnement de guitarre* (*c.*1793). F–Pn.

—— *Air du traité nul. Paroles de Marsollier . . . chanté par Mlle Rolando. Avec accompt. de guitare par Lemoine* (*c.*1797). F–Pn.

—— *Air de l'amour filial ou des deux Suisses . . . Accompagnement de guitarre par M. Le Moine* (*c.*1797). F–Pn.

—— *La Chanson du jeune pâtre, tirée du roman de Brick Bolding (t. Ii^e) . . . accompagnement de guitarre par Lintant* (*c.*1800). F–Pn.

—— *Chanson de la famille indigente avec accompagnement de guitarre.* F–Pn.

—— *Couplets de Locataire chanté par Solier, paroles de Sevrin . . . accompagnement de guitare ou lyre par Lintant* (*c.*1800). F–Pn.

—— *Couplets de Locataire, chanté par Moreau, paroles de Sevrin . . . accompagnement de guitare ou lyre par Lintant* (*c.*1800). F–Pn.

—— *Romance de Locataire, chantée par Mme Gavaudan, paroles de Sevrin . . . accompagnement de guitare ou lyre par Lintant* (*c.* 800). F–Pn.

—— *Vaudeville de Locataire, paroles de Sevrin . . . accompagnement de guitare ou lyre par Lintant* (*c.*1800). F–Pn.

—— *Couplets du trompeur trompé chantés par Mlle Lesage, paroles de B. Valvile . . . accompt. de guitare ou lyre par Lintant* (*c.*1800). F–Pn.

—— *Air du trompeur trompé. Paroles de B. Valvile . . . accompt. de guitare ou lyre par Lintant* (*c.*1800). F–Pn.

—— *Romance du trompeur trompé, chantée par Mlle Lesage, paroles de B. Valvile . . . accompt. de guitare ou lyre par Lintant* (*c.*1800). F–Pn.

Genty, Mlle, *Recueil de chansons avec un accompagnement de guittare . . .* F–Pn. RISM G 1584.

—— *IIe recueil de chansons avec accompagnement de guitarre par musique et par tablature . . .* (1761). F–Pn. RISM G 1585.

Godard, *Premier recueil d'airs choisis, avec accompagnement de guitarre . . . par Mr. Godard* (1762). F–Pc; F–Pn. RISM G 2920.

Gougelet, Pierre-Marie?, *Premier [–deuxième] recueil d'airs choisis avec accompagnement de guitarre . . . par Mr. Gougelet . . .* (1766–7). B–Bc; F–Pn. 2 vols. RISM G 3213.

—— *Troisième recueil d'airs choisis avec accompagnement de guitarre . . . par Mr. Gougelet.* I–Nc. RISM GG 3213a.

Gouriet fils, *Hymne des parisiens, chantée sur différents théâtres avec accompagnement de guithare. Paroles du Cn Morambert . . .* (1793). F–Pn.

Guichard, François, *Les Loisirs d'Apollon ou Nouveau recueil d'ariettes, romances, chansons nouvelles etc. avec accompagnement de guitarre et basse chiffrée pour le clavecin ou piano forte . . . œuvre VII . . .* (*c.*1775). F–Pn. RISM G 5021.

—— *Nouvelles chansons, romances, ariettes etc. avec accompagnement de guitarre et basee chiffrée pour le clavecin ou piano forte pour servir de suite aux Loisirs d'Apollon . . . œuvre VIII* (*c.*1778). F–Pn. RISM G 5022.

Guichard, Louis Joseph, *C'est l'honneur qui vous guide nouveaux. Aux soldats nationaux. Romance avec accompagnement de guitare* [Air: Charmante Gabrielle]. F–Psen. RISM GG 5036a.

Guillaume, Simon, *Air de M. Guillaume avec accompagnement de guittare du Cn Lintant: 'Époux imprudent, fils rebelle!'*. F-Pn.

—— *Air de M. Guillaume avec accompagnement de guittare du Cn Lintant: 'Fuyant et la ville et la cour'*. F-Pn.

—— *Air de M. Guillaume avec accompagnement de guittare du Cn Lintant: 'Qui l'aspect de la nature'*. F-Pn.

Lagarde, Pierre de, *Ier recueil de brunettes avec accompagnement de guittare, de clavecin ou de harpe . . . Les brunettes sont tirées du Journal de musique . . .* (1764). GB-Lbl; F-Pn. RISM L 227.

—— *IIe recueil de brunettes avec accompagnement de violon, guitare, clavecin ou harpe . . . Ces brunettes sont tirées du Journal de musique . . .* (1764). GB-Lbl; F-Pn; F-Po. RISM L 228.

—— *IIIe recueil de brunettes avec accompagnement de violon, guitare, clavecin ou harpe . . . Ces brunettes sont tirées du Journal de musique . . .* (1764). GB-Lbl; F-Pn; F-Po. RISM L 229.

—— *Soyez toujours songes charmans. Ariette . . . avec accompagnement de guithare par Mr Guichard*. GB-Lbl. L 234.

Lemoine, Antoine-Marcel, *La Comparaison. Chansonette, avec accompagnement de guitare, par le citoyen Lemoine*. GB-Lbl. RISM L 1876.

—— *Le Buveur. Chanson de table . . . accompagnement de lyre ou guitarre*. A-Wn. RISM LL 1875a.

—— *Le Tems et l'amour. Chansonette . . . accompagnement de lyre ou guitare*. US-PHu. RISM LL 1876a.

—— *Air du secret* [arr. Lemoine] (1800). GB-Lbl.

Le Moyne, Jean-Baptiste, *Ier recueil d'ariettes de l'opéra de Phèdre avec accompagnement de guitare . . . Par M. Alberti* (1787). F-Pn. RISM L 1903.

—— *Air de Nephté avec accompagnement de guittare 'O toi que j'ai perdu'* (c.1790). F-Pn. RISM L 1896.

—— *Air de Nephté avec accompagnement de guittare 'Tout me trouble, tout m'épouvante'* (c.1792). F-Pn. RISM L 1898.

—— *Les Vertus à l'ordre du jour. Stances contre l'athéisme. Air* [à v/guitare] *du vaudeville de La soirée orageuse*. US-PHu. RISM LL 1885a.

—— *Mon fils vole aux champs de l'honneur. Air de Miltiade à Marathon, avec accompagnement de guitarre*. GB-Lbl. RISM L 1890.

—— *On danse bien à la ville. Ronde des Pommiers et le moulin, avec accomp^t de guitare*. GB-Lbl. RISM L 1910.

—— *Oui, mettons nous à l'ouvrage. Air des Pommiers et le moulin, avec accomp^t de guitare*. GB-Lbl. RISM L 1912.

—— *Vivent les noces pour danser. Ronde . . . avec accomp^t de guittare*. GB-Lbl. RISM L 1930.

—— *Vivent les noces pour danser. Ronde . . . avec accomp^t de guittare*. US-PHu. RISM LL 1930a.

Lintant, C., *Romance d'Ariodant variée pour la guitare ou la lyre*. CZ-Pnm. RISM L 2570.

Merchi, Giacomo, *Raccolta d'ariette francesi ed italiane per la chitarra li acompagnamenti sono in musica e tavolatura . . . Opera quarta* (c.1760). F-Pn. RISM M 2285. [facs. repr. Florence: S.P.E.S., 1981].

Merchi, Giacomo, *Recueil d'airs avec accompagnement de guitarre . . . VIe livre de guitarre. Œuvre VIIIe* (1762). F-Pn; US-CA. RISM M 2288.

—— *La Guitare de bonne humeur, ou Recueil de vaudevilles badins; avec accompagnement de guitarre, VIIe livre de guitarre, œuvre X^e.* GB-Ckc. RISM M 2289.

—— *Recueil d'airs avec des accompagnemens de guitarre faciles et à la portée des commençans . . . VIIIe livre de guitarre, œuvre XIe.* (1764). F-Pn. RISM M 2290.

—— *Choix d'ariettes avec accompagnement de guitarre . . . X^e livre de guitarre. Œuvre XIIIe* (1764). F-Pn. RISM M 2291.

Paisible, Mlle, *Premier recueil d'ariettes choisis avec accompagnement de guitarre par Melle. Paisible et de violon a volonté par Mr. son frère avec basse chiffrée dédiés aux amateurs . . .* (1766). F-Pc.

Patouart, *La Muse lyrique dédiée à Madame la Dauphine. 1er [–4è] Recueil d'airs avec accompagnement de guitarre par Mr. Patouart fils* (monthly 1770–6). B-Bc (1774); F-Dc (1773–4); F-Pa (1770–1); F-Pn (1770–2, 1774–5); F-Psg (1774); GB-Gm (1774); GB-Gbl (1774); NL-DHk (1774); S-Skma (1771–5); US-BRp (1774); US-Wc (1771). RISM P 1030.

—— *La Muse lyrique dédiée à la Reine. Recueil d'airs avec accompagnement de guitarre par Mr. Patouart fils* (1777–89). F-Dc (1776–7, 1786); F-Pn (1778, 1780–3, 1785–6, 1789); GB-Lbl (1781); US-U (1779); US-Wc (1783). RISM P 1031.

Phillis, Jean-Baptiste, *Nouveau recueil de romances, airs, contredances, valzes, arrangé pour la lyre ou guitare . . . les airs sont arrangés pour deux lyres ou guitares.* D-KIl. RISM P 2003.

—— *Ah! combien la nuit a de charmes. Les charmes de la nuit. Romance . . . accompagnement de guittare par M. Phillis.* GB-Lbl. RISM P 2004.

—— *Les remords de David. Romance, avec accomp^t de guittare.* GB-Lbl. RISM P 2005.

Poirier, *La Suitte du réveil du peuple ou les cris de la nature contre les agens du crime avec accompagnement de guitthare par le Cn Poirier, la taille. Chantée sur les théâtres* (1793). F-Pn.

Porro, Pierre, *Six romances nouvelles, avec accompagnement de guitare ou lyre, violon ou flûte à volonté . . . opera 34.* I-Mc. RISM P 5125. [facs. repr. Florence: S.P.E.S., 1982].

—— *Journal de guitarre, ou choix d'airs nouveaux de tous les caractères avec préludes, accompagnements, airs variés, &c . . . pincé et doigté marqués pour l'instruction . . . par Mr. Porro . . . 12 cahiers et les étrennes de guitarre* (1788). F-Pc (incomplete); US-NYp. RISM P 5150. [facs. repr. Florence: S.P.E.S., 1982].

—— *A dieu. Air du petit matelot* [no title page, but appears to be pp. 48–9 of *Journal de guitare, en 48 nos . . . 10e année*, No. 23]. D-LÜh. RISM P 5151.

—— *Le Dormeur éveillé* [music by N. Piccini, acc. by Porro]. GB-Lbl.

Tarchi, Angelo, *Air du Cabriolet jaune* ['Il fallait voir dans Angoulême'] . . . *avec accompagnement de guitare par Lemoine* (c.1798). F-Pn.

—— *Air du Cabriolet jaune* ['Je dis quand je vois dans la rue'] . . . *avec accompagnement de guitare par Lemoine* (c.1798). F-Pn.

—— *Air du 30 & 40* ['Morbleu! je ne peux plus me taire'] . . . *chanté par le C^n Martin avec accomp. de guitare par Lemoine* (1799). F-Pn.

—— *Polaque du 30 & 40* ['On dit que j'ai de grands défauts'] *chanté par le C^n Elleviou . . . avec accomp. de guitare par Lemoine* (1799). F-Pn.

—— *Romance du 30 & 40* ['*Pardonnez-moi si mon cœur coupable*']. *Paroles du Cⁿ Duval* . . . *chantée par la Cne Jenni Bouvier, accompagnement de guitare par Lemoine* (1799). F–Pn.

—— *Air d'auberge en auberge. Paroles de Dupaty* ['*Chez nous les hommes, les coquettes*'] . . . *Arrangé pour la lyre ou guitare par Phillis professeur* (1800). F–Pn.

—— *Romance d'auberge en auberge chantée par Mme St Aubin. Arrangé pour lyre ou guitare par Phillis professeur* (1800). F–Pn.

—— *Romance d'auberge en auberge. Paroles de Dupaty* ['*On reconnaît qu'on est près d'une fleur*'] . . . *Arrangée pour la lyre ou guitare par Phillis professeur* (1800). F–Pn.

Tissier, *Troisième recueil d'airs d'opéra et autres avec accompagnement de guittare par Mr. Tissier de l'Académie royalle de musique . . . œuvre 7è* (1775). F–Pc.

—— *VIe recueil d'airs et ariettes tirés des opéra, opéra comiques et autres morceaux choisis. Avec accompagnement de guitarre par Mr. Tissier de l'Académie royale de musique. Œuvre XIIè . . .* (1780). F–Pc.

—— *IVe recueil d'ariettes d'opéra comiques et autres avec accompagnement de guitarre et autres airs connus par la guitare seule par Mr. Tissier . . . œuvre 8è . . . (c.*1780). B–Bc.

—— *Recueil de romances, chansons et vaudevilles arrangés pour la guitarre, dédiés à la Reine par Tissier . . .* F–Pc.

Vidal, B., *IIe recueil d'airs d'opéra comiques et autres avec accompagnement de guitarre par Mr. Vidal* (1772). B–Bc. RISM V 1444.

—— *V^e recueil de petits airs variés pour la guitare* (1786). F–Pn. RISM V 1448.

—— *Ariette ou romance avec accompagnement de guitare (c.*1788). F–Pn. RISM V 1439.

Recueils (various authors), *Recueil d'airs des opéras-comiques avec accompagnement de guitare par MM. Alberti, Tissier, et autres (c.*1778–9). D–HR (62 nos.); GB–Lbl (45 nos.).

—— *Les Après-soupers de la Société . . . petit théâtre lyrique et Moral avec accompagnement de guittarre et un violin ad libium* (1781–2). [no copy located].

—— *Étrennes de Polymnie* (1785). GB–Lam, ex-Spencer.

—— *Étrennes chantantes ou choix des plus nouvelles ariettes, romances et vaudevilles avec accompagnement de guitare. Dédiées aux dames pour l'année 1787* (1787). B–Bc; F–Pn; F–TLm; NL–DHk; US–CAe. [145 pp.].

—— *Journal d'airs italiens et français avec accompagnement de guitare (c.*1789). B–Bc (nos. 25inc., 49–180); F–Pc (some missing) [nos. 1–180, 744 pp.].

—— *Amusement de société ou choix d'ariettes, romances, vaudevilles . . . avec accompagnement de guitarre par divers auteurs (c.*1790). F–Pn. [193p].

—— *Étrennes chantantes ou choix des plus nouvelles ariettes, romances et vaudevilles avec accompagnement de guitarre. Dédiées aux dames pour l'année 1793* (1793). F–Pc.

APPENDIX VI

Guitar Methods, 1750–*c*.1800

This appendix contains all known guitar methods of the period (all countries, published and manuscript, in chronological order).

1752   Minguet y Yrol, Pablo, *Reglas y advertencias generales para tañer la guitarra* (Madrid, 1752). US-Wc MT582.M32. [facs. repr. Geneva: Minkoff, 1981].

c.1758   Don ****, *Méthode pour apprendre a jouer de la guitarre par Don ***** (Paris, *c*.1758). US-Wc MT582.M375 (Case).

1760   Sotos, Andre de, *Arte para aprender con facilidad y sin maestro a templar y tañer rasgado la guitarra* (Madrid, 1760). US-Wc MT582.A2 S7. [facs. repr. Valencia: Librerias Paris, 1991].

1761   Merchi, Giacomo, *Le Guide des écoliers de guitarre* (Paris, 1761). F-Pc. [facs. repr. Geneva: Minkoff, 1981].

1762   Corrette, Michel, *Les Dons d'Apollon, méthode pour apprendre facilement à jouer de la guitarre par musique et par tablature* (Paris, 1762). GB-Lbl.

1773   Bailleux, Antoine, *Méthode de guitare par musique et tablature* (Paris, 1773). [facs. repr. Geneva: Minkoff, 1980].

1776   Vargas y Guzmán, Juan Antonio, *Explicación para tocar la guitara de punteado, por música o sifra* (Veracruz, 1776, MS).

1777   Merchi, Giacomo, *Traité des agrémens de la musique* (Paris, 1777). F-G. [facs. repr. Geneva: Minkoff, 1981].

c.1778   Vidal, B., *Méthode de guitare* (Paris, *c*.1778). [A copy was possibly in GB-Lam, ex-Spencer, but I have so far been unable to locate it.]

1781   Baillon, Pierre Joseph, *Nouvelle méthode de guitarre selon le système des meilleurs auteurs* (Paris, 1781; repr. Geneva, 1977).

1786   Alberti, Francesco, *Nouvelle méthode de guitarre* (Paris, 1786). F-Pn.

1789   Ribeiro, Manoel da Paixão, *Nova arte de viola* (Coimbra, 1789). GB-Lbl. [facs. repr. Geneva: Minkoff, 1985].

c.1790   Lemoine, Antoine-Marcel, *Nouvelle méthode courte et facile pour la guitare à l'usage des commençans contenant plusieurs petits airs et des variations* (Paris, *c*.1790). GB-Lam, ex-Spencer.

1792   Moretti, Federico, *Principj per la chitarra* (Naples, 1792, MS; repr. Florence: S.P.E.S., 1983).

1795   Chabran, Felice, *Compleat Instructions for the Spanish Guitar* (London, 1795). GB-Lbl.

1799   Abreu, Antonio, and Prieto, Victor, *Escuela para tocar con perfección la guitarra de cinco y seis órdenes* (Salamanca, 1799). US-Wc MT582.A2.

Rubio, Juan Manuel García, *Arte, reglas armónicas para aprehender a templar y puntear la guitarra española de seis órdenes* (Madrid?, 1799, MS).

Ferandiere, Fernando, *Arte de tocar la Guitarra española por Música* (Madrid, 1799). GB-Lam, ex-Spencer. (repr. Tecla, London, 1977).

Moretti, Federico, *Principios para tocar la guitarra de seis órdenes* (Madrid, 1799). GB-Lbl.

1801   Doisy, Charles, *Principes généraux de la guitare* (Paris, 1801; repr. Geneva: Minkoff, 1979).

c.1802   Lemoine, Antoine-Marcel, *Nouvelle méthode courte et facile pour la guitare à l'usage des commençans . . . deuxième édition augmentée de principes pour la lyre* (Paris, c.1802). D-DEsa, F-Pn. [facs. repr. Geneva: Minkoff, 1980].

Non-Parisian Guitar Music, 1750–*c.*1800

This list does not pretend to be more than a starting point for further research, as a great deal of late eighteenth-century manuscript guitar music is undoubtedly still awaiting rediscovery.

Ballasteros, Antonio, *Obra para guitarra de seis órdenes* (Spain, 1780). [now lost]

Boccherini, Luigi, [Twelve quintets for guitar and strings, adapted by the composer from his piano quintets in 1798–9. The original manuscripts have been lost, as have four of the quintets. Eight have survived: Gérard catalogue nos. 445–50, 451, and 453.]

Chabran, Felice, *Compleat Instructions for the Spanish Guitar* (London, 1795). GB-Lbl. [Contains a short *fandango*, a setting of *Folies d'Espagne*, and a *Sigadilia*.]

Ferandiere, Fernando, *Arte de tocar la guitarra española por música* (Madrid, 1799; repr. London: Tecla, 1977). GB-Lam, ex-Spencer. [Contains several short dances for solo guitar, and a *seguidillas boleras* for voice and guitar.]

—— *12 Minués, 12 Rondos, 18 Sonatas, 6 Diálogos de violin y guitarra, 18 Duos de violin y guitarra, 6 Duos de dos guitarras, 6 Piezas de guitarra sola, 40 Trios de guitarra, violin y baxo, 40 Quartetos de guitarra, violin, viola, y baxo, 18 Quintetos de dos guitarras, dos violines y baxo, una ópera instrumental, 6 Los quatro tiempos de el año en quartetos, 6 La Historia de el hijo Pródigo, dividida en seis quartetos, 6 Conciertos de guitarra á grande orquesta, 6 Adagios en quartetos para las iglesias, 6 Polacas de guitarra y baxo, 6 Boleras para cantar y tocar, 6 Minués con sus rondós, 6 Duos de flauta y guitarra, 6 Tiranas para cantar, con acompañamiento á la Guitarra, Un Tema con variaciones para los tocadores de guitarra, Obra instrumental, titulada: El Ensayo de la naturaleza, explicada en tres quartetos de guitarra, violin, flauta y fagót.* [All these works, which were listed by Ferandiere in his 1799 guitar method, have been lost.]

Hainglaise, J. B., *Journal d'airs italiens, français et russes avec accompagnement de guitare par J. B. Hainglaise . . .* [*1re–3e année*] (St Petersburg, 1796–8). RUS-Lsc; RUS-Ml.

Merchi, Giacomo, *Scelta d'arietta* [sic] *francesi, italiane ed inglesi, con accompagnamento di chitarra, opera XV* (London). GB-Lbl. RISM M 2292. [NB. Most of Merchi's London publications are for the English guittar.]

—— *A Collection of the most favourite Italian, French, and English songs, with an accompaniment for the guitar* (London). GB-Lbl. RISM M 2293.

—— *Dodici suonate per la chitarra, sei a due chitarre o con accompagnamento di violino e sei a solo . . . opera XVI* (London). GB-Lbl; S-Skma. RISM M 2294.

—— *Twelve divertimentos for two guittars or a guittar and violin . . . opera 21st* (London). GB-Lbl. RISM M 2296.

—— *A Collection of the most favorite Italian, French & English songs & duets for the guittar, with an accompanyment for an other guittar . . . op. XXII* (London). GB-Lbl; GB-Ckc. RISM M 2297 [op. 22a].

—— *Collection of the most favourite Italian, French, and English songs, with an accompaniment for the guitar* (London). D-KIl. RISM M 2303.

Merchi, Giacomo, *A Collection of the most favourite Italian, French & English songs and duets with an accompaniment for the guitar . . . book second* (London). GB-Ckc. RISM M 2304.

—— *Twelve divertimentos for two guitars or a guitar and violin* (London). DK-Sa. RISM M 2306.

—— *Six lessons and six duets for one and two guitars . . . book first. N.B. These duets may be play'd by a guitar and violin.* (London). DK-Sa. RISM M 2307.

Millico, Giuseppe, *Sei ariette italiane con parole allemande per l'arpa, o piano-forte o guitarra dedicate alle dame composte dal sigr. Giuseppe Millico* (Bonn, 1795). GB-Lbl. [As far as I am aware, this is the earliest six-string guitar music to be published in Germany.]

Negri, M. A., *Raccolta di musica vocale italiana de' più celebri autori ridotta coll'accompagnamento di fortepiano, e parte anche di chitarra da M. A. Negri, no 1 [–2]* (Hamburg). D-Bds

Recueils (various authors), *Journal de musique allemand, italien & français pour le chant avec accompagnement de piano-forte ou de guitarre par différents auteurs. No. 1er* (Hamburg). S-Skma.

Ritter, D., *A Choice Collection of XII of the most favorite songs for the guittar sung at Vaux Hall and in the Deserter . . . with an addition of the overture in the Deserter [P. A. Monsigny], two favorite rondeaus & six cotillons properly adapted for that instrument with an easy bass throughout by D. Ritter* (London). GB-Lbl. RISM R 1754. [Apparently for English guittar.]

Ritter, Peter, *Notturno pour guitarre, flûte et alto* (Mainz). D-Mmb. RISM R 1765.

Suin, Nicolas, *Recueil d'airs choisis pour la guitare avec accompagnement de violin ad libitum* (Lyons, 1768). [Announced in *Affiches de Lyon*, 16 June 1768. No copy located.]

Vidal, B., *Collection of easy pieces for the guitar* (London). CZ-Pnm (guitar, guitar/violin). RISM V 1454.

Manuscripts formerly in the Spencer collection

Bevilacqua, Matteo, *Nun 2 Duetti e A Cavatine ridotti per chitarra francese e dal sig.r Matteo Bevilacqua.* (MS). GB-Lam, ex-Spencer. [Six songs for voice and guitar.]

Caruso, Luigi, *Duetto con chitara francese obligat ho verduto una civetta del Sig. Luigi Caruso* (MS). GB-Lam, ex-Spencer. [Song with violino, chitarra francese, canto, and basso.]

—— *Duettino or siam pur del cielo irato per chitarra fran:e del sig:r Luigi Caruso* (MS). GB-Lam, ex-Spencer. [2 voices and guitar.]

Gazzaniga, Giuseppe, *Duettino Lieti voci che tanto esultate per chitarra francese del Sig.r Giu.pe Gazzaniga* (MS). GB-Lam, ex-Spencer. [2 voices and guitar.]

Millico, Giuseppe, *Canzoncina per chitrra* [sic] *francese del sig.r Giuseppe Milico* (MS). GB-Lam, ex-Spencer.

Trentin, Gregorio, *Un tema con sei variazioni per chitarra francese di Gregorio Trentin umiliato alla nobile signora Lauretta Co: Papafava Dotto . . . Conselve li 24 Genjo 1799* (MS). GB-Lam, ex-Spencer. [All the manuscripts from the Robert Spencer library listed in this section were previously in the Papafava collection, Padua, and appear to date from 1799.]

A Selection of Pieces for Guitar,
c. 1750–*c.* 1800

PL. App. VIII. 1. First movement of *Duetto IV* for two guitars by Merchi (*Quatro duetti a due chitarre . . .* Op. 3, Paris 1757)

Chasse de Mr de Lagarde

PL. App. VIII.2. *Chasse de M. De Lagarde* for violin and guitar by Baillon (*Nouvelle méthode de guitarre,* Paris, 1781)

Pl. App. VIII.3. *Gigue* for two guitars by Alberti (*Nouvelle méthode de guitarre*, Paris 1786)

PL. App. VIII.4. *Les Remords de David* for voice and guitar by Jean–Baptiste Phillis (Paris *c*. 1800)

PL. App. VIII.4. *continued*

PL. App. VIII.4. *continued*

2.ᵉ

De mon devoir, déplorable victime,
Longtems je n'ai fait que languir ;
J'ai succombé, j'ai vécu dans le crime,
Mais pouvais-tu mieux m'en punir ?
Grand Dieu ! ta puissance suprême,
N'a plus de coups à me porter :
On n'a plus rien à redouter,.
Quand on a perdu ce qu'on aime.

3.ᵉ

Si je l'aimai, cette amante adorable,
Si j'oubliai tous tes bienfaits,
C'est toi grand Dieu qui m'a rendu coupable,
En lui donnant autant d'attraits.
A mes sermens toujours fidelle
Et toujours soumis à ta loi
Je n'eus jamais aimé que toi
Si je n'avois brulé pour elle.

4.ᵉ

Elle n'est plus, la mort impitoyable,
A moissonné ses jeunes ans,
Hélas ! au fond d'un sépulchre éffroyable
Elle captive encore mes sens,
En t'implorant, mon cœur t'outrage.
Mon Dieu, mes vœux sont criminels,
Puisque j'apporte à tes autels
Un cœur rempli de son image.

A Paris Chez Imbault au Mont d'or rue St Honoré N° 627.

PL. App. VIII.4. continued

BIBLIOGRAPHY

Treatises and Guitar Tutors

****, DON, *Méthode pour apprendre a jouer de la guitarre par Don **** (Paris: Le Menu, c.1750).

ABREU, ANTONIO, and PRIETO, VICTOR, *Escuela para tocar con perfección la guitarra de cinco y seis órdenes* (Salamanca: Imprenta de la Calle del Prior, 1799).

AGUADO, DIONISIO, *Méthode complète pour la guitare* (Paris, 1826).

ALBERTI, FRANCESCO, *Nouvelle méthode de guitare dans laquelle on y trouve différentes variations, une sonate, 12 menuets et 6 ariettes . . .* (Paris: Camand, 1786).

AMAT, JUAN CARLOS [y], *Guitarra española de cinco ordenes . . .* (Lérida: viuda Anglada y Andrés Lorenço, 1626).

ANON. [BONAVENTURE DES PÉRIERS?], *Discours non plus melancoliques* (Poitiers: Enguilbert de Marnef, 1556).

BAILLEUX, ANTOINE, *Méthode de guitare par musique et tablature* (Paris: L'éditeur, 1773; facs. repr. Geneva: Minkoff, 1980).

BAILLON, PIERRE JOSEPH, *Nouvelle méthode de guitarre selon le système des meilleurs auteurs* (1781; facs. repr. Geneva: Minkoff, 1977).

BERMUDO, JUAN, *El libro llamado declaracion de instrumentos musicales* (Osuna: Juan de Leon, 1555).

BRICEÑO, LUIS DE, *Metodo mui facilissimo para aprender a tañer la guitarra a lo español . . .* (Paris: Pierre Ballard, 1626; facs. edn., Geneva: Minkoff Reprint, 1972).

CAMPION, FRANÇOIS, *Traité d'accompagnement et de composition* (Paris: veuve G. Adam, 1716).

—— *Addition au traité d'accompagnement* (Paris: veuve Ribou, 1730).

CARULLI, FERDINANDO, *Méthode de guitarre ou lyre* (Paris, 1810).

—— *Méthode complète pour parvenir a pincer de la guitare* (Paris, 1825).

CERRETO, SCIPIONE, *Della prattica musica vocale e strumentale* (Naples: Giov. Jacomo Carlino, 1601).

CHABRAN, FELICE, *Compleat Instructions for the Spanish Guitar* (London: Culliford, Rolfe & Barron, 1795).

—— *A New Tutor for the Harp and Spanish Guitar* (London, 1813).

—— *A Complete Set of Instructions for the Spanish Guitar* (London, 1816).

[CORBETTA, FRANCESCO, *Guitarra española y sus diferencias de sones, c.1650*].

CORRETTE, MICHEL, *Les Dons d'Apollon, méthode pour apprendre facilement à jouer de la guitarre par musique et par tablature* (Paris: Bayard, 1762).

DEROSIER, NICOLAS, *Les Principes de la guitarre . . .* (Paris: Christophe Ballard, 1689; facs. edn., Bologna: Forni Editore, 1975).

DOISY, CHARLES, *Principes généraux de la guitare* (1801; facs. repr. Geneva: Minkoff, 1977).

DOIZI DE VELASCO, NICOLAO, *Nuevo modo de cifra para tañer la guitarra . . .* (Naples, 1640).

FERANDIERE, FERNANDO, *Arte de tocar la Guitarra española por Música* (Madrid: Pantaleon Aznar, 1799; repr. Tecla: London, 1977).

GATAYES, GUILLAUME, *Seconde méthode de guitare à six cordes* (Paris, *c.*1807).

GUERAU, FRANCISCO, *Poema harmonico, compuesto de varias cifras por el temple de la guitarra española* . . . (Madrid: Manuel Ruiz de Murga, 1694; facs. edn. London: Tecla Editions, 1977 and Madrid: Editorial Alpuerto S.A., 2000).

LEMOINE, ANTOINE-MARCEL, *Nouvelle méthode courte et facile pour la guitare à l'usage des commençans contenant plusieurs petits airs et des variations* (Paris, *c.*1790).

LIGHT, EDWARD, *A Tutor with a Tablature for the Harp-Lute-Guitar* (London, *c.*1810).

MATTEIS, NICOLA, *The False consonances of Musick* (London: J. Carr, 1682; facs. edn., Monaco: Éditions Chanterelle S.A., 1980).

—— *Le false consonanse della musica per poter apprendere a toccar da se medesimo la chitarra sopra la parte* . . . (London, *c.*1680).

MERCHI, GIACOMO, *Le Guide des écoliers de guitarre ou préludes aussi agréables qu'utiles, sur tous les modes, les positions et les arpégemens avec des airs et des variations . . . V*ᵉ *livre de guitarre, œuvre VII*ᵉ (Paris: l'auteur, 1761; facs. repr. Geneva: Minkoff, 1981).

—— *Traité des agrémens de la musique exécutés sur la guitarre . . . œuvre XXXV*ᵉ (Paris: l'auteur, 1777; facs. repr. Geneva: Minkoff, 1981).

MERSENNE, MARIN, *Harmonicorum libri XII* . . . (Paris: Guillaume Baudry, 1648).

—— *Harmonie universelle* (Paris: Sebastien Cramoisy, 1636; facs. edn., Paris: CNRS, 1965).

MINGUET Y YROL, PABLO, *Reglas y advertencias generales para tañer la guitarra* (Madrid: J. Ibarra, 1752; facs. edn., Geneva: Minkoff Reprint, 1981).

MORETTI, FEDERICO, *Principj per la chitarra* (Naples: Luigi Marescalchi, 1792, MS; repr. Florence: S.P.E.S., 1983).

—— *Principios para tocar la guitarra de seis órdenes* (Madrid: Josef Rico, 1799).

MURCIA, SANTIAGO DE, *Resumen de acompañar la parte con la guitarra* . . . (Antwerp, 1714; facs. edn., Monaco: Éditions Chanterelle S.A., 1980).

PHILLIS, JEAN-BAPTISTE, *Nouvelle méthode pour la lyre ou guitarre à six cordes . . . œuvre 6* (Paris, n.d.).

PITA DE ROCHE, JOÃO LIETE, *Liçam instrumental da viola portugueza ou de ninfas, de cinco ordens* . . . (Lisbon, 1752).

PRAETORIUS, MICHAEL, *Syntagma musicum*, ii (Wolfenbüttel: Elias Holwein, 1618).

RIBEIRO, MANOEL DA PAIXÃO, *Nova arte de viola* (Coimbra: Real officina da universidade, 1789; facs. repr. Geneva: Minkoff, 1985).

RUBIO, JUAN MANUEL GARCÍA, *Arte, reglas armónicas para aprehender a templar y puntear la guitarra española de seis órdenes* (Madrid?, 1799, MS).

RUIZ DE RIBAYAZ, LUCAS, *Luz y norte musical para caminar por las cifras de la guitarra española* . . . (Madrid: Melchor Alvarez, 1676; facs. edn., Geneva: Minkoff Reprint, 1976).

SANZ, GASPAR, *Instruccion de musica sobre la guitarra española* . . . [and] *Documentos, y advertencias generales* . . . (Zaragoza: herederos de Diego Dormer, 1674; 3rd edn., 1675; 4th edn., 1675).

SILVA LEITE, ANTÓNIO DA, *Estudo de guitarra, em que se expoem o meio mais fácil para aprender a tocar este instrumento* (Oporto: Antonio Alvarez Ribeiro, 1795).

Sor, Fernando, *Méthode pour la guitare* (Paris, 1830).

Sotos, Andre de, *Arte para aprender con facilidad y sin maestro a templar y tañer rasgado la guitarra* (Madrid: Imprenta de Cruzada, 1760; facs. repr. Valencia: Librerias Paris, 1991).

Vargas y Guzmán, Juan Antonio, *Explicación para tocar la guitara de punteado, por música o sifra* (Veracruz, 1776, MS).

Vidal, B. *Méthode de guitare* (c.1778). [A copy is believed to have been in GB-Lam, ex-Spencer, but I have so far been unable to locate it.]

Secondary Sources

Acutis, Cesare (1971). *Cancioneros musicali spagnoli in Italia (1585–1635)*. Pisa: Università di Pisa.

Anthony, James R. (1973). *French Baroque Music from Beaujoyeulx to Rameau*. London: B. T. Batsford Ltd.

Artigas, Josep Maria Mangado (1998). *La guitarra en Cataluña*. London: Tecla Editions.

Azevedo, João Manuel Borges de (1987). Introduction to *Uma tablatura para guitarra barroca: 'O Livro do Conde de Redondo'* (facs. edn. of P-Ln, F.C.R. MS Ne. 1). Lisbon: Instituto Português do Património Cultural.

Baak Griffioen, Ruth van (1991). *Jacob Van Eyck's Der Fluyten Lust-Hof (1644–c1655)*. Utrecht: Vereniging voor Nederlandse Muziekgeschiedenis.

Baines, Anthony (1966). *European and American Musical Instruments*. New York: Chancellor Press.

Baron, John H. (1975). 'Les Fées des Forests de S. Germain: ballet de cour, 1625', *Dance Perspectives*, 62/16: 1–53.

—— (1977). 'Secular Spanish Solo Song in Non-Spanish Sources, 1599–1640', *JAMS* 30: 20–42.

Becherini, Bianca (1959). *Catalogo dei manoscritti musicali della Biblioteca Nazionale di Firenze*. Kassel: Bärenreiter.

Benoit, Marcelle (ed.) (1992). *Dictionnaire de la musique en France aux XVIIᵉ et XVIIIᵉ siècles*. Paris: Fayard.

Bobri, Vladimir (1956). 'Gypsies and Gypsy Choruses of Old Russia', *Guitar Review*, 20: 26.

Boetticher, Wolfgang (1978). *Handschriftlich überlieferte Lauten- und Gitarrentabulaturen* (RISM B/VII). Munich: G. Henle Verlag.

—— (1979). 'Zur inhaltlichen Bestimmung des für Laute intavolierten Handschriftenbestands', *AcM* 51: 193–203.

Boyd, Malcolm (ed.) (1992). *Music and the French Revolution*. Cambridge: Cambridge University Press.

Boye, Gary R. (1997). 'Performing Seventeenth-Century Italian Guitar Music: The Question of an Appropriate Stringing', in Coelho (ed.) (1997: 180–94).

Branco, João de Freitas (1959). *História da Música Portuguesa*. Mem Martins: Publicações Europa-America.

Brooks, Jeanice (1999). 'Catherine de Médicis, *nouvelle Artémise*: Women's Laments and the Virtue of Grief', *EM* 27: 419–35.

BROWER, ROBIN (1992). 'The Guitar Books of Adrian Le Roy and Robert Ballard (1551–1555): An Anthology'. MA thesis, University of Southern California.

BROWN, HOWARD MAYER (1965). *Instrumental Music Printed before 1600: A Bibliography*. Cambridge, Mass.: Harvard University Press.

—— (1981). 'The Geography of Florentine Monody: Caccini at Home and Abroad', *EM* 9: 147–68.

BROWN, DR JOHN (1757). *An Estimate of the Measures and Principles of The Times*. London.

BRUNI, A. (1890). *Un Inventaire sous la terreur*. Paris.

BUDASZ, ROGÉRIO (2001). 'The Five-Course Guitar (Viola) in Portugal and Brazil in the Late Seventeenth and Early Eighteenth Centuries'. Ph.D. diss., University of Southern California.

BURNEY, CHARLES (1771). *An Eighteenth-Century Musical Tour in France and Italy*, 2 vols. London.

BUTTON, STEWART (1989). *The Guitar in England, 1800–1924*. New York: Garland Publishing, Inc.

CARDAMONE, DONNA G. (1981). *The* Canzone villanesca alla napolitana *and Related Forms, 1537–1570*, 2 vols. Ann Arbor: UMI.

CARTER, TIM (1985). '*Serate Musicali* in Early Seventeenth-Century Florence: Girolamo Montesardo's *L'Allegre Notti di Fiorenza* (1608)', in A. Morrogh et al. (eds.), *Renaissance Studies in Honor of Craig Hugh Smyth*. Florence: Giunti Barbèra, i. 555–64.

—— (1987). 'Giulio Caccini (1551–1618): New Facts, New Music', *Studi musicali*, 16: 13–32.

—— (1988). 'Caccini's *Amarilli, mia bella*: Some Questions (and a Few Answers)', *PRMA* 113: 250–73.

CAVALLINI, IVANO (1978a). 'L'intavolatura per chitarrino alla napolitana dal *Conserto Vago*—1645', *Quadrivium*, 19/2: 227–63.

—— (1978b). 'Sull'opera "*Gratie et affetti amorosi*" di Marcantonio Aldigatti (1627)', *Quadrivium*, 19/2: 145–203.

—— (1989). 'Sugli improvvisatori del Cinque-Seicento: persistenze, nuovi repertori e qualche ricoscimento', *Recercare*, 1: 23–40.

CHARNASSÉ, HÉLÈNE, REBOURS, G., and ANDIA, R. (eds.) (1999). *Robert de Visée, Les deux livres de guitare, Paris 1682 et 1686* (tablature, transcription, interpretation). Paris: Éditions Transatlantiques.

CHAUVEL, CLAUDE (1984). Introduction to the facs. edn. of *Angelo Michele Bartolotti: Libro primo et secondo di chitarra spagnola*. Geneva: Minkoff Reprint.

CHORON, ALEXANDER ÉTIENNE, and FAYOLLE, F. J. M. (1810). *Dictionnaire historique des musiciens*. Paris.

CHRISTIANSEN, KEITH (1990). *A Caravaggio Rediscovered: The Lute Player*. New York: The Metropolitan Museum of Art.

COELHO, VICTOR (1983). 'G. G. Kapsberger in Rome, 1604–1645: New Biographical Data', *JLSA* 16: 103–33.

—— (1995a). *The Manuscript Sources of Seventeenth-Century Italian Lute Music*. New York: Garland Publishing.

—— (1995b). 'Raffaello Cavalcanti's Lute Book (1590) and the Ideal of Singing and Playing', in Jean-Michel Vaccaro (ed.), *Le Concert des voix et des instruments à la Renaissance*. Paris: CNRS, 423–42.

—— (ed.) (1997). *Performance on Lute, Guitar, and Vihuela: Historical Practice and Modern Interpretation*. Cambridge: Cambridge University Press.

COGGIN, PHILIP (1987). ' "This Easy and Agreable Instrument": A History of the English Guittar', *EM* 15: 205–18.

COLLINS, DAVID (1976). 'A 16th-Century Manuscript in Wood: The Eglantine Table at Hardwick Hall', *EM* 4: 275–9.

CORONA-ALCADE, ANTONIO (1990). 'The Vihuela and the Guitar in Sixteenth-Century Spain: A Critical Appraisal of Some of the Existing Evidence', *The Lute*, 30: 3–24.

CORRETTE, MICHEL (1772). *Nouvelle Méthode pour apprendre à jouer en très peu de tems de la mandoline*. Paris; facs. repr. Geneva: Minkoff, 1985.

COX, PAUL WATHEN (1978). 'Classic Guitar Technique and its Evolution as Reflected in the Method Books c. 1770–1850'. Ph.D. diss., Indiana University.

CRAWFORD, TIM (1993). Introduction and concordances to *The Goëss Lute Manuscripts II.*, facs. edn. of A-KLse goëss II. Munich: Tree Edition.

—— and GOY, FRANCOIS-PIERRE (1997). Introduction and concordances to *Goëss Vogl*, facs. edn. of A KLse goëss-vogl. Munich: Tree Edition.

CUMMING, W. P., et al. (1971). *The Discovery of North America*. London: Elek Books Ltd.

DANNER, PETER (1974). 'Giovanni Paolo Foscarini and his *Nuova Inventione*', *JLSA* 7: 4–18.

—— (1979). 'Bibliografia delle principali intavolature per chitarra', *Il Fronimo*, 7/29: 7–18.

DELL'ARA, MARIO (1979). 'Giovanni Battista Granata chitarrista, compositore e barbiere chirugico', *Il Fronimo*, 7/26: 6–15.

DENIS, FRANÇOISE-EMMANUELLE (1978–9). 'La Guitare en France au XVIIe siècle: son importance, son répertoire', *RBM* 32–3: 143–50.

DOBBINS, FRANK (1992). *Music in Renaissance Lyons*. Oxford: Clarendon Press.

DOBSON, CHARLES, SEGERMAN, EPHRAIM, and TYLER, JAMES (1974). 'The Tunings of the Four-Course French Cittern and of the Four-Course Guitar in the 16th Century', *LSJ* 16: 17–23.

ELKIN, ROBERT (1955). *The Old Concert Rooms of London*. London.

Encyclopédie (1751–76), ed. Denis Diderot. Paris.

ESPINOSA, DAWN ASTRID (1995–6). 'Juan Bermudo "On Playing the Vihuela (*De tañer vihuela*)", from *Declaración de instrumentos musicales* (Osuna, 1555)', *JLSA* 28–9 [entire issue].

ESSES, MAURICE (1992). *Dance and Instrumental 'Diferencias' in Spain during the 17th and Early 18th Centuries*. Stuyvesant, NY: Pendragon Press.

ETZION, JUDITH (1988). 'The Spanish Polyphonic Cancioneros, c.1580–c.1650: A Survey of Literary Content and Textual Concordances', *RdMc* 11/1: 1–43.

EVANS, TOM and MARY ANNE (1977). *Guitars: Music, History, Construction and Players from the Renaissance to Rock*. London and New York: Paddington Press Ltd.

FABRIS, DINKO (1981). 'Danze intavolate per chitarra tiorbata in uno sconosciuto manoscritto napoletano (Na, Cons., Ms. 1321)', *NRMI* 15: 405–26.

—— (1982). 'Prime aggiunte italiane al volume *RISM* B/VII', *Fontes artis musicae*, 28: 103–121.

FABRIS, DINKO (1987). *Andrea Falconieri napoletano: un liutista-compositore del Seicento.* Rome: Edizioni Torre d'Orfeo.

—— (1995). 'Voix et instruments pour la musique de danse: à propos des airs pour chanter et danser dans les tablatures italiennes de luth', in Jean-Michel Vaccaro (ed.), *Le Concert des voix et des instruments à la Renaissance.* Paris: CNRS, 389–422.

FAILLA, SALVATORE E. (1979). 'La nuova chitarra composta da Don Antonio Di Micheli della città di Tusa', *AnMc* 19: 244–71.

FENLON, IAIN (1979). Review of RISM B/VII, in *MT* 120/1636: 489.

—— and HAAR, JAMES (1988). *The Italian Madrigal in the Early Sixteenth Century: Sources and Interpretation.* Cambridge: Cambridge University Press.

FÉTIS, FRANCOIS-JOSEPH (1873). *Biographie universelle des musiciens.* Paris.

FINK, MICHAEL (1993). 'Boccherini: Guitar Quintets', in booklet accompanying *Boccherini: Les Quintettes avec guitare.* Philips CD 438 769-2.

FISKE, ROGER (1973). *English Theatre Music in the Eighteenth Century.* London; 2nd edn., Oxford: Oxford University Press.

FORRESTER, PETER (1987). '17th-c. Guitar Woodworks', *FoMRHI Quarterly*, 48: 40–8.

FOUSSARD, MICHEL, et al. (1980). *Guitares: chefs-d'œuvre des collections de France.* Paris: La Flûte de Pan.

GARROS, MADELEINE, and WALLON, SIMONE (1967). *Catalogue du fonds musical de la Bibliothèque Sainte-Geneviève de Paris.* Catalogus musicus, 4; Kassel: IAML/IMS.

GERBER, ERNEST LUDWIG (1790). *Historisch-biographisches Lexicon der Tonkünstler.* Leipzig.

—— (1812–14). *Neues historisch-biographisches Lexicon der Tonkünstler.* Leipzig; repr. 1966.

GILL, DONALD (1960). 'James Talbot's Manuscript: V. Plucked Strings—The Wire-Strung Fretted Instruments and the Guitar', *GSJ* 15: 60–9.

—— (1978). 'The de Gallot Guitar Books', *EM* 6: 79–81.

GOY, FRANCOIS-PIERRE (1996). Introduction and concordances to *Berliner Lautentabulaturen*, facs. edn. of D-B Mus. Ms. 40600 and PL-Kj Mus. Ms. 40626. Mainz: Schott.

—— MEYER, CHRISTIAN, and ROLLIN, MONIQUE (1991). *Sources manuscrites en tablature: luth et théorbe (c. 1500–c.1800). Catalogue descriptif,* i: *Confoederatio Helvetica (CH), France (F).* Baden-Baden and Bouxwiller: Éditions Valentin Koerner.

GRASSINEAU, JAMES (1740). *A Musical Dictionary.* London: J. Wilcox.

GRIFFITHS, JOHN (1997). 'The Vihuela: Performance Practice, Style, and Context', in Coelho (ed.) (1997: 158–79).

GRUNFELD, FREDERIC V. (1969). *The Art and Times of the Guitar: An Illustrated History of Guitars and Guitarists.* London: The Macmillan Company.

La guitarra española/The Spanish Guitar [Exhibition catalogue; The Metropolitan Museum of Art, New York, and Museo Municipal, Madrid, 1991–2.]

HALL, MONICA (1980). Introduction to the facs. edn. of *Joan Carles Amat: Guitarra española (c.1761).* Monaco, Éditions Chanterelle.

—— (1983). 'The Guitar Anthologies of Santiago de Murcia'. Ph.D. diss., Open University.

HAMILTON, MARY NEAL (1937). *Music in Eighteenth-Century Spain.* Urbana: University of Illinois Press.

HAMMOND, FREDERICK (1983). 'Cardinal Pietro Aldobrandini, Patron of Music', *Studi musicali*, 12: 53–66.

—— (1994). *Music and Spectacle in Baroque Rome: Barbarini Patronage under Urban VIII*. New Haven and London: Yale University Press.

HEARTZ, DANIEL (1960). 'Parisian Music Publishing under Henry II: A Propos of Four Recently Discovered Guitar Books', *MQ* 46: 448–67.

—— (1963). 'An Elizabethan Tutor for the Guitar', *GSJ* 16: 3–21.

—— (1972). '*Voix de ville:* Between Humanist Ideals and Musical Realities', in Laurence Berman (ed.), *Words and Music: The Scholars's View*. Cambridge, Mass.: Harvard University Press, 115–35.

HECK, THOMAS F. (1995). *Mauro Giuliani, Virtuoso Guitarist and Composer*. Columbus, Ohio: Editions Orphée.

HIGHFILL, PHILIP, JR. (1978). *A Biographical Dictionary of Actors, Actresses, Musicians, Dancers, Managers, and other Stage Personnel in London 1660–1800*. Carbondale, Ill.: Southern Illinois University Press.

HILL, JOHN WALTER (1997). *Roman Monody, Cantata, and Opera from the Circles around Cardinal Montalto*, 2 vols. Oxford: Clarendon Press.

HODGSON, MARTIN (1985). 'The Stringing of a Baroque Guitar', *FoMRHI Quarterly*, 41: 61–7.

HOGARTH, GEORGE (1836). 'Musical Instruments—The Harp and Guitar', *Musical World*, 3: 32.

HOLMAN, PETER (1993). *Four and Twenty Fiddlers: The Violin at the English Court, 1540–1690*. Oxford: Clarendon Press.

ISHERWOOD, ROBERT M. (1973). *Music in the Service of the King: France in the Seventeenth Century*. Ithaca and London: Cornell University Press.

JACOBS, CHARLES (1978). *Miguel de Fuenllana: Orphénica Lyra (Seville 1554)*. Oxford: Oxford University Press.

JEFFERY, BRIAN (1977). Introduction to the facsimile and translation of *Francisco Guerau: Poema harmonico (Madrid, 1694)*. London: Tecla Editions.

—— (1994). *Fernando Sor: Composer and Guitarist*. London, 1977.

JENSEN, RICHARD (1980). 'The Development of Technique and Performance Practice as Reflected in Seventeenth-Century Italian Guitar Notation'. MA thesis, California State University, Northridge.

JOHANSSON, CARI (1955). *French Music Publishers' Catalogues of the Second Half of the Eighteenth Century*. Stockholm.

KASTNER, JEAN GEORGES (1837). *Traité general d'instrumentation*. Paris.

KEITH, RICHARD (1966). 'La Guitare royale: A Study of the Career and Compositions of Francesco Corbetta', *RMFC* 7: 73–93.

KENYON DE PASCUAL, BERYL (1983). 'Ventas de instrumentos musicales en Madrid durante la segunda mitad del siglo XVIII (parte II)', *RdMc* 6: 1–2.

KIRKENDALE, WARREN (1972). *L'Aria di Fiorenza id est Il Ballo del Gran Duca*. Florence: Olschki.

—— (1993). *The Court Musicians in Florence during the Principiate of the Medici*. Florence: Olschki.

KIRSCH, DIETER, and MEIEROTT, LENZ (1992). *Berliner Lautentabulaturen in Krakau*. Mainz: Schott.

KOCZIRZ, ADOLF (1926). 'Eine Gitarren- und Lautenhandschrift aus der zweiten Hälfte des 17. Jahrhunderts', *AMw* 8: 433–40.

—— (1933). 'Eine Gitarrentabulatur des Kaiserlichen Theorbisten Orazio Clementi', in *Mélanges de musicologie offerts à M. Lionel de la Laurencie*. Paris: Librarie E. Droz, 107–15.

LAFARGUE K, VÉRONIQUE (1998). 'Adrian Le Roy: Those Accompaniments which Resemble Solo Music', *The Lute*, 38: 65–82.

LARSON, KEITH A. (1985). 'The Unaccompanied Madrigal in Naples from 1536 to 1654', Ph.D. diss., Princeton University.

LATHAM, ROBERT (ed.) (1989). *Catalogue of the Pepys Library at Magdalene College, Cambridge*, iv. Woodbridge: D. S. Brewer.

LE COCQ, JONATHAN (1995). 'The Status of Le Roy's Publications for Voice and Lute or Guitar', *The Lute*, 35: 4–27.

LEDHUY, A., and BERTINI, H. (1835). *Encyclopédie pittoresque de la musique*. Paris; repr. London: Tecla Edition, 1994.

LESURE, FRANÇOIS (1957). *Pierre Trichet: Traité des instruments de musique (vers 1640)*. Neuilly-sur-Seine: Société de Musique d'Autrefois.

—— (ed.) (1981). *Catalogue de la musique imprimée avant 1800 conservée dans les bibliothèques publiques de Paris*. Paris: Bibliothèque nationale.

—— and SARTORI, CLAUDIO (1977). *Bibliografia della musica italiana vocale profana pubblicata dal 1500 al 1700* (Vogel B). Pomezia: Staderini.

LIBIN, LAURENCE (1992). 'A Remarkable Guitar by Lorenzo Alonso', *EM* 20: 643–6.

LORIMER, MICHAEL (1987). *Saldívar Codex No.4: Santiago de Murcia Manuscript*, facs. edn. Santa Barbara, Calif.: Michael Lorimer.

LOSPALLUTI, LEONARDO (1989). 'Consideratione su Giovan Battista Abatessa e su manoscritto per chitarra del Seicento a Bitonto', *Il Fronimo*, 17/67: 27–33.

LUYNES, DUC DE (1860). *Mémoires* (extracts repr. Paris, 1970, ed. Norbert Dufourcq).

LYONS, DAVID B. (1975). 'Nathanael Diesel, Guitar Tutor to a Royal Lady', *JLSA* 8: 80–94.

MABBETT, MARGARET (1986). 'Italian Musicians in Restoration England (1660–90)', *ML* 67: 237–47.

MACCLINTOCK, CAROL (1965). *The Bottegari Lutebook*. Wellesley: Wellesley College.

—— (1979). *Readings in the History of Music in Performance*. Bloomington and London: Indiana University Press.

MCCUTCHEON, MEREDITH ALICE (1985). *Guitar and Vihuela: An Annotated Bibliography*. New York: Pendragon Press.

MCVEIGH, SIMON (1993). *Concert Life in London from Mozart to Haydn*. Cambridge: Cambridge University Press.

MASON, KEVIN (1981). 'François Campion's Secret of Accompaniment for the Theorbo, Guitar, and Lute', *JLSA* 14: 69–94.

—— (1989). *The Chitarrone and its Repertoire in Early Seventeenth-Century Italy*. Aberystwyth: Boethius Press.

—— (1997). '*Per cantare e sonare*: Accompanying Italian Lute Song of the Late Sixteenth Century', in Coelho (ed.) (1997: 72–107).

MEE, JOHN H. (1911). *The Oldest Music Room in Europe*. London: John Lane.

MEYER, CHRISTIAN (1994). *Sources mauscrites en tablature: luth et théorbe (c.1500–c.1800). Catalogue descriptif*, ii: *Bundesrepublik Deutschland (D)*. Baden-Baden and Bouxwiller: Éditions Valentin Koerner.

MILLER, ROARK (1996). 'New Information on the Chronology of Venetian Monody: The "Raccolte" of Remigio Romano', *ML* 77: 22–33.

MILLIOT, SYLVETTE (1970). *Documents inédits sur les luthiers Parisiens du XVIIIme siècle*. Paris.

MISCHIATI, OSCAR, and TAGLIAVINI, LUIGI F. (1975). Appendix to *Due Messe: Girolamo Frescobaldi*. Opere, i; Milan: Edizioni Suvini Zerboni.

MOLITOR, SIMON, and KLINGER, R. (*c.*1811). *Versuch einer vollständigen methodischen Anleitung zum Guitare-Spielen*. Vienna: Chemische Druckerei.

MOOSER, R. ALOYS (1948–51). *Annales de la musique et les musiciens en Russie au XVIIIme siècle*. Geneva: Mont-Blanc.

NEWCOMB, ANTHONY (1980). *The Madrigal at Ferrara*. Princeton: Princeton University Press.

OLIVEIRA, ERNESTO VEIGA DE (1982). *Instrumentos Populares Tradicionais Portugueses*. Lisbon: Fundação Calouste Gulbenkian.

—— (*c.*1982). *Instrumentos Musicais Populares dos Açores*, Lisbon: Fundação Calouste Gulbenkian.

OPHEE, MATANYA (1998). *Luigi Boccherini's Guitar Quintets: New Evidence*. Boston: Editions Orphée.

OSBORN, JAMES M. (1962). *The Autobiography of Thomas Whythorne*. London: Oxford University Press.

PALISCA, CLAUDE V. (1989). *The Florentine Camerata*. New Haven and London: Yale University Press.

PANDOLFI, VITO (1957–61). *La commedia dell'arte: storia e testi*, 6 vols. Florence: Edizioni Sansoni Antiquariato.

PAOLINI, PAOLO (1980). Introduction to the facs. edn. of *Francesco Corbetta: Varii capricci per la ghitara spagnuola . . . (1643)*. Florence: S.P.E.S.

—— (1983). Introduction to the facs. edn. of *Francesco Corbetta: Varii scherzi di sonate per la chitara spagnola (1648)*. Florence: S.P.E.S.

PARETS I SERRA, JOAN (2000). 'Guerau, Francisco', *NG II*.

PARISI, SUSAN (1989). 'Ducal Patronage of Music in Mantua, 1587–1627: An Archival Study', Ph.D. diss., University of Illinois at Urbana-Champaign.

PASSARO, COSIMO (1992). 'Manoscritto per chitarra Spagnola 2951 della Biblioteca Riccardiana di Firenze', *Il Fronimo*, 20/80: 35–43.

PENNINGTON, NEIL D. (1981). *The Spanish Baroque Guitar with a Transcription of De Murcia's Passacalles y obras*, 2 vols. Ann Arbor: UMI.

PERNETY, ANTOINE JOSEPH (1770). *Histoire d'un voyage aux isles Malouines, fait en 1763 & 1764*. Paris.

PERUFFO, MIMMO (1997). 'Italian Violin Strings in the Eighteenth and Nineteenth Centuries: Typologies, Manufacturing Techniques and Principles of Stringing', *Recercare*, 9: 155–203.

PIERRE, CONSTANT (1893). *Les Facteurs d'instruments de musique*. Paris.

—— (1975). *Histoire du Concert Spirituel 1725–90*. Paris.

PINNELL, RICHARD T. (1979). 'The Theorboed Guitar: Its Repertoire in the Guitar Books of Granata and Gallot', *EM* 7: 323–9.

—— (1980). *Francesco Corbetta and the Baroque Guitar.* Ann Arbor: UMI.

—— (1993). *The Rioplatense Guitar: The Early Guitar and its Context in Argentina and Uruguay*, i. Westport: The Bold Strummer, Ltd.

PRICE, CURTIS (1979). *Music in the Restoration Theatre.* Ann Arbor: UMI.

RISM B/VII, *see* Boetticher (1978).

REBOURS, GÉRARD (2001). *Robert de Visée, catalogue thématique et concordances.* Paris: Symétrie Éditions.

RICHARDS, KENNETH and LAURA (1990). *The Commedia dell'Arte.* Oxford: Basil Blackwell Ltd.

RUDÉN, JAN OLOF (1981). *Music in Tablature: A Thematic Index with Source Descriptions of Music in Tablature Notation in Sweden.* Stockholm: Svenskt musikhistoriskt arkiv.

RUSSELL, CRAIG H. (1981). 'Santiago de Murcia: Spanish Theorist and Guitarist of the Early Eighteenth Century'. Ph.D. diss., University of North Carolina at Chapel Hill.

—— (1982). 'Santiago De Murcia: The French Connection in Baroque Spain', *JLSA* 15: 40–51.

—— (1988–9). 'François Le Cocq: Belgian Master of the Baroque Guitar', *Soundboard*, 15: 288–93.

—— (1989). 'Spain in the Enlightenment', in Neil Zaslaw (ed.), *Man and Music: The Classical Era*, Englewood Cliffs, NJ: Prentice Hall, 350–67.

—— (1995*a*). *Santiago de Murcia's 'Códice Saldívar No.4'*, 2 vols. Urbana: University of Illinois Press.

—— (1995*b*). 'New Jewels in Old Boxes: Retrieving the Lost Musical Heritages of Colonial Mexico', *Ars Musica Denver*, 7/2: 13–38.

SAINSBURY, JOHN (1825). *A Dictionary of Musicians.* London.

SASLOW, JAMES M. (1996). *The Medici Wedding of 1589.* New Haven: Yale University Press.

SAVINO, RICHARD (1997). 'Essential Issues in Performance Practices of the Classical Guitar, 1770–1850', in Coelho (ed.) (1997: 195–219).

SCHMITT, THOMAS (1992). 'Sobre la ornamentación en el repertorio para guitarra barroca en España (1600–1750), *RdMc* 15/1, 1–32.

—— (2000). *Francisco Guerau: Poema harmónico* (a study, transcription, and facs. edn. of Guerau, 1694). Madrid: Editorial Alpuerto, S. A.

SEGERMAN, EPHRAIM (1976). 'Stringed Instruments on the Eglantine Table' (Correspondence), *EM* 4: 485.

—— (1992). 'Shelley's Guitar and 19th-Century Stringing Practices', *FoMRHI Quarterly*, 67: 41–2.

—— (1994). 'Stringing 5-course Baroque Guitars', *FoMRHI Quarterly*, 75: 43–5.

SILBIGER, ALEXANDER (1980). *Italian Manuscript Sources of 17th-Century Keyboard Music.* Ann Arbor: UMI.

SPENCER, ROBERT (1976). 'The *Chitarrone Francese*', *EM* 4: 165–6.

—— (1981). Introduction to modern edn. of *Six Sonates pour la Guitare avec accompagnement de violon . . . par Mr. Porro. Oeuvre XI*. Monaco: Éditions Chanterelle.

STARKIE, WALTER (1958). *Spain: A Musician's Journey through Time and Space*. Geneva: Edisli at Éditions René Kister.

STEIN, LOUISE K. (1987). 'Accompaniment and Continuo in Spanish Baroque Music', in Emilio Casares Rodicio, Ismael Fernández de la Cuestra, and José López-Calo (eds.), *España en la música de occidente: Actas del congreso internacional . . . Salamanca . . . 1985*. Madrid: Instituto Nacional de las Artes Escéncias y la Música, ii. 357–70.

—— (1993). *Songs of Mortals, Dialogues of the Gods*. Oxford: Clarendon Press.

STEVENSON, ROBERT M. (1968). *Music in Aztec and Inca Territory*. Berkeley: University of California Press.

—— (1979). 'A Neglected Mexican Guitar Manual of 1776', *Inter-American Music Review*, 1: 205–10.

STRIZICH, ROBERT (ed.) (1971). *R. De Visée: Œuvres complètes pour guitare*. Paris: Heugel.

—— (1974). 'A Spanish Guitar Tutor: Ruiz de Ribayaz's Luz y Norte Musical (1677)', *JLSA* 7: 51–81.

—— (1981). 'L'accompagnamento di basso continuo sulla chitarra barocca', *Il Fronimo*, 9/1: 15–27; 9/2: 8–27.

TESSARI, CARLA (1989). Introduction to the facs. edn. of *Stefano Pesori: Galeria Musicale*. Verona: Antiquae Musicae Italicae Studiosi.

TIMMERMAN, ALEX (1994). *De mandoline en de gitaar*. Zwolle: AETii-Producties.

TIMOFEYEV, OLEG V. (2000). 'Guitar' (8 (I)), *NG II*.

TREADWELL, NINA (1991). 'On the Use of Fingernails when Playing the Baroque Guitar', *Context*, 2: 16–19.

—— (1992). 'The Guitar Passacalles of Santiago de Murcia (c1685–1740): An Alternative Stringing', *Musicology Australia*, 15: 67–76.

—— (1993). 'Guitar Alfabeto in Italian Monody: The Publications of Alessandro Vincenti', *The Lute*, 33: 12–22.

—— (2001). 'Restaging the Siren: Musical Women in the Performance of Sixteenth-Century Italian Theater'. Ph.D. diss., University of Southern California.

TURNBULL, HARVEY (1974). *The Guitar from the Renaissance to the Present Day*. London: B. T. Batsford Ltd; 2nd edn., Westport: The Bold Strummer, Ltd, 1991.

TYLER, JAMES (1974). 'A Checklist of Music for the Cittern', *EM* 2: 25–9.

—— (1975a). 'The Renaissance Guitar', *EM* 3: 341–7.

—— (1975b). 'Further Remarks on the Four-Course Guitar', *LSJ* 17: 60–2.

—— (1979a). Introduction to the facs. edn. of *G. B. Granata: Soavi concenti di sonate (1659)*. Monaco: Éditions Chanterelle.

—— (1979b). Introduction to the facs. edn. of *Adrian Le Roy & Robert Ballard: Five Guitar Books (1551–1555)*. Monaco: Éditions Chanterelle.

—— (1980a). *The Early Guitar: A History and Handbook*. London: Oxford University Press.

—— (1980b). Introduction to the facs. edn. of *Nicola Matteis: The False Consonances of Musick (1682)*. Monaco: Éditions Chanterelle.

—— (1980c). Introduction to the facs. edn. of *Simon Gorlier & Guillaume Morlaye: Four Guitar Books (1551–1553)*. Monaco: Éditions Chanterelle.

TYLER, JAMES (1980*d*). Introduction to the facs. edn. of *Alonso Mudarra: Tres libros de musica en cifras (1546)*. Monaco: Éditions Chanterelle.

—— (1984*a*). Introduction and modern edn. of *Gasparo Zanetti: 'Il Scolaro' (1645)*. Brighton: London Pro Musica Edition (DM5 and DM6).

—— (1984*b*). *A Brief Tutor for the Baroque Guitar*. Helsinki: Chorus Publications.

—— (2000*a*). 'Cittern', *NG II*.

—— (2000*b*). 'Guitar' (3) and (4), *NG II*.

—— (2000*c*). 'Mandore', *NG II*.

—— (2000*d*). 'Mandora', *NG II*.

—— (2000*e*). 'Cithrinchen', *NG II*.

—— and SPARKS, PAUL (1989). *The Early Mandolin*. Oxford: Clarendon Press.

VACCARO, JEAN-MICHEL (1981). *La Musique de luth en France au XVI⁰ siécle*. Paris: CNRS.

VALLAS, LÉON (1908). *La Musique à l'Académie de Lyon au dix-huitième siècle*. Lyons.

—— (1932). *Un Siècle de musique et de théâtre à Lyon 1688–1789*. Lyons: P. Masson.

VANNES, RENÉ (1951). *Dictionnaire universel des luthiers*. Repr. Brussels: Les Amis de la Musique, 1975.

VECCHI, GIUSEPPE (1977). 'La monodia da camera a Bologna e *I Pietosi affetti* (1646) di Domenico Pellegrini', *Quadrivium*, 18: 97–106.

WALKER, D. P. (ed.) (1963). *Les Fêtes du marriage de Ferdinand de Médicis et de Christine de Lorraine*, i: *Musique des intermèdes de 'La Pellegrina'*. Paris: CNRS.

WALKER, THOMAS (1968). 'Ciaccona and Passacaglia: Remarks on their Origin and Early History', *JAMS* 21: 300–20.

WARD, JOHN M. (1979–81). 'Sprightly and Cheerful Musick: Notes on the Cittern, Gittern and Guitar in 16th- and 17th-Century England, *LSJ* 21 [entire issue].

—— (1982). 'Changing the Instrument for the Music', *JLSA* 15: 27–39.

—— (1983). 'The Relationship of Folk and Art Music in 17th-Century Spain', *Studi musicali*, 12: 281–300.

—— (1992). *Music for Elizabethan Lutes*, 2 vols. Oxford: Clarendon Press.

WEIDLICH, JOSEPH (1978). 'Battuto Performance Practice in Early Italian Guitar Music', *JLSA* 11: 63–86.

WENLAND, JOHN (1976). 'Madre non mi far Monaca: The Biography of a Renaissance Folksong', *AcM* 48: 185–204.

WHISTLING, CARL FRIEDRICH, and HOFMEISTER, FRIEDRICH (1817–27). *Handbuch der musikalischen Literatur*. Repr. New York, 1975.

WOLF, JOHANNES (1919). *Handbuch der Notationskunde II. Teil*. Leipzig; repr. Wiesbaden: Breitkopf & Härtel, 1963.

WOLZIEN, CHARLES (1983). 'Battle Music for the French Renaissance Guitar', *Guitar Review*, 54: 2–11.

—— (1993–4). 'Early Guitar Literature: Baroque Song Literature', *Soundboard*, 20/3: 77–80; 20/4: 67–70; 20/5: 79–82.

YAKELEY, M. JUNE (1999). 'The Life and Times of José Marín', *The Lute*, 39: 16–26.

—— and HALL, MONICA (1995). 'El estillo Castellano y estillo Catalan: An Introduction to Spanish Guitar Chord Notation', *The Lute*, 35: 28–61.

Eighteenth- and Early Nineteenth-Century Periodicals Consulted

Affiches de Lyon (Lyons, 1759–72)

Allgemeine musikalische Zeitung (Leipzig, 1798–1848)

Almanach de Lyon (Lyons, 1756, 1761)

Almanach musical (Paris, 1775–83)

Annonces, affiches, et avis divers (Paris, 1760–72)

L'Avant-coureur des spectacles (Paris, c.1760–80)

Avis divers (Paris, c.1760–91)

Calendrier musical universel (Paris, 1788–9)

The Giulianiad (London, 1833)

Journal de musique (Paris, 1770–7; facs. repr., Geneva: Minkoff Reprint)

Journal de Paris (Paris, 1783)

Mercure de France (Paris, 1749–85)

Tablettes de renommée des musiciens (Paris, 1785)

INDEX

Index

Index

Ernst Augustus of Brunswick, Prince Palatine 128
Espagnol, l'Abbé (*fl. c.*1780?) 224
Evelyn, John 121

Fabricatore, Giovanni Battista (*fl. c.*1785–1807) 219,
    256–7
Fachoni, Gioseppe 43
fado 239
Falconieri, Andrea 80, 96
fandango, *see* grounds and popular tunes
Fardino, Lorenzo 152
Fasolo, Giovanni Battista 98
Fedele, Giacinta 98
Felix, J. S. (*fl. c.*1770–3) 272, 277
Ferandiere, Fernando (*c.*1740–*c.*1816) 230–2, 234–5,
    258, 261, 283, 284
Ferdinand Karl, Archduke of Austria 70
Ferdinand Maria, Elector of Bavaria 142
Ferdinando de' Medici, Grand Duke of Florence 32–3,
    35
Ferdinando, Viceroy of Naples 149
Ferré (*fl. c.*1763) 205
Festa, Sebastiano 21
Fétis, François-Joseph 248–9
Fezandat, Michel 12, 14
figured bass, *see* basso continuo
Fiorini, Giovanni Alberto 62 n. 27, 95
Fioroni, Gio. Francesco 92
Fontanelli, Lodovico (*fl.* 1733) 90
Fontei, Nicolo 99
Forqueray, Anthoine 112
Foscarini, Giovanni Paolo (*fl.* 1620–49) 57, 60, 63–7,
    69, 86, 107–8, 129, 141, 152, 153 n. 20, 168,
    169–70, 185
    Intavolatura di chitarra (1629) 60, 65, 86
    Il primo, secondo, e terzo libro (*c.*1630) 63–5, 88,
        175–6, 178, 180, 181
    I quarto libri (*c.*1632) 65–6, 88, 116
    Li cinque libri (1640) 66, 88
    Inventione di toccate (1640) 67, 88
Fossa, François de (1775–1849) 237, 269
Fourier, Nicolas François (*fl. c.*1790–5) 245, 256
Fra João (*fl.* early 18th c.) 156
Franci, Andrea 94
François I, King of France 13 n. 7, 14
Frederick V, Elector Palatine 109
frémissement 267–8
Frescobaldi, Girolamo 54, 80, 83
frets:
    gut (tied) 6, 7, 42, 200, 216, 255–6
    metal (fixed) 199, 216, 219, 228, 236–7, 254–6
Fuenllana, Miguel de (*c.*1525–*c.*1605) 8
    Libro de musica (1554) 8–9
Furioso, Il 60; *see also* Foscarini, Giovanni Paolo

G****, Mr (*fl. c.*1770–80?) 277
Gabrieli, Giovanni 139

Gabrielli, Francesco (1588–1636) 57, 99; see also *Aria
    di Scapino* and Scapino
Gaffino, Joseph (*fl. c.*1750–60) 204
galant, see *style galant*
Galilei, Michelangelo 66
Gallot, Henry François de (*fl. c.*1660–*c.*1684) 116
    'Pieces de guitarre' (GB-Ob Mus. Sch. C 94) 116,
        120
Garcia, Miguel, *see* Basilio, Padre
Gautier, Ennemond (?) 66, 101, 117, 120, 133, 138
Gatayes, Guillaume-Pierre-Antoine (1774–1846) 238,
    245–6, 248, 277
Gaude (*fl. c.*1788) 272
Gaveaux, Pierre (1760–1825) 278
Gazzaniga, Giuseppe (1743–1818) 285
Geminiani, Francesco Saverio (1687–1762) 207
Genty, Mlle (*fl. c.*1762–84) 204, 278
Gervaise, Claude 18
Gervasio, Giovanni Battista (*fl. c.*1762–84) 261
Ghizzolo, Giovanni 97
Giaccio, Orazio 96
Giamberti, Giuseppe 97
Gianfelippi, Felippo 95
Giardini, Felice de (1716–96) 227
Ginter, Franz 147
Giordani, Tommaso (*c.*1730–1806) 227
Giuliani, Girolamo (*fl. c.*1585) 32 n. 13
    Intavolatura de chitarra (*c.*1585) 32 n. 13
Giuliani, Mauro (1781–1829) 134, 242–3, 250–2, 261–3
glissade 268–9
Gloucester, Duke of 124
Godard (*fl. c.*1761–2) 204–5, 278
Godoy, Manuel de 231
Gomes 156
Gonzaga, Carlo II, Duke of Mantua 67
Gonzaga, Vincenzo, Duke of Mantua 43
Goretsky (*fl. c.*1659) 210
Gorlier, Simon (*fl.* 1550–84) 12, 13, 22
    Le troysieme livre (1551) 12–13
Goudimel, Claude 17
Gougelet, Pierre-Marie (1726–90) 278
Gouriet *fils* (*fl. c.*1793) 278
Goya, Francisco de 193, 212
Gragnani, Filippo (1768–1820) 242
Granata, Giovanni Battista (*c.*1625–*c.*1685) 74–5, 130,
    131, 152
    Capricci armonici (1646) 74, 88, 178
    Nuove suonate (*c.*1650) 74, 89
    Nuova scielta (1651) 74, 89
    Soavi concenti (1659) 74, 89
    Novi capricci (1674) 74–5, 89, 142, 178
    Nuovi sovavi [sic] *concenti* (1680) 89
    Armonici toni (1684) 89
Granadino, El (*fl. c.*1760) 195
Grandi, Alessandro 59, 80, 98
Granjon, Robert 12
Grassineau, J. 184, 185, 206
Grenerin, Henry (*fl.* 1641–80) 111, 117, 119